THE AGE OF THE GODS

DEMETER THESMOPHOROS

The relief depicts the consecration of Triptolemus, the hero of Eleusis, who is being sent forth by the Mother Goddess to teach mankind the mystery of agriculture and the rudiments of civilisation. Demeter is shown placing in his hand the sacred corn-stalks, while Kore, the Queen of the Underworld, who holds the torch of the Eleusinian mysteries in her left hand, sets a crown upon his head.

[*Frontispiece*

THE AGE OF THE GODS

A STUDY IN THE ORIGINS OF CULTURE IN PREHISTORIC EUROPE AND THE ANCIENT EAST

BY CHRISTOPHER DAWSON

New York · HOWARD FERTIG · 1970

First published in 1928 by John Murray Ltd.

Howard Fertig, Inc. Edition 1970
Published by arrangement with The Society of Authors, London

Library of Congress Catalog Card Number: 68-9653

PRINTED IN THE UNITED STATES OF AMERICA
BY NOBLE OFFSET PRINTERS, INC.

PREFACE

DURING the last thirty years the great development of archæological and ethnological studies has prepared the way for a new conception of history. The old separation and mutual distrust that existed between prehistoric archæology and ancient history have disappeared, and the historian is to-day working hand in hand with the archæologist, while on the other hand, the anthropologist and the ethnologist are more and more developing the historical methods which were so completely neglected by the older evolutionary school. Thus we are witnessing the rise of a new science which will study man's past, not as an inorganic mass of isolated events, but as the manifestation of the growth and mutual interaction of living cultural wholes. In the present work I have attempted to make a brief survey of the whole problem of the origins of our civilisation from the standpoint of the new methods. Although these methods are still young, the labours of specialists have already provided rich materials for a cultural interpretation of history—materials which are, however, widely scattered in learned periodicals and monographs. It is unnecessary to emphasise my debt to these scholars, since my whole work is entirely dependent upon them. I must, however, acknowledge the help that I have derived from the writings of Professor Langdon, Professor Breasted, and Professor Gordon Childe, as well as from such co-operative works as Ebert's *Reallexikon der Vorgeschichte* and *The Cambridge Ancient History*.

I must express my thanks to the Clarendon Press and to the Trustees of the British Museum for the permission to reproduce illustrations from their pub-

94-162

lications. I am also greatly indebted to the publishers for their help in the preparation of the maps. In the case of Map IX I have made use of the invaluable material and maps contained in Mr. de Navarro's article on Prehistoric Amber Routes in the *Geographical Journal* for December 1925. Finally, I must thank my friend Mr. E. I. Watkin for his kindness in undertaking the compilation of the index.

CHRISTOPHER DAWSON.

CONTENTS

CHAPTER I

THE GLACIAL AGE AND THE BEGINNINGS OF HUMAN LIFE IN EUROPE

CHAPTER II

LATER PALÆOLITHIC CULTURE AND THE RELIGION OF THE HUNTER

CHAPTER III

THE DAWN OF THE NEOLITHIC AGE AND THE RISE OF THE PEASANT CULTURE IN EUROPE

CHAPTER IV

ASIA AND THE ORIGINS OF THE HIGHER CIVILISATION

CONTENTS

CHAPTER IX

CHAPTER X

CHAPTER XI

CHAPTER XII

LIST OF ILLUSTRATIONS

LIST OF MAPS

INTRODUCTION

AFTER a century and more of historical specialism and archæological research, of the minute criticism of documents and sources, the time has come when it is becoming possible to reap the fruits of this intensive labour, and to undertake some general synthesis of the new knowledge of man's past that we have acquired. It is a truism that we cannot understand the present without a knowledge of the past or the past without the whole, but previous to our own age it has been difficult to realise this. Men were forced to rest content with the history of a few favoured peoples and exceptional periods—like classical Greece and Rome or our own immediate past—that were islands of light in a sea of darkness. But now, thanks not only to the sensational discoveries of the great civilisations of the Ancient East, but even more to the patient investigation of the dry bones of archæology—literal bones and fragments of pottery and rude implements—a general vision of the whole past of our civilisation has become possible. There is still no lack of gaps in our knowledge, there is an infinity of problems that still await solution, but at least the broad outlines are there, and no educated person need any longer be ignorant of the primary foundations on which our civilisation has been built up.

The practical importance of this knowledge is obvious. If we have not a general framework into which to fit our knowledge of history, we are forced to fall back on some lesser unity in relation to which we order our ideas, and this lesser unity will of course be the national state. During the last two centuries the history of Europe has been given an almost exclusively national interpretation. And since the unit is a political one, the method of interpretation has tended to be political also, so that history has often sunk to the level of political propaganda and even some of the greatest of nineteenth-century historians—such as Macaulay, Froude, Treitschke, even Mommsen himself—have been unashamed political partisans.

This state of things was one of the great predisposing causes of the late War, and it is certain that the peoples of Europe will never be able to co-operate in peace, so long as they have no knowledge of their common cultural tradition and no revelation of the unity of European civilisation. Now the alternative to the nationalist conception of history is the cultural or sociological one which goes behind the political unit and studies that fundamental social unity which we term a culture.

I. *The Nature of Culture.*—What is a culture ? A culture is a common way of life—a particular adjustment of man to his natural surroundings and his economic needs. In its use and modification it resembles the development of a biological species, which, as Dr. Regan pointed out in his address to the British Association in 1925, is primarily due, not to change in structure, but to the formation of a community, either with new habits, or in a new and restricted environment. And just as every natural region tends to possess its characteristic forms of animal and vegetable life, so too will it possess its own type of human society. Not that man is merely plastic under the influence of his material environment. He moulds it, as well as being moulded by it. The lower the culture the more passive it is. But the higher culture will express itself through its material circumstance, as masterfully and triumphantly as the artist through the medium of his material.

It is true that three of the main influences which form and modify human culture are the same as in the case of the formation of an animal species. They are (1) race, i.e. the genetic factor ; (2) environment, i.e. the geographical factor ; (3) function or occupation, i.e. the economic factor. But in addition to these there is a fourth element—thought or the psychological factor—which is peculiar to the human species and the existence of which frees man from the blind dependence on material environment which characterises the lower forms of life. It is this factor which renders possible the acquisition of a growing capital of social tradition, so that the gains of one generation can be transmitted to the next, and the discoveries or new ideas of an individual can become the common property of the whole society. In this way a human culture is able to modify itself more rapidly and adapt itself more successfully to a new environment by an inheritance of acquired characteristics, such as does not seem to exist under the purely biological law of development which governs animal species. The formation of a culture is due to the interaction of all these factors ; it is a four-fold community—for it involves in varying degrees a community of work and a community of thought as well as a community of place and a community of blood. Any attempt to explain social development in terms of one of these to the exclusion of the rest leads to the error of racial or geographical or economic determinism or to no less false theories of abstract intellectual progress.

At present perhaps the dominant fashion is to look to the racial factor as the *deus ex machina* of the human drama. Yet race is itself but the product of the process of interaction that we have mentioned. In the address to the British Association to which I have already referred, Dr. Tate Regan shows how various species and subspecies of fishes have been differentiated owing to their segregation in particular areas and the corresponding variation of their habits. Thus the plaice of the Baltic have become differentiated from those of the North Sea, and the colonies of freshwater char in the lakes of Great Britain and Ireland, which have been segregated since the glacial period, have acquired each their special group characteristics.

Now the same process occurs in the formation of human races. A particular way of life in a particular environment produces a specialised human type if it is continued over a long enough course of time. Thus the Mongol is the result of a uniform way of life on the steppes of Eastern Central Asia, a totally different way of life in the tropical forest has produced the Negro, and so on. In other words, the primitive cultures of the nature peoples have endured for such vast periods that their human products have become stabilised as fixed racial types, which have remained the raw material, as it were, of all the later developments. And every subsequent culture, in so far as it involves a way of life peculiar to itself, tends to produce a new racial type, even though it does not enjoy uniform conditions long enough to become fixed. It may be that the unscientific habit of talking about " the Latin race " or " the Anglo-Saxon race," instead of the Latin or " Anglo-Saxon " culture, is due to a half-conscious popular realisation of this fact.

It must of course be admitted that many racial characteristics, such as skin colour, and probably nose form, are due to a purely passive reception of climate and geographical influences. Nevertheless, in the formation of any culture even of the lowest type, such as the ways of living of the prehistoric Negro or Mongol, human activity and spontaneous co-operation with Nature take a leading part. Perhaps no culture is more completely controlled by, and in harmony with, its environment than that of the Esquimaux. He belongs to the Arctic no less than the animals on whom he is a parasite—the seal and the reindeer. At every point —in his use of skin for boats and tents and clothing, of bone for weapons and tools, of blubber for warmth and light—he is bound down to an absolute dependence on the little that Nature has given him. Yet his culture is not a necessary result of climatic and economic determinism, it is a work of art, a triumph of human inventiveness and endurance, and it is the fruit of an age-long cultural tradition, which may well stretch back as far in time and space as the Magdalenian culture of the European glacial age.

And here, too, we see that a culture may be no less a fixed type than is a race. When once a new way of life has been discovered, when man has attained some permanent state of equilibrium with the external world, he will preserve it indefinitely from age to age, and any change will come, not from within, but from the foreign pressure of some external culture. To-day the Esquimaux are learning a new manner of life, they are becoming civilised, but at the same time and for the same reason they are a dying race.

II. *The Problem of the Change and Progress of Cultures.*—In spite of this tendency towards the fixation of culture in unchanging social types, it is impossible to deny the reality and importance of cultural progress. This progress is not, however, as the philosophers of the eighteenth century believed, a continuous and uniform movement, common to the whole human race, and as universal and necessary as a law of nature. It is rather an exceptional condition, due to a number of distinct causes, which often operate irregularly and spasmodically. Just as civilisation itself is not a single whole, but a generalisation from a number of historic cultures each with its own limited life, so Progress is an abstract idea derived from a simplification of the multiple and heterogeneous changes through which the historic societies have passed.

Hence in place of a single uniform law of Progress it is necessary to distinguish the following main types of social change :

(A) The simple case of a people that develops its way of life in its original environment without the intrusion of human factors from outside. This is exemplified in those primitive race-forming " pre-cultures," of which we have spoken above.

(B) The case of a people which comes into a new geographical environment and readapts its culture in consequence. This is the simplest type of cultural change, but it is of great importance. There is a constant process of steppe peoples entering the forest, and vice versa, of mountaineers descending into the plains, and inland peoples coming into contact with the sea. The consequences are most striking when the climatic differences of the two regions are widely different, as in the case of the invasion of India by peoples from the steppes and plateaux of Central Asia.

(C) The case of two different peoples, each with its own way of life and social organisation, which mix with one another usually as a result of conquest, occasionally as a result of peaceful contact. In any case, this involves the preceding factor (B) also, for at least one of the two peoples.

This is the most typical and important of all the causes of culture change, since it sets up an organic process of fusion and change, which transforms both the people and the culture, and produces a new cultural entity in a comparatively short space of time. It is the origin of practically all those sudden flowerings of new civilisation, which impress us as almost miraculous (e.g. " le miracle Grec "). It is possible to compare this process of fusion of peoples and cultures in very numerous instances in different ages and in different parts of the world, and everywhere we see the cycle of change passing through the same phases and lasting for an approximately similar time. First there comes a period of several centuries of silent growth during which a people lives on the tradition of the older culture, either that which they have brought with them, or that which they found in the land. Secondly there comes a period of intense cultural activity, when the new forms of life created by the vital union of two different peoples and cultures burst into flower ; when we see the re-awakening of the forms of the old culture fertilised by contact with a new people, or the creative activity of a new people stimulated by contact with the old autochthonous culture. It is a time of great achievement, of abounding vitality, but also of violent conflicts and revolts of spasmodic action, and brilliant promise that has no fulfilment. Finally the culture reaches maturity, either by the absorption of the new elements by the original people and its culture, or by the attainment of a permanent balance between the two, the stabilisation of a new cultural variation.

(D) The case of a people that adopts some element of material culture which has been developed by another people elsewhere. This is a comparatively superficial change compared with the last one, but it is of great importance as showing the close interdependence of cultures. We see how in the past the use of metals, agriculture and irrigation, a new weapon or the use of the horse in war, have spread from one end of the Old World to the other with amazing rapidity. Moreover, such material changes bring with them profound social changes, since they may alter the whole system of social organisation. We have seen instances of such change almost in our own times ; in the case of the adoption of the horse by the Indians of the Plains, and the spread of the use of firearms and of European clothing among primitive peoples. But it is remarkable how often such external change leads not to social progress, but to social decay. As a rule, to be progressive change must come from within.

(E) The case of a people which modifies its way of life owing to the adoption of new knowledge or beliefs, or to some change in its view of life and its conception of reality. Up to this point it may seem that the process of culture change is a rigidly deterministic one, and leaves no room for any free moral or intellectual progress.

For it might be thought that if the highest products of a culture are the flowers of a social organism that has had its roots in particular geographical and ethnological circumstances, no permanent and objective progress will be achieved and the greatest works of art and thought will simply reproduce in a more sophisticated form the results of the past experience of the organism. Certainly we must admit that every past condition will express itself in the life-impulses and life-concepts of a society, and that thus the cultural achievements of a people are largely determined by the past. But this does not occur mechanically. The existence of Reason increases the range of possibilities in the fulfilment of instinctive purpose. An old impulse acting in a new environment, different from that to which it was originally adapted, may be not merely a decadent survival, but a stepping-stone to the acquisition of new powers and to some new conception of reality. Thus there is a continual enlargement of the field of experience, and, thanks to Reason, the new does not simply replace the old, but is compared and combined with it. The history of mankind, and still more of civilised mankind, shows a continuous process of integration, which, even though it seems to work irregularly, never ceases. For Reason is itself a creative power which is ever organising the raw material of life and sensible experience into the ordered cosmos of an intelligible world—a world which is not a mere subjective image, but corresponds in a certain measure to the objective reality. A modern writer has said : " The mind of man seems to be of a nature to assimilate itself to the universe ; we belong to the world ; the whole is mirrored in us. Therefore, when we bend our thoughts on a limited object, we concentrate faculties which are naturally endowed with infinite correspondences." [1]

We cannot shut our eyes to the significance of this steadily growing vision of Reality, which is at once the condition and the result of the life-purpose of human society.

It is easy for us to see how in the case of modern

[1] *Times Literary Supplement*, 1923, p. 330.

science or Greek philosophy a culture has been directly moulded by the influence of thought. But the importance of the psychological factor is not confined to purely intellectual knowledge, it is manifested equally in the religious outlook, which dominates even the most primitive cultures. Every religion embodies an attitude to life and a conception of reality, and any change in these brings with it a change in the whole character of the culture, as we see in the case of the transformation of ancient civilisation by Christianity, or the transformation of the society of Pagan Arabia by Islam. Thus the prophet and the religious reformer, in whom a new view of life—a new *revelation*—becomes explicit, is perhaps the greatest of all agents of social change, even though he is himself the product of social causes and the vehicle of an ancient cultural tradition.

And thus the great stages of world-culture are linked with changes in man's vision of Reality. The primitive condition of food-gathering and hunting peoples does not necessarily imply reasonable purpose or any reflective vision of Reality ; consequently it does not imply civilisation. The dawn of true civilisation came only with the discovery of natural laws, or rather of the possibility of man's fruitful co-operation with the powers of Nature. This was the foundation of the primitive cultures of Elam and Babylonia and Egypt. To it belongs the discovery of the higher agriculture, the working of metals and the invention of writing and the calendar, together with the institutions of kingship and priesthood and an organised state.

It governed the progress of civilisation for thousands of years and only passed away with the coming of the new vision of Reality which began to transform the ancient world in the fifth and sixth centuries B.C.—the age of the Hebrew Prophets and the Greek Philosophers, of Buddha and Confucius, an age which marks the dawn of a new world.

THE AGE OF THE GODS

CHAPTER I

THE GLACIAL AGE AND THE BEGINNINGS OF HUMAN LIFE IN EUROPE

THE PHASES OF TERRESTRIAL AND CLIMATIC CHANGE AND THEIR INFLUENCE ON THE DEVELOPMENT OF LIFE.

THE EARLY AND MIDDLE PALÆOLITHIC PERIODS.

THE LATER PALÆOLITHIC PERIOD AND THE APPEARANCE OF NEW HUMAN TYPES.

THE AURIGNACIAN AND SOLUTREAN CULTURES.

THE MAGDALENIAN AND CAPSIAN CULTURES.

CHAPTER I

THE GLACIAL AGE AND THE BEGINNINGS OF HUMAN LIFE IN EUROPE

I. The Phases of Terrestrial and Climatic Change and their Influence on the Development of Life

THE question of the origins of cultural change is hardly less fundamental than that of the mutation of species itself, which remains the fundamental problem of biology. In fact, the development of a new way of life, and that of a new race or species, are, as we have seen, closely bound up together, and form two aspects of a single vital movement. The farther we go back in the history of humanity, the more difficult it is to conceive of any spontaneous development or modification of culture. The way of life of a primitive people is almost as unchangeable as the habits of an animal species. When Tasmania was first discovered by Europeans its natives were living a life which was in all probability essentially the same as that of their ancestors in Pleistocene times, and the coming of the higher civilisation brought with it for them, not progress, but extermination.

In order to be effective, change must come from without—from a change in environment—as well as from within, for if natural conditions are unchanging, life will be unchanging also, and thus the evolution alike of cultures and of species is dependent on the whole process of terrestrial change.

For the history of the earth is not a simple uniform development. It has proceeded by a series of vast cyclic revolutions, true world-ages in which the stages

3

of geological, climatic, and biological change are co-
ordinated and dependent on one another. Behind
the world that we know there lies a whole series of
other worlds, each with its own continents and seas,
and its own types of animal and vegetable life.

This conception of the cyclic process of terrestrial
change was already foreshadowed by the Greek genius,
in one of those flashes of scientific imagination which,
as in the case of the atomic theory or the heliocentric
astronomy, seem to anticipate the laborious experimental achievements of modern science. This is the
Aristotelian theory of the Great Summer and the Great
Winter, according to which the earth passes through a
cycle of climatic change, each phase of which is linked
with a corresponding change in the relative area of land
and sea.

This brilliant guess had to wait for its verification
until the modern sciences of geology and palæontology
had revealed the successive chapters of the earth's
history and had proved that the whole process of terrestrial change is indeed governed by a kind of rhythmic
movement. Not only the oceans, but the " eternal
hills " themselves rise and fall in obedience to this cosmic
law, so that the mountain ranges rise from the floor
of ancient seas, and in their turn fade away again like
snow wreaths under the sun and rain. Owing perhaps
to the gradual accumulation of radio-active heat within
the earth's crust, which ultimately causes the solid substratum of the continents to liquefy, each period of
stability is followed by a slow process of continental
depression and by the advance of the ocean at the
expense of the land. This process culminates in a
period of maximum submergence, which is followed by
an intensification of volcanic activity and a new phase
of orogenesis or mountain building, due mainly to the
lateral pressure of the ocean floor on its continental
margins. This climax reverses the former process
of submergence and leads to a new phase of land elevation

and continental advance. These cycles, each of which takes some forty million years to run its course, likewise form definite epochs in the history of organic life. Here the climatic changes which accompany the alternate phases of land depression and elevation play a leading part. Above all the growing severity of climate, culminating in the glaciation of large parts of the earth's surface, which coincides with the maximum phase of land elevation, following on a period of mountain building and continental uplift, has a most profound influence on the development and distribution of organic life.

Thus the vast glaciation of Permo-Carboniferous times, in which the ice sheets extended almost to the equator, marks the end of the Primary Palæozoic world, which was dominated by the lower forms of plant and animal life, such as the giant spore-bearing plants and the trilobites, and was followed by the first great expansion of land vertebrates and by the spread of coniferous trees and cycads. The passing of the Secondary Mesozoic world, with its giant forms of reptilian life, is more difficult to explain, but it is probable that the slight fall of temperature that accompanied the minor glaciation of Eocene times was sufficient to render conditions unfavourable for the survival of the cold-blooded reptiles, while the warm-blooded mammals and birds, with their coats of fur and feathers, were able to increase and multiply.

Finally the relatively modern glaciation of Pleistocene times, in the waning of which we ourselves live, witnessed the end of the reign of the beasts, and the rise to supremacy of the human race.

It was no doubt in the antediluvian world of the Tertiary Age, with its mild climatic conditions and its vast development of mammalian life, that the earliest forms of man first came into existence. It is true that we have no certain evidence for this, apart from Mr. Reid Moir's discoveries of flint implements in late

Pliocene deposits at Foxhall in Norfolk, which have as
yet not gained universal acceptance among archæologists.

To the archæologist man is essentially a tool-using
animal, and he is apt to conclude that where stone
implements are absent, man is non-existent. Yet it
is probable that just as the Stone Age far surpasses
the Age of Metals in duration, the age before man learned
to fashion stone implements was the longest of all.
Even to-day there are tribes like the Semang of the
Malay Peninsula, the Kubu of Sumatra,[1] and the
Veddahs of Ceylon, who are still in a pre-palæolithic
stage of culture, and it is suggestive that the region in
which these peoples survive is that in which there has
been least change of climatic conditions since Pliocene
times, and in which the flora and fauna of the Pre-
Glacial Age still flourish. Thus it was probably only
after the expulsion of man from the Paradise of the
Tertiary World, with its mild climatic conditions and its
abundance of animal and vegetable life, that he made
those great primitive discoveries of the use of clothing,
of weapons, and above all of fire, which rendered him
independent of the changes of climate and prepared
the way for his subsequent conquest of Nature.

But the effect of the Glacial period was not only to
increase the severity of the struggle for existence and
to lead to the extermination of the less adaptable species,
it also produced a growing tendency to racial and
cultural differentiation. It is necessary to remember
that the Pleistocene Glaciation was not a simple uniform
change of climate. It was rather a vast series of oscillations, which shifted the climatic zones alternatively
backwards and forwards, so that as Northern Europe
became a desert of ice, the modern desert areas of North
Africa and Central Asia became moister and more
temperate. Each swing of the pendulum was accompanied by a change in fauna and flora, and in the human

[1] Cf. H. O. Forbes in *Nature*, April 24, 1926.

population and culture. And it was during these successive changes that the human type seems to have developed most rapidly, for while a period of glaciation involved retrogression and death in one region, it gave fresh opportunities for life and progress elsewhere ; and with the ebbing of glacial conditions, there was a returning wave of new life and more highly developed types. Moreover, these climatic changes led in some cases to the permanent isolation of certain regions which became areas of racial segregation and differentiation. Thus the glaciation of the highlands of Central Asia led to the separation of the East Asiatic steppes— the cradle of the Mongolian race—from the rest of Asia, and in the same way the breaking up of the tropical forest belt which had formerly been continuous caused the isolation of the tropical region of South-eastern Asia from that of Africa.

II. The Early and Middle Palæolithic Periods

Unfortunately it is as yet impossible for us to trace the resultant process of human differentiation in detail. Though Europe was but the extreme outer margin of the inhabited world, and was certainly not the earliest or the most important centre of human development, we owe our knowledge of primitive man almost entirely to European evidence, and it is the typology of the stone implements of prehistoric Europe which serves as our standard of interpretation for palæolithic culture throughout the world. Nevertheless, even the partial and incomplete evidence that we possess does tend to illustrate the process of racial and cultural differentiation which we have just described. The lower palæolithic cultures, the Pre-Chellean, the Chellean, and the Acheulean, of which the first two are contemporary with the warm climate of the inter-glacial periods, represent a uniform type of culture, which is almost world-wide in extension, being found not only in West and Southern

Europe, but also in Western and Central Asia and
India, in North and South Africa, and in North and
South America. This uniformity of cultural type
undoubtedly points to a similar uniformity of racial
type, since cultural borrowing is hardly conceivable
at that period. Unfortunately we have no satisfactory evidence to show what this primitive type was
like. The only human remains that go back to the
Chellean age are these of the Piltdown Man (*Eoanthropus
dawsoni*) in England, and the Mauer Jaw from near
Heidelberg, in Germany. It is possible that the Piltdown
man belonged to the Chellean culture, but as his remains
are not associated with Chellean implements, and as
England itself lies on the extreme frontiers of the
Chellean province, it is equally probable that he represents the survival of an even more primitive type. On
the other hand, the Heidelberg man was undoubtedly
non-Chellean, for Central and Eastern Europe lay outside the limits of Chellean culture, and even at that
date formed part of another culture province, that of the
so-called Pre-Mousterian.

This was the forerunner and ancestor of the Mousterian
culture which spread southwards into Western and
Southern Europe with the fresh advance of glacial
conditions. The Chellean period had been characterised
by a warm climate and a semi-tropical fauna, including
the hippopotamus, the ancient straight-tusked elephant,
and Mercks rhinoceros, and these conditions still
existed during the early stages of the Acheulean culture,
which appears to have developed directly from the
Chellean without any abrupt change of race or culture.
During the later Acheulean period, however, there was
a gradual deterioration of climate which ultimately
led to the extinction of the earlier warm flora and fauna
and the appearance of a new semi-Arctic fauna—the
woolly rhinoceros and the mammoth, the musk ox
and the reindeer, as well as hosts of small Arctic rodents,
such as the lemming and the tailless hare. At the same

time it would seem that the earlier human population was driven out by the increasingly rigorous climate, and gave place to a new type of man, the Neanderthal race, which was probably derived from the Heidelberg man, who, as we have seen, existed in Central Europe at an earlier period.

This is the first human type, of which we possess plentiful and positive evidence. Its remains have been discovered not only in Central and Western Europe, but as far south as Gibraltar and Malta, and recently as far east as Galilee, while the corresponding culture— the Mousterian—is as world-wide in extent as its Chellean and Acheulean predecessors. The evidence suggests that a specialised type of race and culture, which had been developed under temperate conditions in Central Europe or farther east, was forced to migrate southwards before the fresh advance of the ice-sheets, thus taking the place of the population which had inhabited Western and Southern Europe during the previous period of warm climate. Either in continuation of this movement, or in consequence of the growing severity of climatic conditions during the maximum of the last glaciation, Neanderthal man passed on into South-west Asia and into Africa, where he probably continued to exist long after his disappearance from Europe, for the famous skull discovered at Broken Hill, Rhodesia, proves that a type closely allied to Neanderthal man existed in South Africa in Post-Glacial times.[1]

III. The Later Palæolithic Period and the Appearance of New Human Types

But in spite of the almost world-wide extension of the Mousterian culture, which, at least in Europe and Palestine, is everywhere associated with the Neanderthal

---

[1] The Rhodesian skull is non-fossilised, and consequently may date from a comparatively recent age. M. Boule has even suggested that Rhodesian man may have lingered on in out-of-the-way parts of the Continent, like the okapi, down to modern times.

race, it is certain that the latter was in no sense the
ancestor of modern man.   In spite of the almost bestial
appearance of his skull, with its massive chinless jaw,
its enormous brow ridges and receding forehead, Neanderthal man was not a primitive, undifferentiated type of
humanity.   He was rather an over-specialised by-
product, a side path or blind alley on the road of
human development.   Modern man descends from other
unknown types which must have existed somewhere in
the Old World, both before and during the dominance
of the Neanderthal race in Europe.   There is no gradual
transition from the latter to more modern types.   When
the climax of the last glacial phase began to pass,
and Europe became a land of cold, dry steppes, ranged
by vast herds of bison and reindeer and wild horse,
Neanderthal man and his culture disappear entirely,
and their place is taken by a new culture and by new
types of man.   This is the greatest turning-point in the
human history of Europe, for it marks the coming of
modern humanity.   Henceforward, however great may
be the changes in environment and culture, there is no
complete break.   The process of development is
continuous, and we have to do with essentially the same
kind of man as that which inhabits the world to-day.

Indeed, judged by purely physical standards, such
as the size of their brain, fossil men of the later palæolithic period were equal and sometimes even superior
to the average modern man.

The modern average of cranial capacity lies between
1,400 and 1,500 cubic centimetres, while that of the
fossil man of Cromagnon has been estimated at 1,650 c.c.,
that of Chancelade at 1,710 c.c., and that of Barma
Grande, near Mentone, higher still.

This result is not flattering to our pride in the progress
of modern man, but it is curiously borne out by the
recent discoveries of fossil man outside Europe.   In
South Africa, remains have been found at Boskop and
Tsitzikama of a prehistoric race, somewhat resembling

the Cromagnon type and probably of similar age. The
cranial dimensions of the skulls are most remarkable
and were estimated by the discoverer of the Boskop
specimen at 1,832 c.c., and by Professor Elliot Smith at
1,900. This is probably too high, but the lowest
estimate gives over 1,700.

There is reason to think that this race was the ancestor
of the modern South African Hottentot and Bushman,
for the remains of an intermediate type—the vanished
race of Strandloopers—has been discovered and all three
types agree in certain cranial characteristics.   In size
of brain, however, there is a steady diminution from the
1,700 c.c. or more of Boskop through the Strandlooper
skulls with a maximum of 1,500 down to the Hottentot
who averages 1,380, and the Bushman whose cranial
average is only 1,300 c.c.   Just the same phenomenon
is to be found in Oceania, where the ancestral type of the
small-brained modern Australian native goes back to the
large-brained fossil man discovered at Wadjak in Java.

The conclusion seems to be that the last glacial period
was contemporary with a simultaneous development of
humanity, which was not confined to a single race or
a single part of the world. But while in Europe and
Asia the new types of man were the initiators of a
progressive movement which has never wholly ceased,
in South Africa and Australasia, owing to isolation and
the absence of external stimulus, they became stationary
in culture and physically retrograde.

Even in Europe, the successors of Neanderthal man
did not belong to a single type. Among the remains
dating from the Aurignacian period that have been
discovered in Southern France and the Riviera, we can
distinguish at least three different races. The most
important is the Cromagnon type (*Homo priscus*),
characterised by its tall stature and large and lofty
skull, though the face is unsymmetrically short and
wide.

Entirely different to this is the Combe Capelle race

(*Homo aurignacensis*), examples of which have been found, not only in France, but as far east as Brunn in Moravia.   This type is small and delicately made, with a long, narrow head and a low, somewhat receding forehead.   Its features, especially the jaw, show much more primitive characteristics than the man of Cromagnon. It is tempting to see in these contrasting types the ancestral forms of the modern Nordic and Mediterranean races ; but though the skulls found at Obercassel, and classified by German anthropologists with the Cromagnon type, do show decided resemblances to Nordic man, the Combe Capelle race is a far more primitive type than Mediterranean man, though Professor Fleure and other anthropologists believe that it still survives among the modern population of Europe in secluded regions such as Sardinia, North-west Spain, and the moorlands of North Wales.[1]

Finally, in one of the caves of Grimaldi on the Riviera, a region in which the warm fauna of inter-glacial times had survived as late as the Mousterian period, in addition to numerous remains of Cromagnon man, two skeletons have been found which belong to a distinctly negroid type, and may be either the survivors of the human representatives of the old semi-tropical fauna, or more probably new-comers from warmer latitudes.   Moreover, in addition to these three types, all of which co-existed in Western Europe in Aurignacian times, numerous remains of another, distinct race have been found at Predmost in Moravia, dating from the later Aurignacian period.   This Predmost type is characterised by the very heavy brow ridges which give the skull a somewhat primitive appearance.   In other respects, however, it differs little from modern man, and may perhaps be regarded as an ancestral form of the Nordic race.   Thus it is clear that in later palæolithic times Europe was already a

---

[1] Cf. Fleure, " Some Early Neanthopic Types," in *J. R. Anthrop. Inst.*, vol. 50, 1920.

meeting-ground of different races, which must have developed elsewhere, and the same diversity characterises the later palæolithic cultures.

IV. The Aurignacian and Solutrean Cultures

The Aurignacian culture, which replaced the Mousterian after the passing of the climax of the last glacial phase, was of a relatively uniform type, and is found not only in Western, Central, and Eastern Europe, but in North Africa and Spain, and possibly also as far as Siberia, India, and South Africa.

While the earlier palæolithic industry had been characterised by large and usually coarsely worked flint implements, such as " hand axes " and scrapers, that of Aurignacian times was marked by the development of small, finely worked flint blades, which attained an extraordinary degree of elaboration and complexity of type in the Middle Aurignacian period in Europe. It is the industry of a highly developed hunting culture, which possessed the lance and the bow, weapons which enabled their possessors to hunt down the swifter kinds of game, such as the horse, the bison, and the deer, whereas the men of the older palæolithic culture seem to have depended mainly on the hunting of the large, slower-moving pachyderms, such as the elephant and the mammoth, which were presumably either trapped in pits or tracked down when wounded or sick as the modern African pygmies follow up a wounded elephant.

But the most striking features of the later palæolithic period is the rise of Art, which alone is sufficient to mark off the Aurignacian culture from all that preceded it. This art consists mainly of sculpture in ivory or stone, as well as reliefs and rock engravings. There is as yet none of the wonderful cave painting that characterises Magdalenian times, but Aurignacian art already shows remarkable artistic gifts, and is far superior to

the work of modern savage peoples. The sculpture is
often highly realistic, and as a rule represents female
figures of extreme corpulence with an accentuation of
the sexual characteristics, which is probably due to
religious or magical ideas regarding fecundity. Some
writers, however, impressed by the realistic spirit of
the art, have seen in it a racial characteristic of Aurignacian man. A similar extreme development of adipose
tissue is, in fact, found among the women of several
modern African peoples, such as the Hottentots, and
the Hamitic Watusi of Ruanda in East Africa ; and since
the Aurignacian culture seems to have entered Europe
from North Africa, a connection between the primitive
non-negroid African stock and Aurignacian man is not
improbable. The same feature reappears in neolithic
times in the art of the South-east Mediterranean and
Malta. In palæolithic times, however, this figure
sculpture is confined to Europe, and is one of the marks
which distinguishes the Aurignacian culture of Europe
from the sister culture, known as the Capsian, which
embraced North Africa and South-eastern Spain. The
latter culture possessed a very distinctive art of its
own, which is known to us from the numerous rock
paintings of South-eastern Spain, and it developed
without a break through the whole of the later palæolithic period down to the beginnings of the neolithic
age.

The Aurignacian culture of Europe, on the other hand,
came to an abrupt end, and was replaced by the sudden
intrusion of a new culture—the Solutrean—which
originated in Eastern Europe or Asia. Its appearance
coincides with an increase of cold and dryness, which
may have rendered the eastern steppes uninhabitable,
and forced their population to migrate west and south.
The Solutrean culture is in fact an isolated episode,
which has no connection with the general course of
cultural development in prehistoric Europe, and it is
impossible to estimate its real meaning and importance,

until we know more concerning the later palæolithic cultures of Western and Central Asia. The great characteristic of the Solutrean period is the perfection that it attained in the working of flint, above all in the famous " laurel leaf " javelin points, which surpass in regularity and delicacy of workmanship every other product of palæolithic industry. They have been compared with the finely worked flint implements of neolithic or æneolithic date from Elam and Egypt, but it is doubtful whether the resemblance is close enough to justify any theory of inter-connection, unless perhaps there was a common West-Asiatic tradition of flint working, which maintained itself with modifications through the ages.

V. The Magdalenian and Capsian Cultures

The Solutrean culture in Europe passed away as suddenly as it had appeared, and gave place to a revival of the old cultural traditions which had obtained in Aurignacian times. This new culture, known as the Magdalenian, did not, however, like its predecessors, enter Western Europe fully formed from without. It was a purely local development which had its origin and centre of diffusion in the region of the Pyrenees, whence it ultimately extended eastward through France and Germany as far as Hungary and Poland. It is thus the first specifically European culture to come into existence.

So far as we know it was not due to the coming of a new people. The Cromagnon race, which had inhabited Western Europe in Aurignacian times, still continued to exist, and it is to this period that the skeletons of Les Hoteaux, Duruthy, Laugerie Basse, and Obercassel belong. There is one skeleton, however, that of Chancelade, which belongs to a completely different type. It is short and squat, with a large head which bears some resemblance to that of the modern Esqui-

maux.[1] This is specially interesting, as the Magdalenian
is a culture of definitely " Arctic " character, comparable
in some respects with that of the modern hunting peoples
of the Arctic regions, such as the Esquimaux. Its
flint work is poor, and not to be compared with the Solutrean, but it is characterised by a great development
in the use of bone implements and weapons such as the
propulsor or spear thrower, especially the harpoon.
Above all, it possessed a very remarkable and distinctive
artistic tradition, entirely devoted to the portrayal of
animal forms. There are hardly any sculptures of the
human figure, as in the Aurignacian period, but the
bone implements are often beautifully carved or
engraved, and there are carvings in the round, such
as the figure of a horse from Les Espélungues, and
the even finer head of a neighing horse from Mas
d'Azil, as well as the great animal sculptures in high
relief on the walls of the cliff at Cap Blanc, near Les
Eyzies.

But most important of all is the wonderful art of
the cave paintings, which are the peculiar glory of the
Magdalenian culture. It is more than half a century
since these were first discovered, but their full importance
was not at first realised, and it was even doubted
whether such works could date from so remote a period
as the later palæolithic age. For the most striking
feature of this art is its naturalism and realism. There
is none of the stiffness and childishness which is usually
associated with the art of primitive peoples. It does
not need a sophisticated taste to appreciate it, as is the
case with the art of many far more advanced cultures.
It conveys to the most untrained observer an extraordinarily vivid impression of animal life and energy.
The great bison and the wild boar of Altamira are as
powerful and full of vitality as any animal paintings
of modern times, certainly there is nothing to be com-

[1] Cf. Sollas, *Ancient Hunters*, pp. 513–16, and recently Karl Pearson
in *Man*, vol. 26, no. 27.

pared with them in Europe until we come to the best
age of Minoan art in Crete.

The geographical range of the Magdalenian paintings
is very limited, being confined to South-west France
and the adjoining part of Spain.   They fall into three
main groups, one in the Dordogne region, one in the
French Pyrenees, and one on the north-west coast of
Spain (Santander and Asturias).   Entirely distinct from
all of these is the contemporary art of South-east Spain,
the region of the Capsian culture.   The Magdalenian
art consists almost entirely of individual representations
of animals, without any attempt at scenic composition.
On the other hand, human figures play a predominant
part in the art of Eastern Spain, and are often grouped
together with animals in hunting scenes and more
rarely in scenes of fighting and dancing.   The style is
equally different from that of Magdalenian art.   The
human figures are conventionalised and often highly
grotesque, though details of personal adornment are
often carefully shown ;   and in spite of the unnatural
proportions of the figures, the running bowman and the
fall of the wounded chieftain at Barranco del Valtorta
are depicted with extraordinary mastery and vigour.
Taking into account the close geographical proximity
of the two styles, it is possible that Magdalenian art
in its origins owed something to the influence of its
southern neighbour, but there can be no question of
the complete independence of the two cultures.   In
spite of their common ancestry, they had each developed
a distinct type of culture and industry.   In contrast
to the bone harpoons and weapons of the Magdalenians,
the men of the later Capsian culture practised a flint
industry of a peculiar type, in which the old Aurignacian
forms were gradually simplified and reduced in size
until they became minute implements of geometrical
form.   This culture had an enormously wide range,
since it extended from Spain through North Africa as
far as Syria and perhaps farther still, and at the close

of the palæolithic age it was destined to expand into Europe at the expense of the Magdalenian culture. How far the East Spanish art was characteristic of the culture as a whole, it is impossible to say, although hitherto discoveries have been confined to Spain.

A somewhat similar art, however, existed in later palæolithic times in Central India, where rock paintings, depicting hunting scenes, and the figures of animals have been discovered in the Vindhya Hills. Even more remarkable is the resemblance to the East Spanish paintings of the art of the Bushmen of South Africa in relatively modern times, and despite the enormous gap between the two periods it seems not impossible that this resemblance is due to the survival of the Capsian artistic tradition among the hunting peoples of Africa.

The Magdalenian culture, on the other hand, did not survive the glacial period, it passed away with the reindeer and the rest of the steppe fauna. The last relics of its artistic tradition are to be found far to the north in Scandinavia and date from neolithic times, when nothing of the kind existed in the old centres of palæolithic culture in Western Europe. For the close of the glacial period, which we may place somewhere between 12000 and 6000 B.C., produced a complete change in the conditions of European life. A mild, damp climate set in, the old hunting-grounds of the Magdalenian people became forests, and the great herds of bison and reindeer and wild horse disappeared. Europe was no longer a good land for the hunter, for the forest is not friendly to man, and the consequence was a degradation rather than an advance of culture. The successors of the Magdalenians lingered on as hunters of the deer and the wild ox, but largely as a miserable population of shore dwellers, which lived by gathering shell fish, one of the most universal and rudimentary of primitive occupations. At the same time new cultures began to penetrate into Europe from the south and east, and a new age began.

CHAPTER II

LATER PALÆOLITHIC CULTURE AND THE RELIGION OF THE HUNTER

CHAPTER II

LATER PALÆOLITHIC CULTURE AND THE RELIGION OF THE HUNTER

I. The Place of Religion in Primitive Culture

THE later palæolithic period which we have described in the last chapter has an extraordinary importance for the history of culture, not only because it witnesses the appearance of the modern type of humanity, but still more because for the first time it enables us to form some idea of the inner life of primitive culture. Hitherto we have been dealing with the dry bones of vanished cultures. Now for the first time we are able to see something of the life behind. We can at last enter into the mind of primitive man and gain some knowledge of the psychic conditions which influenced the life of prehistoric man. Many attempts—some of them brilliant enough—have been made to reconstruct the whole course of man's social and religious development from the very dawn of humanity, but these are from their very nature incapable of proof or disproof. It is impossible to reconstruct man's early social organisation, and still more his psychic development, from flint hand axes and scrapers, or from the rare fossil remains, whose very physical interpretation is sometimes uncertain.

Even in palæolithic times, we have seen that racial composition of the population of Europe was far from simple, and this renders impossible any attempt to explain culture on purely racial lines. The pure race is at best a scientific abstraction, and the generalisations, in which many anthropologists still indulge, regarding the fixed types of racial psychology, which

lie at the root of all historic cultures, are mere specula-
tions, often influenced by modern national prejudices.
From the first we have to deal, not with pure races,
but with regional types which are the products of social
and cultural influences.   A culture can only be understood from within.   It is a spiritual community which
owes its unity to common beliefs and a common attitude
to life, far more than to any uniformity of physical
type.

Hence the study of primitive culture is intimately
bound up with that of primitive religion.   Throughout
the history of humanity the religious impulse has been
always and everywhere present as one of the great
permanent forces that make and alter man's destiny,
and the deeper we delve in the past, the more evident
it is how inseparable is the religious instinct from
human life and society.   The beginnings of religion are
as old as the human consciousness, and we can no more
go behind the religious stage in human history than we
can go behind the origins of language or of social life
itself.

This, however, presupposes a broader definition of
religion than that which it has sometimes received.   It
would not hold good, if, with Sir James Frazer, we limit
religion to the conciliation and worship of supernatural
and personal beings which control the forces of nature.
Even Tyler's " minimum " definition, " the belief in
spiritual beings," is too narrow, for primitive religion
is something vaguer and more rudimentary even than
the type of thought to which these definitions properly
refer.   Yet we can go back behind this stage and still
find religion—a powerful and living religion—existing.
Wherever and whenever man has a sense of dependence
on external powers which are conceived as mysterious
and higher than man's own, there is religion, and the
feelings of awe and self-abasement with which man is
filled in the presence of such powers is essentially a
religious emotion, the root of worship and prayer.

Taken in this sense the religious instinct is part of the nature of man. It involves both affection and fear, and its power is strongest at times of individual or social crisis, when the routine of ordinary life is broken through and men are face to face with the unforeseen and the unknown. Hence the moments of vital change in the life of the individual—birth, puberty, and death—are pre-eminently religious, and so, too, for a society that lives in close dependence on Nature, are the vital moments of the life of the earth, spring and winter, seed-time and harvest, the yearly death and rebirth of nature.

The earliest form of religious observance of which we possess any real evidence is, in fact, connected with the idea of death. It dates from the time of Neanderthal man, long before the age of Magdalenian art or the rise of the later palæolithic culture. Although to us Neanderthal man may seem so primitive a type as to be scarcely human, there is no doubt about the fact that he cared for his dead. Already in several interments of the Mousterian period—notably at La Chapelle aux Saints and at La Ferrassie—there is evidence that the disposal of the dead was accompanied with practices which point to the belief in some existence in or beyond the tomb. The very fact that a careful interment is made suggests some thought for the welfare of the dead, but far more important is the presence with the corpse of weapons and implements, of food offerings, and in one case of a rhinoceros horn which, from later palæolithic evidence, seems to have possessed some magical significance. Moreover, at La Ferrassie the large block of stone which covered the bones was found on its removal to be covered with artificial cup-markings, such as are found on sacred stones in neolithic and later times.

Here, then, in Mousterian times and in association with the Neanderthal type of man, which has no direct connection with its successors, do we find the first evidence of practices and beliefs that can be called religious. It is, however, clearly impossible to argue from this evidence that the origins of religion are to be looked for in the cult of the dead. Our knowledge of the Mousterian culture is too fragmentary for us to form any general ideas about primitive religion and its relation to social life. This only becomes possible in the later palæolithic period, when a flood of light is thrown on prehistoric culture by the art of the Magdalenian cave paintings and the Aurignacian figure sculptures and fine engravings, as well as by the human remains and the objects associated with interments. From these it is possible to form a picture of the culture of the later palæolithic inhabitants of Europe—the external conditions of their life and their mental reaction to their environment—which is capable of being compared in its main features with that of existing peoples of primitive type, such as the Bushmen of Africa and the Australian aborigines, and even more advanced peoples, such as the hunting peoples of North America.

It is, of course, a very controversial question how far it is possible to regard modern savages as representatives of truly primitive conditions. On the one hand, it is held that the most backward existing peoples, for example the Australians, are practically unchanged survivals of prehistoric culture, social fossils from an extremely remote past which can be used, as they have been by Professor Sollas in his book on *Ancient Hunters and their Modern Representatives*, to reconstruct the life of our prehistoric forerunners in Europe. On the other hand, it is believed by an increasingly numerous school (e.g. Dr. Rivers and Professor Elliot Smith) that the so-called primitive peoples owe the greater part of their social and religious institutions to the influence of civilising currents transmitted from the ancient historic cultures.

Certainly it is impossible to deny the extremely primitive character of the Australian race. The fossil skulls found at Wadjak in Java and Talgai in Queensland point to the development of a separate human type in Australasia which has some affinities to Neanderthal man, and is more archaic in type than anything to be found elsewhere. It would, therefore, not be surprising that such a primitive anthropological type should preserve a correspondingly primitive form of culture and religion—perhaps even an earlier type than that which the large-brained and talented men of the later palæolithic age in Europe already possessed. But for that very reason, Australia is not a safe analogy. The difference of physical type and geographical environment is so great that we are not warranted in supposing that their past followed the same lines of development as our past. For it is not possible to take any savage people just because they are primitive as a parallel to the later palæolithic inhabitants of Europe. We must take account of differences in physical type and geographical environment. The Andaman Islanders or the Tasmanians of modern times belong to a lower stage of culture even than the Aurignacians, as well as to a lower physical type.

II. The Religious Conceptions of the Hunting Peoples

It is rather in the Northern Steppe region of Asia and America—the domain of what has been called the Arctic culture—that we find the closest analogies to the Europe of the later glacial age. It may seem paradoxical to suggest that peoples like the North American Indians, who possess some knowledge alike of agriculture and of the use of metals, can be better representatives of primitive conditions than the Australian natives who were completely ignorant of both. But it is in the tundra and steppes of Siberia and Canada that the natural conditions of later palæolithic Europe are most closely paralleled, alike in climate, in fauna, and in flora, and it would seem to follow that the reproduction of the psychological conditions of the primitive hunter are to be looked for in the Indian of the North, who, like his Magdalenian forerunner, was a parasite of the bison and the reindeer, than in the food-gatherers of the Australian bush or of the tropical jungle.

The remarkable resemblances between the different hunting cultures of the Arctic region, of North Siberia, and North America, and those of later palæolithic Europe, are too great to be fortuitous.   Underlying them all there is not only a common way of life, but a common psychology—a common religious foundation which is the key to the interpretation of the culture, and which, if not primitive in the strict sense of the word, is at least the earliest human religion of which we have knowledge.

For the primitive peoples belonging to the hunting culture are in no sense pre-religious or a-religious.   They are on the contrary more religious than the peoples of the higher cultures, since the essential religious attitude —the sense of dependence on mysterious external powers—is stronger with them than it is in the case of civilised societies.   The culture-peoples even at their lowest have conquered a certain autonomy and security against the external world.   Nature is to them partly external and foreign—the forest and the jungle as against the village and the field—partly conquered and harnessed as in the case of the domesticated animal and the artificially raised crop.   But the hunter lives always in a state of utter dependence on Nature, such as we cannot conceive.   Nature is always and everywhere his mistress and mother, and he is a parasite living on her bounty through her elder and wiser and stronger children, the beasts.   Hence the religion of the primitive hunter is characterised by universality and vagueness. He does not single out particular powers of Nature to be divinised and worshipped as do the men of the archaic civilisations, nor is he, strictly speaking, an animist, who looks on every manifestation of Nature as the work of individual personal spirits. He is rather a kind of primitive pantheist or " hekastotheist," as Powell calls him, who sees everywhere behind the outward appearance of things a vague undifferentiated supernatural power which shows itself alike in beast and plant, in storm and thunder, in rock and tree, in the magic of the shaman, and in the spirits of the dead. This is the type of religion which Professor Marett first described as Pre-Animism, and to which M. Durkheim and his school have given the name of the Religion of Mana. The latter, however, is not the ideal term, since in Polynesia and Melanesia, excepting only in the Banks and Torres Islands, Mana is used almost exclusively to describe the magical powers of individual men, especially chiefs.

It is rather among the relatively advanced hunting tribes of North America that this conception has been most fully developed and can be most clearly recognised.

Thus, Swanton writes of the Tlingit Indians in Alaska :

" The Tlingit do not divide the universe arbitrarily into so many different quarters ruled by so many supernatural beings. On the contrary, supernatural power impresses them as a vast immensity, one in kind and impersonal, inscrutable as to its nature, but whenever manifesting itself to men taking a personal, and it might be said a human personal form in whatever aspect it displays itself. Thus the sky spirit is the ocean of supernatural energy as it manifests itself in the sky, the sea spirit as it manifests itself in the sea, the bear spirit as it manifests itself in the bear, the rock spirit as it manifests itself in the rock, etc. It is not meant that the Tlingit consciously reasons this out, or formulates a unity in the supernatural, but such appears to be his unexpressed feeling. For this reason there appears to be but one name for this spiritual power, *Yok*, a name which is affixed to any specific manifestation of it, and it is to this perception or feeling reduced to personality that the ' Great Spirit ' idea seems usually to have affixed itself. This supernatural energy must be carefully differentiated from natural energy and never confused with it.   It is true that the former is supposed to bring about results similar to the latter, but in the mind of the Tlingit the conceived difference between the two is as great as with us.   A rock rolling down hill or an animal running is by no means a manifestation of supernatural energy, although if something peculiar be associated with these actions, something outside the Indian's usual experience of such phenomena, they may be thought of as such." [1]

This cosmic supernatural power was everywhere recognised by the peoples of North America under many different names, Orenda, Wakan, Manito, etc., and it is obvious that while it is neither theism nor animism it has considerable affinities to both.

This idea of a diffused supernatural cosmic power is found almost everywhere amongst primitive peoples— among the decadent remnants of the Palæo-Siberian tribes, among the Melanesians and the Australians, and among the least advanced of the African peoples.   It is often almost indistinguishable from Animism properly so called, for example, among the Lango and other Nilotic peoples where Jok, usually translated God, is conceived at once as a power behind Nature and as the accumulated force of the spirits of the dead.   It lies at the root of primitive magic, which consists essentially in the experimental knowledge and control of this supernatural force.

So, too, according to a writer in the *Journal of the Royal Anthropological Institute,* among the Yao of Nyassaland the word Mulungu is applied alike to the ancestral spirits and to the creative power behind Nature, and it is very remarkable that when the same word is taken over by the missionaries to describe the personal God of their teaching, the natives added to it a personal prefix " Che "—" Mr. Spirit " as it were—

---

[1] J. R. Swanton, " Social Conditions, Beliefs and Linguistic Relations of the Tlingit Indian," in *Twenty-Sixth Annual Report of Bureau of American Ethnology,* pp. 451–2, note.

to distinguish it from the undifferentiated and impersonal meaning that the word had hitherto borne.

Moreover, some peoples who possess a fairly well-defined personal deity, like the Koryaks of North-east Siberia, have preserved a religious terminology which points to the former existence of much wider and vaguer religious conceptions. According to Jochelson, the Koryak apply the following names to their god: (1) Universe or world—lit. Outer One, (2) Supervisor, (3) Something existing, (4) Existence or Strength, (5) The One on High, (6) The Master on High, (7) The Master, (8) The Dawn, (9) The Thunder Man. Among the Siberian peoples, the general belief, however, is in a number of powers behind the phenomena of Nature, which are distinct from the (evil) spirits and from the souls of the dead, and are known as " Beings " by the Chukchi, and as " Masters " or " Owners " by the Gilyak. Thus there is the Owner of the Mountain, the Owner of the Sea, the Owner of the Reindeer ; and these powers are propitiated by the hunter and the fisherman, as the Animal Guardian Spirit is in North America.[1]

III. The Worship of Animals among the Hunters

For the peoples of the hunting culture always see this vague cosmic power above all manifested and incarnated in the animals. It might seem at first sight that the conditions of primitive life, in which the hunter lives at war with Nature, are irreconcilable with any feelings of religious reverence towards his prey. Yet we have only to turn to modern savages to see that this is not so. The beasts are looked on as stronger and wiser than man. They are the first-born of Nature, the real lords of the land ; while man is a new-comer—an intruder.

And since he must kill the beasts in order to live, it is necessary for him in some way to secure the favour of

[1] Czaplica, *Aboriginal Siberia*, p. 262 and *passim*.

the lords of the beasts themselves, that he may do so by their permission.

There still exist among the hunting peoples widely spread customs and ceremonies designed to secure the favour of the animal spirits before hunting, or to placate the beasts that have been killed.

Especially among the northern people from Finland and Lapland throughout Siberia and North-eastern Asia to North America, we find these peculiar customs in connection with the hunting and the killing of the bear, the most formidable of northern animals, and the one most apt to inspire reverence and awe. Some tribes of American Indians prepared for the hunt by fasting and religious rites, and by the offering of expiatory sacrifice to the souls of the bears already killed. Among the Tlingit of Alaska, when a dead bear was brought into camp, " its head was carried indoors and eagle down and red paint put upon it. Then one talked to it as if to a human being, saying, ' I am your friend, I am poor and come to you.' Before the entrails were burned he talked to them saying, ' I am poor, that is why I am hunting you.' When one came to a bear trail, he said, ' My father's brother-in-law, have pity upon me, let me be in luck.' " [1]

Among the Koryaks of North-east Siberia, when a bear is killed, " the bear-skin is taken off along with the head and one of the women puts on the skin, dances in it, and entreats the bear not to be angry, but to be kind to the people." At the same time they offer meat on a wooden platter to the dead beast, saying, " Eat, friend." Afterwards a ceremony is performed with the object of sending the dead bear, or rather his spirit, away back to his home. He is provided with provisions for the journey in the shape of puddings or reindeer flesh packed in a grass bag. His skin is stuffed with grass and carried round the house, after which he is supposed to depart towards the rising sun. The inten-

[1] Swanton, *The Tlingit Indians*, p. 455.

tion of the ceremonies is to protect the people from the wrath of the slain bear and his kinsfolk and to secure success in future bear hunts.[1]

Among the Gilyaks of the Amur, every clan has a captive bear cub which is kept for a year or two, until it is killed and eaten in a solemn feast of the clan ; after which its soul is dispatched to the Owner of the Mountain, laden with offerings, in order that he may send more bears for their hunting in the future, and the sharing of this " common bear " is an important element in the social organisation of the Gilyaks.

And if this attitude to animals obtained even in the nineteenth century among American Indians and Siberians with their incomparably greater resources against Nature, how much more must it not have been so for palæolithic man, armed with his poor implements of flint and bone, in the presence of the mighty prehistoric fauna of the steppes—the bison and the elk, the cave bear and the lion, the mammoth and the woolly rhinoceros ! And this is proved not merely by a priori reasoning, but by the evidence of palæolithic art, which consists almost entirely of animal paintings and sculptures.

We can be certain that the primitive hunter did not create these works of art in the depth of dark and inaccessible caverns for the sake of amusement. Their origin is undoubtedly magical or religious, and is to be explained by beliefs and practices regarding the animal spirits, of the type of those we have just described. Indeed, the very use of cave sanctuaries, such as Magdalenian man used, seems to survive among the modern hunting peoples, for we read that Apache medicine men before a hunt " used to resort to certain caves where they propitiated the animal gods whose progeny they intended to destroy." [2] The palæolithic animal paint-

---

[1] Jochelson, "The Koryak," p. 88, in Frazer, *Spirits of the Corn and the Wild*, vol. ii, p. 223.

[2] N. W. Thomas, s.v., "Animals in Hastings," *E. R. E.*, i., 511 b.

ings were in fact the magical means by which man acquired power over the beasts. It was only by the spirit of the animal that man could overcome the animal. He must magically conquer and make his own the force of the bison, the swiftness of the horse, the cunning of the lynx and the wild cat. And this mysterious transference of power could only be accomplished, in the eyes of primitive man, through the image—either the dream image or the dramatically represented image or finally the painted or carved image.

Many of the cave paintings of Magdalenian times show clear signs of having been used for magical purposes. The animals, especially the buffalo, are often marked with signs, intended in all probability to represent spears, or with " cupulas " which seem to represent wounds, or else with " tectiform " signs in the shape of a single rectangular structure, of which the explanation is more obscure. But there can be little doubt that all these marks were magical signs by which the operator " put his power " on the animal, and secured its capture by the hunter.[1]

IV. The Cult of the Animal Guardian Spirit in Modern and Prehistoric Times

But this is not the only explanation of the palæolithic animal paintings and sculptures. Many of the caves seem to have been true sanctuaries, and the figures in them the object not merely of utilitarian magical practices, but of a real cult. For example, the Tuc d'Audou-

---

[1] Similar practices are found among the Indians of North America. They also made drawings of animals with arrow marks on the side or in the heart, or carved figures upon which they bound a flint arrow head. And in their case we have the actual charms that were recited by the magician, such as—

" I shoot your heart ; I hit your heart,
O Animal—your heart—I hit your heart."

See illustrations and references for the Zuni and Ojibwa Indians in Sollas' *Ancient Hunters*, pp. 424–7.

bert cave, with its famous clay-modelled bison, has impressed every observer as an " inner sanctuary " which has been the scene of prehistoric religious rites. And in the case of the modern hunting peoples of North America the use of animal paintings, though not without its utilitarian magical side, is primarily connected with a circle of ideas which even Sir James Frazer recognises as religious in the full sense of the word.

This is the belief in the Animal Guardian Spirits, a belief which was almost universal among the hunting tribes of North America, and was specially powerful in the regions where agriculture was unknown, such as Northern and Western Canada.[1]

Every individual, but particularly the shaman and the chief, was supposed to possess such a guardian, whom he received through a dream or revelation in times of fasting and religious exaltation. Among the Blackfeet, a man who wished to acquire supernatural power would go away by himself into the wilderness, to some place of terror and mystery—a mountain peak, an island in a lake, a burial ground, or some place abounding in bears and wild beasts. Here he would remain for days without food or covering, lying for two nights on his right side and for two nights on his left, fasting and praying to the helpers. At last, often at the end of the fourth day, a secret helper would appear to him in a vision—usually, but not always, in the form of an animal—and would impart to him its power, and give him counsel, marking for him his course in life.[2]

Among the Omaha, according to Fletcher, a boy on attaining the age of puberty went through a similar

---

[1] This belief was observed by the Spaniards centuries before Totemism had been discovered, and was named by them *Nagualism*, from the word for the guardian spirit—Nagual—which was generally used in Central America.   Cf. D. G. Brinton, " Nagualism, a Study in American Folk Lore and History," in *Pr. American Philosophical Society*, vol. xxxiii.

[2] Frazer, *Totemism and Exogamy*, iii, p. 389.

ordeal.   When he had reached a secluded spot among the hills, " he must chant the prescribed prayer, uplifting his hands, wet with his tears, to the heavens, and then he must place his hands on the earth and fast, until he falls asleep or into a trance.   Whatever he sees or hears while in this state is the being through whom he can receive superhuman aid and comfort."   Later on it is his duty to seek until he finds the animal or bird seen in his revelation, which he must kill, retaining a small part of it as a concrete link with the power that he had seen in his vision.   The writer adds :

" This ceremony of initiation rests on the assumption that man's powers and activities can be supplemented by the elements and the animals, only through the grace of *Wakonda*, obtained by the rite of vision, consisting of ritualistic acts and a fervent prayer of humility explaining a longing for something not possessed, a consciousness of insufficiency of self, and an abiding desire for something capable of bringing welfare and prosperity to the suppliant." [1]

The mode of preparation varied in character and severity among the different peoples.   The Mandans even went so far as to cut off the joints of their fingers, so that, according to the Prince of Wied in 1833, some finger was mutilated amongst all of them, a practice which suggests comparison with the famous mutilated hand prints in the palæolithic cavern of Gargas in the Pyrenees.

In Western Canada and Alaska, as well as among the Omaha, it was more often a regular initiation ordeal, which every youth had to undergo, and in some cases, as among the Shuswap, the making of rock paintings of the animal guardians was a normal part of the ceremony.   But in every case, the dream image or vision was essential.   Writing of the Western Dene of the

[1] *Handbook of the American Indians North of Mexico*, vol. ii, p. 790, art. "Totem."

Yukon, Fr. A. G. Morice refers to the importance
that they attach to dreams. He says :

" It is while dreaming that they pretended to communicate with the supernatural world, that their
shamans were invested with their wonderful power
over nature, and that every individual was assigned his
particular nagual or tutelary animal genius. Often-
times they painted this genius with vermilion on
prominent rocks in the most frequented places, and
these rough inscriptions are about the only monuments
that the immediate ancestors of the Dene have left us."

Elsewhere he says the tutelary spirits

" are the link which connects man with the invisible
world, and the only means of communing with the
unseen : these are the personal totems of the Denes,
and I cannot help thinking of most of the American
aborigines as well. It has been said that Totemism is
a purely social institution. I feel absolutely no hesita-
tion in denying this, at least as far as the Denes are
concerned. Totemism among them is essentially and
exclusively connected with their religious system, and
I am inclined to believe that the gentile totem is
nothing else than an extension to the entire clan of
an institution which was originally restricted to the
individual.

" The personal totem revealed itself usually in
dreams, when it appeared to its future protégé under
the shape of an animal, etc., which was to be thenceforth
his tutelary genius. . . . Thenceforth the most intimate
connection existed between the two. The native
would be careful to carry on his person and expose
in his lodge the spoils of that animal, its entire skin,
or part of it, which he would not suffer to be treated
lightly. Occasionally he would even carve a rough
representation of the totem. He would treasure any
object—such as a stone or a vegetable excrescence—
between which and his totem he fancied he saw a striking
resemblance. He would paint its form or symbol in

bright vermilion on conspicuous rocks along lakes or rivers, etc. Under no circumstances would anything induce him wilfully to kill or at least to cut the flesh of the being, the prototype of which had become, as it were, sacred to him. In times of need he would secretly invoke its assistance, saying, ' May you do this or that to me.'

" Before an assault on his enemies or previous to his chase of large game, he would daub its symbol on his bow and arrows, and if success attended his efforts he would sometimes thank it by destroying any piece of property on hand, food or clothing, or in later times tobacco, which he would throw into the water or cast into the fire as a sacrifice." [1]

These descriptions suggest parallels in several respects with the hunting cultures of prehistoric Europe,[2] and there is no doubt that the existence of a similar circle of ideas in palæolithic times would afford a more satisfactory explanation than is otherwise forthcoming of the art of the European cave paintings. The wealth of animal paintings, their variety, and their reduplication one upon another, are such as might be expected, if the religious ideas and ceremonies centred round the conception of animal guardians and the importance of the visible image. A great artistic movement such as that of the palæolithic cave paintings presupposes a powerful emotional foundation in the psychic life of the people, such as we have seen to exist where the belief in the Animal Guardian Spirit is still prevalent. A purely utilitarian magic is incapable of producing a great art—in fact, among primitive people, even more than elsewhere, a great art requires a strong religious impulse to bring it into being. Hence the great age of

---

[1] Rev. A. G. Morice in Frazer, *Totemism and Exogamy*, iii, 440–2.

[2] Cf. also the Indian custom of a shaman or an initiate wearing the skin or mask of his tutelary animal in religious dances or ceremonies with the palæolithic paintings of men disguised as animals, such as the famous figure of the " sorcerer " from the grotto of the Trois Frères (Ariège).

palæolithic art may well represent the formative period of a new type of religion-culture, which has survived among the hunting peoples of the North ever since. A totemic origin has often been suggested for the palæolithic paintings, for example, by S. Reinach, but to this it has been rightly objected that there are no signs of selection of one particular type of animal, such as we should expect if a tribal totem was being depicted. This objection, however, does not hold good against the view that the painting represents animal guardians. Moreover, this view would also explain the existence of figures of animals which are not good for food, such as the cat or the lion, and which consequently cannot be explained on purely utilitarian grounds.

V. The Animal Guardian and the Origins of Totemism

The idea of the animal guardian cannot, however, be entirely separated from the question of Totemism. In North America, at any rate, the two seem to be closely connected. Not only do many tribes, such as the Dene, possess at once naguals or individual guardians and clan totems as well, but also there are certain institutions intermediate between the two. First of all there are the widespread and important secret societies, of which the bond of union is the possession of a common guardian spirit—which therefore appears as a kind of non-hereditary totem; and secondly, among some of the tribes of British Columbia, the individual guardian can in some cases become hereditary, passing from father to son— so that it appears as a kind of family totem.

In consequence of these facts a connection between the two beliefs is universally admitted, but while the majority of American ethnologists, such as Boas, have seen in Totemism simply the extension to the community of the conception of the individual Animal Guardian Spirit, European writers have almost universally adopted the opposite view, and they maintain that the belief in guardian spirits is the last trace of a decadent and disappearing Totemism.

This view is, however, difficult to reconcile with the actual distribution of the two institutions in America. As Sir James Frazer has pointed out, totemic institutions in North America are most fully developed in the more highly developed and sedentary cultures—for example, in the Pueblo culture of the south-west, and among the Haida and Tlingit of the North Pacific coast—while they are absent among the primitive and barbarous peoples of California, and the territories to the northward. On the other hand, the cult of the guardian spirits and the beliefs concerning the dream image are strongest among the hunters of the plains and the northern forests, and are also found among the Californians and the primitive western peoples, while they are entirely absent among the Pueblo Indians, and almost so among the Haida.

Now the origin of the belief in guardian spirits among a hunting people is simple. It arises directly from their psychic environment, and, as we have shown, forms an essential part of the hunting culture. The origins of Totemism on the contrary remain obscure, in spite of half a century of study and research. To view the belief in the guardian spirits as a relic of Totemism would be to derive the simple from the complex, and the primitive from the advanced. It is easy to understand how the belief in the guardian spirits of the hunter should pass away among a sedentary agricultural people like the Pueblo Indians, or among the trading and fishing villages of the North Pacific coast, while Totemism, even though it owed its origin to the same circle of ideas, when once it is embodied in a settled social organisation, will endure as long as the society continues to exist.

Judging the North American evidence by itself, it seems clear that the Religion of the Hunter—the belief in Animal Guardian Spirits—lies at the root of the whole development. First comes the guardian spirit of the shaman, then that of the ordinary individual ; finally, as population increases and the primitive groups become more complex, the same idea becomes the principle of social organisation, and we have, on the one hand, the religious confraternity of men who own a common guardian spirit, i.e. the secret society, on the other, the group of kinsmen that inherit a common guardian, i.e. the regular totemic clan.

This relatively simple explanation, which adequately covers the evidence as it exists in North America,[1] has, however, met with little favour in Europe, partly because it conflicts with the view that Totemism is essentially a non-religious institution, but still more because European students of the question almost invariably assume that in Australia alone do we find Totemism at its purest. Yet there are insuperable difficulties in the way of the view upheld by some writers that Australia is the original home and centre of diffusion of Totemism and all that it stands for. The fact that Totemism extends from West Africa to North America, and was one of the constituent elements in pre-dynastic Egyptian culture, is fatal to the claims of Australia, and appears rather to favour the idea of some prehistoric wave of cultural influence, starting perhaps in North Africa and gradually extending by South Arabia and India to South-eastern Asia and Oceania. It is equally difficult, however, to believe, with Professor Elliot Smith and his school, that this diffusion was due to the influence of the historic Egyptians. Totemism in Egypt bears all the marks of a survival from a far earlier type of culture. It belongs essentially not to the archaic kingdom with its mastery of agriculture and

---

[1] The belief in animal guardians is, however, not confined to America. On the contrary, it is perhaps even more widespread than the totemic institution itself. It is found among the Siberians, the Melanesians and Polynesians (the so-called " spirit animals "), the Australians, and many African peoples. It even appears in a degraded form in European folklore and magic, i.e. the animal " familiar " of the wizard.

irrigation, but to the hunting tribe, the society that lives in complete dependence on the life of untamed Nature. It would be an amazing paradox if the most characteristic institution of the religion-culture of the hunters and the food-gatherers had come to them at second hand from agriculturalists and traders of the higher culture. It seems far preferable to suppose that it formed part of a distinct culture-complex, which was developed by hunting peoples as far back as the later palæolithic period and was subsequently diffused through India to South-eastern Asia and Australasia, and through Siberia to North America, either owing to racial movements or to culture transference, existing down to the present day, wherever the conditions of life remain similar to those under which it was produced, although it has been overlaid by accretions and modifications due to the influence of other cultures. According to this view the cult of Animal Guardian Spirits is an older and more universal stage than that of Totemism properly so called. The latter arises naturally when a primitive hunting people attains a higher form of social organisation, owing to the adoption of agriculture or the influence of higher cultures. In this stage of society, which is that of the modern Pueblo peoples or the prehistoric Egyptians, each local or tribal subdivision possesses a common guardian, which is the symbol and consecration of their social solidarity. But at the same time the religious vitality of the institution tends to disappear. The totem either loses its religious significance and becomes an heraldic symbol of purely social significance, or else, as in ancient Egypt, it may develop into a local deity, which gradually acquires personality and wider attributes. In all the earlier civilisations, but most of all in Egypt, we find animal gods occupying an important place in the pantheon, along with the divinised powers of Nature, but in almost all cases these belong in origin to a much earlier and more primitive stage of culture. As soon as a people becomes sedentary the vital emphasis is transferred from the life of the hunter to that of the cultivator of the soil, and the earth takes the place of the wild things as the great cosmic mystery which arouses religious awe and veneration. This is the Religion of the Peasant, which, as we shall see, accompanies the rise of the higher culture, alike in Europe and throughout the East.

CHAPTER III

THE DAWN OF THE NEOLITHIC AGE AND THE RISE OF THE PEASANT CULTURE IN EUROPE

THE POST-GLACIAL PERIOD AND THE EPIPALÆOLITHIC CULTURES OF EUROPE.

THE COMING OF THE NEOLITHIC CULTURE.

THE PEASANT CULTURES OF CENTRAL AND EASTERN EUROPE.

(a) THE ALPINE LAKE-DWELLING CULTURE.

(b) THE DANUBIAN CULTURE.

(c) THE PAINTED POTTERY CULTURE OF EASTERN EUROPE.

(d) THE NEOLITHIC CULTURE OF THESSALY.

GENERAL CHARACTER OF THE PEASANT CULTURE.

CHAPTER III

THE DAWN OF THE NEOLITHIC AGE AND THE RISE OF THE PEASANT CULTURE IN EUROPE

I. The Post-Glacial Period and the Epipalæolithic Cultures of Europe

The change of climate which resulted from the passing of glacial conditions, and the emergence of Northern Europe from the great ice-sheets that had covered it, did not, as one might suppose, lead to any immediate progress in European culture. On the contrary, the passing of the glacial age seems to have been in many respects a time of retrogression and cultural decadence. The highly specialised hunting culture of Magdalenian times could not survive the passing of the cold, dry steppe conditions to which it had adapted itself, and it was many centuries and probably thousands of years before the higher form of civilisation, known as neolithic, was able to acclimatise itself to European conditions. The palæolithic age was characterised by a purely hunting culture, by the use of chipped flint and carved bone implements and by a semi-nomadic way of life, in which the only permanent forms of habitation were caves and rock shelters. The men of the neolithic culture, on the other hand, followed a settled way of life in huts and villages, practising agriculture and the breeding of domestic animals, and manufacturing pottery and implements of ground and polished stone. It was formerly believed by the earlier students of prehistory that there was an actual gap between the disappearance of palæolithic man and the coming of the new culture, in which Europe was an uninhabited desert. Modern discoveries, however, have shown that there was no such hiatus, and that there exists a whole series of cultures which belong to the intermediate period, and are known as mesolithic or epipalæolithic. They are characterised on the one hand by the survival of the native tradition of the later palæolithic European cultures, and on the other by the introduction of new cultural influences from outside. The most important of these was due to the great expansion of the late Capsian culture from the south, to which we have already referred, and which is known outside its original home as the Tardenoisian culture. It is characterised by the use of minute flint implements of geometrical form, which are found throughout Western Europe, and as far east as Poland and South Russia. This culture spread north with the change in climatic conditions and the advance of the forests, and it undoubtedly marks the coming of a new wave of population from the Mediterranean region or North Africa, perhaps the ancestors of the modern Mediterranean race. The actual human remains that date from this period are, however, curiously mixed. A small number of broad-headed (brachycephalic) men are found both at Ofnet in Bavaria and at Mugem in Portugal, and mark the first certain appearance in Europe of the broad-headed type of man to which the Alpine race of modern Europe belongs. The majority of the Mugem skulls, however, are dolichocephalic and belong to a curiously primitive type with a prognathous jaw and a small brain, which differs alike from the races of palæolithic Europe and from the true Mediterranean type.

The earlier Magdalenian population of Europe did not, however, entirely disappear, though the change in climatic conditions rendered the preservation of its old culture impossible. It was partially submerged by the wave of new population, and the mingling of the two streams of influence gave rise to the mixed forms of culture known as the Azilian and the Maglemosian.

The former is widely distributed in a sporadic way

from Southern France and Scotland to Switzerland and South Germany. Like the Magdalenians, the Azilians used bone implements, especially flat harpoons made of deers' horn, though the forms are coarse and degenerate, but they also possessed the minute flint implements of geometrical form that are characteristic of the Capsian-Tardenoisian culture. The most remarkable remains of the Azilian culture, however, are the pebbles painted with conventional signs and ornaments, which are found in Southern France. These are evidently connected with the conventional designs of the Spanish rock paintings which belong to the last phase of Capsian art. Their significance is undoubtedly religious, and it is possible that they served a similar purpose to the churingas or " ancestor stones " of the modern Australian natives, with which they have often been compared.[1]

Owing to the uniformity of climatic conditions during the post-glacial period it is difficult to form any estimate of the duration of the Azilian and Tardenoisian cultures. It is only in the Baltic that the post-glacial climatic and geographical changes constitute a series of successive phases, which can be clearly distinguished, and consequently this region forms an invaluable bridge between palæolithic and neolithic times.

First of all, when the ice-sheet that covered Scandinavia had withdrawn to the north, the Baltic became an open Arctic sea, connected with the White Sea on the north-east, as well as with the North Sea, as at present. During this " Yoldia " period, which corresponds in date to the Magdalenian age, there are no signs of human occupation in Scandinavia. This age was followed by a period of land elevation, which gradually converted the Baltic into a freshwater lake,

[1] These signs often resemble alphabetical characters, and it has been suggested by G. Wilke, and recently by S. Reinach, that an alphabetical script was actually developed from them in neolithic times. But the evidence on which this view rests (i.e. the inscribed tablets of Alvão and Glozel) is of more than doubtful authenticity.

the Ancylus Sea, so named from the presence of the freshwater snail. At the same time the climate became milder and Denmark and Southern Sweden were covered with pine forests. It is to this period that the first Baltic culture, named from the settlement discovered at Maglemose in Seeland, belongs. Its inhabitants lived not on dry land, but on a raft moored to the shore of the lake, a kind of primitive prototype of the lake village. In physical type some of their remains seem to belong to the old Cromagnon race, though a broad-headed element was also present, as in Portugal and Bavaria. Like the Azilians, they possessed minute flint implements, and bone harpoons, as well as fish spears and bone needles, but the survival of the Magdalenian tradition is more strongly marked. They showed considerable artistic propensities and decorated their bone implements with engravings and patterns, which are sometimes of a decadent Magdalenian style and sometimes resemble the conventional designs of post-Capsian art. This Maglemose culture had a considerable extension, and traces of it are found, not only throughout the Baltic region, but as far as Belgium and Holderness in Yorkshire.

At the end of the Ancylus period a new movement of land depression set in, which once more united the Baltic with the North Sea. At the same time the climate of Scandinavia became much warmer, owing perhaps to a change in the ocean currents, and the oak and the hazel flourished. This is the Litorina stage, named after the periwinkle which now inhabited the warmer waters of the Baltic. This period was accompanied by a new phase of culture, typical examples of which are the stations of Ertebolle in Denmark and Nöstvet in Norway. The inhabitants of these stations lived by hunting and fishing, like their predecessors, but above all by shell-gathering, and their settlements are marked by enormous deposits of cockles and oyster shells, from which the Danish culture derives its usual name of

the Kitchen Midden Culture.   Unlike the earlier Maglemose and Azilian cultures, this phase possesses few links
with the older European cultures of late palæolithic
times.   Its typical implements are the large flint picks
and hatchets which had already begun to appear towards
the end of the Maglemose epoch, as well as other flint
implements, which resemble in workmanship the rude
tools of the early palæolithic cultures.   There is no trace
of artistic development, but a rude kind of pottery makes
its appearance for the first time in Europe.   This culture
seems to be merely a local variation of a very widely
extended type known as the Campignian, which is
represented not only in Western Europe, especially in
Belgium, but also in Italy and Syria.   It is usually
supposed to have entered Europe from the south-east,
from some region in which the tradition of early palæolithic industry had survived through the ages, so radically
do the Campignian flint picks and hatchets differ from
all the later types of palæolithic industry.   It was from
this source that they were borrowed by the men of the
Maglemose culture, who in the main still inherited
the later palæolithic tradition.   A somewhat similar
stage of culture has recently been discovered in North-
west Spain, in the shell mounds of Asturias.

II. The Coming of the Neolithic Culture

But though the Campignian culture is usually termed
proto-neolithic, it shows none of the typical neolithic
features, except a rude type of pottery.   It possessed
no domestic animal except the dog, and it is very improbable that even the most primitive agriculture was
practised.   In fact all the European cultures of the
period with which we have been dealing leave a greater
impression of poverty and barbarism than any of the
cultures of the later palæolithic age.   Man was entirely
at the mercy of Nature—a mere scavenger who eked out
a miserable existence as a food-gatherer and an eater of
shell fish.   While in other parts of the world higher

forms of civilisation were being developed for the first time, Europe had become a mere cultural backwater, like Patagonia or the Cape of Good Hope, into which backward races were pushed aside to stagnate in squalid savagery. The coming of the true neolithic culture did not take place till a relatively recent period, perhaps late in the fourth millennium, when a new phase of land elevation had set in in Scandinavia and the Baltic was assuming its present form. This is the Mya (clam) phase, and it was accompanied by a change in flora, the red pine and the beech taking the place of the oak as the typical trees.

Even then the coming of the higher culture was due not to any spontaneous progressive movement on the part of the European population, but to the advent of more civilised peoples from without. Indeed, the very term " neolithic " is open to serious objection. What we term the neolithic age in Europe was really the first stage in the diffusion of the higher metal-using culture of the Near East. Where the contact was most direct, as in Western Mediterranean countries, the barbarous natives of the interior still followed the old cultural tradition, which had descended without a break from palæolithic times, at the same time that the coastal regions, which were in touch with the higher culture centres of the Eastern Mediterranean, were in the full Age of Metals. It is only in Northern and Central Europe, where the process of contact was more gradual and indirect, that we find a non-metal-using culture of the higher type, which we may call neolithic, and even there the tradition of epipalæolithic barbarism still lived on down to the Age of Metals, as in the case of the microlithic culture of Poland with its Tardenoisian antecedents, and the cultures of inner Scandinavia and the Eastern Baltic, which represent the survival of the old Kitchen Midden and Maglemose types.

Hence the extraordinary heterogeneity of cultural conditions in Europe in the " Neolithic Age." There was no uniform European culture, but only diverse streams of colonisation and cultural influence, which were widely different in type and origin, and which co-existed with barbaric survivals of the old native cultures, just as in recent times in South Africa the primitive cultures of the Hottentot and the Bushman lingered on, while the Bantu agriculturalists were pressing in from the north, and the Portuguese and Dutch traders were establishing themselves on the coasts.

The new cultures which entered Europe in neolithic and æneolithic times followed two main lines of diffusion. There was a movement along the Mediterranean and Atlantic coasts, which was due to maritime influences, and there was an inland movement of agricultural colonisation and settlement, which entered Europe from the east and the south-east, and gradually expanded into Central Europe. The Atlantic movement is characterised by the great monuments of unhewn stone, known as dolmens and megaliths, which have given their name to the culture. It reached the Baltic and the British Isles from the south-west, where the western part of the Iberian Peninsula seems to have been its earliest centre of diffusion, but similar monuments, perhaps of later date, are found also in the Black Sea and in Palestine, as well as far to the east in India and the Pacific. Consequently many archæologists have looked to some intermediate region in the Near East, such as Phœnicia or Egypt, as the original source of the whole megalithic culture, both in the East and West.

This movement was not, however, the main channel through which the higher culture affected Europe. Its influence was somewhat superficial, as would naturally be the case if it was due, as has been supposed, to the influence of seafarers or traders, and not to a migration of new peoples. It was not in the West, but in Central and Eastern Europe that we first find a true agricultural civilisation, with domestic animals, fine pottery, and settled villages.

III. The Peasant Cultures of Central and Eastern Europe

This neolithic culture was not, however, uniform. It may be divided into three or four different types. There are the Painted Pottery cultures of Eastern Europe, one province of which extended from the Ukraine to Rumania and Transylvania, while the other lay to the south in Thessaly and mainland Greece ; there is the Danubian culture, which occupied the greater part of Central Europe ; and finally there is the Lake-dwelling Culture of the Alpine Region.

(a) *The Alpine Lake-dwelling Culture*

The latter was the first type of neolithic culture to be discovered and fully studied, and it was long believed to be due to the migration of a new people of Alpine race from Asia, who brought with them all the elements of the new culture. In racial type, the Swiss lake-dwellers certainly belong mainly to the broad-headed Alpine stock, which still predominates in Central Europe, though there is a considerable admixture of long-headed dwarfish people of a primitive type, which has often been compared to that of the palæolithic negroid skeletons of Grimaldi. But the traces of lake dwellings in the East are scanty and late, while in Europe this form of settlement goes back to the stations of the Maglemose culture on the Baltic in very remote times. Raft and pile settlements of a primitive type are widely distributed through the region of the Baltic and North Germany, as well as in Holland and North-east England (Holderness), and it is easy to understand how they may have gradually spread southwards up the Rhine until they reached the Alpine region where the Swiss and Austrian lakes afforded specially favourable circumstances for their establishment. Here they acquired all the elements of the higher culture, practising agriculture, weaving, and the making of pottery, and possessing every type of domestic animal except the horse. It is, however, difficult to believe that the lake-dwelling culture was in its origin that of an agricultural people. The type of pile settlement seems to have arisen in a densely forested region in which the rivers and lakes afforded the only open channels by which man could move freely, and on the banks of which the primitive population of hunters and fishers fixed their settlements. In this environment an agricultural society cannot have developed as early as on the open lands of Eastern Europe, and it is probably from the latter direction that the lake-dwellers first acquired their domestic animals together with the higher neolithic culture.

(b) The Danubian Culture

It is certainly in the Danubian region that we find the most complete and typical example of an early peasant culture. Here, except in its extreme western extremity (at Ofnet), there is no evidence of the survival of the epipalæolithic stage of culture. The earliest inhabitants after the true palæolithic hunters seem to have been the bearers of the new full neolithic culture. These belong to a distinctive physical type, which resembles the Mediterranean race in build and stature, but differs in the shape of the skull, the latter being an intermediate form between the long-headed Mediterranean and the broad-headed Alpine. Owing, however, to its uniformity, it cannot be due to a cross between the two races ; it belongs to a distinct and independent variety of man. Their settlements are found just where we should expect an early type of agriculture to develop —not in the swamps and on the sea beach like the Baltic people, nor in the wet forest like the Alpine lake-dwellers, but on the fertile loess soil, the result of the accumulation of wind-blown dust from ancient deserts, which holds sufficient moisture to enable crops to be raised, but is not damp enough to permit the growth of

forest. These open lands extend from Hungary through
Moravia and Bohemia, to Galicia and Silesia on the
north, and into Central and Southern Germany on the
west, where they form limited corridors and islands
interspersed among the sea of forest. Here there
developed a true peasant culture, which possessed the
domestic animals, the ox, the goat, the sheep, the pig,
and possibly the hare, and which cultivated wheat,
barley, millet, and flax. Polished stone implements
were used, the typical example of which is the so-called
shoe-last celt, a long instrument flat on one side and
rounded on the other.[1] The smaller examples were
hafted and used as hoes for cultivating the ground, the
larger ones, which appear later, were probably plough-
shares. The absence of weapons, apart from a disk-
shaped mace-head, points to the peaceful character of
the people, and this is borne out by the nature of their
settlements, which lay in the open valleys near a stream
and were unprotected by moat or rampart. For ornaments they had bracelets, made of sea shells (Spondylus)
from the Mediterranean, and their pottery, which is of
a fine type, was decorated with incised irregular patterns
of spiral and meander forms. This pottery, the Band or
Ribbon Ceramic of the German archæologists, has
given its name to the culture, and is characteristic of
the Danubian area. No less important are the small
clay figures or idols, which usually represent a female
figure, though clay figures of animals are also known,
especially of the ox.

The earliest centres of settlement seem to have been
Moravia in the north and the region round Belgrade
in Serbia to the south, but as the population increased
the culture steadily advanced, and early in the third
millennium B.C. it had spread not only into Poland
and Silesia, but southwards into Bosnia and westwards
into Germany, both through Saxony and Thuringia,
and up the Danube, until the Rhineland was reached

[1] Cf. Plate III, Fig. 1.

and settled, and the bearers of the culture finally penetrated into Eastern France and Belgium, where they
were the first to introduce the true neolithic culture.

In the Danube valley itself and in Bohemia and Saxony
a later and more advanced stage of this culture began,
probably before the middle of the third millennium.
New forms of pottery with coloured embossed mouldings
appear, and the clay figures are much more developed,
female figures seated on a kind of throne being common.
Copper axes and ornaments also began to come into use,
and curious stamps with a spiral design were used for
painting the body.

All these new elements seem to have come in from
the East, from the third great province of neolithic
culture which we have mentioned above.

(c) *The Painted Pottery Culture of Eastern Europe*

The home of this culture was the Black Earth region
of the south-east, the most fertile agricultural land in
Europe. Its chief centres were in Transylvania in the
Upper Alt valley, where twenty-two settlements have
been explored, farther east in Moldavia and Northern
Bulgaria, and northwards in Eastern Galicia, as well as at
Tripolye, near Kiev, in South-west Russia, while outlying
colonies of the same culture occur as far as Eastern
Thessaly and across the Adriatic in Apulia. In its
broad lines this culture resembles the Danubian. It
also belonged to an agricultural people, and it possessed
the shoe-last stone implements, the clay figures of
women and animals, and the spiral and meander decoration which are all so characteristic of the Danubian
culture. But in other respects it differs widely. It is
less primitive, both in date and in character. Copper
is known, at least in small quantities, from the beginning,
and gold is plentiful. Some of the settlements in Transylvania were strongly fortified, and the houses instead
of being mere oval huts partly excavated out of the
ground, as with the Danubians, were solid rectangular

structures with raised hearths and painted plaster decoration. The forms of pottery are peculiar and quite different to the Danubian—pedestalled bowls and binocular vases something like a double egg-cup being particularly common—in fact, it is a highly advanced ceramic art, which does not suggest the imitation of earlier vessels of wood or leather or wickerwork, as is usually the case with primitive pottery. Moreover, the designs, instead of being incised, are elaborately painted, so that the whole culture is commonly known as the Painted Pottery Culture. Paint was also used for decorating the body, a custom which spread to the Danubians only in the later stage of their development. The clay figures, which usually represent erect or seated female figures, some of them nursing children, are found in Russia chiefly on the site of the curious buildings or platforms known as " ploshchadki," which seem to have had a religious object. The whole problem of the origin and affinities of this culture is a very important one, and must be dealt with more fully hereafter. For the moment it is sufficient to say that it was probably of Asiatic origin and seems to be connected with the cultures that lie on the other shores of the great Asiatic steppes, in Turkestan, and even far to the east in China, while its resemblances to the Danubian culture are due mainly to later contact and mutual influence. Nothing definite is known of the racial character of the people responsible for its introduction. The civilisation seems to have appeared in Europe by the early part of the third millennium, and its decline and fall were undoubtedly due to the coming of warlike nomads from the steppes. The first attack took place during the third millennium, and after a revival of prosperity the final catastrophe followed several centuries later. The people may have gone west and fused to some extent with the later Danubians, and there are features in the Copper Age Culture of Thrace which point to a survival there of the earlier culture traditions.

Indeed it was no doubt from this source that the Thracians of Herodotus' day inherited the custom of painting themselves.

(d) *The Neolithic Culture of Thessaly*

The other neolithic culture - province of Eastern Europe lies to the south in Thessaly and mainland Greece. The Central and Southern Balkans have been less fully explored, and the possibilities of agricultural settlement were no doubt considerably limited by the large proportion of forest and mountain. But the civilisation that we find in Thessaly is essentially of the same type as those of the provinces farther north. Here also we find an agricultural people cultivating the ground with the same shoe-last type of polished stone implement, and possessing the same domestic animals. They also manufactured fine pottery, originally a thin red polished ware, which gave place at a very early period to a more elaborate type with red-painted decoration on a white ground. The designs, however, are not of the spiral and meander type that we find in the north; they are rectilinear and perhaps suggest an imitation of wickerwork.

These earliest inhabitants of Greece lived in open villages, consisting of huts built of unbaked brick which developed before the end of the first period into rectangular houses with stone foundations, inner brick buttresses to support the roof beams, and wattle-and-daub partitions.

Like the Danubians, and the dwellers in the Black Earth region, they also possessed the small clay female images, usually erect, and in some cases with a child in their arms. Later on we find curious clay figures with a detachable stone head on which the features were painted grotesquely. In addition to the shoe-last celt, they also used a bevelled form of celt which is peculiar to this region, and they had knives and razors of obsidian, which must have been imported from Melos,

or perhaps from Argos in the Peloponnese. For ornaments they had shell bracelets and clay beads, as well
as clay and stone stamps which may have been used
for painting the body.

Now in the second stage of this culture, some time in
the course of the third millennium B.C., a new people
suddenly appears in East Thessaly in the region of
Iolcos and the Pagasæan Gulf, the home of the legendary
Argonauts. Here they established themselves in fortified settlements, as at Sesklo and Dimini, which are the
first walled " towns " of Greece, and the earliest forerunners of the historic Greek Polis. There is no doubt
as to their origin, for they are practically identical in
culture with the people of the Black Earth Region in
Rumania and South Russia. They made the same
painted pottery with spiral decoration, and they had
the same forms of vessels, which differ from those of
the native Thessalians as well as from those of the
Danubians. They possessed copper and gold in small
quantities, and they brought with them a new type of
house, with a pillared porch opening into a single large
room or hall. This is the so-called Megaron house,
which was characteristic of the early Greeks, and which
we find as the typical royal dwelling in Homer. This
was not the only contribution the new-comers made to
the civilisation of the Ægean world, for it was through
them that the spiral ornament was brought south and
became incorporated into the art of the Ægean and
Cretan civilisation.

The new culture, however, was confined to Eastern
Thessaly. In the West and in Central Greece the old
tradition remained and continued to develop until the
Bronze Age.

IV. General Character of the Peasant Culture

But in spite of these regional differences between the
three main provinces of Central and Eastern European

culture, it is clear that there is a considerable element that is common to them all.

All of them are essentially peasant cultures, which are on the one hand completely unwarlike and peaceful, but on the other have not attained to the higher culture of Western Asia, which is characterised by the existence of the city. All three cultures possess the same domestic animals, cultivate the same grains, and—as is even more remarkable—use the same type of polished stone agricultural implement—the shoe-last celt. All of them make fine pottery, though it is here that the regional types differ most widely ; and finally all of them agree in the—apparently religious—use of clay figurines or idols, which are often closely similar in the different regions and which are equally characteristic of the early civilisation of Western Asia.

These peasant cultures were the source of a fundamental transformation of European culture, which gradually affected the greater part of the continent. The natural increase of an agricultural population led to a continued expansion—a movement of peasant colonisation, which, as we have just seen, passed westward and northward through the European continent bearing with it the neolithic culture and the peasant religion. This is the true foundation of all the subsequent development of European culture. History as a rule takes account only of the warrior peoples and the conquering aristocracies, but their achievements were only rendered possible by the existence of a subject peasant population of which we seldom hear. Underneath the successive changes in the dominant element, the peasant foundation remains intact with its own culture and its own traditions. Up to a few years ago in Eastern Europe, we could still trace the separate existence of these two elements. We could see a German or Magyar upper class with the traditions and culture of the great European capitals ruling over peasant populations of a different language and a primitive, incalculably ancient cultural tradition. We may call these peasants Slavs or Rumanians or Germans, but these are often only artificial linguistic distinctions due to later historical movements, while the peoples themselves are in many cases far more ancient, and are the bearers of the original tradition of neolithic peasant culture.

We are only now beginning to realise the extraordinary stability and persistence of the peasant culture, through which even the life of modern Europe rests on foundations which were laid in the prehistoric period. For the agricultural civilisation which was firmly established in the Danube region and in Moravia in early neolithic times became the centre of diffusion of the new type of culture throughout continental Europe. It was thence in all probability that the inhabitants of the lake villages of the Alpine region received the principal elements of their characteristic culture, and that agriculture and domestic animals reached not only Poland and Germany, but also the Baltic, the Nether-lands, and Eastern France; while later on in the Bronze and Iron Ages it was from the same region that the new influences were derived which transformed the culture of France and Great Britain. Thus the cultural development of neolithic Europe proceeded in the reverse direction to that which it has followed in modern times, in what has often been called the Atlantic Age of civilisation. In neolithic times there is a steady advance in culture as we pass from west to east. It was in the west that the epipalæolithic cultures of the hunters and the food-gatherers survived the longest. In Central Europe the culture of the Alpine lake-dwellers, while retaining traces of its barbarous origin, had acquired the neolithic arts and agriculture of its more civilised Danubian neighbours. The Danubians themselves prob-ably derived their original culture from Western Asia either by way of Asia Minor or through the Eastern Mediterranean, and they owed their further advance in

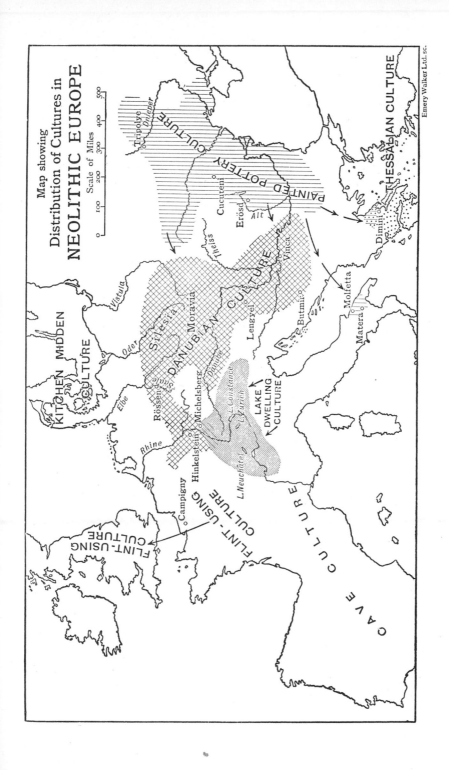

Map showing
Distribution of Cultures in
NEOLITHIC EUROPE

Scale of Miles

0   100   200   300   400   500

THESSALIAN CULTURE

PAINTED POTTERY CULTURE

Tripolye
Dnieper

Cucuteni

Erösd

Alt

Theiss

Vistula

Oder

Silesia

Moravia

DANUBIAN CULTURE

Lengyel

Vinča

Butmir

Molfetta

Matera

Dimini

Elbe

Saale

Rössen

Michelsberg

Hinkelstein

Danube

L. Constance

L. Zürich

LAKE
DWELLING
CULTURE

Rhine

L. Neuchâtel

Campigny

FLINT-USING
CULTURE

FLINT-USING
CULTURE

KITCHEN MIDDEN
CULTURE

CAVE CULTURE

Emery Walker Ltd. sc.

civilisation to their eastern neighbours of the Painted Pottery Culture. Finally the latter, which represents the apex of the continental neolithic development, was itself the most westerly off-shoot of a great Asiatic culture. Thus we are inevitably led back to Asia as the source and cradle of the civilising movement which transformed the life of neolithic Europe.

CHAPTER IV

ASIA AND THE ORIGINS OF THE HIGHER CIVILISATION

THE BEGINNINGS OF CULTURE IN ASIA.

THE PAINTED POTTERY CULTURES.

THE RISE OF THE HIGHER CULTURE IN THE MIDDLE EAST.

THE PROBLEM OF THE INFLUENCE OF ASIATIC CULTURE ON EGYPT.

THE SUMERIANS AND THE ORIGINS OF ASIATIC CULTURE.

CHAPTER IV

ASIA AND THE ORIGINS OF THE HIGHER CIVILISATION

I. THE BEGINNINGS OF CULTURE IN ASIA

WHILE Europe was passing through the stages of culture which were described in the first chapter, what was happening in Asia ? There can be no question of the importance of the Asiatic developments, for there is every reason to think that the traditional belief in Asia as the original cradle of the human race is true, but the study of Asiatic prehistory is in its infancy, and the whole course of palæolithic development is still obscure. There is no doubt that the palæolithic cultures were widely spread in Asia. Industries corresponding to those of the older palæolithic cultures of Europe have been found in connection with remains of the pleistocene period, not only in the Near East, but in India and Farther India, in Siberia to the north of the Altai Mountains, and quite recently in Western China.

Later palæolithic types are less fully known, but the Capsian Culture, which is parallel to the Aurignacian, embraced practically the whole Mediterranean basin and a similar type of culture seems to have extended to India, where there exist interesting rock paintings of hunting scenes, perhaps of similar date to our Magdalenian cave art.

But there is an almost complete lack of human remains. Apart from the skulls found at Wadjak in Java, and the Neanderthal man just discovered in Galilee, there is practically nothing of palæolithic date, and this is especially unfortunate not only in view of the problems of early human evolution, but also because

Asia was certainly the scene of most important developments during the Glacial Age itself.

At that time the position that Europe now occupies was held by the great region to the south-east, the land that lies between the Mediterranean and the Iranian plateau, and between the Caspian and the Indian Ocean. For in the Glacial Age the geographical and climatic conditions of this region were totally different from what they are at present and had more resemblance to those of modern Europe. The Black Sea and the Caspian were probably united in a great inland sea, which extended north-eastward to the Sea of Aral and far beyond. The Persian Gulf was much larger than at present, and this, together with the glaciation of the Lebanon, the Armenian, and West Iranian highlands, as well as the great mountain mass of Central Asia, caused the climate of the whole area to be cooler and moister. On the other hand, the Black Sea, and probably at times also the Red Sea and the Persian Gulf, were inland seas, and communications were consequently easy between Western Asia and Africa, as well as between Asia Minor and the Balkans. The whole of this Western Asiatic region, in fact, was a great land bridge between Asia and Africa on the one hand and Asia and Europe on the other, and the manifold variety of sea and mountain, of forest and steppe, of high plateau and alluvial valley, made it possible for the different regions to develop a corresponding variety of human and cultural types which were afterwards brought into fruitful contact with one another by the gradual change in climatic conditions and the development of new channels of communication and mutual influence.

We can divide the whole area into three main regions, each of which possessed its own human type. First of all there is the great highland bridge itself, the main mass of which runs east and west from the highlands of Asia Minor through Armenia to Persia with a north-eastern extension in the Caucasus and a south-western one in Syria and Palestine. For the most part this region must have been uninhabitable in the glacial epoch, but in post-glacial times it has been the home and centre of diffusion of Alpine man—the tall, muscular, broad-headed type which has been so important in history.

Secondly, there is the great region of desert and steppe which lies to the south of the highlands, and is connected with a similar region in North Africa. This is the home of the long-headed, brown-skinned, dark-haired Semitic race, which closely resembles the Hamitic race of North-eastern Africa.

Thirdly, there is the great lowland region to the north of the highlands—the Central Asiatic steppe. This region has been completely transformed in post-glacial times by the drying up of the great inner Asiatic sea, of which we have spoken. At first it must have been little more than an extensive coastal strip, afterwards a region of moist and fertile grass lands, and finally after many oscillations it has reached its present condition of semi-aridity. And there has been a corresponding change of human types, due largely to the successive waves of people driven outwards from the interior of Asia by the growth of aridity and the conversion of habitable lands into desert. The first inhabitants seem to have been a dark, long-headed race. At the beginnings of historic times we find the region occupied by peoples of Indo-European speech, and probably of Nordic race. Finally, there comes the flood of Turkish and Tartar peoples, who have occupied the region ever since the beginning of the Christian era.

In addition to those three main regions there are two important sub-types. The alluvial valleys, in which the great historic civilisations of Babylonia and India grew up, and the coast lands, especially the littoral of the Eastern Mediterranean and that of the Persian Gulf and the Indian Ocean.

II. THE PAINTED POTTERY CULTURES

The whole of this great region is of the first importance for the history of human culture, but up to recent times the only archæological evidence was derived from the valleys of the Euphrates and the Tigris, the home of the historic Sumerian and Babylonian cultures. Of late years, however, new discoveries have unveiled a whole series of prehistoric cultures, extending far and wide through Asia from the Persian Gulf to the Caspian and from North-west India to Northern China. All of them are due to settled agricultural peoples who cultivated the ground with stone implements and were beginning to acquire the use of copper, and all of them are characterised, like the Eastern European culture described in the last chapter, by the manufacture of painted pottery, often of a very fine type.

Whatever view is taken of the origin of these cultures and of their relation to one another, they at least prove the existence of a relatively high type of prehistoric culture extending throughout Asia and into South-eastern Europe in very early times, and they throw a new light upon the beginnings of the higher Asiatic civilisations of historic times, the origins of which have hitherto remained a mystery.

The first important discoveries were made in South-western Persia. Here at Susa, the capital of the ancient kingdom of Elam, the French mission under de Morgan discovered in the years 1897–1908 the remains of the earliest known civilisation of Asia. It belonged to a people who had already learnt to domesticate animals as well as to practise agriculture. They could weave linen, and possessed a little copper, though the majority of their implements were of stone. Their high artistic powers are shown by the beautiful painted pottery that they made, the finest prehistoric ware in existence. It is wheel-made and extremely thin and fragile, with elaborate decoration in black paint on a light ground, consisting of geometrical patterns and highly stylised representations of animals and plants. At a later period this fine pottery gives place to a thick ware with polychrome decoration and naturalistic designs, quite unlike the abstract and conventionalised ornament of the earlier style. This second style shows resemblances to the type of painted pottery which is characteristic of North Syria and Eastern Asia Minor, and which certainly dates back to a very remote period, as has been shown by the excavations at Carchemish and Sakjegeuzi.

As soon as this primitive culture was discovered, the problem of its connection with Mesopotamia at once aroused attention, and it was generally concluded that this was the original source of the historic Sumerian culture, and that the settlement at Susa marked a stage in the expansion of a primitive civilisation that had developed either in Elam itself or farther north in Central Asia. This belief was strengthened by the discovery at Anau in Western Turkestan, east of the Caspian, of a series of ancient settlements characterised by fine types of painted pottery. As at Susa, the earliest inhabitants were agriculturalists, who used stone implements, together with a little copper, but their culture probably belongs to a considerably later period than that of Susa, and certainly does not date back to the enormous antiquity (8000 B.C.) postulated by their discoverer. It may well be contemporary, however, with the Painted Pottery Culture of Eastern Europe, which was described in the last chapter and with which it has been connected by Professor Myres and other writers.

Even more remarkable are the points of resemblance between each of these cultures and that discovered in recent years (1921, ff.), in North and West China. Here also we find the traces of an agricultural people, who cultivated the ground with stone hoes, manufactured fine painted pottery in large quantities, and were beginning to acquire the use of copper. Like the peoples of Anau and Eastern Europe, they had domesticated the pig, though not apparently the ox, the sheep, or the horse. Settlements of this culture have already been discovered in Kansu, Honan, and Chihli, and they seem to mark the first introduction of the higher culture in the Far East, just as the Painted Pottery Culture of the Ukraine·and Rumania does in Europe.

Finally, discoveries of even greater importance were made in India in 1924, revealing the existence of an ancient civilisation in the Indus valley, dating back at least to the early part of the third millennium. This was not a mere peasant culture, like those of Anau and North China. It was a true city civilisation, resembling that of the Sumerians, with a highly developed art and architecture and a pictographic script. Here also painted pottery was manufactured, but the finest types were found farther west at Nal in Baluchistan, a site which belongs to an earlier, less advanced stage of the same culture.

Isolated discoveries of painted pottery of early type but of uncertain date have also been made in Seistan and Khorasan in Persia, in Eastern Afghanistan, and in Transcaucasia.

Taken as a whole these discoveries have suggested to many minds the existence of a great focus of primitive civilisation situated in Central Asia, from which radiated all the different types of culture with painted pottery in Western Asia, and Europe and the Far East.[1] At first sight the discontinuity of these cultures and the vast distances which separate them from one another seem to make the supposition of a common origin less

---

[1] Thus Mr. Gordon Childe writes : " At the very dawn of the food-producing era the shadowy but stately outlines of a mysterious civilisation, majestic in its range, transcendental in significance for human progress, are to-day beginning to emerge from the morning mists that cover the scene of history as the last glaciers retreat. It appears from the Yellow Sea to the Adriatic as the first manifestation of men who had made the great advance from a food-gathering to a food-producing economy."—V. G. Childe, *The Aryans*, p. 103.

probable than that of a number of independent local developments. On the other hand, both in China and in Europe, the Painted Pottery Culture appears as a new departure, without any earlier development leading up to it, and with no links with an older indigenous culture. Moreover in every case the finest type of pottery is found fully formed at the earliest stage, while the later development is artistically inferior.

There is, of course, a danger of overlooking vital differences in style and type when we are dealing with a whole series of cultures which belong to different periods as well as to different regions, and in the first enthusiasm of discovery there was a natural tendency to exaggerate points of similarity. Thus the latest and most careful student of the subject, Mr. H. Frankfort, has shown that the earlier comparisons between the pottery of Susa and that of Anau rested largely on false analogies and that the two wares differed profoundly in style and technique. This could hardly be otherwise, however, when we remember that the two cultures may be separated by a gap of a thousand years or more. Nevertheless, there are links between even the most distant members of the group of Painted Pottery Cultures which can hardly be explained as the accidental result of independent evolution. Thus we find a curious type of vessel—a tripod with hollow legs—occurring both in Eastern Europe and in China, where it seems to have been the prototype of the bronze tripods that appear later in the historical period. Moreover, the spiral and meander decoration, which is so characteristic of the East European province, also appears, though less frequently and in a less-developed form, in China. Even more remarkable is the similarity in type between the shallow bowls on a high pedestal, often perforated with small holes, which occur not only in Eastern Europe and in China, but in the deepest levels of the Sumerian temple at Assur and in the earliest dynastic tombs of Egypt. Closely allied to these are the hollow perforated vase-supports or

" offering stands," which are common to Europe, Mesopotamia, and Egypt.   There is also a considerable resemblance between the clay images of the goddess found at Assur and the female figurines so widely distributed in Eastern Europe.

III. The Rise of the Higher Culture in the Middle East

In spite of these detailed points of similarity, however, we can distinguish a broad difference in civilisation, and probably also in date, between the provinces of the Painted Pottery Culture which lie to the north of the great mountain axis of Central Asia and those to the south.   The practice of agriculture is common to them all, and, alike in Mesopotamia, China, and Europe, the domestic pig takes an important place in the economic life of the people ; but while the northern development is that of a purely peasant culture, in the south the Painted Pottery Cultures of Mesopotamia and India are associated with such unmistakable features of the higher civilisation as inscribed seals, the use of a picto-graphic script, and the rise of the city state.   It is true that the direct connection between the Painted Pottery Culture and the historic Sumerian civilisation is not universally admitted.   Mr. Frankfort goes so far as to distinguish three successive and independent periods of culture in Elam and Mesopotamia, which he ascribes to distinct racial elements.   First comes the earliest culture of Susa, that of the makers of the fine pottery of the first style.   Secondly, there is the later culture characterised by the thick polychrome ware, which he ascribes to a people coming from the west, from the region of North Syria, the centre of the later Semitic culture.   These two cultures he believes to have been separated by a considerable gap during which the site of Susa was deserted owing to a period of drought. Finally, there appears the historic Sumerian civilisation, which is later in date and which Mr. Frankfort believes

to have entered Mesopotamia from the south up the
Persian Gulf. Recent discoveries, however, seem to
show that all these phases of culture are the result of a
single homogeneous process of evolution. It is admitted
on all sides that the first civilisation of Susa did penetrate into Mesopotamia, for similar types of pottery have
been discovered, together with stone implements and
a few seals on the sites of later Sumerian settlements in
Southern Mesopotamia, such as Tell el Obeid, close to
Ur, and Abu Shahrein or Eridu, as well as at Bender
Bushire on the Persian Gulf, and far to the west at
Tell Zeidan on the lower Balikh valley,[1] almost on the
frontiers of North Syria. Further, in Northern Mesopotamia, in Assyria and the region of Kerkuk, painted
ware of a later type with some resemblances to that of
the second period at Susa is found intermingled with
the plain incised pottery of the early historical period.
Finally, at Jemdet Naz'r, near Kish, the Weld expedition
during the last season, 1925–6, has discovered pottery
which, alike in form and decoration, has elements that
are common to both the styles at Susa, and which thus
seems to supply the necessary transitional link between
the earlier and the later periods. With this were
found clay tablets with pictographic inscriptions, so
that its connection with the Sumerian civilisation
seems established.

The use of the seal also seems to point to a continuity
between the different phases of culture. Stamp seals of
primitive design are already found in the later stages of
the first culture at Susa. Mr. Frankfort regards the
stamp seal as an essentially Syrian type, and sees in its
presence at Susa the proof of western or Semitic influence.
But the early seals of Susa and Mesopotamia are far
older than the most ancient examples known from
Syria or Cappadocia, and the recent discoveries in
India have shown that the same type was characteristic
of the Painted Pottery Culture in that region.

[1] Described by W. F. Albright in *Man*, 1926, no. 25 (vol. 26, 3).

The stamp seal is in fact common to the whole area from the Mediterranean to the Indus. Only in Babylonia and the regions under Mesopotamian influence was it replaced by the specifically Mesopotamian invention of the cylinder seal, in which the design was engraved in a continuous frieze on the sides, instead of at the end of the seal, but the wide distribution of the other type outside this central area, from Asia Minor and Crete on the one side to Northern India on the other, suggests that the stamp seal was the original form.

The inscribed seal is of the greatest importance for the early history of civilisation, for its use is closely bound up with the origins of writing. The earliest pictographic scripts arose in the same areas as those in which the use of the seal was prevalent, and it seems probable that the sacred symbols which were used as devices upon the seals were the earliest written characters —they were in the literal sense of the word hieroglyphs.

From the earliest times the seal seems to have served a double purpose. On the one hand it was a signet, which might be the badge of an individual owner, or, as in the case of the Great Seal of the English Chancellor, the symbol of public office. But on the other hand it had a religious value. It was an amulet or talisman, which possessed magical properties and ensured to its possessor the protection of the deities whose sacred signs it bore. Hence the ancient inscribed seals, which have been discovered in such large numbers throughout Western Asia, are an invaluable source of information regarding the religious symbolism of early oriental civilisation.

So far as it is possible to judge from the little that has hitherto been published, the newly discovered seals from the Indus valley, which probably date from the third millennium B.C. or later, stand in a class by themselves. For the most part they depict single figures of animals characteristic of India, such as tigers, elephants, zebus, and bulls, each with a sort of trough beneath the head.   The sacred pipal tree (*Ficus religiosa*) is also represented with animals' heads springing from the stem. All these are native types, with a long independent tradition behind them.   The art of the Western Province, however, which includes Syria and Asia Minor, shows a great resemblance to that of Mesopotamia and Elam, and the earlier the examples, the closer is the similarity. The same animal motives, the same religious symbols, and even the same figures of deities and heroes occur from Susa and Babylonia to Syria and Cappadocia, and the number of the examples found seem to preclude the possibility of foreign importation.   The whole of this great area, in fact, formed a single cultural region, and during the third millennium B.C. there existed a common West Asiatic civilisation of Mesopotamian origin, from which the later separate cultures of the Hittite Empire and Northern Syria and Assyria were developed by a process of differentiation.   To some extent this cultural community was no doubt due to Mesopotamian conquest and trade in the third millennium itself.   But the painted pottery of the Western Province goes back to an even earlier period, when the higher culture of Mesopotamia first penetrated this region.   The discovery of painted pottery of the earlier Susian style on the River Balikh proves the coming of this civilising current to the west at a date which can hardly be put lower than 3500 B.C. at the latest, and from the River Balikh to Carchemish, where the Syrian painted ware occurs at the very beginnings of the settlement, is but a step. Nor did the movement stop here.   Northern Syria became a great secondary centre of culture, from which civilising influences radiated in all directions.   We can trace the expansion of the Painted Pottery Culture southwards as far as Palestine, and across the sea to Cyprus.   On the other hand, the Painted Pottery Culture reached the plateau of Asia Minor, probably not through Syria, but directly from Northern Mesopotamia by way of the upper valleys of the Tigris and the

Euphrates. Here it formed the earliest stage of the peculiar Anatolian type of civilisation, often loosely known as " Hittite," which subsequently extended throughout that region, and which was characterised by the cult of the Mother Goddess and her consort, and by its own types of art and pictographic script.

Moreover it is impossible to separate this movement of expansion from the great wave of civilising activity which spread over the Eastern Mediterranean and the Ægean at the dawn of the Age of Metals, for the later development of civilisation in this area bears unmistakable signs of its Asiatic affinities. Here also the worship of the Mother Goddess and her youthful companion occupies the central place in the religion of the people, and not only the animal attributes of the divinities, above all the bull, the lion, the dove, and the serpent, but even the symbols and objects of their cult, such as the cross, the double axe, and the sacred tree, are the same as in Asia Minor.

The use of inscribed seals is equally characteristic of the Ægean culture, and their symbols show the gradual development of a pictographic script which bears some resemblance to those of Asia Minor as well as to the early Egyptian hieroglyphics. Painted pottery also makes its appearance in the Ægean at the beginning of the Age of Metal and attains a magnificent development in Crete by the end of the third millennium. The painted ware of the Cyclades, with its geometrical or conventional figures of birds, and human beings, has a much closer resemblance to the art of Western Asia than the more independent and original Cretan style. But even in its Cretan form, the Copper Age Culture of the Ægean was not a purely native growth. Alike in Cyprus, in Crete, and in the Cyclades, its abrupt appearance points to an external origin, and its introduction was probably due to the coming of foreign traders in search of the copper of Cyprus and the emery and obsidian of Naxos and Melos. It is true that we

have also to reckon with Egyptian influences, especially
in the case of Crete. But these influences are not
altogether mutually exclusive, since there is reason to
think that even Egypt itself was affected by the Asiatic
Culture.

IV. The Problem of the Influence of Asiatic Culture on Egypt

In predynastic times there existed a powerful kingdom
with its centre in the Western Delta, which appears to
have been culturally in advance of the predynastic
communities of Upper Egypt. It was here, in all
probability, that the Egyptian pictographic script,
as well as the use of inscribed seals, were first developed
and that the Cypriot forms of copper implements,
which characterise the early dynastic period, were
introduced into Egypt. It was in the Delta also that
the cult of Isis and Osiris, with its strong resemblance to
that of the Asiatic Mother Goddess and her consort,
had its centre. The people of the Delta seem to have
been traders and seafarers, for they certainly had
contact with Crete and Syria, and Sir Arthur Evans
even goes so far as to suppose that the beginnings of the
Minoan civilisation in Crete were due to an actual
settlement on their part. Moreover, there is some
reason to think that the dominant element in the
population of the Delta was itself of Asiatic origin, for
we find a distinctly non-Egyptian type with broad heads
and powerful, massively built frames forming an important element in the population of Lower Egypt in the time
of the Old Kingdom. This is the " Armenoid " type
discovered at Gizeh by Professor Elliot Smith, and it is
well represented among the statues of the ruling class
of the age of the Pyramids, such as the famous Sheikh
el Beled at Cairo or Prince Hem On at Hildesheim. This
element must have already been present in the Delta
in predynastic times, and it undoubtedly played an

important part in the development of the historic
Egyptian culture.[1]

Finally, in addition to these general signs of Asiatic
influence there is evidence of specific contact between
Egypt and the Sumerian culture during the period of
the rise and establishment of the Egyptian Kingdom.
The art and culture of the proto-dynastic age shows
a striking number of points of similarity, such as do
not occur either in earlier or later times, with Mesopotamian types.[2] We find characteristically Sumerian
artistic motives, such as the hero between two lions,
the lion attacking a bull, the confronted animals with
long interlaced necks, as well as cylinder seals, carved
votive mace-heads, and " offering stands " of the type
that we have seen to be characteristic of the Painted
Pottery Cultures.

These parallels are so detailed and so numerous that
they have suggested to many Egyptologists and historians the hypothesis that the actual unification of
Egypt was the work of foreign conquerors from Elam
or Mesopotamia, who reached Egypt by way of the
Red Sea. It is true that the Sumerians were not
primarily a sea-going people, and we know nothing of
the existence of early ports in Southern Mesopotamia,
but in Arabia, probably on the western shore of the
Persian Gulf, there existed a country known to the
Sumerians as Magan, " the land of the ships," which
was undoubtedly in relation with the civilisation of
Mesopotamia from a very early period. Its inhabitants
were a seafaring people, renowned for their skill as
shipwrights, and they seem to have acted as inter-

[1] Dr. Hall writes : " There can be no doubt now that the impetus
to the development of civilisation was given by these Armenoids from
the north. . . . In Lower Egypt we find them as the dominant civilised
aristocracy at the beginning of things, and it is by no means improbable
that the ruling race of Upper Egypt, to which the unifiers of the
Kingdom belonged, were of Armenoid origin."—*Cambridge Ancient
Hist.*, vol. i, pp. 263–4.

[2] These are discussed at length by Mr. Frankfort in his *Studies in
the Early Pottery of the Near East*, vol. i, pp. 117–72.

mediaries between Sumer and the lands from which the Sumerians derived their supplies of hard stone, such as diorite, as well as copper and gold. One of these regions was no doubt the Yemen, the land of gold and spices, where the later states of Saba and Ma'an were situated. The other was the land of Melukka, which included the peninsula of Sinai, and also perhaps the western shore of the Red Sea. Now the new culture of proto-dynastic times had its centre in Upper Egypt near the mouth of the Wadi Hammamat, which has always been the main channel of communication between Egypt and the Red Sea, so that it may well have had some connection with the ancient trade route from Sumer and Magan to Melukka. The coming of a new influence from this quarter would not only account for the Sumerian elements that appear in the Egyptian culture of the period, but would also explain the importance which the region at the southern extremity of the Red Sea—the Land of Punt—always held in Egyptian tradition. Moreover the appearance in proto-dynastic art of a new type of ship with high stem and prow, entirely different from the native type of Nile boat, also suggests some new contact with a maritime people. Even if these signs of foreign influence were not due to an actual conquest, but were merely the result of cultural and commercial contact, they would still be of the greatest importance for the history and chronology of ancient culture. If we accept the evidence of these parallels, we must assume that the historic Sumerian culture, as characterised, for instance, by the use of the cylinder seal, was already fully developed as early as the proto-dynastic period of Egypt. But the cylinder seal was not in common use until after the introduction of the incised unpainted pottery, so the whole development of the Painted Pottery styles in Mesopotamia will be contemporary with the pre-dynastic Egyptian culture. Thus it will be difficult to place its beginnings much later than 4000 B.C., or the

rise of the historic Sumerian culture later than 3500 B.C.
This involves a somewhat higher chronology for Sumerian
history than that usually accepted, but the uncertainty
as to the number and duration of the early dynasties
is so great that little reliance can be placed on any
exact calculation.[1]

It is impossible to make even an approximate guess
at the age of the Painted Pottery Culture in India.   It
was certainly flourishing in the third millennium B.C.,
and an inscribed seal of the Indian type is said to have
been discovered at Kish in the foundations of a building
of the time of Hammurabi (c. 2050 B.C.).   The three
northern provinces of the Painted Pottery Culture—
Eastern Europe, Anau, and China—also seem to have
flourished during the third millennium, but here even
an approximate chronology is out of the question.

V. THE SUMERIANS AND THE ORIGINS OF ASIATIC CULTURE

Thus we see how vast is the extension of the phase of
civilisation represented by the Painted Pottery cultures.
In time they are spread out over a period of some 3,000
years ; in space they reach from the Indus to the
Orontes, and from the Danube to the Hoang Ho.

But what was the source of this great civilising movement ?   Was it diffused from a common original centre ?
And if so, is it possible to identify the race or the people
who were responsible for its origin and diffusion ?   In
Mesopotamia, at least, the region in which the progress
of the higher culture is most marked, there seems good

---

[1] The fluid state of Mesopotamian chronology at present may be
judged from Mr. Albright's attempt to identify Menes King of Egypt
(usually dated 3315) with Manium King of Magan, who was defeated
by Naram Sin of Agade (usually dated c. 2700).   This would involve
a compromise between the higher Egyptian chronology of Borchardt
(1st dyn. 4187 B.C.) and the traditional Babylonian chronology which
placed Naram Sin at 3750 B.C., but the latter date will leave an unex-
plained gap of over a thousand years in the Mesopotamian lists of
rulers.   See, however, the Chronological Tables at the end of the volume.

reason to ascribe its introduction to an historical people, the Sumerians. The latter differed alike in physical type, in language, and in culture from the Semitic peoples who occupied the great lowland region of Western Asia, and by whom they were ultimately absorbed in Mesopotamia itself. The original habitat of the Sumerians was probably in the mountainous region to the east, for it is at Susa in Elam that the earliest type of painted pottery is found, and their religion and art show many reminiscences of a highland origin, such as the association of the gods with mountains, and the depicting of bison and ibex on the early seal cylinders, instead of the later water buffaloes and goats. Undoubtedly there was a native population, which may well have been Semitic, established in Mesopotamia, when the bearers of the higher civilisation first entered the country. For the evidence of recent discoveries has proved the co-existence of two completely different racial elements in Mesopotamia in very early times, a broad-headed minority and a majority with extremely long and narrow skulls. The latter would seem to represent the Semitic or Mediterranean aborigines, and the former the dominant Sumerian element, for the Sumerian portrait statues certainly represent an Alpine or Armenoid type, with broad heads and oblique, up-slanted eyes which give them an almost Mongolian appearance, though it must be admitted that in the earliest interments found (at Kish) the long-headed element is predominant. This composite nature of the population of ancient Sumer is perhaps symbolised in the most ancient and popular legend of Sumerian mythology, the original meaning of which must be looked for in the countless representations on early cylinder seals rather than in the late and sophisticated literary version, which dates from the Babylonian period. Gilgamesh, the semi-divine king and civiliser, who built the great walls of Erech, the tamer of oxen, and the servant of the god of irrigation and agriculture, is the national hero of the Sumerian people, while the half-animal being Eabani, whom Gilgamesh vanquishes and makes his friend and companion, stands for the native population of uncivilised hunters.

Thus the disappearance of the Sumerian people and language in the latter part of the third millennium would seem to be due, not to a wave of Semitic migration from the desert, but to the gradual absorption of a foreign minority by the mass of the native population. This process was no doubt accomplished even more rapidly in the western province of the Painted Pottery Culture, in the region of the Upper Euphrates and North Syria, and it was from this direction—the land of Amurru—that the returning wave of Semitisation first spread into Mesopotamia itself.

This derivation of the Sumerians from the highland region to the east of the Persian Gulf suggests that they may have had a common origin with the founders of the Painted Pottery civilisation of the Indus valley, which itself extended westward into Baluchistan, and perhaps even as far as Seistan.   As yet no reports have been made with regard to the physical type of the human remains discovered there, but the two portrait statues, discovered in 1926 at Mohenjo-daro in Sind, undoubtedly represent the same type of low-browed, oblique-eyed, broad-headed men as that in Sumerian art.

To this civilisation must be ascribed the beginning of the higher culture in India, and it was on this foundation that the later Indo-Aryan culture was built.   The Aryans in India, like the Semites in Babylonia and the Greeks in the Ægean, have long enjoyed an undeserved reputation for the creation of a civilisation which was to a great extent inherited from their predecessors. The Dravidian was pictured as a mere jungle-dwelling savage whose culture had been forcibly imposed upon him by the fair-skinned conquerors from the north, a view which flattered the prejudices alike of the dominant castes in India and of the European ruling class.   It has long been realised by scholars that the non-Aryan element in Indian civilisation was of the greatest importance, and was to be ascribed to the Dravidians. The true aboriginal population of India, however, was not the Dravidians, but the speakers of the Munda group of languages which still survives in Chota Nagpur and the neighbouring region, and which forms part of a great linguistic zone extending through Further India and Indonesia into the Pacific.   The true Dravidians, on the other hand, were probably a broad-headed people, like the modern Dravidian-speaking Brahui, who entered India from the north-west in prehistoric times, bringing with them a higher culture of the Sumerian type.   If this is so, their modern representatives must be looked for in the belt of broad-headed population which extends down Western India as far as Coorg, and whose origin is usually, but unsatisfactorily, attributed to the Scythian invasions of the early Christian era, and not among the long-headed Tamils and Telegu of the south, who would represent an earlier native population, probably of Mundari stock, which had acquired their present language and culture from the higher civilisation of the invading peoples to the north. The Dravidian languages stand in a class by themselves, though attempts have been made to connect them with the equally mysterious languages of Elam and Sumer. Resemblances certainly exist between the Dravidian Brahui and the ancient Elamite tongue, and it is possible that all three languages are early representatives of the Caucasian linguistic group.[1]   Even if this were demonstrated, however, it would not go far towards solving the problems of their origin, since the survival of the Caucasian languages in the Caucasus does not prove that it was their original centre of diffusion, any more

---

[1] For the Caucasian character of Sumerian see Tseretheli, " Sumerian and Georgian," in the *Journal of the R. Asiatic Society*, 1913–16.

than the survival of the Celtic tongue in Wales proves
that the Celts originated there.

In the present state of our knowledge, the origins of
the higher civilisation in Western Asia remain a mystery.
The most plausible hypothesis seems to be that the
creators of the Painted Pottery Culture were a broad-
headed people, who inhabited the highlands of Western
Central Asia, possibly in the region of Seistan, and who
were subsequently driven to migrate by the growing
aridity of that area. This would explain the way
in which we find the different Painted Pottery Cultures
radiating north and south from the central mountain
axis, appearing first on the southern frontiers of the
highland region and later extending far and wide along
the border of the northern steppes. In historical times
we find the influence of the Sassanian culture of Persia
following very much the same paths. It extended
westward through Mesopotamia and Armenia to Asia
Minor and North Syria, eastward to the valley of the
Indus, and northward to Turkestan. Most remarkable
of all is the fact that this later Persian influence appears
in almost the same region of Europe as that of the
prehistoric Painted Pottery Culture, i.e. in the Gothic-
Sarmatian kingdom from the Crimea to the Lower
Danube.

It is difficult to say how far this expansion in prehistoric times was due to racial movements, and how far
to purely cultural influence. We have seen that in
Mesopotamia and even in Egypt the rise of the higher
culture was accompanied by the appearance of a broad-
headed minority among a long-headed native population,
and the scanty human remains that have been found
at Anau and in Eastern Europe show that the two
different elements existed in those regions also, though
in what proportions it is impossible to say. In China,
however, the human remains discovered at Yang-Shao
and elsewhere all belong to the broad-headed type and
appear to differ little from that of the modern population

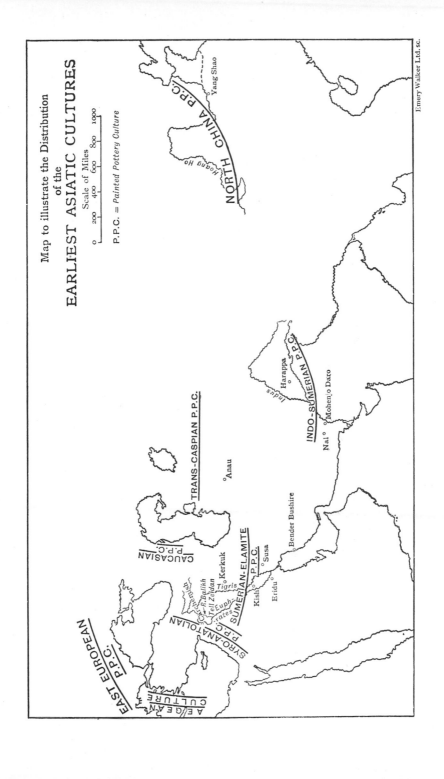

Map to illustrate the Distribution
of the
EARLIEST ASIATIC CULTURES

Scale of Miles

0   200   400   600   800   1000

P.P.C. = *Painted Pottery Culture*

NORTH CHINA P.P.C.

Yang Shao

Hoang Ho

INDO-SUMERIAN P.P.C.

Harappa

Indus

Mohenjo Daro

Nal

TRANS-CASPIAN P.P.C.

Anau

CAUCASIAN P.P.C.

Kerkuk

SUMERIAN-ELAMITE P.P.C.

Bender Bushire

Susa

Kish

Eridu

Tigris

R. Balikh

Tell Zeidan

Euph-rates

SYRO-ANATOLIAN P.P.C.

EAST EUROPEAN P.P.C.

AEGEAN CULTURE

Emery Walker Ltd. sc.

of the country. Nevertheless it would be premature to deny the possibility of the new culture having been introduced by a foreign minority, since the population of Northern China is far from uniform, and is believed by some anthropologists to contain Alpine and even Nordic elements. Certainly the new discoveries do tend to strengthen the case of writers such as Terrien de Lacouperie and the late C. J. Ball, who have maintained a connection between the culture of the Sumerians and that of ancient China.[1]

Yet in spite of all the gaps and obscurities in our knowledge, the discovery of this group of Painted Pottery Cultures throws a very remarkable light on the origins of ancient civilisation. We see that the same type of culture lies at the root of the development of all the higher civilisations of Asia—in India and Persia, in Mesopotamia and Northern Syria, in Turkestan and North China, as well as in those parts of Europe—the Lower Danube and Greece—which were to play so vital a part in the rise of Western civilisation. Nor was this community of cultural origins limited to a purely external parallelism. In all the regions in which the Painted Pottery Culture flourished there is evidence of a similar type of religion and a corresponding social organisation, which form the moral and intellectual foundations of the new way of life.

---

[1] These attempts have, as a rule, met with severe criticism on the part of sinologists. Nevertheless there remain certain minor points, such as the use of the same expression to describe the common folk alike in Sumerian and Chinese, i.e. the black-haired or dark-headed people—which are curious and difficult to explain.

CHAPTER V

NEOLITHIC CULTURE AND THE RELIGION OF THE PEASANT

Primitive Culture and the Origins of Agriculture.

The Religion of the Mother Goddess in Mesopotamia.

The Religion of the Mother Goddess in Western Asia.

The Religion of the Mother Goddess in Prehistoric Europe.

The Religion of the Mother Goddess in India.

Influence of the Cult on the Development of Civilisation.

CHAPTER V

NEOLITHIC CULTURE AND THE RELIGION OF THE PEASANT

I. Primitive Culture and the Origins of Agriculture

It is obvious that the gap between the culture of the palæolithic hunters and that of the neolithic and æneolithic peoples of the Near East is a very wide one. It involves something far deeper than the mere change in the type of stone implements which is implied in the term "neolithic." The ordinary classification of human cultures in Stone, Bronze, and Iron Ages is a convenient one for practical purposes, but it is extremely superficial. The change from the palæolithic to the neolithic culture—one of the greatest changes in the whole range of human history—is not a mere change in the manufacture of stone implements ; in some cases, that change hardly took place and the old palæolithic technique was continued right into historic times. The true change was a change of life. Man ceased to be a parasite on Nature, like the hunter. He learnt to co-operate with Nature—to govern and direct her. From a food-gatherer, he becomes a food-producer. And that change involved a revolution in his whole way of life, in his social organisation and manner of settlement, in his relation to his environment and to his fellow-men, in his religion and thought.

This change in its simplest form must have taken place at a very remote period. In palæolithic Europe it was rendered impossible by climatic conditions, but in other parts of the world it was probably already achieved before the end of the glacial epoch. In a tropical environment, vegetable food is the chief source of human nourishment. And from digging for roots, such as yams, and collecting fruit and edible seeds, the transition is easy to making a transplantation of the wild plant and finally to cultivating it. We find the earliest stage among such primitive food-collecting peoples as the Australians and the Veddahs of Ceylon, where the women when they dug for wild yams used to cut the root and replace part of it in the earth so that it might grow again. A more advanced stage is reached when the seeds of the fruits that have been eaten are intentionally planted near the settlement, as is done to-day by some of the most primitive tribes of the Malay Peninsula. Hence the earliest type of food-production was probably not agriculture in our sense of the word, but horticulture, as it is practised to-day by so many primitive peoples in tropical Africa and Asia. Man's earliest agricultural tool was not the plough, but the hoe and the digging stick.

In this primitive form food-production was essentially a feminine task. As among the lower savages the man is the hunter and the woman the food-gatherer ; so in this more advanced stage we find the woman cultivating the garden while the man, apart from doing the rough work of clearing the ground for the garden plot, remains a hunter as before.

Of course, as this artificial food-supply becomes overwhelmingly important, there is a tendency for the men to share in the work of cultivation, or even to replace the women entirely ; but this is a later stage, sometimes due to the influence of peoples who practise the higher agriculture, and the cultivation of the garden by the woman is undoubtedly the primitive phase.

It is clear that this development adds largely to woman's social importance. The cultivation of land involves the fixing of the settlement, and it is the woman who cultivates, not the hunting male, that is the stable element in the society. This, I believe, is the real reason

for the rise of the widely spread system of social organisation, which is based on female descent and reckons
kinship in the female line—the so-called system of
Mother-right or Matriarchy.   It is not, as has been
commonly taught, the universal primitive system, for
it is conspicuously lacking amongst many of the most
primitive hunting peoples.   Its highest development is
always found in regions where the hoe- or garden-
agriculture that we have just described is dominant,
e.g. in West Africa, among the agriculturalists of
North America, especially the Pueblo Indians, and
in Indonesia.   And the reason for this is obvious, since
even among non-matriarchal peoples in Africa the
garden is usually looked on as in a sense the property
of the woman who cultivates it, and is inherited by her
own children, to the exclusion of the other children of her
husband.   From this starting-point it is easy to see how
the whole system of social organisation would come more
and more to rest on kinship through the woman, until
finally we reach the extreme development (which
curiously enough is found among the most warlike of all
peoples, the Iroquois), where the government of the
clan, i.e. the actual electing and deposing of the chiefs,
is actually in the hands of the older women.

And a corresponding development is found in the
sphere of religion.   Primitive peoples all over the world
regard the earth, which is the mother of the crops and
of every growing thing, as a female principle—the
Earth Mother.   Some writers have even held that
there is a direct connection between this belief and the
fact that the earth is cultivated by women—the human
mothers ; but however that may be, it is certain that
the primitive peoples who depend on agriculture attach
great importance to the female principle in Nature, as
embodied in the earth, and in some cases also in the
moon.

The highly developed religion of Mkissi Nissi, " the
Earth Mystery," in Loango, is a remarkable example of

this cult, and it is found in various forms all over the domain of the primitive hoe-agriculture in South Asia and Indonesia and as far as America, but nowhere is it more important, as we shall see, than it was in the ancient cultures of the Near East. In fact it lies at the root of the development, not only of the higher form of agriculture, but also of that whole complex of beliefs and institutions which we may name in Mr. W. J. Perry's phrase, the *Archaic Civilisation*.

The lower agriculture that I have been describing is not characterised by the use of domestic animals. Their origin is just as important for the history of civilisation as that of agriculture itself, but it is far more obscure. The dog was certainly domesticated very early, in a sense it tames itself, for it may become a parasitic dependent on the hunter, as the jackal is on the tiger. But it is not of great importance for culture like the food-producing animals—the pig, the sheep, the goat, and above all the ox. How and when these were tamed is a very difficult problem. They are found at an early date in Egypt and among the peoples of the Painted Pottery Cultures, though the earliest settlers at Anau did not at first possess them, and in China only the pig was known. In Susa and Mesopotamia, however, they appear from the first, and it was perhaps in this region that the great discovery was made by which the tamed animal was put to labour, and the ox was taught to draw the plough.

There are, in fact, many reasons for supposing that this discovery was made at some definite period by a single people. For while hoe-agriculture is spread widely in different parts of the world, and is everywhere different as regards the plants that are cultivated and the methods of cultivation, plough-agriculture is remarkably uniform. Apart from recent developments, such as European colonisation, the domain of plough-agriculture covers a single continuous area from Europe to China, outside which it does not exist.

In all parts of this area the ox was the original plough animal, and the typical cultivated grains are wheat and barley, plants which in their wild state are found in just those regions of the Near East where the new culture is most likely to have originated. And the coming of this new discovery wrought a profound change in culture. Everywhere the taming and tending of beasts is men's work, just as hunting had been. And so when animals were used for the cultivation of the fields, agriculture became men's work too. The old idle life of the savage, in which the women do the bulk of the work, and the men hunt or fight, gave place to a life in which all the productive forces of the community were employed—the men in the fields and the women at home, with more time for rearing their children and for spinning and weaving. There was not only a great heightening of economic productivity, there was a new organised social activity, which prepared the way for a further division of labour, and for new forms of work and of leisure. Man had become an organiser and an economist, as well as an adventurer and an artist.

The ruling power in the new culture belonged not to the secular chief or war leader, but to the priest.[1] For if the earlier types of garden-agriculture had its religious side, this was so in a far higher degree with the developed agricultural economy of the Near East, where the whole culture was founded on a religious basis and inter-penetrated by religious ideas.

At the root of it there lay the same cult of the Earth Mother which had obtained in more primitive times, but now there is added a second figure, that of her divine son and lover, who is the personification of the vegetative life of Nature, as seen in the trees and the harvest, in the growth of the field and the garden.

---

[1] Thus even down to the present day among the peasant peoples of the Lower Niger, the chieftainship often belongs ex officio to the high priest of the Earth Goddess, and he was known as " The Owner of the Land."

This conception is the fundamental note of the early religions all over the Near East, and goes back to prehistoric times, except perhaps in Egypt, where the primitive animal gods survive into historical times.

II. THE RELIGION OF THE MOTHER GODDESS IN MESOPOTAMIA

The earliest literary evidence for the cult is to be found in the Sumerian hymns and liturgies, but in its origins it undoubtedly dates back to a far earlier period before the rise of the historical civilisation.

The religion of the Sumerians in historic times was a highly developed polytheism with a hierarchy of gods and goddesses who control the different provinces of Nature. But underlying this, there are everywhere traces of an earlier type of religion characterised by the cult of the goddess of fertility and birth and her consort the earth god.   In her earliest form the Mother Goddess seems to have been a bisexual serpent deity, who was worshipped under the names of Kadi and Izir at Der, east of the Tigris, and this dual character survived to some extent in later times, as we see from Gudea's invocation of his " mother-father " Enlil and his father-mother Ninlil, and by the fact that Tammuz himself is described as the " lady " of the city of Kinunir.[1]   In the course of time, however, this primitive type was differentiated according to the nature of its attributes and the place of its cult.   There was the Lady of Heaven at Erech, the Lady of the Mountain at Nippur, the Great Lady of Ur, the August Lady or the Lady of Birth at Kish, the Lady of the Harvest of Umma, and countless others.   Her consort and son Izir underwent a similar process of development, but in his aspect of the dying god of vegetation he was identified above all with the prehistoric King Dumuzi or Tammuz, the centre of whose cult was at Erech, the holy city of the Mother Goddess Innini or Ishtar.

[1] Zimmern, *Tammuz-lieder*, pp. 251 f.

The Mother Goddess herself has two main aspects. On the one hand, she is the goddess of agriculture, the mother of the harvest and the patroness of civilised life ; on the other, she is the goddess of the wild, the virgin huntress and the mistress of the wild beasts—like the Greek Artemis and the Cretan Britomartis and Dictynna.

This latter aspect would seem to be the more primitive, for it goes back to the world of the hunter and to the untamed life of Nature. And similarly the god appears, not only as the embodiment of the corn and the harvest, but also, at least in Asia Minor and Syria, in an animal form, and is represented by the pig and the bull.

In its developed form, however, as we see it among the Sumerians at the dawn of history, the religion is essentially an agricultural and civilised one. It embodies the great cosmic mystery of the annual death and resurrection of Nature—the cycle of winter and spring that make up the farmer's year.

It has its two great moments in the festival of the divine marriage, i.e. the annual wedding of the god, and in the yearly lamentation for the dying god, Tammuz, which held an even more important place in the religious life of the people. Every year as the divine son descends into the underworld all the life of Nature ceases and the great mother is widowed :

" In Eanna, high and low, there is weeping,
  Wailing for the house of the lord they raise.
  The wailing is for the plants, the first lament is they grow not.
  For the habitations and the flocks it is ; they produce not.
  For the perishing wedded ones, for perishing children it is; the dark-
    headed people create not.
  The wailing is for the great river ; it brings the flood no more.
  The wailing is for the fields of men ; the grain grows no more.
  The wailing is for the fish ponds ; the dasuhur fish spawn not.
  The wailing is for the cane-break ; the fallen stalks grow not.
  The wailing is for the forests ; the tamarisks grow not.
  The wailing is for the highlands ; the masgam trees grow not.
  The wailing is for the garden store-house ; honey and wine are pro-
    duced not.
  The wailing is for the meadows ; the bounty of the garden, the
    sihlu plants grow not.
  The wailing is for the palace ; life unto distant days is not."

And again :

> " The lord shepherd of the folds lives no more,
>   The husband of the heavenly queen lives no more,
>   The lord of the cattle stalls lives no more.
>   When he slumbers, the sheep and lambs slumber also,
>   When he slumbers, the she goats and the kids slumber also." [1]

The Mother Goddess wanders through the land lamenting his loss and at last descends herself to Hades in search of him :

> " To the land without return Ishtar, the daughter of Sin, directed her
>   mind,
>   To the dark house, the dwelling of Irkalla,
>   To the house whence those who enter do not return,
>   To the road from which there is no path leading back,
>   To the house in which those who enter are deprived of light,
>   Where dust is their nourishment, clay their food,
>   They do not see light, they dwell in darkness,
>   Clothed like a bird with feathers as a covering ;
>   On door and lock, dust has settled." [2]

There she moves the pity of the god of the underworld and awakens Tammuz from the sleep of death.
Then, with the return of Tammuz, Nature lives again :

> " Innini to her sacred women cried ;
>   In heaven there is light, on earth there is light,
>   In the bosom of the mother she gave him rest.
>
>   .   .   .   .
>
>   In her bosom his wife Innini gave him rest."

> " In Erech its brick walls reposed ; upon Erech a faithful eye he cast.
>   The figs grew large ; in the plains the trees thrived.
>   There the valiant in his boat descended, from Hades hastening,
>   The holy husband of the queen of heaven in a boat descended, from
>   Hades hastening.
>   Where grass was not, there grass is eaten,
>   Where water was not, water is drunk,
>   Where the cattle sheds were not, cattle sheds are built." [3]

---

[1] Tr. S. Langdon, *Tammuz and Ishtar*, pp. 11 and 14–15.
[2] From the Babylonian poem on the " Descent of Ishtar to Hades," tr. Jastrow.
[3] Trs. S. Langdon, *Tammuz and Ishtar*, pp. 22 and 23.

III. The Religion of the Mother Goddess in
Western Asia

This drama of the death and the return of the divine
consort of the Mother Goddess, who is the principle of
the life of Nature, is common to the whole of Western
Asia from the dawn of history, and so great is the
similarity in the form that it takes in the different
regions that there can be little doubt of its origin from
a common centre. This is true even in Egypt, though
the Egyptian religion as a whole is utterly different
from that of Asia, and seems to belong to a more primitive world. The Egyptian Mother Goddess and her
consort, Isis and Osiris, Asat and Asar, however, are
utterly alien to the animal gods of the original Egyptian
pantheon ; they are intruders from without, from some
region of the higher Asiatic culture. They had their
earliest homes and cult centres at Busiris and Perhebt,
near the Damietta mouth of the Nile, in that kingdom
of the Western Delta of which we spoke in the last
chapter. Even the name of Osiris—Asar—resembles
that of his Sumerian compeer Izir or Isir,[1] the original
form of Tammuz. Like the latter Osiris is both a dead
king and a representative of the vegetative life of
Nature, and in both countries the death of the god is
celebrated in the annual ceremonies which commemo-
rate the lamentation of the goddess for her consort
and her pilgrimage through the lands in search of him.
In Egypt, however, the death of the god takes a peculiar
form. It is due to the enmity of his rival Set, the god
of Upper Egypt, who appears to represent the desert
and the destructive forces of Nature ; and peculiar to
Egypt also is the great development of the cult of
Osiris as the lord of the dead and the patron of immortality. Nevertheless even in its later form the Egyptian

[1] The form Asar-ri also occurs in one of Gudea's inscriptions, and
also in the Babylonian Epic of Creation, Tablet vii, 1, as the name
of a vegetation god, the Sumerian prototype of Marduk, cf. Dhorme,
Choix de Textes Religieux, pp. 68-9, and notes 1 and 2.

legend of Osiris bears traces of his connections with Asia, for it was at Byblus on the coast of Syria that Isis finds the body of her lord enclosed in an erica tree in the royal palace.   Now Byblus was from the earliest times a great centre of the cult of the Phœnician vegetation god, Eshmun or Adonis, and it was thence in later times that his cult passed to Cyprus and finally to European Greece.[1]   But the worship of the dying god was not confined to Byblus ;   Ezekiel describes the women mourning for Tammuz in the temple of Jerusalem itself, and even to-day the tenth month of the Jewish year still bears his name.   Moreover, the very foundations of Syrian religion rest on the cult of a mother goddess Ashtart—the biblical Ashtoreth—and of a Baal on whom the fertility of the land depends. At Hierapolis, the great shrine of the Syrian mother goddess, she was served, as at Erech, by eunuch priests, and the darker side of the religion, as shown in the sacrifice of the first-born children to the god, and the prostitution of virgins and married women at the shrines of the goddess, was even more in evidence than in Babylonia.

But it was above all in Asia Minor that the religion of the Mother Goddess best preserved its original character, and most completely dominated the culture of the land.   Wherever an advanced city culture had developed, as in Mesopotamia itself, it tended to be overshadowed by theological speculation and by the multiplication of divinities.   Asia Minor, on the other hand, was always a region of peasant culture, and consequently it maintained the peasant religion intact down to the beginning of the Christian period.   It is true the advanced culture of the Hittite Empire tended to develop a polytheistic pantheon such as we find in Mesopotamia, but with its fall the primitive simplicity

---

[1] He was identified with the River Adonis which flows into the sea south of Byblus, and which is annually coloured red, as though by the blood of the god, owing to the nature of the soil through which it flows.

of Anatolian religion reasserted itself. The native conception of the divinity is well seen in the famous rock carving of Ibriz in Southern Cappadocia, which depicts a king in the act of adoration before a colossal figure of the god of the corn and the vine. The king is dressed in rich attire, but the god wears the short tunic and high boots of the peasant and his arms and legs are bare. But in Asia Minor the foremost place always belongs to the Mother Goddess, whether under the name of Cybele or Ma or the Great Goddess, and the subordinate position of the god is shown by the legend of Attis— the Anatolian counterpart of Tammuz and Adonis— whose union with the goddess is purchased by the sacrifice of his virility. In the third century A.D. the death and resurrection of Attis were celebrated by the eunuch priests of Cybele at Rome in an annual ceremony of which we possess considerable information. On the 22nd of March the pine tree which symbolised the god was cut in the woods and brought down to the temple by the sacred guild of the Tree Bearers. The 24th was the Day of Blood, on which the priests and devotees, to the sound of cymbals and flutes, gashed themselves with knives like modern Dervishes and sprinkled the tree with their blood. At night an image of the god was laid upon a bier and mourned over by the worshippers. Finally, a light was brought in, and the priest anointed the faces of the mourners, saying, " Take courage, O mystæ, for the god is saved, and for you too there will be salvation after travail." The following day was given up to rejoicing—the festival of the Hilaria— and on the 27th the ceremonies closed with the procession of the image of the goddess and her solemn lustration outside the walls of Rome in the waters of the Almo.

The central idea of these rites undoubtedly belongs to the original cultus of the Anatolian peasant religion, but the introduction of the hope of immortality for the initiates is probably a later development, common to the other mystery religions of the Roman period.

It was probably only in Egypt that the vegetation god
was conceived from early times as the giver of immortality.   In Asia Minor religion always centred in the
mystery of the life of Nature, on which man's physical
existence depends.   A similar evolution took place,
probably at a much earlier date in the case of the
mysteries of Eleusis, which, like the Sumerian and
Egyptian ceremonies that we have described, com-
memorated the mourning of the Mother Goddess on the
descent of her child—in this case a daughter—into the
underworld, and her sorrowful pilgrimage in seach of
her.   It was an autumn ceremony of sowing, and so its
primary association was with the death of Nature, but
the mysteries also included a sacred marriage and the
announcement of the birth of a divine child—the resurrection of the seed in spring.   Eleusis was itself a
Mycenæan foundation, and there can be little doubt
that these rites go back in part to the pre-Hellenic
civilisation.   For prehistoric Greece also belonged to
the domain of the ancient vegetation religion, which
even in historic times still underlay the official civic
cultus of the Olympian pantheon.   The Mother Goddess
appears under a multitude of forms and names, like
her prototype the Babylonian Ishtar, who was at once a
city goddess and a goddess of war, an agricultural goddess
and a goddess of untamed Nature, a virgin goddess and a
goddess of sexual love.   Thus in Greece we find Athene,
the great city goddess, who was also a virgin warrior,
Artemis the huntress, and Aphrodite, the goddess of
love, as well as a multitude of half-forgotten figures,
such as Britomartis and Dictynna, Ariadne and Ata-
lanta, Ino and Pasiphæ, all of whom were originally forms
of the Mother Goddess.   Most important of all, however,
was the goddess of agriculture, the fundamental type
of the Mother Goddess, who for the most part possessed
no name but only titles.   She was the Mother, or the
Great Mother, Ge, the Earth, Kore the Maiden, Despoina
the Mistress, Themis the Oracle.   She was Thesmo-

phorus the Lawgiver, Karpophorus the Fruit Bearer, or Pandora the Giver of All. But whether the names are Greek as with this latter class, or non-Hellenic in origin like Athene and the rest, all these types undoubtedly belong to the prehistoric religion. How far they are native to Greece, and how far they are derived from Crete or Asia Minor, it is usually impossible to say, since all three regions belong essentially to the same religious province. In Crete the supreme importance of the Mother Goddess is obvious from all that has been discovered of the Minoan culture. Here too, as in Asia, she was accompanied by a youthful consort whose symbol, like that of Attis, seems to have been the sacred tree which so often appears in Minoan art; and one gem, which shows the breaking of the tree and the lamentation of the goddess, probably represents a ceremony which resembles the mystery of the death of the vegetation god in Asia Minor and Syria.

IV. The Religion of the Mother Goddess in Prehistoric Europe

Undoubtedly the full development of this religion in its higher form in the Ægean world belongs to the Bronze Age, and probably owes much to Anatolian influence, but there is reason to think that even in neolithic times the worship of the Mother Goddess was characteristic of the Painted Pottery Cultures of Greece and Eastern Europe, and even penetrated with the peasant culture far into Central Europe. Throughout this area, but above all in Rumania, Thessaly, and Jugo-Slavia, we find clay figures of women, sometimes standing with the arms uplifted or held under the breast, sometimes seated on a chair or throne. They are usually accompanied by rude figures of animals, oxen, or pigs. Male figures are rare, but not unknown, and there are one or two examples in which the female figure is shown nursing a child. Now in Cyprus and

Western Asia images of this type are known to have been connected with the worship of the Mother Goddess —for example, they are found in the extremely ancient Sumerian temple of Ishtar at Assur, so that it can hardly be doubted that their appearance in Europe points to the existence there of a similar cult. Their centres of diffusion are, in fact, the same as those of the higher neolithic culture, the origins of which were described in a previous chapter. For agriculture and the domestication of animals did not arise in Europe as independent discoveries, nor were they isolated borrowings from a higher culture, as has sometimes been the case with a new invention or a new type of weapon. They formed part of an organised culture-complex which contained spiritual as well as material elements. Hence it is reasonable to suppose that the Peasant Culture brought with it into Europe the same peasant religion or cult of the Mother Goddess which formed such an essential part of the development of the higher culture in Western Asia.

Even to-day we still find abundant traces of the old Peasant Religion of prehistoric times in the customs and superstitions of the European country folk. Wilhelm Mannhardt in his great study of the peasant customs of Germany and Central Europe has shown how all the leading rites and ideas of the Asiatic vegetation religion have their parallel in the spring and harvest customs of the European peasants. In Western Europe, apart from exceptional regions, such as Brittany and Portugal, these customs survive only in a weak and degraded form, but as we go east they become stronger and more primitive. In Central and Northern Europe, the spirit of vegetation is embodied in such forms as the Corn Mother or the Corn Maiden, in Czecho-Slovakia there is the annual ceremony of the carrying of Death out of the village in the form of a straw image, and the bringing in of Life ; while in the Ukraine and Galicia the death and resurrection of the life of Nature is symbolised by figures, such as Kostrobonko, Yarilo, and Lada, which undoubtedly have their origin in the pre-Christian mythology of the people. But it is in Rumania and the Eastern Balkans, the old region of the Painted Pottery Culture, that the tradition of the Peasant Religion is most firmly rooted. It was from that direction—from Thrace—that the vegetation religion in the form of the worship of Dionysus re-entered Greece triumphantly in classical times, and even to-day, or quite recently, in the Thracian villages at Carnival time, the drama of the death and revivification of the god is enacted by a man clad in the skins of goats and fawns, who is slain, and mourned over and comes to life again, while a plough is dragged through the village and prayers are said for the fructification of the crops.[1] Moreover, in Rumania the folklore of the peasants is full of reminiscences of the old vegetation religion, and some of their songs, in spite of a veneer of Christian imagery, show an extraordinary similarity to the Sumerian hymns which describe the sorrowful pilgrimage of the Mother Goddess in search of her son, and the effects of his death upon the life of Nature.[2]

V. The Religion of the Mother Goddess in India

But these, after all, are but faint echoes from a vanished world. All over Western Asia and Europe the spread of the higher religions, Christianity and Mohammedanism, has swept away the old religious foundations on which the life of primitive culture rested. There remains, however, one great civilisation in which the religion of the Mother Goddess is still living and powerful in spite of the many religions that have come and gone. In India the great gods of the Rig Veda, Varuna the Righteous Lord, and Indra the Celestial Warrior, are now but names, the religion of

[1] Frazer, "Attis, Adonis, and Osiris" II 99 from R. M. Dawkins, "The Modern Carnival in Thrace and the Cult of Dionysus," *Journal of Hellenic Studies,* 1906, p. 191.
[2] Cf. Dr. Gaster in *Folklore,* vol. xxxiv, pp. 45–86.

Buddha has vanished from the land that saw its birth, but the Mother Goddess still reigns supreme alike among the primitive tribes of the jungle and the civilised and educated population of Bengal. In the Dravidian lands of the south, where the classical Aryan-Hindu culture has made least impression on the life of the people, the village deities are always feminine : they are the Ammas or mothers, and the gods who are the husbands or tenants occupy a thoroughly subordinate position. But even in the north and in orthodox Hindu circles, the worship of the Great Mother, Durga or Kali or Uma, takes a prominent place by the side of the great deities, and sometimes even tends to supersede them. A modern Bengali poet has written :

" I have searched the Vedas and the Vedantas, the Tantras and the
    Mantras, yet nowhere have I found thy fullness.
  As Rama thou dost take the bow, as Syama the Black (Krishna)
    thou dost seize the sword. . . .
  O Mother, Mother of the Universe, art thou male or female ?   Who
    can say ?   Who knows thy form ?
  Nilkantha's mind ever thinks of thee as chief of Creators." [1]

As in Mesopotamia and Syria, the Goddess has both a beneficent and a destructive aspect, but in India it is the latter that seems to predominate. In the Dravidian South the village goddesses are worshipped above all as " Disease Mothers," like Mariamma, the goddess of smallpox, and Ankamma, the goddess of cholera. Throughout India the most popular form of the Goddess is Kali the Black, who is depicted garlanded with skulls and stained with blood, dancing in triumph on the body of her husband Siva, and she is worshipped with bloody offerings, and even at times with human sacrifices. Yet this terrible goddess is also " the Mother of the World, the Shelter of the shelterless," whose worship appeals to that which is deepest in the mind of the Indian people, and whose praises are sung in countless religious lyrics. In Bengal, especially, it is to her that

[1] Tr. E. J. Thompson and A. M. Spencer, *Bengali Religious Lyrics,*
Sakta, p. 78.

the people turn in times of trouble and necessity, and even the modern nationalist movement has taken as its watchword " The Mother is calling us ; let us go back to the Mother." Thus even in the worship of Kali, the sinister aspects of her cult are far from excluding the elements of benevolence and affectionate trust. And it would be a great mistake to assume that they are characteristic of the religion of the Mother God in its original form. They correspond to the complex nature of the Indian culture itself, in which the highest development of a refined civilisation stands side by side with the wild life of the primitive jungle. Thus they are due in part to the subtle tendency of Indian thought to place the divine " beyond good and evil," and in part to contamination with the barbarous rites and beliefs of primitive tribes of hunters. In the same way Sumerian religion probably underwent a process of degradation when it was brought into contact with the less-civilised Semitic peoples of Syria.

VI. Influence of the Cult on the Development of Civilisation

In its early form the central ideas of the Peasant Religion was undoubtedly that of the beneficent power of the divine nature as manifested in the fruitfulness of the earth, and the entire dependence of man upon its bounty. It was only by obedience to the laws of the Great Mother and by an imitation of her mysteries that man could learn to participate in her gifts. Thus every agricultural operation was a religious rite or a sacramental act through which divine powers were brought into activity. Men opened the earth with their ploughs to receive the miraculously quickened seed. They irrigated and rendered it fruitful with the help of the fertilising god of fresh water. Finally with rites of propitiation and lamentation they reaped the harvest and ground the grain, taking, in a sense, the life of the god of vegetation that they themselves might live.

Thus all the primitive agricultural implements, the plough, the sickle, and the cart, were sacred things ; and the same is true of the domestic animals, the goat, the sheep, and the pig—all are sacred to the Great Mother. But most of all the cow, the representative of fertility, and the bull, who, like the vegetation god himself, is the embodiment of the vital force of Nature, but who must sacrifice his male force and freedom in order that he may labour as the patient plough ox in the service of the Great Mother.

It is in this point that the severe and even cruel aspect of the Peasant Religion is most apparent. The Goddess in the Phrygian form of the legend destroys the virility of her divine lover, Attis, of whom the bull was perhaps the animal embodiment ; and even at Erech, the great centre of her cult in Babylonia, she is served by eunuch priests.

" They were summoned to Eanna the eunuchs and the eunuch singers,
    Whose virility Ishtar turned to effeminacy to terrify the people,
    They who bear the dagger, who bear the razor, the sword, and
        the stone knife,
    They who eat . . . to make glad the mood of Ishtar." [1]

For a moment she almost seems to resemble the terrible Mother Goddesses of India, the blood-stained Kali and Durga.

But even in its most repulsive forms, this cult bears witness to a profound consciousness that the increase of life could only be obtained by sacrifice, whether it was the sacrifice of virility, as in the case of Attis and his eunuch priests, or of the first-born children, as in Syria, or of the king himself, who was forced in Phœnicia and Cyprus to lay down his own life for the life of his people.

Nevertheless, the prevailing aspect of the Mother Goddess is a beneficent one ; she is

" Ishtar, creatress of peoples.
    She that passes before the cattle, who loves the shepherd.
    She is the shepherdess of all lands.
    They are content and before Thee bow down and seek Thee."

---

[1] Tr. S. Langdon, *op. cit.*, p. 77.

She is

" The fruitful mother, who knows lamentation, who abides among
    her people.
  The divinity who surveys mankind, mother of the fruitful breast."
" She gives drink to the young cattle of the stalls, she gives food to
    the feeble ones in the nests."

" Without Thee no stream is opened, no stream is closed,
  Which brings life. Without Thee no canal is opened,
  No canal is closed, which gives the wide-dwelling peoples to drink." [1]

Hence it is easy to see how great a civilising influence
her cult must have had, and how the great advance in
civilisation, which marked the early Peasant Culture of
Asia, was directly connected with it. The chief German
authority on primitive agriculture, Ed. Hahn, holds
that agriculture and the domestication of animals
originated in Western Asia by the religious observation
and ritual imitation of the processes of Nature ; that
animals were first tamed as sacred animals, dedicated
to the Mother Goddess, and that the utilitarian development of the discovery was a secondary consequence.
And Sir William Ramsay, writing of Asia Minor, says :
" The art of agriculture was there taught almost by
Nature herself, who thus revealed herself as mother and
teacher of her people. Step by step and precept upon
precept, the Goddess Mother, the Thesmophoros or
law-giver of the Bœotian and Athenian plain, educated
her people and showed them how to make the best of
the useful animals, swine, ox, sheep, and goat, and
later also of the horse, by proper nurture and careful
treatment and breeding. The history of the education which she gave remains for us in the Anatolian
religion, in which lies the key to an extremely early
stage of human development." [2]

[1] Tr. S. Langdon, *Tammuz and Ishtar*, Chapter II, *passim*.
[2] Sir W. Ramsay, " The Religion of Greece and Asia Minor " in
Hastings' *Dictionary of the Bible*, vol. v, p. 135.

CHAPTER VI

THE CITY STATE AND THE DEVELOPMENT OF THE SUMERIAN CULTURE

THE RISE OF THE SACRED CITY.

    (i) THE RELIGIOUS ORIGINS OF THE CITY.

    (ii) THE DIFFUSION OF THE CITY STATE IN THE NEAR EAST.

THE SUMERIAN CITY STATE AND ITS CULTURE.

    (i) THE SUMERIANS AND THE SEMITES IN MESOPOTAMIA.

    (ii) THE MESOPOTAMIAN CITIES.

    (iii) THE THEOCRATIC CHARACTER OF THE SUMERIAN AND BABYLONIAN STATE.

    (iv) THE ECONOMIC DEVELOPMENT OF MESOPOTAMIAN CULTURE.

    (v) ITS INTELLECTUAL AND SCIENTIFIC TRADITION.

CHAPTER VI

THE CITY STATE AND THE DEVELOPMENT OF THE SUMERIAN CULTURE

I. THE RISE OF THE SACRED CITY

(i) *The Religious Origins of the City*

ACCORDING to the view put forward in the last chapter, the earliest agriculture must have grown up round the shrines of the Mother Goddess, which thus became social and economic centres, as well as holy places, and were the germs of the future cities.[1]

Now we know from the Sumerian evidence that in later times the temples were great landowning corporations. Moreover, the god or the goddess was in a sense the owner of the whole city territory. The actual cultivators were tenants of the divine landlord, and paid part of the produce of the land into the temple storehouses.

These were, of course, in historic times situated in the cities and had all the marks of a highly organised urban economy, but the earliest temple that we know, the recently excavated shrine of the Mother Goddess of Ur, Nin Kharsag, stood some miles outside the city in the midst of the cultivated lands. It is decorated by a frieze in copper relief, and it is thoroughly characteristic of the culture that we have been describing, that this earliest monument of Sumerian religious art—dating from about 3000 B.C.—consists not of mythological figures or scenes of warfare, but of pastoral occupations

---

[1] Even in modern times in the Caucasus, among the Mountain Georgians, the Holy Place or Chat'i exercised a theocratic rule over the whole community, and the Georgian is the slave (*mona*) of his local sanctuary.

—a cattle shed and lines of oxen, milking scenes and perhaps butter-making, while below the main frieze stood statues of oxen, made of copper with golden horns.

In Asia Minor even in later times, the social unit was not the city state, but the temple state, and the vast temple estates of Cappadocia and Phrygia, ruled by the representatives of the goddess or the god, lasted right down to Roman times.

The temple with the temple estate is in fact the foundation of the whole archaic culture of Western Asia.

It was the germ of the city, which was essentially a sacred city, the dwelling-place and throne of a god. It was the germ of the state, and this explains the sacred and theocratic character of political authority, for the king was a priest king, the vicegerent of the city god, with whom he ultimately came to be identified, so that his power rested not on the right of conquest or the choice of the people, but on divine right or the choice of the god, a conception which is of enormous importance for subsequent history.

Further, the temple was the basis of economic development, it alone possessed the resources and the authority that are necessary for a highly developed economic organisation. The great works of irrigation, which above all rendered possible the increase of population and the growth of cities in Babylonia, involved a vast control of labour and a unity of direction to which a population of peasants could never have attained by themselves. It was the superhuman authority and the express mandate of the god that alone rendered these great communal enterprises possible. And hence we note the importance of the divinities of canals and irrigation in the early Sumerian religion.

Finally, the temple with its staffs of priests and servants permitted the growth of a peaceful leisure class, by whom knowledge could be cultivated, and the beginnings of science achieved. The origin of writing was, as the name hieroglyphics implied, a kind of sacred symbolism, and was connected with the use of seals and amulets engraved with sacred symbols. Similarly the elaboration of a liturgical calendar, which was bound up with the changes of the agricultural years, first led to an exact observance of the Seasons, and their correlation with the movements of the heavenly bodies. For example, the Elamites evolved a year of 584 days, based on the apparent revolutions of the planet Venus, and the priests of Heliopolis in Lower Egypt had at an early period attained to a solar year of 365 days, which was correlated with the heliacal rising of the Dog Star, so as to give a cycle of 1,460 years by which the calendar was regulated.[1]

(ii) *The Diffusion of the City State in the Near East*

In all these ways, the temple and the religious conceptions which it stood for supplied the basis of the new cultural development which transformed the ancient world about the fourth millennium B.C. All over the East, from Crete and Egypt to South-west Persia, and even to India, the Sacred City appears at the dawn of history as the essential organ of the higher civilisation. It is true that in Egypt it is overshadowed in historical times by the growth of a great unified state, but even there the cities of the Delta seem to have played a decisive part in the development of the higher culture which preceded the rise of the dynastic kingdom. Above all, Heliopolis, which was the home of Egyptian science and theology from very early times and the source of the solar religion of the Old Kingdom, was a true temple city of the same type as Nippur or Erech in Babylonia. In Minoan Crete, on the other hand, the Temple is absent, and its place is taken by the Palace. But the Minoan Palace was itself a sacred edifice, which was the religious as well as the secular centre of the community. It was the residence of a priest king, like those of Asia Minor ; indeed the throne-

[1] Cf. pp. 149–50 *infra.*

room of the Palace at Cnossus finds a remarkable parallel in the shrine of the God Men near Antioch in Pisidia. Cnossus and Phæstus are, in fact, sacred cities no less than those of Sumer. They differ only in that the secular and religious aspects are more closely united, as was also the case in Assyria and Asia Minor.

In the latter area the origins of the city state are obscure. We know from the Cappadocian tablets of the latter part of the third millennium that there already existed a number of cities in Eastern Anatolia, Kanesh, Burushanda, and more than twenty others, many of which reappear in later times as religious centres of the Hittite Empire. It has, however, not yet been agreed whether these places were native Anatolian states, in which the writers of the tablets resided as foreign merchants, or whether, as J. Lewey maintains, they were dependencies of an extensive empire, with its centre in Assyria, which owed its origin to an early expansion of North Mesopotamian culture towards the west.[1]

The Sacred City was equally characteristic of Syria and Palestine, which remained throughout history a land of city states. Here also the origins of the city go back far beyond all recorded history. Jerusalem itself was a sacred city long before historic times, as we see from the Hebrew tradition of the mysterious priest king, Melchisedech, who met Abraham returning from the battle of the kings. Even its name is non-Semitic and contains the Sumerian root Uru = city.[2] But Jerusalem was a much less important place than Jericho, whose great walls date in part from the third millennium, while Jericho itself was probably more recent than the cities of North Syria, such as Carchemish and Kadesh.

[1] Cf. J. Lewey, art. "Kappadokische Tontafeln" in *L. V. G.*, vol. vi, p. 212, and for the contrary view B. Landsberger, "Assyrische Handelskolonien in Kleinasien."

[2] Perhaps Uru Salimu = city of the goddess Salimu, but all interpretations are doubtful. A town Uru Silimma with patron goddess Shulmanitu is recorded.

The Phœnician cities stand in a group by themselves and undoubtedly belong in origin to a very remote period. Herodotus was informed by the priests of Melkarth, " the King of the City," at Tyre that their temple and town were founded in the year 2750 B.C., and this antiquity is by no means incredible, since the recent discoveries, including that of a vase bearing the name of the Egyptian king Mycerinus at Byblus, have proved that the temple of that city goes back to the age of the Fourth Egyptian Dynasty, and perhaps even earlier.

According to their own tradition, as recorded by Herodotus and later writers, the Phœnicians were not a people of Syrian origin. They believed that their original home had been in the Bahrein Islands, and on the west shore of the Persian Gulf, and that they had migrated thence into Syria by way of " the Assyrian Lake," the Dead Sea. Now the region from which they claimed to have been derived belonged to the sphere of the ancient Sumerian culture. It was the land of Magan, which, as we have already seen, was an important centre of trade in early times and possibly played a considerable part in the diffusion of Sumerian culture in the direction of the Red Sea and as far as Egypt. Hence a colonising movement of this sea-going people to Sinai and Akaba, and ultimately by way of the Dead Sea route to the Mediterranean coast, seems by no means impossible, and would explain the national character of the Phœnicians as peaceful traders and middlemen, which they preserved throughout history. In Roman times there was a close connection between the trading states of South Arabia, Abyssinia and Petra, and again in the Assyrian period between Ma'in in the Yemen and its trading colonies in the Hadramaut and in North Arabia. This movement of trade undoubtedly goes back to very ancient times and may have extended from Magan to the Land of Punt and to the Phœnician cities of Palestine.

Thus it is probable that the Sumerian culture was responsible for the beginnings of the higher civilisation in Arabia itself. From the earliest times the fertile regions of South-west Arabia—the Yemen—was renowned as the land of gold and of the precious spices, which were in such request among the ancient Egyptians and Babylonians. During the Assyrian period it was the home of the civilised state of Ma'an, which has left us numerous inscriptions and other archæological remains, and which was known to the Greeks as the land of the Minæans. It is possible that this Ma'an or Ma'in in South Arabia is connected in origin with the ancient Magan on the Persian Gulf, just as the North Arabian trading state of Ma'an Musran, north of Medina, was in turn an offshoot or dependency of the Ma'an in the Yemen. Nothing could be more unlike the nomadic tribal life, that we regard as characteristic of Arabia, than this early civilisation of Ma'an and the neighbouring states of Saba, Hadramaut and Kataban. They were true city states of the Sumerian type, the prosperity of which rested on trade and agriculture, and the ruins of whose temples and irrigation works bear witness to their former wealth and populousness. As in Mesopotamia, the god was regarded as the true ruler of the land. He possessed rich revenues and numerous priests and dependents, and the king himself stood in close relations to the priestly corporation, and was even adopted into the family of the god as his son or nephew. Moreover, private individuals frequently dedicated themselves and their families to the service of the god, as slaves of the deity or temple servants. As in Sumer, the economic life of the people centred in the temple, and even the walls and houses of the city and the irrigation dams were consecrated to the God by a solemn act of dedication.[1]

Thus in Arabia, no less than in Syria or Babylonia,

---

[1] The organisation of the South Arabian State and temple corporation is fully described by N. Rhodokanakis in D. Nielsen's *Handbuch der Altarabischen Altertümskunde*, vol. i (1927).

the sacred temple city lies at the root of the development
of the higher civilisation, and the same probably holds
good of India, though here all written evidence is at
present lacking.   However, the newly discovered prehistoric civilisation of the Indus valley so closely
resembles that of the Sumerians that we can hardly
doubt the existence there of a similar type of city state.
Certainly it is in India alone that the sacred city, like
the religion of the Mother Goddess, has survived down
to the present day, so that the temples of Puri, and
Madura and Benares, seem to carry us back four or five
thousand years to the House of Heaven at Erech, or
the temple of the Lord of the Earth at Nippur.

It almost seems as though we were justified in
assuming that the higher civilisation based upon the
city and its temple had everywhere sprung from a
common root and been diffused from a single original
centre.   Certainly in the East the temple city spread
eastwards from India to Cambodia and Java, and in the
West the city states of classical Greece and Italy go
back through the Mycenæans and the Etruscans to an
Ægean or Anatolian origin.   It is true that there exist
certain isolated types of city culture, the origin of which
it is difficult to explain on these lines—for example, the
Maya cities of Central America, and the Yoruba city
states of West Africa, such as Ibadan and Ife, which
retain down to the present day their sacred character
and their ancient theocratic polity.   It is, however,
equally difficult to explain these as the result of a
spontaneous native development, and the Maya civilisation at least possesses some curious links with the
archaic culture of Western Asia, such as the use of the
Venus year of 584 days which was also known to the
ancient Elamites.   For the present at least their origin
remains an enigma, to which only future discoveries
can supply an answer.

Nevertheless, with the exception of these, and perhaps
also of the cities of Northern China, the higher city

civilisations of the Old World from the Mediterranean to India do form a great unity, and it seems possible to affirm their fundamental community alike in type and in origin.

It was formerly believed—and the idea is still widely current—that the creation of the city state was one of the most original creations of the Hellenic genius. But we now know that both the Greeks and the Romans were the heirs of an Ægean-Anatolian tradition which they received through the medium of their Mycenean and Etruscan predecessors, and that this tradition in turn is based on an even more ancient Asiatic foundation. The true creators of the city state were the Sumerians, and it is to them that we must turn in order to find the earliest and most typical example of the new type of culture, on which all the subsequent achievements of civilisation have been based.

II. The Sumerian City State and its Culture

(i) *The Sumerians and the Semites in Mesopotamia*

In spite of the great antiquity of Sumerian civilisation, our knowledge of its history is extremely deficient. Here there was no great unitary state, such as we find in Egypt, to provide a firm basis for a continuous chronology, but a confused world of city states whose dynasties rose and fell in bewildering succession. From the earliest times the Sumerian cities seem to have recognised the principle of a kind of general hegemony, which was vested in the representative of Enlil, the Earth God of Nippur. This hegemony did not, however, involve the political supremacy of the Nippur city state ; it was exercised by whatever prince was powerful enough to " take the hands of Enlil " and thus receive the investiture of universal rule. In fact, Nippur and its priesthood occupied somewhat the same place in the Sumerian world as that of Rome and the Papacy towards the medieval empire in Europe. In early times this supreme position seems to have been usually held by the rulers of Kish, but both the history and the chronology of the earlier dynasties are exceedingly uncertain, and it is not until the beginning of the third millennium that the city states of Mesopotamia really emerge into the light of history. From that time we possess consecutive records for the city state of Lagash, which under the dynasty of Ur Nina and his successors (c. 2967–2777 B.C.) was the chief centre of power in Southern Mesopotamia.

At that time the north was probably already under the dominance of Semitic dynasties, but we know nothing of the conditions under which the latter first acquired control of the northern Sumerian cities : indeed the whole formative period of the Sumerian culture itself lies in almost complete darkness. About 2750 B.C., the whole of Mesopotamia was united under a Semitic dynasty by the great Sargon of Agade, whose conquests extended from Elam to Mt. Taurus and the Mediterranean. " Enlil gave unto him the Upper Land, Maer, Yarmuti and Ibla, as far as the cedar forests (? Lebanon) and the silver mountains " (Mt. Taurus). He is even said to have " crossed the sea of the setting sun and caused the booty of the Sea Lands to have been brought over," a passage which many historians believe to refer to the conquest of Cyprus. His triumphs were repeated by his grandson Naram Sin, who first took the title of " King of the Four World Regions," in place of the older " King of Universal Dominion." He was the conqueror of Magan and Elam as well as of the northern mountains of Kurdistan and Armenia, and he was renowned in Babylonian history as a great founder and restorer of temples. Nabonidus, the last King of Babylon, has recorded the awe and delight that he experienced when he uncovered the foundation stone of his great predecessor in the Temple of the Sun God at Sippar more than 2,000 years later.

Thus the conquests of the dynasty of Agade were in no sense barbarian invasions of the civilised Sumerian cities by warlike Semitic nomads. Semites and Sumerians were already indistinguishable from the point of view of culture, and the empire of Sargon and Naram Sin was a work of consolidation rather than of destruction.

The danger to Sumer came from the north, from the barbarous land of Gutium, " the habitation of the pest," and it was from this quarter that the flood of destruction descended on the land after the strong hand of the rulers of Agade was removed. The great Patesi of Lagash, Gudea, probably reigned in the interval before the barbarian invasions had affected the south, and under his rule Sumerian art and culture enjoyed a brief age of exceptional prosperity. But this was succeeded by a long period of anarchy and destruction (c. 2541–2416 B.C.) during which the most sacred temples in the land were sacked by the barbarians. The Sumerian culture had received a shock from which it never really recovered, although it was the Sumerian city of Erech which led the war of liberation against the foreign oppressor, " the dragon of the mountain," and there was a brief revival of Sumerian power under the Third Dynasty of Ur (c. 2408–2328). However, the last Sumerian king, Ibi Sin, fell before the combined attacks of the Elamites and the Amorites, and the control of Mesopotamia finally passed into the hands of the Semitic dynasties of Isin, Larsa, and Babylon. The establishment of the Babylonian Empire by Hammurabi, about 2050 B.C., marks the final passing of the Sumerian city state, and Babylon takes the place of the old religious centres, Nippur and Eridu and Erech, as the religious capital of Mesopotamia. But there was no real break in the continuity of Mesopotamian culture. The Babylonian civilisation is the legitimate heir of that of the Sumerians. Hammurabi united in a single religious, legal, and political organisation all the separate elements of the old Sumerian cultural tradition. Hence his work was extraordinarily permanent, so that in spite of hostile invasions, and long periods of foreign domination like that of the Kassites (1746–1169 B.C.), Babylonian civilisation remained for 1,500 years essentially unchanged from what it had been in the age of Hammurabi.

(ii) *The Mesopotamian Cities*

The centre of the land of Sumer lay in the narrow territory between the lower reaches of the Tigris and the Euphrates, in the midst of which lay Nippur, the city of the Earth God Enlil. This was the religious metropolis of Sumer from the earliest times, and it is possible that the name of Sumer itself in its original form—Kiengi—was derived from that of the city territory of Nippur, " the land of the faithful lord."

The earliest Sumerian cities clustered thickly along the course of the Euphrates, and towards its mouth they were but eight or ten miles apart from one another. It was here that some of the oldest and most famous cities of the land were situated, such as Erech (Uruk), Eridu, Ur, Larsa, and Lagash. North of Nippur they were less closely placed, but the region between Nippur and Bagdad contains the sites of many ancient cities, notably Kish, Cuthah, and Sippar, as well as more recent foundations, such as Agade and above all Babylon the Great. All these city states form an almost continuous line up the river, but in addition to this main province, there were outlying Sumerian cities far to the north on the Tigris in the land that was afterwards Assyria— Opis and Assur, and far up the Euphrates to the northwest the land of Maer, as well as an ancient and little-known group east of the Tigris towards Elam—the land of Der and Ashnunak.

Each of these cities lay in the midst of its little territory, surrounded by the irrigated cornfields and gardens in which grew the famous date palms which held such an important place in the Sumerian economy, and beyond lay the pasture lands where great herds of

sheep and goats and oxen grazed. All their prosperity
depended upon the water supply, whether from the
Euphrates direct or by means of the great canals which
even in the days of Herodotus were one of the wonders
of the world. It was this that rendered possible the
dense population and great economic wealth of the
country, which surpassed even that of Egypt ; and when
in the Middle Ages the canal system broke down, the
prosperity of Mesopotamia was destroyed, and it became
the backward and unhealthy country that it is to-day.

Every city possessed its patron god and goddess,
who were conceived respectively as the King and the
Mother of the territory. The goddesses were, in fact,
all forms of the Mother Goddess, and their titles and
attributes are not always easy to distinguish from one
another. Thus Gula, the goddess of life who was worshipped at Larak and Isin, is hardly distinguishable
from Bau, the patroness of Lagash and Kish. The gods,
on the other hand, possess clearly defined characters,
and the different provinces of the land are partitioned
amongst them in a most systematic way. Thus Eridu
on the Persian Gulf, and originally Lagash also, belonged
to Ea or Enki, the water god and patron of civilisation,
and his son Ningirshu, the god of irrigation. Ur and
Larsa were dedicated respectively to the Moon and the
Sun God. Nippur and the cities of the centre were the
domain of the Earth God and the gods of harvest, while
in the north, Kish was the city of Ninurasha, like the
Roman Mars the god of spring and war, Cuthah was
the city of Nergal, the plague god and his consort
the Lady of Hades, and Babbar or Shamash, the sun
god of Larsa, reappears in the north as the patron of
Sippar.

These deities were often referred to by the names
of their cities. Ea was " the King of Eridu," Nergal
" the King of Cuthah," and Ninlil " the Lady of
Nippur " ; and conversely the ideograms which represent
the names of the city refer to their divine protectors :

Nippur was Enlilki, " the land of Enlil," Ur was " the place of Nannar," and Larsa was " the place of the Abode of the Sun," or " the Holy Throne."

The sacred character of the city is reflected in the names of its walls and its gates, its streets and its canals, most of which possess religious or liturgical titles. Thus at Babylon, where the old Sumerian religious customs were still preserved, each division of the famous sixfold wall, and each gate, was dedicated to a different deity, and the streets bore such names as " Marduk is the shepherd of his land," " Ishtar is the guardian of her people," and " Nabu is judge of his subjects." But it was above all in the temple that the sacred character of the Sumerian city found its fullest expression. The temple was the centre and mainspring of the whole life of the community. It was not only the dwelling-place of the god ; it was the palace from which he ruled his people. It contained the dwellings of the priests and the officials, storehouses and granaries, workshops and offices, law court, library, and school. We can compare it to a great medieval monastery, but on an even larger scale, and the city itself grew up under its shadow and in dependence on it, like the monastery towns of the Middle Ages—Peterborough or St. Albans or Bury St. Edmunds. Above the city as a symbol of this religious dominance rose the great staged temple—-pyramid or ziggurat, the proud titles of which—such as the Foundation Stone of Heaven and Earth at Babylon, or the Link between Heaven and Earth at Larsa—recall the Biblical story of the Tower of Babel.

Thus the God was the real ruler of the city, and the Sumerian territories are often described not as the land of such-and-such a city, but the land of such-and-such a god. One of the oldest Sumerian documents that we possess describes a treaty between the city of Lagash and that of Umma, through the arbitration of Meslilim, King of Kish. The document itself, however, says that Ningirshu and Shara—that is to say, the gods of the cities in question—made a delimitation of territory by the word of Enlil the father of the gods, the head of the Sumerian pantheon. So too, Entemena, one of the greatest of the early rulers of Lagash, records how " he made for Ningirshu, the god of Lagash, the king whom he loved, the mighty canal at the boundary of Enlil, i.e. at the boundary of the city territory of Nippur ; for Ningirshu he caused it to come forth from the River of the Prince (the Euphrates) whose name is in foreign lands." [1]   Further, at the command of Enlil, Ningirshu, and Nina, he built a canal from the Tigris to the Euphrates. This was probably the modern Shatt el Hai, the greatest of the canals of Mesopotamia, and it shows how the greatest feats of ancient engineering were inspired and consecrated by religious motives.

(iii) *The Theocratic Character of the Sumerian and Babylonian State*

The Sumerian state was a pure theocracy. Its ruler, like Melchisedech, was a priest as well as a king. He was the vicar (*patesi*) and representative of the god, and the interpreter of the divine will to his subjects. He owed his authority not to his power or to the choice of the people, but to the divine will and calling. This conception goes back to the earliest times of Sumerian history, and was handed on to the later Semitic civilisations of Mesopotamia and Syria. The story of Etana speaks of the royal insignia—the crown, the sceptre of lapis lazuli, and the pastoral staff that are laid up in heaven in presence of Anu awaiting the coming of the just king whom Ishtar and Enlil seek throughout the world that he may be " the Shepherd of Men." So, too, Sargon of Agade in the ancient legend describes how he was chosen by the goddess Ishtar to rule her people when he was a humble gardener, a waif and a castaway, whose father's name no man knew ; and Hammurabi

---

[1] Quoted by S. Langdon, *Cambridge Ancient History*, vol. i, p. 382.

declares that when the gods first laid the foundations of Babylon, they had chosen him by name for the royal office. But it is from the later Assyrian period that we possess the fullest evidence of these ideas, above all in the prayer of Assur Nasir Pal I, the restorer of the Assyrian kingdom in the eleventh century.

" I was born," he says, " in the midst of the mountains that no man knows.
I knew naught of thy dominion and I did not pray.
The Assyrians knew naught of thy divinity and did not beseech thee.
But thou, O Ishtar, mighty queen among the gods,—
Thou didst mark me with a look of thine eyes and thou hadst a desire to see me rule,
Thou didst take me from the midst of the mountain, and didst call me to be the Shepherd of Men,
Thou didst grant me the sceptre of justice."

Even the Persian conquest which finally put an end to the independence of Mesopotamia was explained on the same principle. Marduk had taken pity upon his people. " He considered all the lands, he saw them and sought for a just king, a king according to his heart whom he would lead by the hand. He called his name Cyrus, King of Anzan, and he appointed his name for a universal royalty." [1] And this finally leads us to the sublime conception of the greatest of the Hebrew prophets : " Thus saith the Lord to my anointed Cyrus, whose right hand I have taken to subdue nations before his face and to turn the backs of kings. . . . For the sake of My servant Jacob and Israel My chosen I have called thee by thy name. I have given thee the title of honour, though thou hast not known Me." [2]

This dependence of human authority on the divine will was symbolised in the early Babylonian period by the ceremonies of the great annual feast of the Akitu. The king was led into the presence of the god Marduk by a single priest. He was stripped of his royal insignia,

[1] Cylinder of Cyrus, lines 11 seq., tr. Dhorme, La Religion Assyro-Babylonienne, p. 157.
[2] Isaiah xlv. 1–6.

which were laid before the god.   He was smitten on the
face and forced to prostrate himself.   Finally, after
he had made a humble confession of his devotion to
Marduk, the priest raised him up saying, " Be without
fear.   The Lord will bless thee for ever, and will destroy
thine enemies before thy face."   His crown and sceptre
were restored to him, he was again smitten upon the
face, and was brought forth weeping into the presence of
his subjects.

But if towards the great gods the king was but a
servant, towards men he was himself a god.   " Man is
the shadow of God, the slave is the shadow of a man, but
the king is like God," says the Assyrian proverb.   The
deification and cult of kings goes back to the Sumerian
epoch when the human ruler was seemingly identified
with the dying god Tammuz.   Temples were built in
their honour, and men took them as their individual
patron deities.   Hence the royal office possessed an
almost Messianic character.   The gods chose the king
to be the Shepherd and Saviour of his people, and even
external Nature shared in the life-giving effects of his
advent.   Thus Dungi, the king of the last Sumerian
dynasty of Ur, is conceived as the son of the Mother
Goddess, Ninsun, who has come to restore the Golden
Age which had been lost by man's wrongdoing—he is the
" Breath of the life of the Land."   And a little later
we have the fine hymn of Lipit Ishtar of the Dynasty
of Isin (c. 2200) :

" Anu in his secret mind predestined him to be king,
   He made due proclamation to him as offspring of royalty,—
   ' Lipit Ishtar, by me art thou endowed with power.
   As a raging storm, that lifts up its head, mayest thou be clad with
      terror afar,
   May thy storm flood cover thine enemies and the lands that are dis-
      obedient.
   Dealing justice for Sumer and Akkad, saving the life of the land,
   Lipit Ishtar, child of Enlil, go forth shining as the Day.
   The houses of mortals, the houses of the settlements shall verily be
      obedient to thee,
   The dark-haired people shall verily be led aright by thee, as a lamb
      is led by its mother.

Lipit Ishtar, be thou king over the distant lands of the earth.
The desired child of Enlil art thou, every good thing has he done for
  thee.' " [1]

And in the later Assyrian period we have an even clearer presentation of these ideas :

" The God, king of Gods, has named the name of the king my lord, for the royalty over the land of Assur. . . . Prosperous government, durable days, years of equity, abundant rains, full rivers, prosperous commerce. The old men dance, the children sing, the maidens are joyful, the women conceive. They give birth to boys and girls. Child-bearing is easy. In their joy they say to the children, ' The King, our Lord, has made him.' The prisoners thou hast delivered. Those who were long sick revive. The hungry are satisfied, the thin become fat, the naked are clothed." [2]

It is natural that these beliefs should lead to a high moral ideal of the kingly office, and consequently Babylonia became from very early times the land of great lawgivers and of the earliest written codes. Hammurabi calls himself the King of Law to whom Shamash has accorded justice, and declares that he has been called by Anu and Bel (Enlil) " to establish the welfare of mankind, to create justice in the land, to destroy the wicked and the perverse, that the strong may not oppress the weak, to rise like the Sun God on men for the illumination of the land," and the existence of his great Code, the masterpiece of ancient jurisprudence, proves that these were no empty boasts.[3]

This, however, is but the final stage of an age-long process of development which stretches far back into

---

[1] Published and translated by H. Zimmern. *Proceedings of the R. Saxon Society of Science. Phil. Hist. Klasse*, 1916, vol. lxviii.

[2] From the letter of Adad Shume Usur, trans. Dhorme, *op. cit.*, 172–3.

[3] The bas-relief on the Code itself shows Hammurabi standing in an attitude of adoration before Shamash the Sun God and lawgiver of the gods, who holds forth to the king the ring and the staff, the symbols of his divine investiture.

Sumerian times. From the beginnings Justice and Law—Kettu and Mesharu—were the corner stones of Mesopotamian civilisation. In Sumerian times the city temple was the law court and the supreme source of jurisdiction, and men brought their wrongs and their disputes before " the throne of the god." One of the earliest Sumerian codes that has come down to us is entitled, " the laws of Nisaba and Hani," i.e. of the Mother Goddess and her consort. So, too, Gudea the great Patesi of Lagash entitles Bau, " the lady judge of her city," and describes how he has installed " the sublime throne of her divinity " in " the place of her judgments."

Not only were the gods the supreme lawgivers, they were also the governors of mankind, and human destiny was believed to be fixed in accordance with the unalterable decrees of the divine powers. On the Great Mountain of the East Enlil and the assembly of the gods met together to decide the lot of men, and so too on the feast of the New Year at Babylon Marduk entered the council house of the temple—the Dul Azag— to decree the annual destiny of his city. Hence the importance that the Sumerians and Babylonians attached to divination or the scientific ascertainment of the divine will by the observation of omens and portents, so that no business of importance could be undertaken without first taking measures to discover the will and purpose of the gods.

The whole of social life was interpenetrated by religion and it was impossible to separate loyalty to the city and the king from devotion to the gods. The following lines express the early Babylonian ideal of the duty of a good citizen :

" Prayer was my meditation, sacrifice was my law.
    The day in which men honoured the gods was the joy of my heart.
    The day on which they followed the Goddess was my gain and my
        riches.
    The prayer of the king was my joy,
    And his music was for my pleasure.

I taught my land to keep the name of the god,
I taught my people to honour the name of the Goddess,
I caused the praises of the king to resound on high,
And I instructed the people to venerate the palace." [1]

Nor was religion limited to the public cult of the city gods. Every man and every woman had their private divinities which were conceived as personal protectors and helpers, like the guardian angel and patron saint of the Christian. Hence the use of those " theophoric " names, which go back to Sumerian times. A man would be called the servant or the animal of such a god, as Ur Bau, Subar Bau, or his name might contain an invocation or a pious formula such as " My god is my father," " Who is like my god ? " " Enlil is my defence," or " Have pity on me, my god."

This custom became universal among the Semitic peoples, and is familiar to us in the Old Testament in such forms as Micah, Samuel, Isaiah, etc.

(iv) *The Economic Development of Mesopotamian Culture*

Nevertheless in spite of the intensely religious and theocratic spirit which governed Sumerian civilisation, it was far from being unpractical or otherworldly. Unlike the Egyptians, the people of Mesopotamia seem to have devoted but little attention to the after-life. Their religion was a religion of the present, and it was directed towards very concrete and material ends. Even the temple was essentially a great economic corporation and the centre of the business life of the city. The recent excavations at the great temple of the Moon God at Ur of the Chaldees throws a remarkable light on the businesslike spirit in which the temple economy was conducted. In the temple archives have been found the detailed accounts of the payments of the god's farmers and tenants, carefully balanced month by month, and for everything brought in, even down to six pounds of butter, a written receipt was made out on a

[1] Tr. Dhorme, *op. cit.*, 219–20.

clay tablet. Even more interesting is the industrial side of the temple economy. Weaving was carried on in the temple precincts on a large scale both by women votaries attached to the temple and by slaves. As many as 165 women were employed in the building Ekarzida alone, and full accounts have been found of the amount of yarn issued to each worker, the amount of cloth produced, and the daily rations of food which took the place of wages.[1] It is clear that we are not dealing with mere domestic industry for the needs of the temple community, but with a production on a large scale for commercial ends. The poverty of Babylonia in timber and building stone, but above all in metals, had led to the rise of an extensive commerce even in prehistoric times. Lapis lazuli was known to the Sumerians at a very early date, which suggests that they may have had relations with Central Asia, since at the present day lapis lazuli is not found west of Badakshan north of the Hindu Kush. Copper was obtained from Elam and Cyprus, silver and lead from Asia Minor, cedar wood from Armenia and the Lebanon, and building stone and gold from Arabia. Originally the state and the temple corporation were the only bodies which possessed the necessary stability and resources for establishing widespread commercial relations. Temple servants were sent on distant missions, provided with letters of credit which enabled them to obtain supplies in other cities. Moreover the temple was the bank of the community, through which money could be lent at interest and advances made to the farmer on the security of his crop. Thus in the course of the third millennium there grew up in Mesopotamia a regular money economy, based on the precious metals as standards of exchange, which stimulated private wealth and enterprise and led to a real capitalistic development. The temple and the palace remained the centres of the

---

[1] Cf. Mr. L. Woolley in *The Antiquaries' Journal* and in *The Times*, April 16, 1925.

economic life of the city, but by their side and under their shelter there developed a many-sided activity which found expression in the guilds of the free craftsmen and the merchants, and the private enterprise of the individual capitalist.

The great merchant usually remained at home in the city, which was his centre of business, and carried on his distant enterprises through an agent, who was entrusted with a capital sum and who received a commission on the profits of his journey ; but a system of equal partnership was also practised by which the partners swore a mutual contract before the gods of the city temple for a definite period at the end of which the common stock was brought to the temple and redivided by the assessors.

These and all other commercial transactions had to be carried out before legal witnesses and authenticated by the seals of the principals. On these lines it was possible to establish a regular system of credit and banking far in advance of anything that we find elsewhere, even in Egypt, until much later times. The great code of Hammurabi and the numerous legal and commercial tablets that have been discovered provide plentiful evidence of this highly developed commercial economy as it existed in the time of the First Dynasty of Babylon (twenty-first century B.C.). Far more striking, however, is the evidence of the recently discovered tablets from Cappadocia, for they show the same system in full operation at an earlier period and in a land far removed from the historic centres of Mesopotamian culture, in the very region which was later to be the home territory of the Hittite Empire. The Cappadocian merchants seem to have been of Assyrian origin, and stood in close relations with Assur, which they call simply " the City," but they possessed organised settlements in Kanesh and the other cities of Eastern Anatolia from which they carried on a thriving trade in cloth, hides, copper, and lead.

(v) *Its Intellectual and Scientific Tradition*

This remarkable expansion of Mesopotamian trade and civilisation rested not only on the practical capacity of the people, but above all on the higher development of education and intellectual culture. Here, again, it was the temple that led the way. Every sanctuary possessed its library and school—" the House of the Tablet " or " the House of the Seal," in which the temple archives and liturgical texts were preserved, and the young were instructed in the art of writing. Already in the fourth millennium, the Sumerians had developed from their original pictographic writing a cuneiform syllabic script which was imprinted with a reed or a bone stylus on clay tablets which were afterwards baked. This invention put the means of writing within the reach of everybody, and is partly responsible for the wide diffusion of the knowledge of writing in ancient Mesopotamia. At Shuruppak, Nippur, and elsewhere, tablets have been found containing the exercises of pupils in the temple schools, and already in Sumerian times classified lists of words and synonyms were drawn up, for the assistance of scribes and teachers. In later times the co-existence of Sumerian and Semitic led to the compilation of real dictionaries and grammars, which show the existence of systematic philological study.

The same systematic spirit appears in the Babylonian development of weights and measures, and in their system of land measurement and survey. We possess elaborate field plans dating from the time of the Third Dynasty of Ur (twenty-fourth century B.C.), which show the detailed measurement of an irregular area, by division into measured rectangles, triangles, and trapezoids ; and in the time of Hammurabi there existed regular textbooks, dealing with the solution of simple geometrical problems, such as to calculate the length of the diagonal of a measured rectangle, or to find the cubic contents of a clay wall and the number of loads of earth that are necessary to rebuild it. These acquirements are elementary enough and can hardly be dignified by the name of science. Their significance, however, lies in the fact that they should be considered honourable not only for craftsmen and architects, but for priests and princes. The Sumerians seem to have been the first to value knowledge for its own sake, and the tradition of learning which they founded never disappeared. It is only in Mesopotamia that one can find the leader of a great military monarchy like Assur Bani Pal boasting that he can " decipher difficult tablets in the obscure Sumerian and the hard-to-master Accadian," and that he " can solve complicated problems of Division and Multiplication."

In this way the Sumerians and Babylonians became the schoolmasters of the ancient world, and their influence on the development of religion and art, as well as on commerce and law, was enormous. In the second millennium B.C. Babylonian cuneiform was already used as the regular medium of diplomatic and commercial intercourse throughout the Near East, and the Babylonian codes served as a model for Hittite legislation.

The extent and antiquity of this influence is shown by the fact that Sumerian and Accadian loan words for the most common and important objects are common to all divisions of the Indo-European languages and presumably date back to the time before their separation from the parent stem.[1] But it is above all through the Jews and the Greeks that this influence has become part of the heritage of modern civilisation. The Jews traced the very beginnings of their nation to Chaldæa, and in the course of their history came more and more under the influence of Babylonia until it had penetrated their whole culture. With the Greeks the

---

[1] Examples of such words are the Sumerian urud=copper (Latin, raudus), gu = ox (Sanskrit, go), and the Assyrian pilakku = axe and shuru = steer (Sanskrit, staora). Cf. W. G. Childe, *The Aryans*, 87.

contact was less direct and passed through the medium of Anatolian culture.   Nevertheless the Greek vocabulary preserves many traces of influence, above all in the naming of stars and plants, such as the cherry, the rose, and the crocus, as well as in such common terms as the words for gold, hour, measure, rule, sack, and tunic, many of which have passed over to modern English.[1] Even to-day it is to the Sumerians that we owe our divisions of time, and the sexagesimal system of reckoning by multiples of six and ten, which still survives in our coinage, and many of our weights and measures, as well as in the 360 degrees of the circle.

But the worldwide influence of the Babylonian culture can be seen most clearly in the remarkable diffusion of the Babylonian theory of divination and astrology, which extended through the whole of the Old World from Europe to China.   These pseudo-sciences were held in higher honour by the Babylonians themselves than the more utilitarian branches of knowledge, and indeed it was in them rather than in the humble beginnings of mathematics and geometry that the scientific tradition finds its origin.   The idea of a fixed cosmic order which can be understood only by patient observation is the very foundation of science in the modern sense of the word, and it is in Babylonian astrology that this view of the world makes its first appearance. From very early times the Sumerians seem to have believed that there was an intimate correspondence between human life and the external order of Nature, so that the destinies of the individual are reflected in the disposition of the whole, and vice versa.   The earliest example of this belief is to be found in the practice of divination through the inspection of the liver or entrails of the sacrificed victim, a system which was handed on from the Babylonians through the

---

[1] E.g. χρυσός = khuraṣu, ὥρα = beru, κόρος = gur, κανών = kanu, σάκκος = shaḳḳu, χιτών = kitinnu, etc.   Cf. R. Campbell Thompson, " The Influence of Babylonia," in *Cambridge Ancient History*, vol. iii, p. 249.

Hittites and the Etruscans to the peoples of classical Greece and Rome. Readers of Herodotus will remember how at the battle of the Himera, Hamilcar the Carthaginian general stood apart from the battle, sacrificing and inspecting the entrails of the victims, until at last, when all the omens had failed, he cast himself on the sacrificial fire as a last propitiation to destiny—an impressive example of the ancient Babylonian belief that victory depends not on human effort, but on the decrees of the gods.

As early as the age of Gudea, however, the more advanced idea that the destinies of men were written in the heavens had made its appearance, and from this there gradually developed the systematic observation and naming of the chief constellations, and the theory of planetary influences. It is true that a really scientific astronomy did not develop until much later, but from the Assyrian period onwards there was a steady progress in the observation of eclipses and of the planetary movements, which culminated in the age of the great astronomers of Persian and Hellenistic times, who succeeded in calculating the exact duration of the synodic and sidereal months, and in constructing perpetual ephemerides of the planetary movements. It is now generally recognised that Greek astronomers owe far more to their Babylonian predecessors than was formerly believed, and even the discovery of the Precession of the Equinoxes seems to have been known to the great astronomer of Sippar, Kidennu (Kidenas), more than a century before the time of its reputed Greek discoverer Hipparchus.[1] Already in the fourth century Babylonian astronomy, and the astrological theory of the world on which it was based, were beginning to penetrate the Greek world. Thus Plato himself, or one of his immediate successors, has given classical expression in the Epinomis to the fundamental Babylonian doctrine that astronomy is the one perfect

[1] Cf. Meissner, *Babylonien und Assyrien,* vol. ii, pp. 416–18.

science, and that the celestial harmony is at once the prototype and the source of order in the terrestrial world. During the following centuries this astronomical mysticism became, as M. Cumont has shown, the dominant religion of the educated Hellenistic world, and the prestige that Babylonian learning acquired in this way enabled a few centres of the old culture to survive. Even as late as the Seleucid era the priests of the great sanctuary of the Mother Goddess at Erech were still collecting and transcribing liturgical documents which had been carried away from their temple centuries before. Yet more remarkable is the survival of the old religion and culture at Harran, the sacred city of the Moon God in Upper Mesopotamia, through the ages of Christian and Zoroastrian dominance down to Mohammedan times. When the Abbasid Khalifs founded " the House of Wisdom " at Bagdad, it was men of Harran, like Thabit ibn Qurra, who acted as the instructors of the Arabs in astronomy and mathematics, so that there is an unbroken tradition reaching from the temple schools of Sumerian times to the scientists of the Mohammedan world who were in turn to be the teachers of medieval Europe.

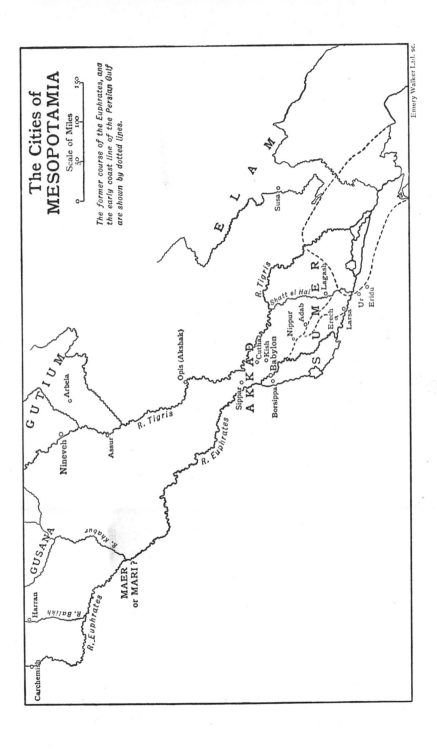

The Cities of
MESOPOTAMIA

Scale of Miles

50   100   150

The former course of the Euphrates, and
the early coast line of the Persian Gulf
are shown by dotted lines.

E L A M

Susa

R. Tigris

Shatt el Hai

SUMER

Nippur

Adab

Lagash

Erech

Ur   Eridu

Larsa

Cutha

AKKAD

Kish

Opis (Akshak)

Sippar

Babylon

Borsippa

GUTIUM

Arbela

R. Tigris

Nineveh

Assur

R. Euphrates

GUSANA

R. Khabur

Harran

R. Balikh

MAER
or MARI?

R. Euphrates

Carchemish

Emery Walker Ltd. sc.

CHAPTER VII

THE ARCHAIC CULTURE IN EGYPT AND THE DEVELOPMENT OF THE GREAT STATE

The Nile Valley and its Prehistoric Cultures.

The Civilisation of the Delta and the Origins of the Egyptian Monarchy.

The Unification of Egypt and the Early Dynastic Culture.

The Age of the Pyramid Builders and the Rise of the Solar Monarchy.

Ancient Egypt and the Tradition of the Great State.

CHAPTER VII

THE ARCHAIC CULTURE IN EGYPT AND THE DEVELOPMENT OF THE GREAT STATE

I. The Nile Valley and its Prehistoric Cultures

Vast as is the importance of Mesopotamia for the development of ancient civilisation, it does not stand alone. No less imposing and original is the creative genius of the Egyptian culture, and even if the latter was, as we have suggested, indebted to the fertilising influence of Asiatic civilisation, it nevertheless preserved its originality and its ancient indigenous culture-tradition. It is, in fact, in Egypt that it is possible to trace back the continuous history of civilisation farther than anywhere else. Owing to the dryness of the climate a far larger mass of archæological evidence has been preserved, and owing to the rapid achievement of political unity the beginnings of an historical tradition are exceptionally early and reliable.

The land of Egypt seems predestined by nature for the development of a unique civilisation. Nowhere else in the world are the natural conditions so simple and uniform, and the resources of the whole land so amenable to human control, and nowhere is there so abrupt a contrast between the intense fertility of the inhabited area and the utter desolation of the surrounding deserts. For Egypt is the creation of a single river, which gives unity and life to the whole country, and human existence is absolutely dependent on the fertilising water of the annual inundation. From the point at which the Nile leaves the open plains of the Sudan to traverse the high lands of North-eastern Africa, its course lies in a narrow channel bounded on either side by the precipitous walls of the desert plateau until it reaches the Delta. As long as the river cuts its way through the sandstone and harder primary formations of Nubia, the valley is little more than a ravine, and the course of the stream is interrupted by frequent cataracts. South of Assuan, however, it enters a softer limestone formation and the valley widens sufficiently to sustain a considerable population. Finally, below Cairo the walls of the valley disappear and the river enters the wide alluvial plain of the Delta. Thus the land falls into two distinct parts—the narrow rainless valley of Upper Egypt, with its desert climate, and the broad fertile Delta, which enjoys the winter rains and more temperate conditions of the Mediterranean countries. These are " The Two Lands" which nominally preserved their separate identity throughout the historical period. The centre of gravity of Lower Egypt lies in the North-western Delta, the region of Sais and Buto, and later of Alexandria, the capital of all Egypt during the period of Greek and Roman dominance. On the other hand, the centre of Upper Egypt lies far to the south in the region of the Thebaid, and it is here that the capital was situated—at Hierakonpolis or at This or at Thebes itself—in periods when the national Nilotic tradition was strongest. At other times, however, when neither Upper Egypt nor the Delta is predominant, the whole country finds its natural centre at the junction of the Delta and the Upper Valley, the region of Memphis and Cairo. In spite of its great length, the habitable region is very restricted, indeed its total area is less than that of Belgium, and of this more than half lies in the Delta. Owing to natural conditions, practically the whole of the archæological evidence is derived from the upper valley between Cairo and the cataracts, which we are apt to regard as almost identical with ancient Egypt ; but it is important to remember that the richest, the most populous, and perhaps even the most civilised part of the country has always lain in the Delta, though all material record of it is irretrievably lost.

In prehistoric times, however, the face of the land was entirely different. The valley was a swampy jungle, the haunt of the hippopotamus and the crocodile, such as is now found only far south in the Bahr el Ghazel, and the desert plateau was a grassy steppe, teeming with game, and capable of supporting a population of hunters whose palæolithic implements are still scattered plentifully over its surface. The first people of the higher culture to enter the country seem to have come from the north, perhaps from Asia, and their settlements are found on the borders of the Nile valley as far south as Badari, between Assiut and Sohag, the site which has given its name to the culture. They were an agricultural people, and the remains of wheat have been found in their settlements, as well as the flint-toothed sickles that they used in harvest. They possessed fine flint implements of a type that has been compared with the European Solutrean industry, and they manufactured pottery and glazed stone beads, as well as ivory and clay figures of women, and slate palettes on which they ground malachite for painting the eyes.[1] This Badarian culture is undoubtedly of great antiquity, though it is difficult to accept Sir Flinders Petrie's estimate of 12,000 years ! In fact it suggests comparison with the neolithic cultures of Crete and the Danube, rather than with the Solutrean culture of palæolithic Europe, and it is possible that all three are variants of an early type of Mediterranean culture, no less ancient than the Painted Pottery Cultures of the Middle East. But its northern origin seems probable, and it may well be the source of many of the characteristic features of the predynastic Egyptian culture that succeeded it. The latter is common to the whole valley south of Assiut, including Nubia, and

---

[1] A similar, but less advanced, type of culture has been discovered in the Northern Fayum desert. The discoverer, Miss Caton-Thompson, regards this Fayum culture as somewhat earlier than the Badarian which already used a little copper, and attributes both of them to " an autochthonous proto-Libyan origin."

possesses a very uniform character throughout the whole area. Its beginnings can hardly be later than the fifth millennium, since it passed through a long process of evolution before the rise of the dynastic kingdom. It represents a phase of civilisation not unlike that of the Painted Pottery Cultures of Asia. As in the latter, the use of copper was not unknown, and painted pottery was manufactured, though the designs and technique are entirely different from any of the Asiatic types. The artistic powers of the predynastic people are shown in the elaborately carved ivory combs, and above all in the perfection of their work in flint, in which they fashioned not only weapons and implements but ornaments and bracelets of remarkable delicacy.

This First Predynastic Culture forms the foundation of the later Egyptian development, and was no doubt due, in the main, to the native Hamitic population of North-east Africa carrying on the tradition of the higher type of culture that had been introduced into the Nile valley by the Badarian people. It underwent a still further development at a later period owing to the appearance in Egypt of the new type of civilisation known as the Second Predynastic Culture. This culture is distinguished from its predecessor by new forms of weapons and ornaments, such as the pear-shaped mace (in contrast to the earlier disk-shaped type), amulets in the form of animals, and glazed beads. Above all the white " cross-lined " pottery gives place to a red-painted ware and to drilled stone vases of fine workmanship and material. Some of the new forms of pottery show a considerable resemblance to early Palestinian types, and it is usually supposed that the Second Culture itself originated in close proximity to Egypt among the tribes of the north-eastern frontier region. The most important cemeteries belonging to this culture are situated in the northern part of Upper Egypt, near the Fayum, but it gradually penetrated southwards and the later predynastic period witnessed a fusion of the two cultures in which the second appears to have been predominant. This fusion of cultures no doubt represents the mingling of two peoples and may well explain the union of Hamitic and Semitic elements which went to make up the historical Egyptian people. Linguistic evidence clearly shows the existence of these two elements, for while the ground-stock of the language is undoubtedly Hamitic, it differs from the other Hamitic tongues by the possession of a striking affinity to Semitic which suggests that Egypt had come under strong Semitic influences during the formative period of the language. From the anthropological point of view, however, a fusion of this kind would be hardly perceptible, for the Semites, the Hamites, and the Mediterraneans are all so similar in type that Professor Elliot Smith and other anthropologists have regarded them as three variants of a single racial stock.

In physical type the predynastic people were a small, delicately made, long-headed people, and the same type which characterised the predynastic people has survived through historical times with astonishingly little modification. Nevertheless there are traces from the very beginning of the historical period of other racial types, both Alpine and Nordic,[1] which, in spite of their small numbers, may have had a considerable influence in the development of Egyptian civilisation.

The settlements of the predynastic peoples lie along the edge of the desert above the valley and apparently formed independent tribal districts which survived to some extent in the later nomes. In historic times the latter were administrative divisions, consisting of a town, together with the irrigated lands and pastures that were its territory, not unlike the city states of Mesopotamia. Each of them possessed its local cult

---

[1] E.g. there are distinctively Nordic types among the ancient skulls from the Thebaid in the collection of the Department of Human Anatomy at Oxford. The Egyptian Alpines are usually known as " the Gizeh Type," cf. supra, p. 77.

and its own patron deity, who was almost invariably worshipped under the form of an animal. Thus there was the falcon Horus at Edfu, Thoth, the ibis at Hermopolis, Sebek the crocodile in the Fayyum, Nekheb the vulture at Hierakonpolis, and many more. The worship of these animal gods belongs to the earliest stratum of Egyptian culture, and takes us back to the world of totemism and the animal guardian of the hunter, a far more primitive stage than that of the Peasant Religion of the early Asiatic culture. The Egyptian word for a god, " neter," is shown even in historic times by a sign which represents the standard or totem pole of the nome, and these standards appear already in the designs of the prehistoric pottery and the proto-dynastic carved slate palettes, bearing the emblems of the local god. Only in the Delta do we find the local deities worshipped under a human form, as Neit the War Goddess at Sais, and Osiris and Isis at Busiris and Perhebt. And in these cases we are justified in assuming foreign influence, since Neit is in historic times the goddess of the Libyans, and Isis and Osiris are, as we have seen, forms of the Asiatic Mother Goddess and her consort.

II. The Civilisation of the Delta and the Origins of the Egyptian Monarchy

Now it was in the Delta that the higher civilisation, characterised by the city state, the invention of writing, the common use of metals, and the establishment of a fixed calendar, first made its appearance, and it is highly probable that an organised monarchical state already existed in the Western Delta, when the predynastic people of Upper Egypt were still in the stage of village communities organised in independent tribal units. The later Egyptian tradition traced the origins of the Egyptian monarchy to Osiris, who was not only a vegetation god, but also the embodiment of kingship.

Throughout Egyptian history the pastoral staff and the flail or scourge of Osiris are the insignia of the monarch, and at the great Sed festival, which goes back at least to the First Dynasty, the king appeared in the garb of the dead god as though to show that, like Osiris himself, his forces underwent a periodic process of renewal.[1] Nevertheless Osiris remained in a sense outside the true Egyptian pantheon ; there are passages in the Pyramid Texts which refer to the opposition and hostility of the older gods. The vindication of Osiris was accomplished, according to the legend, by his son Horus, who defeats his rival Set, the slayer of his father, and establishes his rule throughout the land. Now Horus did not originally belong to the circle of Osiris, but was the falcon god of a Lower Egyptian nome (Behdet), and his connection with Osiris seems to be due to the share taken by a dynasty, of which he was the patron god, in the expansion of the higher civilisation of the Delta. It is true that a rather late text preserved in the temple of Horus at Edfu, the Behdet of Upper Egypt, describes the conquest of Egypt by Horus and his followers, " the Mesentiu," as having originated in the south. But M. Moret has argued with much plausibility that this is a later southern redaction of an older legend, and that the followers of Horus were " Mesenou " or Harpooners, from the Harpoon nome which formed an important part of the ancient kingdom of the Western Delta, and in which Isis is said to have given birth to the young Horus. This hypothesis of a conquest of the valley from the north would explain, not only the expansion of the higher civilisation in predynastic times, but also the way in which the earlier deities of the nomes of Upper Egypt are overlaid by new cults. For example, in the sign of the 16th nome the falcon of Horus is placed above the oryx of Set, the old god of

---

[1] This ceremony has been thought to represent the killing of the king at the end of a thirty-year reign, but if this was ever so, it had certainly ceased to be the case in historical times.

Upper Egypt; in the 15th the hare, which is another
emblem of Set, has been replaced by the ibis god Thoth;
and so too in later times Osiris himself appears at Abydos
the old home of the native Egyptian god of the dead, the
jackal Khentamenti.[1]

This legendary conquest of Horus was the traditional
source of Egyptian royalty. Every king was the
successor and the divine embodiment of the falcon god.
He assumed on his succession a Horus-name, and every
two years the feast of " the Following of Horus "
recalled the divine origins of the kingdom. In later
times Egypt was regarded as " the Creation of Horus,"
and it existed only to serve and honour the god in the
person of his earthly embodiment, the king. " It is
He (Horus) who has adorned thee," says a hymn of the
Sixth Dynasty :

"It is He who has built Thee,
  It is He who has founded Thee,
  Therefore Thou dost for Him all that He commands in every place
      whither He goes.
  Thou bringest to him everything that is in thee, in every place that
      his heart desires. . . .

"The gates of Egypt stand fast like Inmutef,
  They open not to the Westerners,
  They open not to the Easterners,
  They open not to the Northerners,
  They open not to the Southerners,
  They open not to the dwellers in the centre,
  But they open to Horus.
  For it is He who hath made them,
  It is He who hath set them up,
  It is He who defends them from all the ills that Set would do unto
      them,
  Since it is He who founded thee in thy name of Foundation,
  Since it is He who abased Set for Thee in thy name of City."[2]

But this complete unification of Egypt under a single
Horus-monarch was a gradual process. The dynastic
lists bear witness to a long period in which the Two

---

[1] Cf. Moret, *Le Nil and la Civilisation Égyptienne*, pp. 124–8.
[2] *Pyramid Texts*, [ed. Sethe, § 1587, etc. Moret, *Des Clans aux
Empires*, p. 215.

Lands were ruled by the Followers of Horus—" the dead Demigods "—from their separate capitals at Nekhen in the south, and Buto in the north. Each of these was connected not only with Horus, but with a local Mother Goddess, in the south the vulture goddess Nekheb, the mistress of the high White Crown òf Upper Egypt, in the north the serpent goddess Wazet, the mistress of the Red Crown which bore the sacred uræus on its front. And this twofold division lived on in later times. Egypt remained at least in theory a dual monarchy. The Pharaoh wore a double crown. He had two palaces, the White House of Upper Egypt and the Red House of the Delta Kingdom, and even two tombs. And the whole organisation of government was nominally twofold, with two treasuries and two chanceries, long after it was in practice closely centralised.

It is unfortunately impossible to make any estimate of the length of the period during which the separate kingdoms of Upper and Lower Egypt existed. Undoubtedly the beginnings of the higher civilisation and of an organised state go back to a very remote period, at least in Lower Egypt. The later Egyptian calendar was regulated by a cycle of 1,460 years based upon observations of the heliacal rising of the star Sirius, and astronomical calculations combined with the data of the monuments show that the first of these cycles was introduced in Lower Egypt in the neighbourhood of Memphis or Heliopolis, either in the year 2776/81 or 4236/41 B.C.

According to the generally accepted system of chronology, which places the beginning of the First Dynasty about 3315 B.C., the earlier date for the institution of the calendar, which has been almost universally accepted by Egyptologists, leaves a gap of nearly 1,000 years between the rise of a relatively civilised state in Lower Egypt and the dawn of historical times. Hence there are a considerable number of scholars who are in favour of a much earlier dating for the whole of the

earlier part of Egyptian history. Thus Borchardt, one
of the leading authorities on Egyptian chronology,
places the beginning of the First Dynasty as far back
as 4186, and thus brings it into close relation with the
institution of the calendar. But there are very serious
objections to so early a date, since the parallels that
we have seen to exist between the proto-dynastic culture
of Egypt and the early Sumerian culture of Mesopotamia show that they are nearly contemporary with
one another, and we shall therefore be left with an
unfilled gap of 1,000 years in the chronology of Mesopotamian civilisation. From this point of view, as well
as for other reasons, the lower chronology advocated
by Eduard Meyer seems much to be preferred, but on
the other hand it still leaves us with the vast gap of
1,000 years between the institution of the calendar and
the rise of the kingdom. The only radical solution of
the difficulty is that recently advocated by Dr. Scharff,
namely the abandonment of the higher date, and the
bringing down of the institution of the calendar to the
next Sothic period, which begins in 2776 (or 2781) B.C.[1]
In this case, it would fall, according to Meyer's reduced
chronology, at the beginning of the reign of Zoser, the
actual or virtual founder of the Third Dynasty. This
is an epoch-making point in Egyptian history, for it
marks the final achievement of Egyptian unity, and the
transference of the capital from the south to Memphis,
the region which is proved by astronomical data to have
been the place of origin of the Egyptian calendar.
There is no reason to suppose that Memphis or Heliopolis was of any importance in predynastic times, for
the earliest centres of power in the Delta seem to have
been at Sais and Buto. It was only under the Third
Dynasty that Memphis became the capital of the
kingdom, and Heliopolis a great religious centre in
which the solar cult of the following period had its
origin. Moreover, the reign of Zoser is noteworthy in

---

[1] A. Scharff, *Grundzüge der Aegyptischen Vorgeschichte* (Leipzig, 1927).

other respects. He was the first pyramid builder, and his minister Imhotep was the real founder of Egyptian architecture, and so renowned for his wisdom that he was in later times worshipped as a god and as patron of the sciences. Such a man might well have been the author of so important an innovation as the Egyptian solar calendar with its 12 months of 30 days and 5 epagomenal days, which is so marked an improvement on the Babylonian lunar year, and which is hardly conceivable as the invention of the primitive population of early predynastic times. The twenty-eighth century B.C., on the other hand, was a period of high cultural development alike in Babylonia and Egypt. New religious conceptions were leading men to make careful observations of the movements of the sun and the other heavenly bodies, and thus the introduction of the new calendar would form part of the same movement of culture which expressed itself in the religious sphere in the new solar theology, which also had its origin at Heliopolis. Thus there seems to be a considerable probability, prima facie, in favour of the lower Sothic date, and if that could be accepted, it would no longer be necessary to assume an exaggeratedly high antiquity for the origins of Egyptian civilisation, and it would be possible to correlate the proto-historic Egyptian development with that of the Mesopotamian peoples. It must, however, be admitted that the great majority of Egyptologists are still in favour of the earlier date, and so long as this is so, it seems impossible to rule out the possibility of a higher system of chronology, like that of Borchardt, for the whole of the early historical period.

Unfortunately, this uncertainty throws doubt on the whole chronology of the Archaic Cultures, since Egypt is our main archæological standard of reference for all of them, and accordingly we must be prepared to allow for a margin of error of more than 800 years in dealing not only with the Old Kingdom of Egypt, but also the

Sumerian civilisation of Babylonia and the Minoan culture of Crete, as well as in regard to the chronological data for prehistoric Europe that have been based on archæological comparisons with the latter.

III. THE UNIFICATION OF EGYPT AND THE EARLY DYNASTIC CULTURE

The actual unification of Egypt undoubtedly proceeded from the south, and was accomplished by the rulers of the Horus Kingdom of the upper valley. Nevertheless, the appearance in Egypt of distinctively Sumerian types in the art of this period, and the other signs of Mesopotamian influence described in a former chapter, have led many writers to conclude that the beginnings of the dynastic culture itself were due to the coming of invaders from Asia by way of the Red Sea. The chief link of communication between Egypt and the Red Sea has always been the Wadi Hammamat, which leaves the Nile valley near Koptos, " the town of the caravans," in the very heart of Upper Egypt, which was the starting-point of all the ancient Egyptian expeditions to the Red Sea and the lands to the south, as well as of the pilgrim traffic of medieval and modern times. It is therefore not impossible that adventurers from Mesopotamia or more probably from Arabian lands of Sumerian culture, such as Magan, may have reached Upper Egypt by this route in late predynastic times : indeed, such a movement would explain the religious veneration with which the later Egyptians regarded the mysterious country of Punt, " the land of the gods," which was situated at the southern end of the Red Sea, either in South Arabia or on the opposite coast of Africa. In any case, however, the foreign influence that may have reached Egypt from this direction cannot have been strong enough to transform either the racial type or even the tradition of culture that was already established in the age of the separate kingdoms of the North and South.

Recent discoveries have thrown considerable light on the beginnings of united Egypt, and we now possess some historical evidence regarding the rulers who actually accomplished the work of unification, although up to a few years ago they were hardly less legendary than the " Followers of Horus." These were three kings, the first named the Scorpion, who ruled as far north as the head of the Delta, the second Narmer, the actual conqueror of Lower Egypt, and the third Aha or the Fighter, the first ruler of the united kingdom. The great ceremonial mace head and the carved palette of Narmer are the first actual historical documents that we possess. On the latter we see the king returning in triumph from the conquest of the North, with two rows of beheaded prisoners in front of him, and the hieroglyphics describe his booty, 120,000 captives, 400,000 oxen, and 1,422,000 sheep or goats. Below, the king in the form of a bull is shown trampling on a captive and breaking down the wall of a fortified town. This was probably the actual campaign that brought about the union of the two kingdoms, and the union was consolidated by the marriage of the southern king with a princess from the Delta. Nevertheless, the consolidation of Egypt was not absolutely complete, for the Second Dynasty seems to represent a northern reaction, and the Delta was conquered a second time at the beginning of the Third Dynasty, after which the capital was moved north to Memphis, near Cairo, the common centre of the Two Lands.

The state that was thus founded by Narmer and his successors, and which reached its complete development under the Third Dynasty, was from the first an absolute theocratic monarchy in which everything centred in the person of the king. For the latter was not simply the high priest and representative of the city god, as in Mesopotamia. He was himself a god, separated from his subjects by an unbridgable gulf of sanctity and awe. To the Egyptians the Crown was not a mere badge of office, it was a magical talisman which endowed its wearer with superhuman majesty and terror. It is invoked in the Pyramid texts as a living divinity. " O Red Crown, O Great Magician, O Flame ! Grant that the fear of the King may be as thy fear, that his respect may be as thy respect. Grant that the King may be prayed as thou art prayed, and loved as thou art loved. May his soul preside over the living. May his Power preside over the Spirits and may his knife be strong against his enemies." [1] Even the name of the king might scarcely be uttered; he was described by some circumlocution such as He of the Great House Per-O, the title that is familiar to us as Pharaoh. His chief minister was named the Man by contrast to his own divinity, and his treasurer was known as the Treasurer of the God. The welfare of Egypt, and even the course of nature was held to depend upon his sacred office, so that although his subjects were absolutely without rights towards him, he was bound by a series of ritual obligations which in practice limited his freedom more than that of many constitutional kings. For his primary function was not to transact the practical work of government, so much as to fulfil the sacred rites on which the life of the land depended.[2] With his own hands, as we see on the mace head of the earliest historical ruler, the Scorpion, he broke the ground and traced the channel that inaugurated the period of irrigation, and at his coronation he performed the symbolic rites called the Circuit of the Wall, and the Uniting of the Two Lands, which secured the defence and the union of Egypt.

All the life of Egypt centred in the royal palace, the Great House—and even from the beginning there

---

[1] *Pyramid Texts*, 196, cf. Moret, *op. cit.*, 190.

[2] This idea is a very widespread one among primitive peoples. The Abuan of Nigeria say, " It is for this cause our people chose an Ake-Abua that he might be holy in our behalf, keeping all the laws that ordinary people have not time to remember because of their regular work."—Talbot, *Southern Nigeria*, iii, p. 606.

existed an elaborate court life with stately ceremonial and numerous offices. Even in the days of the First Dynasty we can trace the rise of a bureaucracy. We hear of a vizier and a chamberlain, a chancellor and a master of the ceremonies, the royal architect and the Superintendent of the Inundation, not to mention minor offices like the Keeper of the Wine, and the Keeper of the King's Cosmetic Box. Thus from the first the Egyptian Government was a government of courtiers and bureaucrats. The ruling class consisted not of independent nobles, as in a feudal kingdom, but—apart from the members of the royal house—of men who had served their apprenticeship at the court or in the numerous royal offices. For already under the early dynasties the kingdom possessed an elaborate system of census and tribute, and different taxes in kind were sent up to the great storehouses of the royal residence from the local governors of the nomes, or provinces. The land was, for the most part, the property of Pharaoh himself, and the peasant cultivators were bound to the soil. There was little room for a wealthy middle class, as in Mesopotamia, and the essential elements of Egyptian society were the same then as they have been ever since, whether under the Ptolemies or the Cæsars or the Turks—namely the tax-paying fellahin and the tax-receiving Government.

This extraordinary economic and political centralisation, which makes ancient Egypt one of the most perfect examples of state socialism in history, had its basis in those natural conditions of human life in the Nile valley which were mentioned at the beginning of the chapter. The conversion of the jungles and swamps of the prehistoric valley into the rich cornlands which made Egypt the wonder of the world, was only accomplished by ages of communal co-ordinated effort. The prosperity of the country depends, not as in northern lands on the industry of the individual peasant and his family, but on the organised labour of the irrigation dykes, and on the fertilising waters of the annual inundation, for land in itself is valueless apart from the water which is supplied by the Nile and the irrigation canals. From the earliest times the measurement of the Nile flood and the maintenance of the irrigation works has been the primary duty of every Egyptian Government. The ancient Egyptian year began on July 19, the day that the inundation reached the neighbourhood of the head of the Delta, and as early as the First Dynasty the annual taxation was fixed according to the level of the river, for the yield of the following harvest depends entirely on " a good Nile," which is neither too low to irrigate the fields nor high enough to cause destruction by flood.[1] Hence the power which regulates and controls the inundation is the master of the life and property of the whole population, and the principle of compulsory public labour— the corvée—which elsewhere appears as a tyrannical infringement of the rights of the individual, is in Egypt the necessary condition of all economic life.

IV. The Age of the Pyramid Builders and the Rise of the Solar Monarchy

This concentration of the whole life of the nation in the hands of its ruler gave Egyptian civilisation that unique character of simplicity and grandeur which renders the art of the Old Kingdom so impressive. And it found its expression no less in the sphere of religion and thought than in the achievements of material organisation. The primitive cult of the animal gods of the predynastic communities still subsisted, but it was subordinated to the new state religion which was the inspiration of the Dynastic Culture, and which had its

---

[1] The customs connected with the rise of the Nile have maintained themselves down to modern times, and Lane has given a vivid account of the festival of the Abundance of the Nile or the Breaking of the River, as it was celebrated nearly a century ago.—*Modern Egyptians*, ch. xxvi.

centre in the worship of the Dead King and his celestial father and prototype the Sun God.

Egyptian culture seems to have been marked from its very beginnings by an especial preoccupation with death and the after-life : in fact, never before or since has a people lavished such care and wealth and labour on the service of their dead. But it was in the person of the king that the cult of the dead centred. He was the visible god and all Egypt existed only for his service, so it was natural that he should not resign himself to the common fate of men, but should attempt to rival the gods and continue to reign in the tomb. Consequently every conceivable device that might secure immortality or avert decay was employed. In the later days of the Old Kingdom under the Fifth and Sixth Dynasties, we possess abundant evidence for these rites, and we can trace their gradual rise in the development of the tomb itself. Under the First Dynasty it was simply an enlargement of the grave of prehistoric times—a brick-lined pit with a wooden roof, but even then the body of the king was already surrounded with rich furniture and treasure. With the Third Dynasty there is a great development. Zoser, the second king of this house, built the first pyramid, the step pyramid of Sakkarah, and by the end of the dynasty the nobles and courtiers had also begun to erect great mastaba tombs round the grave of their dead lord. Finally under the Fourth Dynasty the movement reaches its climax in the great pyramids of Gizeh which remain the greatest wonders of the ancient world. They lie out on the desert plateau above the Nile valley, and round them stand the rectangular mastaba tombs of the nobles of their court. In front of each pyramid stood a great mortuary temple in which the service of the dead Pharaoh was carried on, and from this a long covered causeway led down to the valley, where it terminated in a great monumental gateway or pylon. From a purely material point of view these buildings are a marvellous achievement. The Great Pyramid of Khufu consists of 2,300,000 blocks of limestone which average 2½ tons apiece. But even more remarkable is the workmanship, which surpasses anything known in modern masons' work. The construction of these great works must have absorbed the resources and labour of the whole kingdom, and in addition to the actual cost of building, there were also the enormous endowments which were necessary for the upkeep of the mortuary temples and their priesthoods. Indeed, it was impossible to maintain the standard set by King Khufu, and the succeeding royal tombs gradually decline in size and workmanship. The succeeding dynasty, the Fifth, was marked not so much by the greatness of its royal pyramid tombs, as by its temples and by the complete development of that solar religion which gives Egyptian civilisation its final character. From very early times Heliopolis or On, the sacred city near Memphis, had been the centre of sun worship, and it was from this source apparently that the very idea of the pyramid had its origin, for its model seems to have been the sacred sun stone or obelisk, which was the object of the Heliopolitan worship. But at the beginning of the Fifth Dynasty the royal power itself passed into the hands of a priestly family from Heliopolis. Henceforward the Sun God, Re, was the patron and divine ruler of the Egyptian Kingdom. Every Pharaoh, by a pious fiction, claimed to be the actual son of the Sun God by an earthly mother. The old royal god, Horus, was not abolished, he was regarded as himself an aspect of the Sun God, the sun as a divine falcon. Thus there arose a kind of solar monotheism, answering to the sacred monarchy of Pharaoh, whose earthly majesty was conceived as the counterpart of the celestial majesty of the Sun God. And after his death, he did not descend like common men into the region of the dead, the realm of the earth god, Osiris, but was translated to the heavens to dwell with his father, Re. This is the motive that dominates the inscriptions of the pyramids and their mortuary temples, and it is the first appearance that we know of the belief in a celestial hereafter ; but it was a hereafter that at first only the king could enjoy, and its gradual extension to the nobles and to the common people was the result only of long centuries of subsequent development. " Men fall, their name is not," says one of the Pyramid Texts :

> " Seize thou King Teti by his arm,
> Take thou King Teti to the sky,
> That he die not on earth, among men."

This identification of Pharaoh with the Sun God strengthened the Egyptian belief in the divinity and sacredness of the kingdom. They felt that they were a chosen people set apart under the protection of the Sun God. Henceforward Egypt always felt herself to be a land apart ; she had found a religious idea that consecrated her geographical isolation and her separate culture tradition, and thenceforward, like China, she was a country that went her own way and preserved her own peculiar civilisation, even under the stress of invasion or the yoke of foreign conquerors.

Nevertheless Egypt was no hermit kingdom. The high level of civilisation that she had attained led to extensive commercial relations, and, especially in the last period of the old kingdom under the Sixth Dynasty, we hear of distant voyages, and frequent expeditions to foreign lands. Egypt maintained close commercial relations with the Ægean and with Syria, whence came the cedar wood that was used so extensively ; and in the Red Sea region, not only was the mining district of Sinai a direct dependency, but expeditions were sent far to the south, to the Somali coast or to Southern Arabia, to obtain gold and the precious spices that were used in the temples and in the service of the dead. At the same time Egyptian art reached its climax, not only in the great architectural achievements of the Fourth and Fifth

Dynasties, but even more in the statuary and bas-reliefs, which were not merely the ornaments, but the necessary equipment of the tombs and mortuary chapels, especially under the Fourth, Fifth, and Sixth Dynasties. It was from this period that date the wonderfully life-like statues of kings and nobles, which are masterpieces of portraiture and are not surpassed in the later and better-known periods of Egyptian history. This art of portraiture had a definitely religious motive, for it was believed that the life of the dead man in his tomb depended on the life-like image which stood in the tomb chamber to receive the mortuary offerings, and to which his soul attached itself, whereas if the statue was not a good portrait the soul might have difficulty in recognising its old body.

Similar ideas explain the temple reliefs and paintings, which were intended to provide the deceased in the next life with all that he had been accustomed to in his life on earth, property and servants and so forth. It was, in fact, magical equipment for the life beyond the tomb.

During the Sixth Dynasty the same artistic tradition persisted, and the general level of civilisation remained as high as ever, but the first signs of decline begin to appear, and the spirit of omnipotent power that had characterised the great pyramid builders of the Fourth Dynasty has entirely vanished. During the long reign of King Pepi II, who came to the throne when he was only six and lived to be a hundred, the centralised power of the monarchy gradually collapsed. The governors of the nomes were semi-independent, and they became the hereditary governors of local principalities rather than official representatives of the central bureaucracy. And with the close of Pepi II's reign, Egypt enters on a long period of darkness and confusion which lasted from the Seventh to the Eleventh Dynasty. Just as Meso-potamia, about the same time, was overrun by the barbarous hosts of Gutium, Egypt likewise fell a prey to foreign conquerors, either from Libya or from

Northern Syria, like the later Hyksos invaders.   At the same time Negro peoples from Central Africa had penetrated up the White Nile as far as Nubia and already make their first appearance on the scene of history in the later part of the Sixth Dynasty.   During these Dark Ages the history of Egypt is a blank, and the Seventh to the Tenth Dynasties are empty names.   All that we know is that the great unitary state of the Old Kingdom had ceased to exist, and when the historical record begins once more, towards the end of the third millennium, Egypt was a land of independent fiefs, ruled by great families of local nobles, who owed nominal allegiance to a titular monarch.   This is the first example in history of a feudal society, and in Egypt, as afterwards in ancient China of the fifth and fourth centuries B.C. and in medieval Europe and Japan, its appearance represents the relapse of a highly civilised imperial state into the semi-tribal conditions of local separation from which it had been built up.

V. Ancient Egypt and the Tradition of the Great State

Nevertheless the monarchical tradition in Egypt, as in China, was based on religious and natural foundations which could not be entirely destroyed, and after the Dark Ages had passed the Divine Monarchy emerged stronger and more united than ever.   Indeed, the tradition of the Great State maintained itself in Egypt through all the subsequent periods of dissolution and foreign invasion down to the Christian era, and, as Professor Rostovtzeff has shown, it exercised a vital formative influence on the tradition of European state administration through its inheritance by the Hellenistic monarchies and the Roman Empire.   The empire of the fourth century, above all, with its regime of fixed hereditary occupations and forced services, its official hierarchy centring in the Sacred Palace, and its

vast organisation of state ownership and fiscal exploita-
tion, may be regarded as nothing less than an adaptation
to the Mediterranean world in general of a system that
had been inherited by the Cæsars in Egypt as the
successors of the Ptolemies and the Pharaohs.[1]

It is not, however, possible to maintain that Egypt
was the sole original creator of the tradition of the Great
State, for a similar type of social organism arose independently at the other extremity of the Old World in
China.

It is true that we possess practically no archæological
evidence for the period of some 2,000 years that lies
between the age of the æneolithic Painted Pottery
Culture and the historic civilisation of the time of
Confucius, but it is impossible to doubt the existence of
an archaic stage of Chinese culture characterised by the
introduction of the pictographic script, the art of
irrigation, and the foundation of a theocratic monarchy,
which was the basis of the later historical development.
And it was to the maintenance of this theocratic tradition that the Chinese culture and the Chinese state owed
its extraordinary stability and endurance. As in
Egypt, not only the social order, but even the order of
Nature was held to depend on the office of the Son of
Heaven. It was through his actions—the promulgation
of the calendar, the solemn ritual ploughing, and the
annual sacrifices on the Altar of Heaven—that the
rhythm of human life was co-ordinated with the celestial
order. In China alone, among the civilisations of the
Old World, this archaic type of culture survived the
coming of the World Religions, and it is only in the
present generation that it has finally passed away
before the coming of Western civilisation and Western
political ideas.

An even more remarkable parallel to the Egyptian

[1] It is remarkable that in the Roman Empire also, from the reign
of Aurelian to that of Constantine, a solar monotheism was becoming
the official religion of the empire.

development is to be found in comparatively recent times in the Inca monarchy of Peru. Here also there existed a Great State of even more socialistic and centralised type than that of Egypt. The Inca, like the Pharaoh, was regarded as the son of the Sun God, and the purity of the divine blood was preserved, as in Egypt, by the marriage of the ruler with his sister.

The land was divided into three parts, one of which was set aside for the service of the Sun, and another for the service of the Inca, and the whole population was employed, under the supervision of the Government, in organised state labour such as the building of roads and irrigation works, the cultivation of the state and temples land, and the weaving of textiles, and the products of the common labour were distributed among the population in accordance with their needs. The cult of the dead was highly developed. After their death, the bodies of members of the royal race were embalmed and buried in rich tombs, usually in caves, but in the coastal region sometimes under large brick pyramids, and frequent offerings were made to them.

The origins of this remarkable civilisation are no less mysterious than those of the Maya cities of Central America, though it undoubtedly has some connection with the much older culture which created the great megalithic buildings of Tiahuanaco in Bolivia. If it was the result of a purely independent South American development, it is one of the most remarkable examples of convergent evolution in history. According to the hypothesis of Mr. Perry and Professor Elliot Smith, the elements of this culture were actually derived from Egypt, and were introduced into South America by the same race of megalith builders who have left traces of their presence throughout the Pacific from Easter Island to the Carolines. Now the monarchy of Japan, the rulers of which also claimed to be Children of the Sun, was undoubtedly founded by megalith builders who arrived by sea, not long before the Christian era, and it is

not impossible that the same influence may have reached
the Pacific Coast of America.   But the gap in time and
space between this prehistoric Pacific culture and the
historic civilisation of ancient Egypt is so great that it
is difficult to affirm any direct cultural influence on the
part of the latter in the present state of our knowledge.

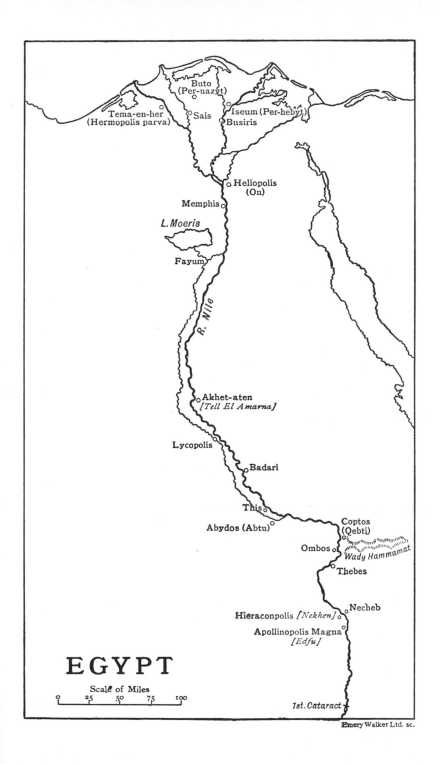

Buto
(Per-uazyt)

Tema-en-her
(Hermopolis parva)

Sais

Iseum (Per-hebyt)

Busiris

Heliopolis
(On)

Memphis

L. Moeris

Fayum

R. Nile

Akhet-aten
[Tell El Amarna]

Lycopolis

Badari

This

Abydos (Abtu)

Coptos
(Qebti)

Ombos

Wady Hammamat

Thebes

Necheb

Hieraconpolis *[Nekhen]*

Apollinopolis Magna
[Edfu]

EGYPT

Scale of Miles

0   25   50   75   100

1st. Cataract

Emery Walker Ltd. sc.

CHAPTER VIII

THE DAWN OF THE HIGHER CIVILISATION IN EUROPE. CRETE AND THE ÆGEAN CULTURE

The Eastern Mediterranean and its Place in the History of European Culture.

The Neolithic Culture of Crete and the Rise of the Minoan Civilisation.

The Palace of Cnossus and the Minoan Culture during the Bronze Age.

The Culture of the Cyclades and Troy and their Maritime Expansion.

The Racial Character of the Early Ægean Peoples.

CHAPTER VIII

THE DAWN OF THE HIGHER CIVILISATION IN EUROPE. CRETE AND THE ÆGEAN CULTURE

I. The Eastern Mediterranean and its Place in the History of European Culture

EUROPEAN civilisation derives its origins from a double tradition—on the one hand from the neolithic Peasant Culture of Central Europe, which was described in Chapter III, on the other from the metal-using culture of the Mediterranean, which was in closer contact with the ancient civilisations of the Near East, and it was the interaction and combination of these two elements that created the European culture of historic times. The neolithic culture of Central Europe was the more truly European tradition, since it influenced the whole continental development, but it did not possess within itself the seeds of progress. It was in the Eastern Mediterranean, on the very border-line between Europe and the East, that there first appears a civilisation of the higher type, characterised by the use of metals, the development of a script and the City-State organisation. This was the foundation of that great Mediterranean culture tradition to which Europe, as a social fact and not a mere geographical expression, owes its very existence. It was in origin a maritime extension of the archaic civilisation of the Near East, but it was by no means lacking in originality. It derived its power and prosperity neither from agriculture nor from war, but from trade and the control of the sea-ways. For the first time in history, we can trace the emergence of maritime influence and sea-power as a decisive factor in the spread of civilisation. This feature was to remain characteristic of the development of European civilisation. For in Europe, alone among the great culture regions of the world, the sea has been the focus of an intense cultural activity. Elsewhere in Asia and Egypt the centres of the higher culture lay in great river valleys or fertile alluvial plains, where the uniformity of natural conditions was favourable to the rise of a homogeneous unified civilisation, based upon irrigation and intensive agriculture, and where the social system tended to acquire the same stability and uniformity as that of its natural environment.

In Europe, however, the possibilities of such a development were limited by the existence of forests and mountains, which formerly rendered communication by land difficult, and tended to segregate each region from its neighbours. Hence the diversity of European regional life, which is most marked in those parts of Europe which have had the strongest influence on its cultural history, such as the Ægean, Italy and the Balkans, the Alpine lands, and Scandinavia. Every valley, every canton, almost every village is an independent whole, a microcosm which is the centre of an intense local patriotism and clan feeling. At first sight this might seem an obstacle to the development of any true civilised life, and so it would undoubtedly have proved, had it not been for the existence of the maritime factor. But in Europe the sea is everywhere, and penetrates deep into the heart of the continent through the basins of the Mediterranean, the Euxine, and the Baltic. The sea-ways have been the high road of European civilisation, for they alone have rendered possible the combination of regional independence with the stimulus of commercial intercourse and mutual influence to which Europe owes the richness and variety of its cultural life.

It is in the Eastern Mediterranean that these conditions attain their highest development. The geological formation of the region is comparatively recent, and owes much to volcanic action and land subsidence. It consists mainly of sharply defined limestone ridges, which run out into the sea as peninsulas, or rise above the waters as islands. There are no great plains or fertile sloping hills. The cultivable areas consist of valleys enclosed by mountain walls, each a little world to itself, like the famous plain of Sparta, or else of narrow strips of fertile coast, like Ionia or Dalmatia or Phœnicia. Behind lie the mountains, rising through forest and scrub to heights of barren arid limestone, which cut off every valley and plain from its neighbours. Everything makes for separation and isolation, were it not for the all-pervading presence of the sea, which has exercised from pre-historic times a controlling influence on the whole development of Mediterranean culture.

The early sailor was tempted to sail from harbour to harbour along the coast, or from island to island, by the steady Etesian winds which blow through the summer months, and when once the practice of navigation was learned, there was an unlimited field open to the men of the Mediterranean. To the south-east lie the centres of ancient civilisation, and Mediterranean shipping could communicate directly with the Egyptian Delta or with the ports of Syria, from which the great caravan routes lead up into Mesopotamia and to Inner Asia. To the north and west lay a wide expanse of barbarous lands, with which enterprising traders might carry on a profitable traffic, like that which our ancestors carried on with the West African coast, for prehistoric Europe possessed not only copper and tin, but substances such as gold and silver, amber and jet, which were precious enough to repay long voyages. Thus the Mediterranean is the natural intermediary between the civilised south-east and the barbarous north-west, and the Mediterranean peoples, when once they had acquired a sufficient level of culture, were especially fitted by the natural conditions of their life to take advantage of their situation. The rocky and mountainous character of their home lands made it difficult to live the self-sufficing laborious life of the agriculturalist. On the other hand, the Mediterranean region is exceptionally fitted for the culture of fruit trees. It is the classical land of the vine, the olive, and the fig tree, and their cultivation not only gives room for long periods of leisure, but also supplies a large surplus production of wine and oil, which is eminently suited for trade and exchange. Even in predynastic times the oil of Palestine was already being brought down into Egypt,[1] and with the rise of the Ægean civilisation in Crete the same products formed the main source of the prosperity of the islanders.

Up to recent times it was believed that the culture of the vine and the olive only dated from classical times and that it was introduced to Greece by the Phœnicians, who were also held to be the predecessors and teachers of the Greeks in trade and navigation. But now we know that the Phœnician traders of the early Greek history were only carrying on an ancient Mediterranean tradition, and that behind what used to be considered the beginnings of Greek history there lies a long and brilliant development of native Ægean culture.

The discovery of this vanished civilisation is one of the most romantic chapters in the history of modern archæology. Its origin was due to a German merchant, Heinrich Schliemann, whose whole life was governed by the ambition to prove by demonstration the historicity of the Homeric poems. The story of the siege of Troy had fired his imagination in childhood, and he spent the early part of his life in earning money with which to carry out his youthful purpose. In 1870 when he was 48 and wealthy, he started his excavations on the site of Troy, and there discovered what he supposed to be the city and the treasure of Priam, though it was really the remains of a far earlier culture— 1,000 years older than the Trojan War. His success aroused the jealousy of the Turkish Government, he

---

[1] Cf. Frankfort, *op. cit.*, pp. 105 ff.

was involved in lawsuits, and finally he turned his attention to Greece. There in 1876 he discovered the shaft graves of the early kings at Mycenæ with their rich treasure—again dating from a much earlier period than the Homeric heroes whose traces he was seeking. In 1880 he went on to Orchomenos, where he discovered the so-called Treasury of Minyas, and in 1884–5 he laid bare the foundations of the great palace of Tiryns. Though Schliemann never realised the full import of his discoveries, he was the real discoverer of a new world.

But the origin of the new type of art and civilisation that he had found at Mycenæ remained a mystery for a long time, and it was not until Sir A. Evans began his great excavations in Crete twenty-five years ago, that the real meaning of the newly discovered civilisation was understood. Not only did Crete prove to be the source of the culture that Schliemann had found at Mycenæ, it was seen to be the home of a far older and more advanced civilisation than that of mainland Greece. Not only at Cnossus, where Evans had discovered the great palace of the prehistoric Cretan kings, but all over the centre and east of the island, the remains were found of a rich city culture, possessing a brilliant and original artistic tradition and a high development of trade and industry.

The chronology of this civilisation, which is usually known as the Minoan, rests upon the archæological synchronisms that it has been possible to establish between prehistoric Crete and ancient Egypt, and thus we have three main periods of Cretan culture, answering to the three main divisions of Egyptian history. The Early Minoan period roughly corresponds to the Old Kingdom in Egypt, i.e. 3200–2100 B.C. according to the minimum chronology. The Middle Minoan period corresponds to the Middle Kingdom (2100–1580 B.C.), and the Late Minoan to the New Kingdom (1580–1200). Each of these main periods again is divided into three sub-periods based on the sequence of artistic types, above all of the pottery, and in this way it has proved possible to attain a detailed and fairly accurate chronology for a civilisation in which the evidence of inscriptions is as yet completely lacking.

II. THE NEOLITHIC CULTURE OF CRETE AND THE RISE OF THE MINOAN CIVILISATION

Ancient as it is, this Minoan civilisation is not the earliest culture of the Ægean world.   It was preceded, at least in Crete, by a long neolithic period, the remains of which lie at the base of the great mound at Cnossus.   This earliest Cretan culture is regarded by Sir Arthur Evans as an insular offshoot of the neolithic culture of Asia Minor, and it also possesses links with the Danubian peasant culture of Serbia and Central Europe.   The neolithic Cretans made the same steatopygous female figures, usually of clay, that are so common on the European mainland, as well as in Asia Minor and pre-historic Egypt, and their pottery was a coarse unpainted ware, decorated with incised patterns, or rippled with a comb, like the early Badarian pottery of prehistoric Egypt.   This neolithic population undoubtedly belonged to the same Mediterranean stock which inhabited the island in later times, nevertheless the new civilisation which appeared in the Ægean at the dawn of the Age of Copper does not seem to have arisen from the spontaneous development of the primitive peasant culture.   Not only in Crete, but also in the Cyclades, where no signs of a neolithic population have as yet been discovered, the coming of the new culture was evidently due to civilising influences from without.   This is suggested by the very situation of the earliest centres of the new culture, which always lie near the sea, and in some cases, as at Pseira and above all at Mochlos, on small barren islands which could never have supported an agricultural population.   But even more conclusive is the evidence of the earliest remains themselves.   The contents of the numerous and rich tombs that have been discovered in the Messara plain in Southern Crete point to a direct connection with the neighbouring coast of Egypt and Libya. Here, as well as at Cnossus and Mochlos, there are stone vases beautifully carved from diorite, liparite and porphyry, as well as softer native stones, such as steatite and alabaster, which undoubtedly represent either importations or imitations of the predynastic and early dynastic stone ware of the Nile valley. The curious peg-shape stone idols and the rectangular stone palettes also resemble early Egyptian types, as well as the ivory seals and amulets, the material for which must have been imported from Africa.

These and other points of resemblance have led Sir Arthur Evans to attribute the foundation of the Early Minoan culture to an actual settlement of colonists from North Africa in Crete, due possibly to the flight of some of the predynastic people of the Delta when the latter was first conquered by the rulers of Upper Egypt. For the Cretan evidence points to a connection with the Western Delta, where Libyan influence was strong, rather than with the culture of the Nile valley itself, and the very form of the tombs of the Messara—stone vaulted structures of beehive shape, sometimes containing hundreds of interments—belong to a type which has a wide distribution in North Africa, and is Libyan rather than Egyptian in origin.

On the other hand, the Asiatic affinities of the Ægean culture are no less strongly marked. The Asiatic worship of the Mother Goddess and her youthful companion is characteristic of Cretan religion from the earliest times, and the symbols of their cult, especially the Double Axe or Labrys, and the sacred doves of the goddess, both of which already appear in early Minoan times, are Sumerian rather than Egyptian in origin. Moreover, we have seen that the predynastic civilisation of the Delta itself was not purely African in character, but probably owed much of its higher development to Asiatic influences.

Thus the ancient Ægean world in its culture as well as in its geographical situation was intermediate between Egypt and Asia.   It owed its prosperity to trade and the control of the sea routes across the Eastern Mediterranean.   The importance of this intercourse is shown by the remarkable wealth of the early Minoan burials, especially at Mochlos, with their abundance of gold and ivory, and their beautiful jewellery and goldsmiths' work.   It was not, however, until the beginning of the Middle Minoan period, which corresponds approximately in date with the rise of the Middle Kingdom in Egypt, that Cretan civilisation definitely reached the higher stage of cultural development which is marked by the possession of a script and the rise of organised states, comparable to the city states of the oriental world. It is possible, as Sir Arthur Evans has suggested, that the advance in Cretan culture was connected with a movement of invasion from Asia Minor, and the establishment of new dynasties of Asiatic origin in the island.

There is no doubt that the dawn of the new age was accompanied by important political and social changes. There was a decline in the old centres of Early Minoan culture.   Mochlos was abandoned and the rich interments of the Messara tombs came to an end, probably owing to the passing of the old trading aristocracy before the new monarchies which had their centre at Cnossus and Phæstus.

III. THE PALACE OF CNOSSUS AND THE MINOAN CULTURE DURING THE BRONZE AGE

The great period of Minoan culture which dawns with the beginning of the second millennium was essentially an age of palaces.   They were the centres of the political, religious, and social life of the whole land, and it is above all from their remains that it has been possible to reconstruct the history of the later Cretan civilisation.

The Cretan palace consisted of a central court round

which were grouped, without much regularity of plan, the various buildings—domestic quarter, offices, warehouses, sanctuaries, and bathrooms—which made up the royal residence. The palaces of Cnossus and Phæstus possessed a great monumental approach—that at Phæstus consisting of a raised causeway leading up to a platform from which broad flights of steps ascend to the palace portico.

The palace at Cnossus, especially, covers about six acres of ground, and its size and wealth show that it was the centre of a powerful state. But it was no less a religious centre, for the sanctuary forms an integral part of the palace and the sacred emblem of the Double Axe is carved on the walls and pillars. The ruler who resided here was in fact, no less than in the sacred cities of Sumer, a priest as well as a king. This sacred character of Cretan royalty appears most clearly in the throne-room of the later palace which has a remarkable resemblance to the shrine of the god Men, near Antioch in Pisidia, the centre of one of the Anatolian temple states.

On one side there is a raised throne, guarded on each side by painted griffins. Opposite it, just as in Pisidia, is the lustral basin or tank, with a flight of steps descending into it, and on the other side a door, also flanked by griffins, leads into the inner sanctuary where stood the altar.

Equally characteristic of the religious aspect of the palace are the temple repositories or shrines of the goddess, situated in the west part of the palace. They contain cult objects such as a faience figure of the goddess, girdled with snakes and crowned with a high tiara, and most remarkable of all, a large flat cross of polished marble with equal arms which seems to have been fixed to the wall of a shrine.

The secular side of the palace life was equally developed. The Cretan palace had not the monumental grandeur of the Oriental palace, but it was just as luxurious and probably more comfortable to live in. The drainage and sanitary system was in advance of anything before modern times. It consists of main drains and culverts with proper air shafts and manholes, and there are clay water pipes with collar and stop ridge which, unlike most modern pipes, are not parallel in section, but of tapering form, so that they cause an irregular flow which prevents the formation of sediment.

From the plentiful material we possess from the later periods we can form a very good idea of the life that went on in the palace. Like the Egyptian palace of the Old Kingdom, it contained great magazines and warehouses in which were stored the tributes in kind which served as currency before the invention of coinage. The excavators found the rows of colossal oil jars still ranged in order in the palace storehouses, and the elaborate system of inscribed tablets and official seals shows that there was a fully developed official hierarchy, organised in different departments, which supervised the different branches of government. Moreover, the palace, like the Babylonian city temple, also contained workshops in which craftsmen produced the works of art and the wonderful painted pottery which is one of the finest achievements of the Minoan civilisation. This pottery, known as Camares ware, reached its highest perfection in the Second Middle Minoan period. Later it gave place to a new naturalistic style, which became known throughout the Ægean world and was in request from mainland Greece to Egypt, where in the tomb paintings of the Eighteenth Dynasty we see processions of Ægean islanders, bearing these great vases as tribute to the Egyptian vizier.

The manufacture of faience was also highly developed, and by Middle Minoan III period beautiful naturalistic pottery figures were being produced, such as the group of a goat with kids, or the images of the snake goddess and her votaries which were found in the Temple Repository of the palace at Cnossus.

But the palace was also the scene of a brilliant court life, as we see from the remains of the frescoes which decorated the palace walls, and which must have depicted the religious ceremonies and the dances and spectacles at which the court assisted. The costume of the Minoan ladies was very elaborate, and as different as possible from that of the Greeks of classical times. It consisted of a close-fitting bodice, cut very low, and a very full skirt which accentuated the smallness of the waist. In contrast to the simplicity of the Greek tunic or robe, the Cretan fashions affected brilliant colours and rich material, and aimed at the greatest variety in effect. In fact they resembled the dress of the ladies of the Renaissance and of modern Europe far more than that of the other peoples of antiquity.

Moreover, the civilisation of ancient Crete resembled that of modern Europe in another respect. The women were not secluded, as in ancient Greece and among the oriental peoples ; they shared fully in the life of the court, especially the dances and spectacles which played such a large part in Cretan life.

The most popular of all these amusements, and the one which appears to have taken place at the great feasts, was a kind of bull-fight in which male and female performers baited a wild bull, leaping across its back and turning somersaults over its horns, as it charged them. This sport is a favourite subject in Minoan art, and it may have given rise to the later Greek legend according to which a tribute of youths and maidens had to be paid by the Athenians every nine years to the Bull Monster, the Minotaur, who lived in the labyrinth at Cnossus which the craftsman Dædalus had built for King Minos.

Wrestling and boxing were also popular sports, and it is probable that the athletic contests of later times which were common alike to the Greeks and the Etruscans are the final product of this ancient tradition of the Ægean culture.

This brilliant civilisation only reached its full development in the Later Minoan period, but even in Middle Minoan II (1900–1750 B.C.) Cretan culture was of a very high type. It was already a true city civilisation, far in advance of anything to be found on the continent of Europe for more than 1,000 years. The predominantly peaceful character of the civilisation is shown by the fact that the Cretan towns were unfortified. The narrow streets and closely packed houses which are to be seen, for example, at Gournia are due not to the need for defence, as in the medieval European town, but to the concentration of population and the high development of commerce and industry.

One of the most interesting discoveries in the earlier palace of Cnossus is a large mosaic depicting a city, and from this we can form some idea of the external aspect of an ancient Minoan town. It shows a type of house quite unlike the low, straggling buildings of the later Greek city, but rather resembling the modern European form with two or three stories, and with door and windows facing outwards towards the street instead of into the inner court.

The age of the First Palace of Cnossus came to an abrupt end at the close of Middle Minoan II (c. 1750 B.C.), when both Cnossus and Phæstus were destroyed by some sudden catastrophe. This took place about the same time as the fall of the Middle Kingdom in Egypt, and it is possible that it was connected with the same wave of invasions which brought the Hyksos kings into Egypt from Asia. But this was only a passing storm. Almost immediately the palaces of Cnossus and Phæstus were rebuilt on a grander scale than before, and ancient Crete enters on its final period of prosperity (c. 1700–1420 B.C.). The great feature of the new age is the absorption by the Minoan civilisation of the other provinces of the Ægean culture of the islands and in mainland Greece. A uniform civilisation which takes its tone from Cnossus spreads over the whole Ægean world, and this was probably due to the actual establishment of a Cretan Empire, based on sea-power and ruled by the King of Cnossus. It was from this time that the palace of Cnossus in its latest and most magnificent form dates. We have already described the main features of the palace and of the brilliant court life that centred there, and throughout the centre and east of the island Cretan civilisation was at its highest. There were important towns at Phæstus and Tylissos, Mallia and Gournia, and in the east, at Pseira, Palaikastro, and Zakro. The system of writing was highly developed, the old pictograph characters being replaced by a linear script. Trade and industry were flourishing, and Cretan art reached its highest expression in the frescoes and painted stucco reliefs of the different palaces, and the pottery, jewellery, and goldsmiths' work, which have been found far and wide throughout the Ægean area.

So long as the Cretan script remains undeciphered, it is impossible for us to know much about the organisation of the Government. The power that centred in the palace of Cnossus seems to have been a centralised monarchy with a developed bureaucratic administration, but it is difficult for us to say what were the exact relations between this central government and the provinces or dependencies, if such indeed they were, of the Cretan Empire in Greece and the islands.

In the seventeenth century B.C. the mainland centres —Tiryns, and Orchomenos, and above all Mycenæ— were already the seats of powerful princes, and throughout the later period of Minoan culture their power and importance were steadily increasing until finally mainland Greece takes the place of Crete itself in the hegemony of the Ægean world. For the last great age of Minoan culture ended suddenly and disastrously. A little before the close of the fifteenth century B.C. (c. 1420 ?) complete destruction fell upon the great palace of Cnossus, and all the old centres of Cretan civilisation were plundered and burnt. The Minoan culture still lingered on in an impoverished and weakened form, but it had lost its imperial power. Crete had sunk into a dependency of mainland Greece, and the last period of the Ægean culture was not Minoan, but Mycenean.

IV. The Culture of the Cyclades and Troy and their Maritime Expansion

The brilliance of the Minoan civilisation of Crete is apt to throw the development of the rest of the Ægean world into shadow. It is true that during the Bronze Age the culture of the other islands was almost entirely dependent upon that of Crete, and Cnossus was the cultural, and probably also the political, metropolis of the whole of the Ægean world. But in the earlier period of the Ægean culture, during the third millennium, this was not the case. The Northern Ægean world possessed its own cultural development which was parallel but not subordinate to that of Early Minoan Crete. The small fertile islands of the Cyclades were naturally suited to be intermediate stations in the sea-going trade of the Ægean world, and they were rich in minerals, such as the marble of Paros, the copper of Seriphos, the gold of Siphnos, the obsidian of Melos, and the emery of Naxos which were in wide request in very early times. Thus there arose in the Cyclades a maritime civilisation closely similar in type to the Early Minoan culture of Crete.

Like the latter it shows some traces of Egyptian influence, such as the palettes and toilet tweezers that are found in the Early Cycladic tombs, but relations were closest, as might be expected, with the western coast of Asia Minor : indeed, so far as can be judged from the rather scanty results of excavation on the mainland, Western Anatolia and the Cyclades seem to have formed part of a single cultural province,[1] characterised by similar types of pottery and by the curious fiddle-shaped

[1] Cf. D. Hogarth in *Cambridge Ancient History*, vol. ii, pp. 554-5.

marble idols which probably represent the Mother Goddess. The Cyclades were also in close contact with Crete, and the similarity in culture between the two regions is shown by the resemblance of the Early Cycladic jewellery to that of the Mochlos tombs. Ultimately, as we have seen, the influence of the Minoan culture entirely dominated the little islands to the north, but in the third millennium Crete received from them no less than it gave. It was probably from the Cyclades that the spiral ornament, which became so characteristic of Minoan art, first reached Crete, and Cycladic imports, such as obsidian, pottery, and marble idols, are common in Crete, particularly towards the end of the Early Minoan Period. The most remarkable feature of the Early Cycladic culture is, in fact, the wide commercial intercourse to which it testifies. During the third millennium these little islands seem to have been the centres of a movement of trade and maritime expansion which has left its traces, not only throughout the Ægean world, but as far as the Black Sea and South Russia on the one hand, and the Western Mediterranean on the other.

So, too, the new metal-using culture of the early Ægean type, which makes its appearance in mainland Greece in the first half of the third millennium, is closely allied to that of the Cyclades, and may have been due to an actual colonisation by Cycladic or West Anatolian people. The earliest settlements of this so-called Helladic culture are found on the eastern coast, in Argolis and the Isthmus of Corinth, especially at Tiryns, and thence they gradually expanded westward throughout the Peloponnese and northward to Attica and Bœotia. These were the regions which were subsequently to be the centres of the Mycenæan civilisation, which, like the Early Helladic culture itself, was due not to the spontaneous evolution of the native mainland culture, but to the coming of foreign influences from the higher civilisation of the Ægean world.

Moreover, the influence of the maritime culture of the Ægean was also making itself felt farther north in the region of the Hellespont. About the middle of the third millennium, a powerful state had arisen in Northwestern Asia Minor, with its centre at Troy. Unlike the peaceful unwalled cities of Crete, Troy was a powerful fortress with great walls and gateways, protected by towers and bastions. It owed its importance to its strategic position on the Dardanelles, which enabled it to command the sea route from the Ægean to the Black Sea and the land route from Asia Minor to the Balkans. Thus, in spite of its warlike character, it was also an important centre of trade and the home of a wealthy community. The treasure discovered by Schliemann is rich in gold and silver, crystal, lapis lazuli, and ivory, and the jewellery is even more elaborate in workmanship than that of Mochlos in Crete. But the Trojan civilisation belongs to the continental rather than the Ægean type. The spiral, which is so characteristic of the East European peasant culture, is the favourite motif in Trojan goldsmiths' work, and it is perhaps from this source that the Ægean world first acquired this type of ornament. Moreover, the Trojan palace is entirely unlike the Ægean type. It is a Megaron house, consisting of a large hall with an external porch and a central hearth such as was common in the Painted Pottery of Transylvania. An even more striking sign of northern influence is to be seen in the fine ceremonial stone axes of European type, which can hardly have been imported by a metal-using people in trade, but which may well have been preserved by a warrior people of northern origin as the traditional insignia of chieftainship, or as religious emblems.

Thus the Trojan civilisation seems to mark the first intrusion into the Mediterranean world of the warrior peoples from the north, but on the other hand, it owed its importance to trade rather than to war, for it acted as an intermediary between the maritime civilisation of the Ægean and the European cultures of the Northern Balkans and Central Europe. There are plentiful signs of Trojan influence in the later stages of the Danubian culture and even more in the earliest Bronze Age culture of Bohemia, while, on the other hand, Trojan pottery is found in Eubœa and the Cyclades, and stone idols of the Cycladic type appear at Troy itself. Troy was probably the source from which the peoples of the Ægean obtained their silver and lead and their earliest supplies of tin, and Mr. Gordon Childe has even suggested that it formed part of a maritime confederation of trading peoples which had its centre in the Ægean. Certainly the evidence from Troy and the Cyclades gives the impression of a great development of commerce both by land and sea, which was in full activity during the second half of the third millennium B.C. It shows that the early Minoan civilisation of Crete was not an isolated phenomenon, but formed part of a wider movement of trade and maritime intercourse which embraced the whole Eastern Mediterranean.

Nor was it even limited to this region, for there is considerable evidence that these early Ægean mariners anticipated the exploits of the Hellenic voyagers of later times. Across the Black Sea in South Russia there are signs of Cycladic influence in the graves of the Don and Donetz region, and throughout the Western Mediterranean the beginnings of the Age of Metal is everywhere accompanied by signs of Ægean influence. The earliest metal-using cultures of the west make their appearance in just those regions which are the natural termini of the sea routes from the Eastern Mediterranean, and which were subsequently to be the centres of Greek and Phœnician colonisation, such as the heel of Italy and Eastern Sicily, Sardinia and South-east Spain; while, on the other hand, in the interior of the western peninsulas a very backward type of stone-using culture continued to exist far into the later Bronze Age.

In all these regions the beginnings of the higher
culture is marked by the appearance of new forms of
tomb—above all rock-cut tombs with collective burials,
and new types of pottery and ornaments, which suggest
the coming of foreign influences. Thus, for example,
flat stone idols of the Cycladic type have been found
in Sardinia and at Almizaraque in South-east Spain, a
region which is especially rich in signs of foreign intercourse, such as ivory and alabaster, and beads made
from the shell of ostrich eggs. Again, the carved bone
plaques found in Eastern Sicily and Liguria are practically identical with similar objects discovered at Troy,
and the Sicilian pottery also seems to imitate Ægean
models. Phallic bead amulets which are common in
the tombs of the Cylcades also have a wide distribution
in the west as far as Southern France, and a copper
dagger of Early Minoan type has been found in Etruria
at Monte Bradone.

Thus it is hardly possible to doubt that the influence
of the Ægean peoples had already penetrated to the
Western Mediterranean in the third millennium B.C.
Nor is this surprising when we take account of the
maritime character of their culture, and the wealth of
Spain in precious metals, and of Sardinia in copper, which
was a sufficient inducement for the trading peoples of the
east to undertake the long western voyages.

This early expansion of Ægean influence in the
Western Mediterranean is, in fact, but the first of a series
of similar movements which passed along the natural
highway of the Ægean, the Ionian, and the Tyrrhenian
seas at intervals of about a thousand years. Thus there
was a similar expansion of the late Minoan and Mycenæan
culture in the second half of the second millennium B.C.,
and of the Greek colonial movement in the sixth and
seventh centuries, while more than 1,000 years later the
influence of the Byzantine culture reached Southern
Italy, Sicily, and South-eastern Spain by the same
path.

V. The Racial Character of the Early Ægean Peoples

The problem of the racial and linguistic affinities of the peoples who were responsible for this great expansion of maritime culture is still very obscure, for, as we have seen, the early Ægean culture has links that connect it with North Africa as well as with Asia Minor. The influence of the Egyptian Delta seems to have been strongest at the dawn of the Early Minoan period, while the later movement of maritime expansion which had its centre in the Cyclades stood in much closer relations with Asia Minor. The great increase in the activity of the Cycladic culture and its intercourse with Troy and the Western Mediterranean seem to have fallen in the interval between the decline of the Old Kingdom and the rise of the Middle Kingdom in Egypt, and no doubt there is some connection between the course of events in the Ægean and the disturbances that were taking place during this period on the mainland. It is probable that a great movement of peoples was taking place at this time owing to the invasion of Asia Minor by warrior peoples from the northern steppes whose presence as the ruling element in the Trojan culture we have already noted, and who were also perhaps the founders of the later Hittite power; and that, in consequence, the native peoples of Asia Minor were driven to seek new homes. Thus Mr. C. L. Woolley writes : " The result of this movement was to spread a racial stock native to Asia Minor over North Syria, the Ægean islands, and parts of the Greek mainland, and for the next thousand years these territories were to develop cultures which, however divergent, yet betray their relationship and a certain measure of interdependence." [1] Evidence for this expansion of Anatolian population is perhaps to be found in the appearance

[1] C. L. Woolley, "Asia Minor, Syria, and the Ægean," in *Liverpool Annals of Archæology*, vol. ix, p. 48.

of a broad-headed non-Mediterranean type of man, not only in the Cyclades, but also at Villafrati in Sicily and Anghelu Ruju in Sardinia, where their remains are found in conjunction with the signs of East Mediterranean influence that have already been described, while in Crete itself Sir Arthur Evans believes that during the Middle Minoan period a broad-headed minority of Anatolian extraction constituted the ruling class in the island. Even more important are the signs of a common type of language connecting the islands of the Ægean and mainland Greece with the coast lands of Asia Minor. Names of non-Indo-European origin, especially those ending in "-ndos" or "-nthos," "-ene" and "-ssos," such as Corinth, Cnossus, Halicarnassos, Lindos, Mycenæ, are widely distributed throughout the whole area. Especially remarkable is the word for the sacred Double Axe—Labrys—which forms the root, not only of the Cretan Labyrinthos, the House of the Double Axe, which was probably the actual name of the palace of Cnossus, but also appears in the title of the god of the Double Axe, Zeus Labrandeus, at Mylasa on the mainland of Asia Minor.

No doubt it would be wrong to suppose that all the Ægean peoples belonged to a single stock. Asia Minor itself contained an extraordinary variety of peoples and languages, as we can see from the records at Boghaz Keui, the Hittite capital, which are now beginning to be deciphered. The Greeks themselves preserved the tradition of a number of different peoples who formerly occupied the Ægean islands and parts of the Greek mainland—Carians, Leleges, Termilli, Tyrsenians, and above all Pelasgians, the last being perhaps a generic name for " the Peoples of the Sea," like the similar term used by the Egyptians for the warlike peoples of the Ægean in the thirteenth and twelfth centuries B.C.

The situation is still further complicated by a new series of invasions which took place at the beginning of the second millennium B.C.

°Troy

Dimini
Iolcus
Pagaseticus Sinus
Othrys
△ M. ↙

Myrina
Cyme
△ *Sipylus*
Mt.
Smyrna   Sardes

Orchomenus
L.
Copais

Ephesus

Mycenae
Tiryns

Miletus

CARIA

Syros   *Delos*

Seriphos   *Paros*   Halicarnassus

Siphnos   *Naxos*

Melos   *Amorgos*

C   y   l   a   d   e   s

Ialysus

Rhodus

Crete   *Mallia*
Miletus
Pseira
Mochlos
Gnossus°   °Palaikastro
°Zakro
Phaestus°   MESSARA

CRETE AND THE AEGEAN

Scale of Miles

0   20   40   60   80   100

At that time the flourishing Trojan civilisation ends
abruptly with the complete destruction of the city and
the Greek mainland was conquered by a new people
from the north, the bearers of the so-called Minyan
culture, who installed themselves on the sites of the
earlier Helladic civilisation in Central Greece.   It is
possible—indeed, it is the most widely accepted view—
that in these new-comers we are to see the first appearance of the ancestors of the later Hellenic population
of Greece, and if this is so we must allow for the co-
existence of Indo-European and Anatolian peoples in the
Ægean area as early as the beginning of the second
millennium, or even earlier still if we accept, as seems
necessary, a northern and Indo-European element in
the Trojan culture of the preceding period.

Nevertheless down to the close of the Bronze Age
the Indo-European peoples played no great part in the
life of the Mediterranean.   The dominant element consisted of the Ægean and Anatolian " Peoples of the
Sea," such as the Carians, the Etruscans, and the
Shardana, traders and adventurers, whose influence
extended far beyond the limits of the Ægean.   There is
even reason to believe that these Sea Peoples came into
contact with the other great province of maritime culture
which extended from Spain and the Western Mediterranean to Western and North-western Europe, the
region of the Megalithic Culture.

CHAPTER IX

THE ORIGINS OF THE MEGALITHIC CULTURE AND ITS EXPANSION IN WESTERN EUROPE

Nature and Distribution of the Megalithic Culture.

The Problem of its Origin. The Theory of its Connection with a Movement of Early Trade and Treasure-seeking.

The Megalithic Culture in Malta and the Mediterranean.

CHAPTER IX

THE ORIGINS OF THE MEGALITHIC CULTURE AND ITS EXPANSION IN WESTERN EUROPE

I. Nature and Distribution of the Megalithic Culture

The problem of the Megalithic Culture lies at the root of the whole question of the origins of the higher culture in Western Europe. We have seen that the culture of the west in neolithic times was of a very backward type. It was an outlying region, and the cultural currents transmitted from the great centres of civilisation in the Near East only reached it late and indirectly. While the Eastern Europe and the Danube region already possessed a settled and semi-civilised peasant culture, in the west the conditions of life were hardly in advance of what they had been in palæolithic times— indeed from some points of view, such as art, they were even more retrograde. We can distinguish different types of culture, that of the Kitchen Midden settlements on the Baltic, the Campignian flint-using culture of Northern France, and the Cave Culture of Central Spain, which carries on the old tradition of the Capsian culture, but all of them agree in their poverty and barbarism. Throughout Western Europe a scanty population eked out a bare existence as hunters and food gatherers.

In the later neolithic period, however, we find the sudden appearance of quite a new type of culture. Instead of burying the dead under the dwelling-places without either sepulchre or funeral offerings, as had been done in the Kitchen Midden settlements, great stone graves, constructed with enormous labour, make their appearance, in which the dead are buried with careful rites and numerous offerings. There is nothing

193

to connect these new burial customs with anything that went before, at any rate in North-western Europe, in France, the British Isles, and Scandinavia. They must have been introduced from without, and the fact that the earliest graves of this type are always found on or near the sea-coast suggests that the people who introduced them came by sea.

The simplest type of megalithic grave is a stone chamber formed of three to six upright stones with a single great roofing slab. This is the dolmen or " stone table," and it is usually assumed to be the earliest form. The more elaborate types, consisting of a long corridor leading to a chamber, or of a corridor only, are believed to be the result of a later development. With the partial substitution of dry masonry for great monolithic blocks, a process of degeneration sets in, and the last type of all is the small cist or box, made of flagstones rather than blocks, and usually used for a simple interment, unlike the earlier tombs, which were collective sepulchres. The megalithic structures, which are not tombs, but are usually found in association with them, such as the Menhir or monolith, the stone circle and the stone row, are also believed to be a later development, and generally date from the Bronze Age.

These rude stone monuments, standing generally in desolate places, on barren moors or rocky headlands, are far the most impressive prehistoric remains that are to be found in Western Europe, and it is natural that they aroused men's wonder and curiosity, long before there was any general interest or understanding with regard to prehistoric culture. As the names of the monuments show, all kinds of legends clustered round them from very early times. The Dolmens are "huts of the fairies," or, among the more sophisticated, " Druids' altars," the Long Barrows are " Giants' Graves " in England, " Beds of the Huns" in Germany, "Tombs of the Giants" in Sardinia. From the seventeenth century onwards, Stonehenge, at least, aroused a really scientific

interest, and numerous theories—most of them wild
enough, it is true,—were invented to account for them.

And with the coming of wider knowledge in the
nineteenth century, the mystery of these monuments
only increased. For it was discovered that they were
not confined to a single country or even to a single
continent, but that they extend from the far west of
Europe and Africa to the far east of Asia and even
out into the Pacific.

In Western Europe they form four main groups—one
including the western coasts of Great Britain and the
whole of Ireland, another in Denmark and the Southern
Baltic, a third in Brittany, the Channel Islands, and
Western France, and a fourth in the Iberian Peninsula.
In the Mediterranean they are found in all the western
islands, except Sicily, in South France, South-east Italy,
and in North Africa. In the Black Sea there is a group
in Thrace, and they are numerous in the Crimea and
the Caucasus, where they extend east to the Caspian.

In Asia they are found in Trans-Jordania and Palestine, in Southern and Central India, as well as in Assam
and Manipur, where a degraded form of megalithic
culture still survives among the Naga and Kachin
tribes, and finally in Korea and Japan. There are,
moreover, a number of regions in which similar remains
have been reported, but where they have not been so
thoroughly examined; for instance, in West Africa, in
Abyssinia and the Sudan, in Arabia and Persia, and
in the islands of the Pacific. Furthermore, in South
America there are the vast and imposing megalithic
remains of Tiahuanaco on Lake Titicaca in Bolivia,
which, however, like the Maya culture of Central America,
seem to belong to a more advanced stage of culture than
the megalithic monuments of the west.

It is clear from this distribution that the megalithic
culture was a world-movement, and since the vast
majority of the monuments are situated near the coasts,
it must have been due to a wave or a series of waves

of maritime intercourse. The only alternative is to
assume the independent origin of closely similar forms
in many different centres, but if this were the case,
there is no reason why some of these centres should not
have been situated in the interior of the continents, as
well as near the coasts.

Historical evidence as to the origin of these monuments is of course entirely lacking. The only source
of information is to be found in the monuments themselves, and it is only by studying the distribution of the
different types of monument and their contents that we
can form any idea as to their date, or as to who were
the builders of them.

Now the purpose of the megalithic structure is fairly
clear. The earliest and most typical monument is the
dolmen which is, without any shadow of doubt, a collective tomb. This fact dominates the whole development.
The megalithic culture was a religious movement, and it
centred in the cult of the dead. Its expansion was not
simply the spread of a certain fashion of building, it
involved the spread of religious ideas connected with
the service or placation of the dead. Those megalithic
monuments that are not tombs—for example, the stone
circle and the standing stone or menhir—are usually
found in connection with them. In fact the vast
majority of stone circles in the British Isles consist of an
enclosure surrounding a tomb, or containing interments.

It has frequently been maintained that the great
circles such as Stonehenge were connected with the
worship of the sun, and had some kind of equinoctial
orientation, and this is quite possible since we know
from Scandinavian evidence that the solar cult played
an important part in European religion during the
Bronze Age. But it is, of course, not safe to form any
conclusion from these later types as to the religion of
the earlier megalith builders.

So, too, the menhir is often found in connection with
a tomb, but it may have been an object of worship in

itself, since we know that the stone pillars or Masseboth, like the stone which Jacob set up at Bethel, played a great part in the religion of Palestine in historical times, as well as in Crete and perhaps in early Egypt. It is, however, quite possible, as we shall see, that both the stone circle and the menhir are due to later cultural influences than the dolmens or collective tombs which represent the earliest megalithic movement.

In Europe the Megalithic Culture as a whole belongs to the last phase of the neolithic period and to the Bronze Age. There is no sign of metal in the dolmens of Portugal, or in the early megalithic tombs of Northern Europe. Nevertheless, in some regions, such as Scotland and Ireland, the Megalithic Culture persisted much later, perhaps even as late as the Age of Iron. In the Western Mediterranean, apart from Malta, the megaliths appear to date from the beginnings of the age of metal. In the Caucasus they belong to the full Bronze Age, and in North Africa they are perhaps later still. On the other hand, in Palestine and Moab, they are held to date, as in Western Europe, from the later neolithic and earliest metal-using periods. The megalithic culture of Eastern Asia is undoubtedly later. In India it seems to date from the early Iron Age, and in Japan it actually touches the fringes of recorded history, for the tombs of the early Emperors who reigned between 200 B.C. and A.D. 600 are megalithic in type.

II. The Problem of its Origin. The Theory of its Connection with a Movement of Early Trade and Treasure-seeking

This chronological distribution has led many writers to believe that the source of the movement is to be looked for in North-western Europe, and that it was from the region of the Baltic that the movement spread in neolithic times to the Western Mediterranean, whence it was diffused during the age of metal to the east. But this view, which is based on the priority of the northern neolithic development, leaves out of sight the fact that the Copper Age in the Mediterranean was contemporary with the neolithic phase in Northern Europe. Moreover, it is very difficult to see how a movement originating in the Baltic could have passed through the higher cultures of the Near East, so as to reach Asia and the Pacific. Consequently, the general view, that has been held by Montelius, Sophus Müller, and Déchelette, looks to the Near East for the origin of the movement.[1] Certainly it is easier to explain the great expansion eastward into Asia and westward into Europe if the movement originated in a central position, as in the Near East, rather than at either of the extremities of the Old World. Now of the two great civilisations of the Near East, one of them, that of Babylonia, has obviously no links with the Megalithic Culture. The cult of the dead plays little part in its religion, though of course it was not lacking, for it is only in dying civilisations that men forget their dead. The graves were small and poor, and it was never the custom to use great stone slabs for building. But if we turn to Egypt the case is different. There we see a civilisation in which the cult of the dead was all-important, where infinite thought and labour were lavished on the construction of vast tombs, and where finally the practice of building with great monolithic slabs was highly developed. Moreover, the mastaba, the typical Egyptian tomb of the Pyramid Age, has considerable resemblances to the dolmen. It was a rectangular structure, built originally of brick, but in the Age of the Pyramids of great stone blocks. It consisted of a mortuary chapel, and an inner chamber containing an image of the deceased, which were connected not by a

[1] This view is now generally accepted by Scandinavian archæologists. Thus G. Ekholm writes : " The stone chamber-tombs are to be regarded as barbaric imitations of the great oriental tombs which spread from people to people, along the coasts of North Africa and Western Europe to the North."—*R.V.G.*, vol. ix, p. 36.

doorway, but by a small round opening in the partition slab. These have been compared by many writers to the passage of the megalithic grave and the inner chamber. Moreover, in many parts of the world in India, the Caucasus, and North-west Europe, the partition slab of the dolmen, or cist, is perforated by a round hole, like that of the inner chamber of the Egyptian tomb. Curiously enough, however, the closest parallel to the Egyptian tomb comes from the farthest limit of the Megalithic Culture—from St. Christoval in the Solomon Islands, where mummification is practised, and the megalithic tomb contains, as in Egypt, a statue of the deceased.

Starting from these parallels Professor Elliot Smith and Mr. Perry have put forward an elaborate theory which derives not only the megalithic culture, but all the ancient forms of civilisation from direct Egyptian influence. They believe that the megalithic remains are due to the activity of expeditions sent out from Egypt in the time of the Old Kingdom to seek for gold and pearls and precious stones which were required for the service of the dead. Thus Mr. Perry thinks the Long Barrows on the English downs may be the tombs of ancient Egyptian nobles who travelled to these shores in search of amber or gold.

In this extreme form the theory seems quite impossible to accept, for some traces of Egyptian influence, such as we find in the tombs of Crete and the Cyclades—seals, scarabs, palettes, stone vases, and so forth,—would surely have been found in the megalithic monuments. Actually we have no evidence that Egyptian sailors ever went west of Crete, or east of Aden, and there is hardly any trace of the influence of the Egyptian civilisation in any part of the western megalithic area.[1]

---

[1] In the Bronze Age, however, signs of Egyptian influence do seem to make their appearance in Northern Europe, such as a curved sword of Egyptian type from Sweden, and the folding stool found at Guldhöi in Denmark, as well as the cult of the Sun Disk, and the sacred barque which is associated with it. Cf. *R.V.G.*, vol. ix, p. 73.

The culture of the Portuguese and Danish dolmen builders appears to be purely neolithic; there is no sign in their tombs of the knowledge of metal or of any connections with the civilisation of the Near East.[1]

Nevertheless, it is also difficult to believe in the independent development of the Megalithic Culture in neolithic Portugal or Denmark. As we have already noticed, peoples of primitive culture seldom originate new ideas; they are far more likely to borrow them from the more advanced peoples. On the other hand, the religious beliefs and practices of the higher cultures spread almost automatically among their more primitive neighbours, as we have seen in the case of the religion of the Mother Goddess in Western Asia, and the peasant neolithic cultures of Eastern Europe. Moreover, the distribution of the Megalithic Culture differs in a remarkable way from that of any primitive culture that we know. It suggests not a racial migration or a wave of warlike invasion, but rather a movement of maritime colonisation like that of the ancient Phœnicians or the modern Portuguese. Thus the latter movement has left its traces along the shores of Africa and the coasts and islands of the Indian and Pacific Oceans, choosing the regions that were rich in gold or spices or trade, and never penetrating far into the interior.

Now the megalith builders of prehistoric Europe followed a similar line of expansion. The situation of the early megaliths in Portugal, especially at the mouth of the Tagus, is just where we should expect to find them, if they were due to the influence of traders coming by sea. Ancient Portugal was rich in valuable

[1] It is true that a dolmen at Alvão, one of the earliest groups of Portuguese megaliths, yielded a remarkable discovery in the form of a collection of stones, engraved with figures of animals and alphabetic signs, as well as inscribed schist tablets. These were at the time generally condemned as forgeries, but the recent discovery at Glozel, near Vichy, of large quantities of engraved stones and clay tablets, inscribed with what appears to be alphabetic writing, has drawn fresh attention to the earlier discovery. Unfortunately the authenticity of the Glozel remains is itself extremely dubious.

metals, especially gold. And the same is true of the other centres of the Megalithic Culture in the west, Denmark, Ireland, and Brittany. We know that the amber of Jutland and the gold of Ireland were being sought for and used in very early times, certainly before the end of the third millennium. And the distribution of the earliest megalithic remains closely follows the maritime trade route that connects the Spanish peninsula with Ireland and the Baltic. The Danish dolmens cluster thickly round the amber coast, and are absent in the centre and on the opposite shore. In Brittany they are most numerous on the south coast, and centre on the great estuary of Morbihan and Quiberon Bay, a district which is said to have produced both gold and tin in early times. The Breton tombs are, moreover, especially rich in a kind of turquoise, called callais, which was perhaps found locally, though it no longer exists anywhere in Europe at present, and beads of this substance are found in megalithic monuments throughout Western Europe, in Spain and Portugal, in Southern France, thus giving additional evidence of prehistoric trade.

Great Britain may have acquired the Megalithic Culture simply owing to its geographical situation on the trade route between Ireland and Brittany, and Ireland and Denmark. That is certainly the impression we get from the distribution of the monuments which lie all along the western coasts, while the importance of Salisbury Plain and the southern Cotswolds would be due to a land route from Southampton Water to Milford Haven, which would avoid the long and dangerous sea passage round Cornwall.

The later megalithic monuments of the south-west of Devon and Cornwall in the same way may be connected with the rise of tin mining and the tin trade during the early Bronze Age.

It is true that the megalithic tombs show few signs of advanced culture, and in particular are almost entirely lacking in metals such as copper and gold, which we should expect to find in the graves of traders and prospectors. On the other hand, it must be remembered that collective tombs of the megalithic type are exceptionally easy to rob and have in most cases been repeatedly opened in ancient and medieval times. The great tombs of the Bronze Age in Ireland and Scotland are as barren of valuable contents as the early dolmens, although there can be little doubt that the chieftains of that period were buried with a rich treasure. The more prominent the tomb, the more was it exposed to plunder. Even to-day in West Africa it has been found necessary to set a guard upon the riches of buried chieftains as in the case of the Olu of Aworo in Nigeria, who was buried in 1895, and whose tomb is still guarded.[1]

Hence the actual poverty of the megalithic tombs is not a sufficient reason for denying the possibility of a prehistoric movement of trade and treasure-seeking, in which the Megalithic Culture had its origin. It is, however, difficult to suppose that such a movement could have had its origin among the dolmen builders of Portugal, for the culture of neolithic Portugal is much too poor and isolated to have been the source of a movement of world-wide importance.

It is rather in the Western Mediterranean, with its richer tradition of culture and its wider opportunities of contact with the centres of ancient culture in the Near East, that we may hope to find some key to the origin of the megalithic development.

III. THE MEGALITHIC CULTURE IN MALTA AND THE MEDITERRANEAN

The islands and coasts of the Western Mediterranean from Southern France to North Africa are extraordinarily rich in megalithic remains of every type dating from neolithic times down to the Iron Age. Moreover,

[1] Cf. C. K. Meek, *The Northern Tribes of Nigeria*, vol. ii, p. 126.

it is the one region which shows parallels alike with the early development of the Megalithic Culture in Western Europe, and with the later extension of the movement in South-eastern Asia. Apart from the common types of dolmens, stone circles, and menhirs, we have on the one hand the Giants' Graves of Sardinia, which find a parallel in the horned cairns of Northern Scotland, and, at the other end of the series, the round flat-topped stone tombs of North Africa, which resemble in form the similar structures of the modern megalith builders of the Naga territory in Assam. So, too, the semi-megalithic dry-stone architecture of the Western Mediterranean islands finds a parallel in the same opposite regions. The Sardinian Nuraghi resemble the Brochs of the Orkneys, while the Talayots of the Balearic Islands seem to correspond with the Dahus or solid stone towers which are used as tribal strongholds in Assam.

It is true that these features belong to the latest phases of the megalithic development, and in some parts of the Western Mediterranean, e.g. in North Africa, the bulk of the remains appear not to be earlier than the Iron Age. Nevertheless, the megalithic tradition in the Western Mediterranean culture certainly goes back to very ancient times, and, in contrast to the other regions of Western Europe, its highest development is also the earliest in date.

The chief example in the Mediterranean of a mega-lithic culture which is neolithic in character is to be found in the little islands of Malta and Gozo, which contain an extraordinary wealth of megalithic remains of an exceptionally interesting type. In addition to the dolmens and stone circles, such as are common to other regions of megalithic culture, there are great stone buildings and subterranean structures which have no parallels elsewhere. The former are sanctuaries or temples, consisting of a succession of large oval chambers, and passages, built of great stone slabs, and wholly or partially roofed by corbel vaulting. The apse is usually separated from the body of the hall by a stone screen and contains the shrines which consist of small dolmen-like stone tables, set in a niche or recess of the wall, and within them stands a conical stone pillar or betyl which was no doubt an object of worship.[1]

The great subterranean temple or mausoleum of Hal Saflieni on Gozo, on the other hand, is hewn out of the living rock, but it imitates the forms of a megalithic building, with door posts and lintel cut in high relief.

No less remarkable than the architecture of these structures is the art that accompanies them. The slabs and altar stones are often decorated with carved or painted spiral ornaments or with reliefs depicting rows of animals, goats, pigs, and oxen. There are numerous statuettes, and one large statue 7 feet in height, of human figures of an extraordinary corpulence, which recall the female figures of palæolithic times.

The pottery is very abundant and far surpasses that of the other regions of megalithic culture in fineness and in decoration. There is an extraordinary variety of types, including a fine polished ware with incised curvilinear ornament, and a painted ware with red lines on a pink slip. Maltese pottery shows considerable resemblances to that of Southern Italy and the islands, especially Sicily, and it is probable that it owes something to the influence of the Painted Pottery Culture of Eastern Europe which had reached South-eastern Italy (Matera) from across the Adriatic, and had thence extended its influence to Eastern Sicily.

The Maltese spiral ornament in particular seems to be derived from this source rather than from the Ægean, though in both cases it had a common origin in Eastern Europe. The native Western Mediterranean element, however, predominates, and Maltese civilisation as a whole finds its closest affinities in Sardinia, where

---

[1] Similar betyls are used as objects of worship and fertility charms among many primitive peoples, especially the Naga tribes of Assam.

not only the types of pottery, but also the style of megalithic architecture appear to point to a common tradition.

But it is not possible to derive the Maltese culture from that of Sardinia, for the latter is wholly post-neolithic, and though the later phases of the neolithic period in Malta may correspond with the æneolithic period in Sardinia, its beginnings must be much earlier. The distribution of the Megalithic Culture in the Western Mediterranean shows that it spread from the south northwards, for it appears to have reached the Balearic Islands later than Sardinia, and Sardinia later than Malta. On the other hand, it is impossible to derive the Megalithic Culture of Malta from that of Portugal, on account of the striking difference between the two cultures and the absence of intermediate links in Southern and Eastern Spain. The independent development of the Megalithic Culture in the Iberian Peninsula and in the Western Mediterranean might seem to suggest a common source for the two movements in North Africa, an origin which would explain the curious way in which the culture passes northward in two streams by Portugal up the Atlantic coast and by Malta to Sardinia and the Balearic Islands, without touching Eastern Spain on the one side or Sicily on the other. There are, however, serious objections to a North African origin, for though that region is rich in megalithic monuments, they apparently date for the most part from the Iron Age, while all evidence for the existence of the Megalithic Culture in neolithic times is as yet completely lacking.

The only remaining alternative is that the Megalithic Culture reached Western Europe by sea from an eastern source whether in Egypt or elsewhere. This would explain the importance of Malta which offers exceptional advantages to a sea-going people by reason of its small size, its good harbours, and its great fertility, so that it has on more than one occasion been occupied by strangers who had no connection with the surrounding regions.

The ultimate source of the Megalithic Culture, however, remains a mystery.   There are slight traces of megalithic influence in the Eastern Mediterranean, in the Tholos tombs of South Crete, which have been attributed to settlers from the Egyptian Delta, and in Egypt itself in the form of what appears to be a true dolmen inside a brick tomb of predynastic date at Hierakonpolis,[1] but the appearance of this isolated example in Egypt long before the age of the Mastaba tomb is adverse rather than favourable to the main argument of those who have asserted the claims of Egypt to be the source of the Megalithic Culture.

There remains one other possible region of origin for the Megalithic Culture—the Arabian Peninsula.   From a purely geographical point of view this would be the most satisfactory solution of the problem, for, with Egypt, it is the only region which occupies a central position which would link the western with the eastern expansion of the Megalithic Culture.   In India the latter appears in just that region—the South-western Deccan—which has been in trading relations with the Arabian Peninsula from the earliest historical times. Moreover, as we have seen in Chapter IV, Eastern Arabia was the home of a sea-going people who were in relations not only with Mesopotamia, but also with the Red Sea and possibly with Egypt, as far back as the Sumerian period.   Even in the Mediterranean itself the distribution of the Megalithic Culture follows much the same path of expansion as did the later movements of Semitic Culture in the West, i.e. the Phœnicians in classical times and the Arabs in the early Middle Ages ; whereas the earliest metal-using cultures of the West appear in regions such as Sicily and South-east Italy, which were always the first to be affected by movements which had their source in Anatolia and the Ægean, for instance, the expansion of the Ionian Greeks and that of

[1] Cf. E. Baumgärtel, *Dolmen und Mastaba*, 1926.   This writer is in favour of a North African origin for the Megalithic Culture.

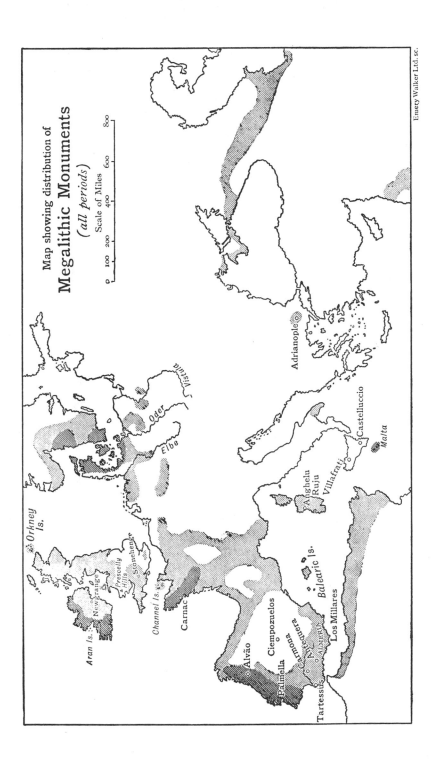

Map showing distribution of
Megalithic Monuments
(all periods)

Scale of Miles

0 100 200   400   600   800

Emery Walker Ltd. sc.

Orkney Is.

Vistula

Oder

Elbe

Aran Is.

Newgrange

Prescelly Hills

Stonehenge

Channel Is.

Carnac

Adrianople

Castelluccio

Malta

Anghelu Ruju

Villafrati

Balearic Is.

Alvão

Palmella

Ciempozuelos

Carmona

Antequera

ALMERIA

Los Millares

Tartessus

the Byzantine Culture in the sixth century A.D.   Nevertheless, there is at present no satisfactory evidence for
the existence of megalithic monuments in the Arabian
Peninsula,[1] though it is rendered probable by the
presence of the neighbouring North Arabian Megalithic
Culture of the region north-east of the Dead Sea. Consequently until the eastern and southern parts of the
peninsula are opened to archæological research, the
theory of an Arabian origin for the Megalithic Culture
must remain, like all the rest, a pure hypothesis.   We
can retain as certain only the significant fact of the
existence of two distinct movements of prehistoric
culture which followed a path of maritime expansion.
One of these, the Æneolithic Culture, undoubtedly had
its source in the Ægean ; the other, the Megalithic
Culture, is of uncertain origin : but both finally met and
blended with one another in the Western Mediterranean
and the Iberian Peninsula, which is the starting-point
of a new development in western culture.

   [1] The tumuli of the Bahrein Islands, which have been recently
investigated, belong to the Bronze Age and are semi-megalithic in
type, like the chambered tumuli of Scotland.   They possess, however,
the peculiarity of a two-storied chamber.

CHAPTER X

SPAIN AND THE LATER DEVELOPMENT OF THE MEGALITHIC CULTURE IN WESTERN EUROPE

THE CULTURE OF THE IBERIAN PENINSULA AT THE DAWN OF THE AGE OF METAL.

THE BELL-BEAKER PEOPLE OF SPAIN AND THEIR ORIGINS.

EAST MEDITERRANEAN INFLUENCES ON THE ÆNEOLITHIC CULTURE OF THE WEST.

THE NORTHERN EXPANSION OF THE BELL-BEAKER PEOPLE.

 (a) BRITTANY.

 (b) THE RHINELAND AND GREAT BRITAIN. THE ROUND BARROW PEOPLE.

THE CULTURE OF IRELAND IN THE BRONZE AGE AND ITS IBERIAN CONNECTIONS.

THE SURVIVAL OF THE MEGALITHIC CULTURE IN LATER TIMES.

CHAPTER X

SPAIN AND THE LATER DEVELOPMENT OF THE MEGALITHIC CULTURE IN WESTERN EUROPE

I. The Culture of the Iberian Peninsula at the Dawn of the Age of Metal

WITH the beginning of the Age of Metal the Megalithic Culture of the West enters on a new phase. Its great development, not only in Spain and Sardinia, but also in France, and above all in Brittany, undoubtedly falls within this period, which we may date approximately to the second half of the third millennium.[1] The starting-point of the movement and its centre of highest development is to be found in Spain, but it was largely due to new influences which did not originate within the domain of the earlier Megalithic Culture. For the latter was far from being characteristic of the Iberian Peninsula as a whole in neolithic times; it was confined to Portugal, or rather to certain districts of Portugal. The greater part of Spain, including the south and the whole of the central plateau, still belonged to the old indigenous culture, which had its roots far back in palæolithic times, as is shown by the continuity of artistic tradition which links the neolithic population of Central Spain with their predecessors of the later Capsian period. Like the latter, the neolithic population still lived, and buried their dead, in caves. The only sign of progress is to be found in their pottery which is decorated with incised patterns or with ornament in relief. On the other hand, the tradition of stone work was decadent, and even flint is rare. This Cave Culture, as it

---

[1] Dr. H. Schmidt dates it considerably higher, while Mr. V. Gordon Childe prefers a later date, 2200–1700 B.C.

is called, undoubtedly represents the native tradition of
Iberian culture, and the megalith builders appear only
on its western borders, as one might expect if they were
an intrusive element which reached Spain from without.

Similarly in the south-east we find another culture
of a much more advanced type established on the
Mediterrancan coast in Almeria.   The people were
agriculturalists who lived in fortified villages, and buried
their dead not in megalithic tombs, but in stone-lined
trenches or cists, or, like the people of the centre, in caves
and rock shelters.   The geographical range of this
culture is very restricted, it is in fact little more than a
coastal colony.   But in spite of this, it had an enormous
influence on the development of Spanish culture, for it
was the link that connected Spain with the higher culture
of the Mediterranean world, and the channel through
which the knowledge of metal first reached the peninsula.

The source of this movement is probably to be found
in the great expansion of the maritime and trading
culture of the Ægean, which has been described in a
previous chapter, and which also affected Sicily and
Sardinia at about the same time; for not only is gold
plentiful, but there are numerous ornaments of ivory,
beads of ostrich egg-shell, and a carved hippopotamus
tusk, which point to trading relations with the East.
The progress of culture in Almeria at this period is seen
in the settlement of Los Millares, on the River Andarax,
with its elaborate system of fortification, its stone-built
houses, and its rough aqueduct which supplied the settlement with water.   The tombs are now quite different
from those of neolithic times and consist of rock-hewn
chambers, of a similar type to those of Sicily, and above
all of megalithic tombs with a corridor and a circular
chamber of beehive shape with corbel vaulting.

This advance of civilisation led to a rapid expansion
of the Almerian culture.   It extended northwards to
Catalonia and the Eastern Pyrenees, and southward
to Grenada and Andalucia.   At the same time there

PLATE I.—IBERIAN AND WEST EUROPEAN TYPES

(From the British Museum)

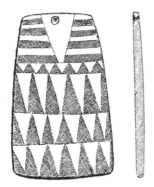

FIG. 1.—Engraved slate idol or
amulet from Portugal (¼).

FIG. 2.—Bell Beaker of Spanish
type from Carnac, Brittany (⅓).

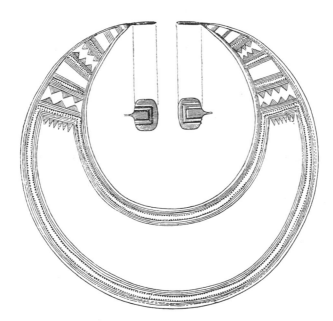

FIG. 3.—Gold Lunula of Irish Type from Carnarvonshire (⅓).

was a great development of the Megalithic Culture of
Portugal. It probably derived its knowledge of metal
from Almeria, but there are also a few signs of contact
with the Eastern Mediterranean, such as the bone knob
found at Nora which resembles those of Troy, and the
segmented beads of Early Minoan type discovered at
Palmella. The native tradition of art is represented
by curious schist plaques or idols, elaborately decorated
with geometrical patterns,[1] and the so-called " croziers."
The latter resemble in form the curved staff or lituus
which was a sacred emblem throughout Western
Asia from Babylonia to Anatolia, but they are made of
schist and ornamented in the same way as the plaques.

Megalithic architecture in Portugal now attained its
highest development, but in addition to the great
megalithic corridor tombs, we find rock-cut chambers
and vaulted cupola tombs of the same type as those of
Almeria. The centre of the development lay in Southern
Portugal, from the region of Lisbon to Cape St. Vincent
and the coast of Algarve. But from Portugal it expanded on the one hand northward through Galicia to
Asturias and the Pyrenees, and on the other eastward
into Western Spain and southward to Andalucia,
where it met and mingled with the advanced province
of the Almerian culture.

II. The Bell-Beaker People of Spain and their Origins

Thus the æneolithic period witnessed a general
transformation of cultural conditions in the Iberian
Peninsula. The two outlying provinces of Iberian
culture in Portugal and Almeria were encroaching on
the domain of the primitive cave-dwellers of the centre,
and were mingling with one another to form a common
civilisation which embraced the whole of the southern
part of the peninsula from Lisbon to Cartagena. Each
of the older cultures contributed its share to the new

---

[1] See Plate I, fig. 1.

development. From the West came the tradition of megalithic architecture, from the East the knowledge of metal, while the type of pottery which is characteristic of the period—the so-called Bell-Beaker ware—developed out of the native tradition of the Spanish cave-dwellers. This common civilisation had its centre in Southern Spain in the provinces of Andalucia and Grenada. The importance of this region is shown by the magnificent tombs, especially those in the neighbourhood of Antequera and Seville, which are perhaps the finest examples of megalithic architecture in Europe. For the most part they consist of cupola tombs surmounted by a great artificial tumulus, but there are also examples of the older type of megalithic tombs, such as the Cueva da Menga at Antequera, the entrance of which is covered by a single slab which is said to weigh no less than 170 tons.[1] The same region, especially the district of Carmona and Ecija, seems to have been the centre of origin of the Bell-Beaker pottery, which is so typical of this civilisation, and of such vast importance for the chronology of prehistoric culture.[2] For its diffusion marks the coming of new cultural influences not only in the Spanish Peninsula itself, but throughout Western and Central Europe from Brittany to the Theiss, and from Sicily to the Rhineland and Thuringia. In the Western Mediterranean the Beakers are characteristic of the earliest phases of the Megalithic Culture of Southern France, and they are also found sporadically in Sardinia, Sicily, and North Italy, especially at Remedello, near Brescia, and to the northwards. In Central Europe the most important groups are situated in Bohemia and Moravia, in Thuringia and Saxony, and on the Middle Rhine ; but they also occur in small numbers on the Danube, in Bavaria and Austria ; on the Oder, in Silesia ; in the north, in

[1] Cf. E. T. Leeds, " The Dolmens and Megalithic Tombs of Spain and Portugal," *Archæologia*, vol. lxx, p. 201.
[2] Cf. Plate I, fig. 2, and Plate II.

Holland and Denmark, and as far east as the region of Budapest and Szenthes on the Theiss. And this remarkable diffusion was not merely due to trade and culture contact, for with the Beaker pottery we find in many cases the remains of a broad-headed type of man which often contrasts with the physical type of the earlier population of the region in question. The importance of this movement in the history of European culture can hardly be overestimated, for it suggests that the dawn of the Age of Metal in Western and Central Europe is to be attributed, at least in part, to the coming of a new people who brought with them the knowledge of the use and working of metals, and who were the first to break down the natural barriers that had separated the cultures of Central Europe from those of the Western Mediterranean and the Atlantic.

Now even at the present day there are traces throughout Western Europe of the existence of a tall, dark, broad-headed population, resembling the Armenoid, or rather Dinaric type. They occur round the head of the Adriatic, and at several points in the Western Mediterranean ; on the coasts of Spain and in Western France, especially in Brittany ; in Devon and Cornwall, the west coast of Wales and the east coast of Ireland ; in the extreme north of Scotland, and the Shetlands and the Hebrides, and finally on the south-west coast of Norway. This distribution corresponds to a great extent with that of the megalithic monuments, and it is explained by Mr. Harold Peake and Professor Fleure as being due to the coming of traders and " prospectors " from Asia Minor or the Ægean in the Early Bronze Age, following the route of the expansion of the earlier Megalithic Culture. Judging from the comparative richness of their graves in gold and amber and other precious substances, as well as from their physical type, and also to some extent from their distribution, the Beaker People have a good claim to be considered as " prospectors " of this type, and if so, it would seem that the

origin of the movement is to be looked for in Spain
rather than in the Eastern Mediterranean.   The problem
of the origin of the Beaker Culture is, however, a very
complex one.   Although there is a small minority of
brachycephalic types among the skulls of mesolithic
date discovered at Mugem in Portugal, the Spanish
Peninsula has always been characterised by the pro-
nounced long-headedness of its population.   In late
neolithic and early mesolithic times, not only the
megalith builders of Portugal and the people of Almeria,
but also the cave-dwellers of the interior were all, so
far as we know, dolichocephalic.   The brachycephalic
element makes its appearance together with the Beaker
pottery at the time of the great expansion of Spanish
civilisation that we have described.   Unfortunately
the great cupola tombs of Almeria have yielded no
human remains, but at Ciempozuelos in Central Spain
brachycephalic skulls have been discovered in association with Beakers, and a certain number also occur in
Portugal and Catalonia.

III. East Mediterranean Influences on the Æneo-lithic Culture of the West

Now if the appearance of this brachycephalic element
in the Iberian population were due to the coming of a
new people from the Eastern Mediterranean, it would
fully explain the sudden advance of Spanish civilisation
at this epoch and the traces of foreign influence which
are so plentiful, especially on the south-west coast.
Even those elements in the Æneolithic Culture which are
most characteristic of the local development are not
irreconcilable with this hypothesis.   For while the new
types of tomb—the rock-cut chamber and the beehive
vault—can, on the one hand, be explained as a natural
evolution of the old megalithic tradition, they also have
their parallels in the Eastern Mediterranean, and they
appear in the West not only in Southern Spain, but
also in Almeria and in Sicily—regions where the true

Megalithic Culture never penetrated. And the same types reappear independently in Italy at a much later period under the influence of a new wave of oriental culture—that of the Etruscans. Similarly the Beaker ware, in spite of its native Iberian antecedents, may well have been taken over and developed by the new-comers, as the Etruscans took over the native Italian pottery of the Iron Age and developed it into their characteristic Bucchero ware.

Moreover, the hypothesis of an East Mediterranean element in South Spanish culture finds some support in the later tradition of the region. In early historical times, the valley of the Guadalquivir, which had been the focus of the Beaker Culture, was the seat of the flourishing kingdom of Tartessus, which was known to the Greeks as the wealthiest and most civilised state of the barbarian West. It was here in the region of Gades that Plato placed the centre of the kingdom of the sons of Poseidon, Atlas and Gadiros, who ruled the vanished western world of Atlantis, as well as all the Western Mediterranean as far as Etruria and Libya; and though the whole story is a typical Platonic myth, it is not improbable that it had its foundation in some vague tradition that recalled the prosperity of the Western Bronze Age, when the influence of the South Spanish culture extended from Sardinia and Italy on the one hand, to Ireland and Brittany on the other. We know, in fact, that such traditions of the antiquity of the Tartessian culture did exist in classical times, for later Greek writers record that the Turdetani (as the people of Tartessus were called in post-Carthaginian times) were the only people of the West to possess a written literature, and an historical tradition which claimed to go back for thousands of years [1]; indeed the Tartessian

---

[1] Strabo writes: "They have an alphabet, and possess ancient writings, poems and metrical laws six thousand years old, as they say. The other Iberians also have an alphabet, but of a different form, nor do they speak the same language."—*Geog.* III, p. 139.

monarchy, like that of ancient Egypt and Japan, derived its origin from the Sun God. The very name of Tartessus suggests an East Mediterranean origin, for it is a typical example of the names terminating in " -essus," which we have seen to be characteristic of the early population of the Ægean and Southern Asia Minor before the Hellenic period, while the similarity of the root to that of Tarsus in Cilicia has often led to confusion between the two places.[1]

But apart from these arguments, it seems impossible to deny the existence of Ægean influences in the culture of the Western Mediterranean during the æneolithic period. For the culture of the Spanish province does not stand alone. It finds a close parallel in the contemporary developments in Sardinia and Sicily. There also the beginning of the Age of Metal is marked by the appearance of new types of tomb, especially the collective interments of the rock-cut chamber tombs, such as Anghelu Ruju in Sardinia and Casteluccio in Sicily, and by new types of pottery and ornament which find their prototypes in the Ægean area. The rise of the new culture is accompanied in Sardinia, as in Spain, by the appearance of a brachycephalic minority in the population, amounting, in the case of the remains found in the tombs of Anghelu Ruju, to about 20 per cent. of the total. A close relation between the Spanish and the Sardinian cultures is proved by the occurrence both at Anghelu Ruju and elsewhere of Beaker

---

[1] There are no signs of Asiatic influence in the remains that we possess of the languages of the Iberians of the historical period, which appear to be connected with the Hamitic Berber linguistic group. On the other hand, the one primitive language of the peninsula, which has survived down to modern times, that of the Basques, in spite of the Hamitic affinities of its vocabulary, possesses a remarkable resemblance to the Caucasian languages in conjugation and grammatical peculiarities. It is, however, impossible to say whether this resemblance, if it is more than fortuitous, is due to the influence of the " Sea Peoples " of the Bronze Age or the æneolithic period, or to that of a prehistoric extension of the Caucasian languages through Continental Europe. Cf. Pokorny, art. " Iberer " in *R.V.G.*, and the literature cited there.

pottery,[1] while on the other hand the flat marble idols of
the Cycladic type, and the carved reliefs of bulls' heads
and high-prowed boats found on the pillars and walls of
one of the Anghelu Ruju tombs, point clearly to contact
with the Ægean. The Sardinian development also
resembles that of Spain in the combination of new
cultural elements with the old western megalithic
tradition, a combination which is characteristic of the
culture of Sardinia throughout the Bronze Age.   Side by
side with the rock-cut tombs, we find the remarkable
megalithic structures, known as " Tombs of the Giants,"
which consist of a long corbel-vaulted chamber closed
by a great stone slab with a perforation in its lower
part, and flanked by a carved façade, terminating in
two projecting horns.   Even more characteristic of the
Bronze Age culture of Sardinia are the Nuraghi, the
massive stone fortresses which occupy almost every
strategic point in the island, and which consist of a
conical two-storied tower, sometimes standing alone,
sometimes fortified by outworks and bastions.

These were the strongholds of the prehistoric chieftains whose bodies were buried in the Giants' Tombs,
and they rise above the stone huts of the village of which
they almost always form the centre, like the keep of a
Norman noble among the dwellings of his serfs.   It is
impossible to say whether their construction was due
to the existence of a foreign ruling class like the Etruscans, which dominated the native population, or to the
prevalence of local feuds, or to the need of defending
the island against the piratical attacks of foreign raiders
from the sea ; but in any case it shows the essentially
warlike nature of the Sardinian culture, in contrast

---

[1] This connection is also reflected in classical tradition according to
which Sardinia was first occupied by settlers from Spain under the
leadership of Norax, the grandson of Geryon King of Tartessus
(Pausanias, x. 17 ; Solinus, iv. 1).   According to Sgr. Pettazzoni, Norax
is to be identified with Sardus Pater, the god and eponymous ancestor
of the Sardinian people, and the name is connected with Nora and
with Nuraghe.

to the predominantly peaceful character of the earlier
type of Megalithic Culture which we find at Malta.
It is maintained by the Italian archæologists, especially
Sgr. Taramelli, the chief authority on the nuraghic
civilisation, that the Sardinian people of the Bronze
Age are to be identified with the Shardana, " The People
of the Sea," who play such a large part in the history
of Egypt under the Nineteenth Dynasty as foreign
mercenaries and piratical raiders, and this view is
supported not only by the warlike character of the
population, but also by the resemblance of the Sardinian types of armour and weapons with those shown
in the representation of Shardana mercenaries in
Egyptian art.   If this be so, it will be necessary to take
account of the possibility of Western Mediterranean
influences in the culture of the Ægean world during the
later Mycenæan period.

IV. The Northern Expansion of the Bell-Beaker People

(a) Brittany

But the chief importance of Western Mediterranean
civilisation lay in the opposite direction along the
line of expansion of Megalithic Culture to Western and
North-western Europe, where it was the source of the
whole later development of the Western Bronze Age.
The æneolithic Spanish culture of the Beaker period
expanded, on the one hand, through Catalonia into South-
eastern France, and on the other, probably by way of
Portugal and the sea, to the Channel Islands and
Brittany, where its appearance is contemporary with
the great development of megalithic architecture in
Morbihan.   The importance of this region is no doubt
due to its having been the meeting-point of the trade
route from the Mediterranean with those to the north-
west, and the contents of the Breton tombs, such as the
stone battle-axes and above all the collared flask found

FIG. 1.—" Bell Beaker " from Pest, Hungary.

FIG. 2.—" Corded Beaker " of Thuringian type from Germany.

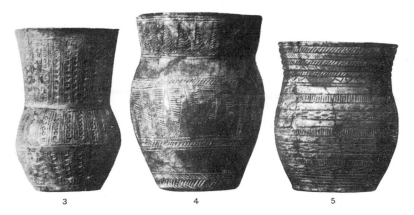

3

4

5

FIGS. 3, 4, 5.—Typical Beaker Pottery of the Round Barrow People in Britain.

at Lann-Blaen, point clearly to a connection with the Baltic. The existence of relations between Southern Scandinavia and the Iberian Peninsula is proved on the one hand by the presence of amber in the tombs of the æneolithic period alike in Portugal and Almeria, and on the other by the signs of Mediterranean influence in the pottery and flint work of the Megalithic Culture of the Baltic. This influence goes back at least as early as the beginning of the period of the passage-graves, which is possibly as early as the rise of the Beaker Culture. Indeed, one of the leading Scandinavian archæologists—Sophus Müller—has recently declared that the great development of prehistoric Scandinavian pottery in the megalithic period is based on loans from the Mediterranean civilisation.[1]   But the most remarkable examples date from the end of the passage-grave-period, when the decoration of the pottery is in some cases almost identical with that of specimens from Los Millares in Almeria.

In spite of its close relations with the Baltic and also, no doubt, with the British Isles, Brittany, or rather the Channel Islands, seems to have been the farthest point which the Beaker people reached in their north-western expansion from Spain.

(b) The Rhineland and Great Britain. The Round Barrow People

The appearance of the Beaker Culture in Great Britain was due to a later movement which had its source, not in the Iberian Peninsula, but in the Rhineland which was one of the most important centres of the expansion of the Beaker People in Central Europe. Here they had come into contact with the vanguard of the Nordic warrior peoples who were penetrating into South-western Germany from Thuringia, as well as with the Alpine people of the Lake-dwelling Culture who

---

[1] S. Müller in *Mémoires de la Société des Antiquaires du Nord*, N.S., 1920–24, pp. 207–94.

were spreading down the Rhine from the south. The
Rhineland was the crucible in which these different
elements met and were mingled together, and from the
fusion there arose not only a new culture, but a new race,
broad-headed like the Southern Beaker People, but with
the heavy build and strongly marked brow ridges of the
Northerners. Socially and culturally the southern
element seems to have been the predominant one, and
their subsequent history shows that they continued
the earlier tradition of the Spanish " prospectors."
This is the type usually known to English archæologists
as the Beaker People ; but in order to avoid confusion
with the original people who brought the Beaker
Culture with them from Spain, it is better to give them
the name of the Round Barrow People, from their
characteristic mode of interment. Their rugged features,
square jaws, and powerful frames must have given them
a formidable appearance, and they inherited equally
the warlike character of their Nordic ancestors and the
adventurousness and enterprise of the Beaker People
from the south.

From their original centre on the Middle Rhine this
people expanded rapidly to the north and west. They
penetrated northwards as far as Denmark, where they
are known as the Borreby type, and north-westward
to Holland. But their most important expansion was
across the seas. They took ship from the mouth of the
Rhine or from North Holland and crossed the North
Sea to Britain. This was, so far as we know, the first
warlike invasion of these islands, the inauguration of
that long series of foreign conquests—Celtic, Saxon,
Danish, and Norman—which has moulded British
history. Both in England and Scotland, their tumulus
graves and their peculiar type of pottery which is due
to the fusion of the Spanish Bell-Beaker type with the
Corded Ware (Schnurkeramik) of the Thuringian Battle-
Axe People, are found all along the eastern coasts.[1]

[1] Cf. Plate II.

They seem to have landed at a number of different points, in the estuaries of the Thames, the Wash, and the Humber, and all along the east coast of Scotland, whence they spread inland by different routes, driving the megalithic people before them, as far as Derbyshire, the Upper Thames, and Salisbury Plain. All over Eastern Britain they became the dominant racial element of the early Bronze Age, so that their invasion of this country, unlike that of Denmark, where their graves are few and scattered, must have been a migration on a large scale. They brought with them into Britain the use of metal, for the earliest bronze and copper weapons have very much the same distribution as that of their graves and their Beaker pottery. Moreover, they developed some skill in metal-working, and through them Britain had a considerable influence on the early phases of the Bronze Age in Germany and Northern Europe. This explains the link that exists between the types of weapons, etc., in England and those in Central Europe, whereas the Early Metal Age in Ireland remained under the influence of the West Mediterranean and Iberian culture.

Nevertheless the Round Barrow People seem to have been in close relations with Ireland and the western megalithic area. Indeed, they themselves adopted the Megalithic Culture in a modified form, and it is to them that we must attribute the most famous of all megalithic monuments, the great circle of Stonehenge.[1] The latter differs from the other megalithic monuments of the British Isles in the advanced style of its masonry, for the blocks are carefully trimmed and the lintels of the trilithons are fastened to their supports with tenons and mortices. The monument is probably contemporary with the great cemetery of Round Barrows which lies around it, and on the neighbouring Normanton Down. These are typical examples of the interments of the invading people from the Continent, and belong for the

[1] See, however, p. 232, note 2.

most part to the Early Bronze Age. It is true that there is no trace of the use of bronze tools in the building of Stonehenge, but at that period metal was far too precious to be used for masons' work. On the other hand, Stonehenge possesses obvious relations with the older Megalithic Culture of the West, for Dr. Thomas of the Geological Survey has shown that the so-called " foreign stones " which form a smaller circle inside the ring of trilithons are composed of a variety of stones which are peculiar to the district of the Prescelly Hills in Pembrokeshire. This is a region exceptionally rich in stone circles and other megalithic monuments, and the stones must have been transported with enormous labour all the way from the south-western extremity of Wales to Salisbury Plain, on account of the sacred character of their place of origin. The " Altar Stone " which lies in the middle of the semicircle formed by the great trilithons was also derived from the same source.

Hence it is clear that Salisbury Plain was the meeting-place of two different streams of culture—that of the Round Barrow People, coming from the Continent by way of the east coast, and that of the western megalith builders, coming from the Irish Channel. It owes its importance to its central position on the over-land trade route between Ireland and Brittany by way of Pembrokeshire, the Bristol Channel, the Cotswolds, and the Christchurch end of Southampton Water—a route which avoided the dangerous sea passage round Land's End. For not only are the most important prehistoric remains of England and Wales—the Round Barrows and stone circles of Salisbury Plain, the Long Barrows of the Cotswolds, and the megalithic graves and circles of Glamorgan and Pembrokeshire [1]—distributed along this route, but to a great extent the finds of the earliest types of metal implements and the Beakers

---

[1] In Wales the Beaker period coincided with that of the megalithic tombs, as is shown by the not infrequent occurrence in the latter of Beaker pottery.

themselves follow the same line. It is probably the existence of this route which explains the appearance in North Brittany and Western Normandy, at the beginning of the Bronze Age, of a new culture somewhat similar in type to that of the Round Barrow People in England. Like the latter, the people of the new Breton culture buried their dead in great round barrows, and their connection with the British Isles is shown by their use of halberds of Irish type and of bronze daggers studded with thousands of gold nails, such as are characteristic of the Round Barrow People in Britain. Beakers are absent, but their pottery appears to derive its origins from the Beaker type. Connected with this culture, but probably earlier, are the tumulus graves of Southern Brittany, such as Mané-es-Hroék, Tumiac, and Mont St. Michel at Carnac, which are among the most imposing remains of that area. They contain neither metal nor pottery, but extraordinary numbers of stone axes of magnificent workmanship and choice materials such as jadeite, chloromelanite, and serpentine, which sometimes resemble in form the metal types of the Early Bronze Age. The builders of these tombs certainly belong to a different tradition from that of the earlier Megalithic Culture of the region, but it is possible that they were also the constructors of the great stone avenues of Carnac, which probably date from the beginning of the Bronze Age. If this were the case, it would afford a remarkable parallel to the building of Stonehenge, which was also the work of an alien people who had come under the influence of the Megalithic Culture in its later stages.

V. The Culture of Ireland in the Bronze Age and its Iberian Connections

Hitherto, except in the case of Sardinia, we have been dealing almost exclusively with the culture of the Beaker People and the different movements which are due to their influence, but it must be remembered that the

Beaker Culture was a comparatively short-lived episode, although this makes it all the more important for chronological purposes. Even in Spain, the land of its origin, it had passed away with the beginning of the Bronze Age, and had been replaced by the El Argar culture, which had its roots in the old south-eastern tradition of Almeria. In that region the great collective tombs of the Beaker period had entirely disappeared, and the dead were buried in separate graves, often in large jars. Elsewhere the later types of megalithic tombs still survived, but everywhere we find the same types of metal implements showing that the culture of the south-east was now dominant throughout the whole peninsula. Spain and Portugal had now become the most important centre of metal production in Europe. Gold and silver were worked, and copper mines dating from this period have been found to exist not only in Almeria and Andalucia, but also in the south of Portugal, Asturias, and Catalonia. The new types of bronze or copper weapons developed in Spain, especially the dagger and the halberd which consisted of a dagger blade fixed at right angles to a staff, were diffused by the movement of trade throughout Western Europe and reached Italy on the one hand and Ireland on the other. The latter became a great secondary centre of Iberian influence during the Early Bronze Age, and it was from there that Spanish types, such as the halberd, were passed on to Denmark and North-west Germany, where they became characteristic of the Bronze Age culture of the region. Hitherto we have left the Irish development on one side, since Ireland alone among the countries of Western Europe seems to have lain outside the direct sphere of influence of the Beaker People. This does not, however, necessarily prove that Ireland was not affected by the people of the Beaker Culture at a later stage in their development. There can, in fact, be little doubt that Eastern Ireland received important influences during the Bronze Age from South-western Scotland which was one of the first districts of Northern Britain to be settled by the Beaker People. Indeed, it is possible that the new ruling element in Eastern Ireland, which was responsible for the great chamber tombs of the Boyne during the Middle Bronze Age, may have originated in that region.

Nevertheless, the connection of Ireland with the Iberian Peninsula undoubtedly goes back to a far earlier period. Its influence is probably to be seen in the finely worked flint arrow-heads of the Irish æneolithic period, and still more in the large gold crescents, or " lunulæ," decorated with chevron patterns which were exported from Ireland to the Baltic, North-west Germany, and Northern France, as well as the western parts of the British Isles.[1] The great gold gorgets which have been found in Portugal,[2] one of which weighs no less than 2,300 grammes, are also decorated with similar patterns, and these probably belong to the same period as the Beakers and the great megalithic graves and cupola tombs, so that it is probable that Ireland was influenced by the Iberian culture even before the beginning of the El Argar period. So, too, the ornamented schist plaques or idols of the æneolithic period in Portugal find a parallel in a stone plaque of similar type that has been found in Antrim.

Later on in the Bronze Age, the influence of the Iberian culture is to be seen in the great chambered tumuli which stand along the banks of the Boyne in sight of the hill of Tara, and which are among the finest examples of the late megalithic tombs in existence. The largest of them all—that of the New Grange—is covered by a great tumulus 280 feet in diameter and 44 feet high, surrounded outside by a stone circle. The tomb itself is reached by a long corridor formed by megalithic slabs, and consists of a central chamber with corbel vault 20 feet high and three side chambers, so

[1] Cf. Plate I, fig. 3.
[2] Cf. S. Reinack, " The Evora Gorget," in *A.J.*, April 1925.

that the whole plan resembles an elongated Latin cross.
The walls are carved with spirals and other ornament
similar to the carvings found in the megalithic tombs of
Brittany, Portugal, and Scandinavia. The cupola tomb,
however, is very rare in Brittany and non-existent in
Scandinavia. It is a characteristically Iberian type,
and its distribution follows the western trade route to
Ireland with an extension in West Scotland and the
Orkneys, where there is a very fine example, similar in
plan to Newgrange, at Maeshowe, close to the great
stone circle of Stennis, the " Stonehenge of Orkney."
The relations between Ireland and Spain are probably
due to the fact that the former had become one of the
main centres of gold production in Europe, and in consequence, during the Early Bronze Age, Irish culture
enjoyed a period of great prosperity—a true " Age of
Gold " the memory of which long survived in Irish
tradition. This is the age to which the ancient historians of Ireland assigned the reign of Tighernmas,
" the lord of Death "—the great legendary king who
first mined for gold in the hills of Wicklow, and divided
the population into six castes or classes, which were
distinguished by the colours of their clothing. It is
no doubt purely a coincidence—though a remarkable
one—that the date, 1618 B.C., or A.M. 3581—given by the
Four Masters for the reign of King Tighernmas, and for
the beginning of the Irish gold mines, corresponds so
closely with that to which modern archæologists assign
the great development of the Irish Bronze Age ; but
nevertheless there are, I think, traces in these legends
of an extremely ancient tradition—a genuine echo,
however faint and distorted, from the strange vanished
world of the Western Age of Bronze. Thus we know
from the great tombs of the Boyne that prehistoric
princes did bear rule in the region of Tara, and the story
of the division of the people into six castes finds a curious
parallel in the seven castes which classical writers
record as existing in the parent centre of the Western

Æneolithic Culture—the region of Tartessus. Similarly the legend of the coming of the children of Miled or Mil from Asia Minor by way of Crete to Spain and thence to Ireland, while obviously mythical as an account of the origin of the Gaelic people, corresponds in a curious way with the history of the expansion of the Æneolithic Culture to the west, which has been described in this chapter. It may be, as Professor MacNeill believes, that the whole story is a concoction of Irish scholars under the influence of classical learning in the eighth century,[1] but it seems equally possible that they merely rationalised a genuine popular tradition, just as the Greek chronologists and logographers had done in the case of the traditions of the Minoan and Mycenæan world.

VI. THE SURVIVAL OF THE MEGALITHIC CULTURE IN LATER TIMES

Moreover, the connection between the cultural development of the Atlantic region and that of the Western Mediterranean appears in an even more remarkable way in that strange island culture of the extreme north, the Ultima Thule of the ancient world, which lived on to Christian times as the last survivor from an older world. Throughout the islands of the Orkneys, the Shetlands, and the Hebrides, and in the two northernmost counties of Scotland, wherever there is fertile land for agriculture, we find the fortress towers known as Brochs which resemble the Nuraghi of Sardinia, not only in their general type, but even in structural details.[2] There are the same staircases and

---

[1] Cf. Leabhar Gabhala, ed. by Professors MacNeill and Macalister, and the discussion of the traditions by the former in his *Phases of Irish History*, ch. iii, and in *Proceedings of the Irish Academy*, vol. xxviii, and by the latter in his *Ireland in Pre-Celtic Times*.

[2] The resemblance is denied by Mr. A. O. Carle (in *Antiquity*, vol. i, p. 295), but this is not surprising, since he regards the Nuraghe as " a sepulchral structure." Actually the Nuraghi, like the Brochs, were fortresses, showing plentiful signs of human occupation, and the only important difference between the two types lies in the fact that the central chamber of the Nuraghe was covered by a stem vault, whereas in the Broch it formed an open courtyard.

galleries in the thickness of the walls, the same narrow
entrance barred by a stone door and flanked by a
guard chamber, and the same fortified outworks
and surrounding groups of stone huts. Even their
contents resemble to some extent that of the Nuraghi,
as in the case of the square-mouthed vessels that are
often found. Only in date are they dissimilar, for the
Brochs belong mainly to the Roman or post-Roman
period, and only cease with the Scandinavian conquest.
Yet in spite of this disparity, the Brochs, like the
Nuraghi, form part of a cultural tradition which goes
back in origin to the dawn of the Age of Metal. The
earliest tombs of Caithness which probably belong to
the æneolithic period present an obvious analogy to
the Giants' Graves of Sardinia in the projecting
horns which usually flank the entrance to the corbelled
tombs chamber, while the stone-chambered cairns of
Orkney, with their central chamber out of which several
smaller cells open, are not without a resemblance in
plan to the rock chamber tombs of Sardinia. The
exceptional richness of this northern region in megalithic
monuments is no doubt due to its importance as a
half-way house on the sea route which connected
Ireland with Denmark in the period before it was
supplanted by the land route from the Baltic through
Central Europe, and while the Irish gold trade was still
flourishing. The shifting of the trade routes which
took place in the later Bronze Age left it as an isolated
and backward region, where the old culture lived on
unaffected by the new influences which had their source
in Central Europe, just as we find in Ireland the great
stone forts of the remote and inaccessible Aran Islands,
which are attributed traditionally to the Fir Bolg or
" Bagmen," the "prospectors "of Irish legendary history.
Throughout the extreme west, in Western Ireland and
the Scottish Islands, in Cornwall and Anglesey, the
tradition of the Æneolithic Culture lingered on into
historical times, as we see not only in the Brochs and

stone forts, but in the corbelled masonry of the beehive huts and in those curious underground dwellings known as Picts' Houses, weems, or coves, which also find their prototype in the Bronze Age culture of the Western Mediterranean, i.e. the covas of the Balearic Islands. Even the later Celtic culture, in spite of its Central European origin, seems to have incorporated considerable elements of the older Western culture. In Western Gaul and the British Isles the Celtic conquerors were an aristocratic minority ruling over a larger subject population which to some extent must have maintained its own traditions, just as, in Asia Minor, the native population of Galatia preserved its own culture after the Gallic conquest in the third century B.C. Here the Celtic element was so completely absorbed that the region became in later times the stronghold of the typically Asiatic cult of the Mother of the Gods with her eunuch priests who were known to the Romans as Galli, in spite of the utterly non-Celtic character of its origin and rites.[1] It is highly probable that a similar process of absorption took place also in the West, and that the Druids of Gaul and the British Isles were no more a native Celtic institution than were the Galli of Asia Minor. There is no evidence for the existence of the Druids in any part of the Celtic world outside the domain of the ancient Megalithic Culture, and the centre of gravity of the Druidic institutions seems to have lain in the West. According to Cæsar, Druidism was introduced into Gaul from Britain, where the Celtic element was, of course, weaker, while in Britain its most important sanctuary was the island of Anglesey, an old centre of the Megalithic Culture.

In Ireland Druidism was even stronger and its influence permeated the whole social system. The members of the sacred order were not mere medicine

---

[1] The title of Gallus is probably of Anatolian origin. But we know that Celtic nobles formed part of the priesthood, or temple corporation at Pessinus, the centre of the cult of the Mother Goddess.

men; they were primarily "Filid," or poets, and the guardians of a tradition of learning, and their schools were the direct ancestors of the bardic schools of medieval Ireland. Here again there is a remarkable parallel to the non-Celtic culture of Southern Spain, where the Turdetani were renowned in classical times for their cultivation of poetry and the care with which they preserved their ancient traditions. It is characteristic of the Irish culture that the privileged classes were not known, among the majority of Indo-European peoples, as the Nobles, but as " the Sacred," Nemed or Nemeth, and this designation included not merely chiefs and warriors, but poets and craftsmen.[1] The Free men or nobles in the ordinary sense, i.e. the Feni, were a subdivision of this sacred order.[2] It is also significant that Nemed was the name of the mythical ancestor of the three peoples—the Fir Bolg, the Tuatha de Danann, and the Milesians, who successively occupied the country according to the Irish legendary tradition.

Another element in the culture of Celtic Ireland which seems to go back to prehistoric times is the institution of the great Fire Festivals of Samin, and Beltane, which took place in the spring and autumn, and that of the aenachs or assemblies, which were held on the site of the great pagan cemeteries and were accompanied by games and markets as well as by celebrations in honour of the dead. The existence of such institutions in the Bronze Age seems to afford the only satisfactory explanation for the existence of Stonehenge and the earthen amphitheatre, or "Cursus," with which it is connected by a wide embanked avenue more than half a mile long. For the importance of Salisbury Plain in prehistoric times was

---

[1] Note the order in O'Mulconry's glossary. " Three superior Nemed, Priests, Poets, and Kings. Four other Nemed, Smiths, Craftsmen, Musicians, and Cattle."

[2] Cf. Professor MacNeill, " Ancient Irish Law," in *Proceedings of R. Irish Academy*, C., vol. xxxvi, p. 273, especially note 3.

no doubt mainly due to the importance of the open downlands as easy ways of communication, and we may suppose that here, by the side of the tombs of their chieftains, the people of the Early Bronze Age had their great centre for religious celebrations and intertribal barter.[1] That the Irish assemblies of this type, such as the great triennial fair of Carman at Wexford, and that of Taillten or Teltown on the Blackwater, should date back to Bronze Age times, is by no means inconceivable, since they survived both the coming of Christianity and the English Conquest, and did not entirely disappear until well on in the nineteenth century, while in Brittany similar survivals of even more primitive type still exist in the great Pardons, such as the Pardon of the Fire.

There is another possible instance of the survival in the Western Celtic region of a tradition which has its roots in the Megalithic Culture—the custom of inaugurating the chieftain upon a sacred stone such as the Lia Fail, or Stone of Destiny, at Tara, and the famous Stone of Scone, which was regarded in the Middle Ages as the palladium of the Scottish monarchy. The story of the bringing of this sacred stone from Egypt to Spain by the daughter of King Pharaoh, and thence to Ireland and Scotland, which reads like a medieval edition of Mr. Perry's *Children of the Sun,* appears to be a later Scottish version of the Irish legend of the origin of the Milesians.[2] But the fact that even to-day the kings

---

[1] Mr. T. D. Kendrick in his recent work on *The Druids* (1927) has put forward the hypothesis that Stonehenge is a Druidic temple, dating from the later Iron Age (La Tène Period). If this view which runs counter to the general opinion of experts should, nevertheless, prove be well grounded, it would afford another remarkable proof of the continuity of the Megalithic tradition, since there can be no doubt that Stonehenge, like Avebury, was an important sacred site some 1500 years earlier.

[2] The earliest evidence (in Latin) for the Scottish story seems to date from the beginning of the fourteenth century, cf. W. F. Skene, *The Coronation Stone,* p. 19, but no doubt the story is considerably older, for it must have had a Gaelic original.

of England are still crowned upon the sacred stone at Westminster provides a curious link with our prehistoric past and is an extraordinary instance of the way in which an element of primitive culture can live on in the most advanced civilisation of the modern world.

CHAPTER XI

THE WARRIOR PEOPLES AND THE DECLINE OF THE ARCHAIC CIVILISATION

The Pacific Character of Primitive Culture.

The Pastoral Society and the Rise of the Warrior Peoples.

The Social Crisis of the Third Millennium in Egypt and Mesopotamia.

The Indo-European Invasions of the Second Millennium and their Origin.

CHAPTER XI

THE WARRIOR PEOPLES AND THE DECLINE OF THE ARCHAIC CIVILISATION

I. The Pacific Character of Primitive Culture

The Archaic Civilisation, which has been described in the preceding chapters, reached its full development in the third millennium B.C. Thereafter the note of the civilisations of the Near East was conservation rather than progress. In fact, in many respects the general level of material culture stood higher in that age than at any subsequent period. All the great achievements on which the life of civilisation rests had been already reached, and there was no important addition to its material equipment until the rise of the great scientific and industrial movement in Western Europe in modern times. The most important inventions which characterise the higher culture, such as agriculture and the domestication of animals, the plough and the wheeled vehicle, irrigation and the construction of canals, the working of metals and stone architecture, navigation and sailing ships, writing and the calendar, the city state and the institution of king-ship, had been already achieved by the fourth millennium, and by the third we find organised bureaucratic states, written codes of laws, a highly developed commerce and industry, and the beginnings of astronomy and mathematics. At first sight it is difficult to understand why a civilising movement that had gone so far should go no further, and why the creative power of the Archaic civilisation should have deserted it when it was still almost in its prime. To some extent, indeed, it was due to the obscure laws that govern the life of peoples and civilisations, above all to the rigidity which seems to characterise a form of culture that has attained a complete equilibrium with its environment. But it also finds an external explanation in the rise of a new type of warlike society, which put an end to the autonomous development of the Archaic Culture, and for a time imperilled its very existence. The close of the neolithic age in Europe and corresponding period in the Near East was marked by far-reaching movements of peoples and warlike invasions which broke down the frontiers of the old culture-provinces and produced new social forms and a new distribution of peoples and cultures. It may be compared to the ages of barbarian invasion, which so often in later history marked the end of one civilisation and the beginning of a new age.   Indeed, it is the earliest example of this process, the first occasion in which we can trace the appearance of organised warfare as a factor in historical development. The earlier changes of culture in Europe had been pre-dominantly peaceful. There is no sign that the transi-tion from the palæolithic to the neolithic age or the expansion of peasant culture in Eastern and Central Europe, or even the beginnings of the age of metal in the Mediterranean, were due in any degree to warlike invasions.   In fact, from their open settlements and the lack of weapons, war can have played little part in the life of the neolithic peasant peoples.   And the same is true, though to a lesser extent, of the Archaic civilisations of the Near East.   There, certainly, war was not un-known, either between the city states of Sumer, or in the early states of the Nile valley, but it was exceptional and of a rudimentary type.   Society was not organised for war as in later times.   There was no military caste. As Professor Breasted points out, the Egyptians of the Old Kingdom were essentially unwarlike.   Their army consisted of an untrained levy of peasants, such as was used equally for the quarrying and transportation of stone for the great monuments, and its command was entrusted by Pharaoh to some leading official who was himself not a professional soldier.

It may seem paradoxical to suggest, as Mr. Perry has done,[1] that war is a comparatively late development in the history of humanity. It has been commonly assumed that the savage is essentially a fighter, and that the early stages of social development were marked by continual warfare. Indeed, many writers have gone further and supposed that man was by nature a beast of prey, and that his progress has been due to a ruthless struggle for existence, in which the weaker were constantly being killed off and possibly eaten by the stronger—Homo homini lupus, as the Romans said—regardless of the fact that even beasts of prey do not usually prey upon each other.

The error has arisen largely from the fact that civilised man, both in antiquity and in modern times has been continuously brought into contact with warlike tribes less civilised than himself—Huns and Tatars, Caribs and Iroquois, Zulus and Maori—and has regarded these as the typical savages. Whereas in reality they are advanced and specialised types, even further removed from the really primitive peoples than they are from the civilised. Even in modern times, in spite of the ages during which men have had to adapt themselves to warlike conditions or perish, the most primitive peoples—the food-gatherers—are predominantly peaceful. Thus in America, while the most warlike peoples such as the Aztecs and the Iroquois were comparatively civilised, the least warlike were the exceedingly backward peoples of California and Tierra del Fuego. In Oceania there is the same contrast between the more advanced Polynesians and Fijians and the primitive natives of Australia and Tasmania. Most remarkable of all is the case of the aborigines of New Zealand and the Chatham Islands, the Moriori, who, in their relation to the warlike

[1] Cf. W. J. Perry, *An Ethnological Study of Warfare* (1917), and *War and Civilisation* (1918).

Maori invaders, adhered to the strict pacifist principle of non-resistance and allowed themselves to be slaughtered without resistance like sheep.

This unwarlike character of the most primitive people depends mainly on the conditions of their life. War is not a paying proposition for them, since it can yield no booty, for hunters and food-gatherers possess no stored-up wealth of goods or cattle. They may fight to defend their hunting-grounds, but unless they are driven to seek new lands by some natural calamity, such as drought, each tribe tends to keep to its own territory, and not to interfere with its neighbours. An attack on the civilised agriculturalists and cattle-keepers would, of course, be profitable, but primitive food-gatherers and hunters are too few and weak to be a serious danger to a settled population. Their relations are like those of gipsies to villagers—a danger to the henroosts, but nothing more. On the whole it is the primitive peoples who are the sufferers and the civilised who are the aggressors, as we have seen in modern times in the extinction of so many defenceless peoples, such as the Tasmanians or the natives of the West Indies at the hands of European colonists.

II. The Pastoral Society and the Rise of the Warrior Peoples

But when the hunters have begun to acquire some elements of the higher culture from their more civilised neighbours, the case is altered. When once they possess flocks and herds, or begin to cultivate the ground, their sparse population increases, and they become numerous enough to be formidable. Originally, as we have pointed out before, the domestication of animals went hand in hand with agriculture, and was probably the discovery of the higher settled culture. But it was an invention, which in the nature of things spread quickly and widely. Tame animals which had strayed or been stolen must sooner or later come into the possession of the hunters, just as the horses of the Spaniards were acquired by the Indians of the plains ; and natural increase would suffice to do the rest. Thus, there grew up a new type of society—that of the nomadic pastoral tribe—based on the combination of the life of the hunter with that of the shepherd, as the ancient agricultural civilisation had been based on the combination of agriculture and the domestication of animals.

In this way there tends to grow up round every centre of the higher civilisation a zone of lower culture which is to some extent dependent or parasitic upon its civilised neighbours, while at the same time possessing a higher degree of mobility and a greater aptitude for war. Thus to the settled Semitic civilisations of Mesopotamia and Syria and South Arabia there corresponds the predatory nomad culture of the Bedouin, and to Egypt the pastoral culture of the Libyans and the other Hamitic peoples of North Africa. So, too, in Eastern Asia we find a similar zone of nomad Mongolian peoples on the north-western frontiers of China, and in Central Asia the peoples of the steppes have owed their culture to the settled civilisation of Persia and Turkestan ; while in prehistoric Europe the same relation existed between the peasant cultures of the Danube and the Dnieper and the warlike peoples to the north and east.

But in spite of their original relation of cultural dependence, the social organisation of the pastoral peoples was in almost every respect a complete contrast to that of the sedentary agriculturalist. Whereas the latter rested on the basis of a fixed territorial settlement and on common labour, the former was characterised by the development of the institutions of property and kinship. The importance of a tribe or a family depended on their wealth in flocks and herds, an ever-varying factor which at once introduced an element of inequality, whereas the amount of land held by a primitive agriculturalist is strictly limited by his powers of cultivation. Any man can take as much land as he wants, by clearing a patch of jungle, but it is not the land itself that is valuable, but the labour which renders it fruitful. Thus the woman who cultivates the ground is, as has been noticed before, as important as or even more important than the man, and the primitive agricultural community often possesses a matrilinear or matriarchal organisation.

On the other hand, the pastoral tribe is patriarchal and aristocratic, and the masculine element everywhere predominates. The shepherd requires no less daring and hardihood than the hunter. He has to defend his flock against the attacks of wild beasts, and the raids of other nomads. The choice of new pastures and the conduct of tribal forays constantly call for the exercise of qualities of leadership and decision.

The pastoral society produces types like Abraham, men rich in flocks and herds, with many wives and children, wise in counsel, and resolute in war. The peasant has only to follow the traditional routine of custom and labour, and he is sure to gain his bare subsistence, but the pastoralist is always an adventurer, and if he fails he is faced in a moment with the loss of his wealth and the scattering of his tribe, like Lot, or Job who lost in a single day his 7,000 sheep and 3,000 camels and all the rest of his flocks and herds.

This contrast between the agricultural and the pastoral societies finds a counterpart in their religions.

Both of them are Nature Religions, and have their origin in the vague undifferentiated religion of primitive peoples that we have described in the second chapter, but each has concentrated its worship on a different aspect of nature. The Religion of the Peasant is concerned above all with the mystery of life, and he sees the divine power embodied in the Earth Mother and the Vegetation God who is her consort or son. The Religion of the Shepherd, on the other hand, is concerned not so much with the Earth as with the Heavens, and it is the powers of Heaven—the Sky, the Sun, and the Storm, that take the first place in his worship.

Among the pastoral peoples all over the world, from Siberia to Africa, we find the Sky God as a vague and often impersonal power which is yet conceived as the creator and supreme ruler of the universe. It is characteristic alike of the ancient Aryans, the Turks, the Mongols, the Hamites, and many of the Negro peoples of Africa,[1] and even among peoples of the higher culture such as the Sumerians and the Chinese it appears as one of the earliest elements in their religion, inherited perhaps from an older phase of barbarism. Even the lower peoples of the hunting culture are not entirely devoid of the conception, and it has a good claim to be considered the oldest and most universal religion of the world.[2]

With the advance of the pastoral culture and the development of the warrior tribe, the Sky God tends to become personified as a celestial hero and chieftain, but at the very end of the development, in classical times, men could still speak of the Sky God in the old undifferentiated way, as in the Roman expression " sub Jove " for " under the open sky."

The Sky God of the warrior peoples is, however, above all the god of the thunderbolt and the storm. He is the Adad and Amor of the Semites, the Teshub of Asia Minor, the Aryan Indra, and the Scandinavian Thor. These are incalculable and formidable powers, whom man cannot control or co-operate with, jealous and arbitrary rulers after the image of their own chieftains who must be feared and obeyed implicitly and blindly. Nevertheless, they have the virtues as well as the defects of the warlike pastoral psychology. They are the guardians of the masculine tribal morality— righteous gods who hate lies and uncleanness and

[1] E.g. Engai among the Masai, Juok among the Shilluk, Leza among the Ba-ila, Nyami among the Ashanti, and many more.

[2] Cf. especially Pettazzoni, *Dio. I, l'Essere Celeste nel Credenze dei Popoli Primitivi.*

disobedience.   While the religions of the settled agricultural peoples were idolatrous and immoral, or at
least non-moral, it was the pastoral peoples who
developed such high conceptions of the divinity as
Varuna, the guardian of righteousness, and Ahura Mazda,
the Wise Lord.   Above all the Jewish people could never
have developed their ethical and monotheist religion
amidst the idolatrous and voluptuous cults of the
agricultural peoples of Syria, had it not been for their
pastoral and tribal tradition, and it was to the desert
that the prophets and reformers turned for inspiration
in the great crises of national history.

It is in fact characteristic of the pastoral peoples
that their intellectual and moral development should be
far more advanced than one would expect from their
material civilisation.   The pastoral life alone frees men
from the grinding necessity of continual labour, while
stimulating the activity of mind and body, so that the
Highland or Montenegrin shepherd is often a man of
higher spiritual culture than the wealthy farmer or
trader of the plains.[1] And even in primitive times,
poetry and reflection on the problems of existence have
been common features among pastoral peoples of a
comparatively rudimentary culture.

III. The Social Crisis of the Third Millennium in Egypt and Mesopotamia

It is clear that the existence of these pastoral societies,
with their intensely masculine and warlike ethics, their
mobility, and the high degree of physical efficiency
which their wandering life entailed, was a great potential
danger to the civilisation of the settled agriculturalists.
The actual materialisation of the danger was delayed by
a number of causes, such as their geographical segregation in the outer steppes, their inferiority in material

[1] Cf. the remarkable description of the characteristics of the warlike
pastoral culture of the Dinaric tribesmen in the Balkans to-day in
Cvijič's *La Peninsule Balkanique*.

equipment, and the prestige of the older and higher civilisation, as well as the mere influence of tradition and routine. It is indeed probable that it was the civilised peoples who were the first aggressors, and that it was from them that the barbarians first learnt the possibilities of organised warfare, as well, no doubt, as the use of weapons of metal. Certainly the great wave of invasion of the men of Gutium from the north which overwhelmed Mesopotamia in the twenty-sixth century B.C. followed close upon the period of Sargon and Naram Sin who were the first to lead Mesopotamian armies into the uncivilised mountainous regions to the north and east of Tigris, and in the same way in Egypt the later days of the Old Kingdom had been marked by expeditions of conquest against " the Sand-dwellers " of the north and the Nubians of the south, which may have helped to provoke the subsequent movement of invasion.

However this may be, the ultimate advantage was all on the side of the barbarians, for every fresh invasion increased their warlike efficiency, whereas the destructive effects of warfare on the higher civilisation were cumulative. Peace and security were essential to the life of the Archaic Culture, and a few years of disorder might cause irreparable damage to the highly organised system of irrigation and canalisation on which the prosperity of Egypt and Mesopotamia rested. Moreover, the psychology of the archaic cultures was essentially unwarlike. Its mainspring was the spirit of unquestioning loyalty and submission to the will of the gods, as incarnated in the divine monarchy or the temple priesthood. The initiative rested with a small ruling class on whom the mass of the peasant population was entirely dependent, so that when, as in the Spanish conquest of Peru, the centre of the government fell into the hands of an enemy, the rest of the people were left as defenceless and unresisting as a flock of sheep.

Hence the age of invasions in the third millennium

B.C. shook the foundations of the Archaic Culture, and produced a wave of pessimism and moral confusion. Men lost faith in the immutable divine order on which the old theocratic state was based. The gods had shown themselves unable to protect their people, or even themselves, from violence and outrage. The temple liturgies which make up so large a part of the later Sumerian and Accadian literature are full of lamentations over the destruction of the holy places of Sumer and the carrying away of the gods into captivity— lamentations which recall those written nearly 2,000 years later on the fall of the Holy City of Jerusalem and the destruction of the Temple.

They describe the deluge of invasion passing over the land. " Order was destroyed. The sacred dynasty was exiled from the temple. They demolished the city, they demolished the temple. The rulership of the land they seized. The divine prince was carried away to a strange land." But above all they depict the evil plight of the Mother Goddess, ravished by unclean hands, chased forth from her shrine, like a bird from its nest, and carried away to a strange land, while the splendid festivals and the solemn rituals cease in the great temple of Eanna.

The Egyptian documents of this period give an even more vivid impression of the social disorder and moral confusion that followed the collapse of the divine order of the Old Kingdom. One of these, known as the Admonitions of Ipuwer, is of especial interest, not only on account of the picturesque detail with which it describes the conditions in Egypt during the period of foreign invasion, but also because it shows that the breakdown of the Archaic Civilisation was marked by the same phenomena of social revolution and class war which have so often accompanied the decline of wealthy and advanced societies in later times.

The document is too long and too fragmentary to quote in full, but it may be condensed as follows :

I. The Ruin of Egypt.

" Behold, strangers have come into the land. The men of Egypt are no longer found anywhere. The people of the desert take their place.

" The land is desolate, the nomes are laid waste. Bowmen from a strange country have come up into Egypt.

" The vessel of Upper Egypt goes adrift. The towns are destroyed. Men flee into the open country ; they dwell in tents.

" The roads are watched. Men lie in ambush by the wayside to put the wayfarer to a shameful death, and spoil him of his goods.

" The cattle are left to stray. There is no man to herd them. When the Nile overflows, none ploughs, for they say, ' We know not what hath come to pass in the land.'

" Blood is on every side. Death ceases not. Men are few, and he who lays his brother in the earth is everywhere. Women become barren, for the Creator fashions not men by reason of the state of the land."

II. The Social Revolution.

" The nobles are in affliction and the base rejoice. Every city saith, ' Come and let us put down those who are in authority amongst us.'

" The land turns like a potter's wheel. Thieves become men of substance, and the wealthy are plundered. The great are hungry and in distress, while those who served now have servants. He who bore messages for others now hath messengers to do his bidding.

" The poor possess riches. He who was wont to go barefoot now hath precious things. He who had not a yoke of oxen possesseth flocks and herds. Luxury is spread abroad among the people. Gold and jewels adorn the necks of slaves ; but the mistresses say, ' Ah ! that we had something to eat ! ' The honourable ladies suffer like servants. Their slaves are the mistresses of their mouth. Hardly will they suffer them to speak.

" Those who built for themselves tombs are become

hirelings ; those who rowed in the boat of the God are under the yoke. Men sail not to Byblus to-day. What shall we do for cedars for our mummies, with the products of which the Pure are buried, and with the oil of which princes are embalmed, as far as the land of Keftiu [Crete]. They return no more. The gold and the precious things are found no more. Men throw their dead into the river. The Nile becomes a burying-place."

III. THE DESTRUCTION OF THE DIVINE ORDER.

" Behold ! that which has never been aforetime has come to pass. The King is taken away by men of naught. Men without faith or understanding have deprived the land of its royalty. They have revolted against the Holy Crown, the defender of Re, which causeth the Two Lands to be at peace. The Serpent is taken from its place, and the secret of the Kings of the Upper and the Lower Land is laid bare.

" As for the sublime Judgment Hall, its writings are carried away, its inner places are exposed. The government offices are opened and their writings carried away, so that serfs become lords of serfs. Woe is me for the evil of this generation ! The writings of the clerks of the census are carried away. The grain of Egypt is for whosoever will come and take it.

" The laws of the Judgment Hall are cast forth. The poor break them open in the public streets. The poor man attains to the greatness of the Divine Ennead, while the children of the princes are thrown into the street.

" The things that were seen of old have perished. The land is exhausted like uprooted flax. Would that there might be an end of men, that conception and birth should fail ! Would that the cry of the land might cease and that strife should be no more !

" Wherefore when Re first created Man, did he not separate the righteous from the ungodly ? It is said that he is the Shepherd of Men. When his flock is scattered, he watches over them and gathers them together.

" Would that he had perceived their nature in the beginning. Then he would have stretched forth his arm and destroyed the evil seed. But in this age, there is no longer any pilot. Where is he ? Does he sleep ? His power is not seen." [1]

This spirit of pessimism finds an even more poignant expression in " The Dialogue of a Man with his Own Soul," which is one of the masterpieces of ancient Egyptian literature. The just man, in despair at the victory of the forces of evil and at his own abandonment by men, turns to death as the one haven of rest.

> " Death is before me to-day (he says)
> Like the recovery of a sick man,
> Like going forth into a garden after sickness.

> " Death is before me to-day
> Like the odour of myrrh,
> Like sitting under the sail on a windy day.

> " Death is before me to-day
> As a man longs to see his house
> When he has spent years in captivity." [2]

But the writer's conception of the after-life is far more spiritual than that of the earlier literature of the Old Kingdom, which is non-moral, and sometimes even utterly barbaric, as in the famous Pyramid Text which describes the dead King Unis as " eating the gods," " the great ones for his breakfast, the middle ones for his dinner, the little ones for his supper " ; " their charms are in his belly, he has eaten the knowledge of every god."

It owes nothing to the belief in the efficacy of the machinery which under the Old Kingdom secured the welfare of the deceased in his tomb. For the writer recognises that this also is vanity ; that the lot of

---

[1] The whole document has been edited and translated by A. H. Gardiner, *The Admonitions of an Egyptian Sage* (Leipzig, 1909). The text is full of difficulties and lacunæ, but I have attempted to convey the general sense, using so far as possible the words of the original as interpreted in the above translation and in the partial extracts given by Breasted in *The Development of Religion and Thought in Ancient Egypt*, pp. 204–15, and by Moret in *Le Nil et La Civilisation Égyptienne*, pp. 261–8.

[2] Breasted, *op. cit.*, p. 195.

those who built for themselves the great Pyramid tombs, who adorned their sepulchres like the dwellings of the gods, is no better than that of " those weary ones who die on the dyke," their bodies a prey to fish and crocodiles.   It is an intensely personal utterance, the earliest emergence of an independent criticism of life on the part of the individual, and the first appeal to the life to come as a deliverance from the injustice and misery of terrestrial existence.   There is no sign of this in the contemporary literature of Babylonia, though that also is marked by the same atmosphere of gloom and disillusionment.   For the Babylonians had no hope of a celestial hereafter.   Their religious outlook was limited to the present life, and when the decline of the Archaic Civilisation threatened the existence of the divine state on earth, they took refuge in a fatalism which was even darker than that of the Egyptian pessimist.   The great epic of Gilgamesh, of which the Babylonian version dates from this period (*c.* twenty-first century B.C.), is dominated by a sense of bitter frustration.   The gods have cheated man of the gift of life.   " When the gods first made man, they allotted to him death, and life they held in their own keeping."   In spite of all the labours of the hero, fate robs him of the one reward he asks, " that mine eyes may continue to see the light of the sun."   When at last his friend returns from the grave, it is only to tell him that there is no escape from the dismal underworld, the House of Hades.   The lot of the hero is even worse than that of other men, for dying in battle or in the desert, he fails to receive the rites of burial or the funeral offerings, and his soul like a dog must lick up " the leavings of the pot, the refuse that is thrown into the street."

In this age of ruin and disillusionment the civilisation of the ancient world came very near to complete destruction—how near we can never know.   It was saved by the work of the great rulers and organisers who appeared at the close of the third millennium, men like Ham-

murabi in Babylonia and the Twelfth Dynasty monarchs
of Egypt, as was predicted (after the event, it is true)
in the almost Messianic utterance of Neferre Hu : " A
king shall come from the South. He shall take the
White Crown and the Red, and the Two Gods who love
him shall take pleasure in him. The Right shall be
restored and Injustice shall be cast forth. Blessed is he
who shall see these things and who shall serve this King."
But the spirit of the new monarchy was different from
that of the old theocracy. Indeed these kings, in whose
veins perhaps ran the blood of foreign invaders, were
warriors rather than priests, and the ideal of kingship
loses the exclusively religious character that it had
possessed under the Old Kingdom. " I have set up my
statue on the frontier," says Senusret III in his Nubian
inscription, " not that ye should worship it, but that ye
should fight for it. I am the King and what I say I
do." And this clear realisation of personal power and
human responsibility is no less clearly expressed in the
admonition to his successor that is attributed to
Amenemhat I, the founder of the dynasty. " Fill not
thy heart with a brother, know not a friend, make not
thyself intimates wherein there is no end, harden thyself
against subordinates, that thou mayest be King of the
Earth, that thou mayest be Ruler of the Lands, that
thou mayest increase good."

And the same ideal of kingship finds expression in
a hymn of gratitude and loyalty to Senusret III :

" How great is the Lord towards his City. He alone is millions, other
   men are but small.
He has come to us : he has seized Upper Egypt and placed the
   White Crown upon his head.
He has united the two countries and joined the Reed [the symbol
   of Upper Egypt] with the Bee [the symbol of the Delta].
He has conquered The Black Land [the Nile valley] and has
   subjected the Red [the desert].
He has protected the Two Lands and given peace to the two banks.
He has given life to Egypt, and abolished her sufferings.
He has given life to men, and made the throat of the dead to
   breathe.

He has trodden down the strangers and smitten the Troglodytes that feared him not.

He has fought for his frontier and driven back the spoilers.

He has granted us to rear our children and to bury our aged [in peace]." [1]

The spirit of heroic energy and lonely power which inspired these Twelfth Dynasty rulers still lives for us in the magnificent art of the Middle Kingdom—in the fierce and virile faces of Senusret III and Amenemhat III, so different from the placid majesty of the God Kings of the Old Kingdom. But in the Middle Kingdom, no less than in the age of the Pyramid Builders, everything depended on the person of the King. The Archaic civilisation remained fundamentally pacific and was incapable of adapting itself to warlike conditions. When the next wave of invasion from the north reached Egypt, there was no longer a royal superman like Senusret III to guard the frontiers, and the short-lived prosperity of the Middle Kingdom ended in darkness and confusion. About the beginning of the seventeenth century, Egypt fell into the hands of the Asiatic conquerors—the so-called Hyksos or Shepherd Kings. These were probably Semites from Northern Syria, but their invasion of Egypt was not an isolated fact. It forms part of a great movement of peoples which was convulsing the whole of the Near East in the first centuries of the second millennium. The power of Babylon had fallen before a Hittite raid, perhaps as early as 1870 B.C., and a whole series of new peoples was making its appearance in the highland regions to the north.

IV. The Indo-European Invaders of the Second Millennium and their Origin

This marks the first appearance of the Indo-European peoples who were subsequently to play so great a part in history, for there is no reason to believe that the earlier northern invaders of Mesopotamia in the middle

[1] Erman, *Literatur der Ägypter*, pp. 179–82.

of the third millennium—the men of Gutium—were of Indo-European stock. Indeed their racial origin is a mystery, for their rulers bear strange names—Irarum, Ibranum, Igesaus, etc., which it is not easy to connect with any known group of languages. However, it is possible that even at that date the period of the Indo-European migrations had already begun, and that the people of the hills were being driven forward on Mesopotamia by the coming of new peoples from the north and west.

The origin of this great movement of peoples may have been due in part to natural causes, such as the growing aridity of Central Asia which may have forced the population to seek new homes, but it was undoubtedly facilitated by another factor which gave a great impetus to the mobility and aggressiveness of the pastoral peoples. This was the taming of the horse and its utilisation as a draught animal, an invention that was to revolutionise the art of warfare in the second millennium. It was probably the peoples of the Painted Pottery Culture of Susa and Anau who were the first to domesticate the horse, for horses' bones are common in their settlements as well as in those of the Painted Pottery Culture of Eastern Europe, and the hunting peoples of the steppe probably acquired it later, by the process of cultural expansion that has been described, and turned the invention to warlike uses. On the other hand, the horse was unknown to the higher civilisations of the Near East. In Mesopotamia it makes its first appearance on the eve of the northern invasions, and its Babylonian name—" the ass from the East "—shows that it was introduced across the mountains from Persia. So, too, in Egypt the horse and chariot were first introduced by the Hyksos invaders, but they were certainly not of Syrian origin, and the Hyksos themselves must have acquired them from the invading peoples from farther north. In fact the appearance of the horse seems to be closely associated with that of the Indo-European peoples, so that the early Aryans, like the Homeric heroes, were above all " tamers of horses " and chariot fighters.   It is remarkable that the earliest known treatise on chariot driving, a document found at Boghaz Keui, and written by a certain Kikulli of Mitanni, uses Indo-European words as part of the technical vocabulary of the charioteer.

The actual period of the invasions is naturally an age of darkness in which historical evidence is almost completely lacking, but in the following period we find traces of Indo-European influence all over the Near East.   The Kassites, who established themselves in Babylonia in the eighteenth century B.C., were not themselves Indo-Europeans, but some of their rulers possessed Indo-European names, and they seem to have worshipped Aryan divinities such as Suryash the Sun God.   Farther west, in the land of Mitanni in North Mesopotamia, the Aryan element is much stronger, and one of the most remarkable discoveries of modern times—a document discovered at Boghaz Keui, the Hittite capital—has shown that some of the gods of the rulers of Mitanni were practically identical with the early Aryan divinities of India—Indara (= Indra), Aruna (= Varuna), Mitra and the two Nashatiya (= the Ashvins), while the rulers themselves bear Aryan names such as Shutarna and Artatama.   Farther south the Egyptian documents of the period of the Eighteenth Dynasty show the existence of Indo-European princes in Palestine in the fourteenth or fifteenth century— Shuwadata of Keilah near Hebron, Yashdata of Taanach, Artamanya of Zir Bashan, Rusmanya of Sharon and Biridashwa of Yenoam, and the occurrence of these names so far south suggests that Indo-Europeans may have played a part in the Hyksos invasion of Egypt. All these names, together with those of the Kassite and Mitannian divinities, belong to the Eastern Indo-Iranian branch of the Aryan linguistic group, but the decipherment of the Hittite archives of Boghaz Keui has shown that the ruling element among the Hittites spoke a language which has remarkable affinities with the western group and especially with Latin.[1] Hence it is clear that the movement of peoples that we are discussing was a very complex one. The old theory of a common " Aryan Cradle " in the steppes of Transcaspia or Turkestan would explain the appearance of Indo-European elements in Western Asia at this time well enough, but the divergence between " Hittite " and the Indo-Iranian language spoken by the ruling element in the land of Mitanni is much too deep to have had a recent origin.

Of course a resemblance between languages does not prove a community of race any more than a similarity of racial type implies a community of speech. Many of the peoples of Indo-European speech, in the West as well as in the East, only acquired their present languages at a comparatively recent date, and these facts have tended to throw discredit on all theorising concerning " the Aryans " as a racial entity. Nevertheless, sometime and somewhere there must have existed an original centre or cradle-land in which the earliest form of Indo-European speech was developed, and from which it spread throughout Europe and through a large part of Asia. Many attempts have been made to locate this original centre, and every kind of argument based on philology, archæology, and anthropology has been employed. The latter is perhaps the least conclusive, owing to the paucity and uncertainty of the evidence, but there is some reason to think that the early Indo-European peoples, or at least the dominant element among them, were Nordic in type, and that their original home must be looked for within the Nordic racial area. The philological evidence, based on the vocabulary common to all branches of Indo-European speech, is,

[1] E.g. Hittite, kuis kuit, Lat. quis quid ; Hittite, genu (knee), Lat. genu. It must, however, be clearly understood that this language was but one of a number of languages spoken by the inhabitants of the Hittite realm.

however, more enlightening. It suggests that the original Indo-Europeans before their dispersion were a pastoral people of patrilinear social organisation, who possessed the horse and waggon, the ox and the sheep, and worshipped a Sky God (Jupiter, Dyaus, etc., and also perhaps Ouranos, Varuna). The common words for metal, as well as other important objects mentioned in Chapter VI, seem to have been borrowed from the higher culture of Mesopotamia or Asia Minor, but on the whole the main features of their common culture point to a neolithic stage of development. The common words for flora and fauna suggest a region of forest and steppe, and the occurrence of common words for the beech, the birch, and the hazel in the European members of the group point more definitely to Central or North-western Europe.

It is, however, the archæological evidence that is the most conclusive. We have seen that the Aryans appear in Western Asia early in the second millennium, as an invading people of warriors and horsemen. Now a similar expansion of peoples of warlike culture occurred in Europe at an earlier period in late neolithic times, overrunning the old peasant cultures of Central and Eastern Europe, and the course of this movement coincides so fully with the distribution of the chief families of Indo-European speech in later times, that it is difficult to avoid the conclusion that the invading peoples were themselves Aryans, and that we must look to Europe for the source of the great movement of peoples which afterwards affected the whole of Western Asia, and even extended as far as India and Eastern Turkestan. Thus the expansion of the Aryans was not a slow and painful movement of peasant colonisation, but the swift advance of victorious warriors, and this explains not only their rapid diffusion over the vast continental region between Northern Europe and India, but also the remarkably homogeneous character of their languages, which offers so complete a contrast to the heterogeneity of speech found among peoples of sedentary peasant culture, such as those of Asia Minor. We find a somewhat similar contrast in Africa between the homogeneous group of Bantu languages which likewise owe their diffusion to the comparatively recent expansion of a warlike pastoral stock, and the settled peasant peoples of West Africa, where almost every district has its own distinct language.

The influence of the Indo-European invasions was not, however, wholly destructive, it was in fact far less so than that of the Turkish and Mongol conquerors of the Middle Ages. They possessed a natural aptitude for assimilating the higher culture of the peoples that they conquered, and the vigorous life of the warrior tribes fertilised the ancient civilisations and gave birth in time to a new and brilliant development of culture. Nevertheless, the civilisation of the warrior was always in a sense parasitic upon that of the Mother Goddess. Even in Europe, it was the influence of the Archaic civilisation which supplied the initial impetus to the native development of culture, and the warrior peoples of the north were not independent of it. First comes the Age of the Gods, to use Vico's phrase, then the Age of the Heroes.

CHAPTER XII

THE NORDIC CULTURE AND THE ORIGINS OF THE WARRIOR PEOPLES IN EUROPE

The Megalithic Culture in the Baltic.

The Battle-axe Culture in Jutland and its Origins.

The Battle-axe Cultures of Central and Eastern Europe.

The Battle-axe Cultures and the Question of Indo-European Origins.

The Interaction of the Warrior and the Peasant Types of Culture, and the Two Elements in the Religion and Culture of the Scandinavian North.

CHAPTER XII

THE NORDIC CULTURE AND THE ORIGINS OF THE WARRIOR PEOPLES IN EUROPE

I. THE MEGALITHIC CULTURE IN THE BALTIC

IN the chapters that deal with the history of the Megalithic Culture little has been said about the most northerly extension of that culture in the Southern Baltic and Northern Germany. It is, however, a region of exceptional importance, not only because it is the terminal point of the expansion of the Megalithic Culture in Europe, but still more because it marks the beginning of a brilliant development of Nordic Culture, which proceeded without a break from neolithic times down to the end of the Bronze Age. With the coming of the Megalithic Culture, the Baltic region ceases to be a cultural backwater, isolated from the main currents of European life, and becomes an active and creative culture centre which has no less importance for the history of Northern and Central Europe than the Spanish æneolithic culture possessed for the Western European region. Like the Iberian Peninsula, the Baltic region was the meeting-point of streams of cultural influence of diverse origin which mingled together and gave birth to a new culture of exceptional vigour and power of expansion. Owing to the comparative wealth of the region in undisturbed burials and other prehistoric remains, and the care with which they have been studied by the Scandinavian and German archæologists, it has been possible to trace the development of this Nordic group of cultures in greater detail and in more continuous sequence than in any other part of Europe. Elsewhere it is often uncertain whether the more rudimentary forms of megalithic grave, such as the dolmens, are actually prior in date to the fully developed type of chamber-tomb.   In the north, however, the contents of the tombs show a regular chronological development from the dolmens to the passage graves, and from the latter to the covered galleries or long stone cists.   Consequently the typology of the Nordic development, as established by Montelius and Sophus Müller, has been accepted as the general standard of comparison for the chronology of prehistoric Europe. So great, in fact, is the importance of the Baltic area from an archæological point of view, that it has given rise to what may be called the Pan-Nordic theory of the origins of culture.   It is the view of a powerful school of German anthropologists and archæologists, led by Professor Kossinna, that the Baltic is the cradle, both of the Nordic race and of the Indo-European peoples, and that the expansion of the latter into Central and Eastern Europe and Western Asia proceeded from this starting-point in neolithic times. Indeed, Kossinna goes further still and believes that the very origins of the higher civilisation—the discovery of agriculture and the domestication of animals—are to be looked for among the inhabitants of the Baltic Kitchen Middens some 7,000 years ago.   But even apart from such exaggerations as this, there are grave objections to the identification *tout court* of the Nordic race with the Indo-European stock, and even to the derivation of the neolithic culture of the megalith builders from the earlier traditions of native Baltic culture.   There is a wide gap between the mesolithic culture of the barbarous food-gatherers who inhabited the Danish Kitchen Midden settlements, and the comparatively advanced type of neolithic civilisation which appears with the dolmen builders.   The latter practised agriculture and possessed domestic animals ; above all their advanced style of pottery, which includes specialised types such as the collared flask, the amphora, and the funnel-necked beaker, bears little resemblance to the rude round-bottomed pots of the older Baltic population. If the former had arisen from the spontaneous development of the native Baltic tradition, we should expect the new stage of culture all over the Baltic region. But as a matter of fact it is confined to the same restricted area as the dolmens themselves, i.e. to the east and north coasts of Jutland, the southern coasts of Sweden, and the Danish islands. Outside this region, in Norway, in Northern and Central Sweden, and in the Eastern Baltic, the old culture tradition of mesolithic times continued to exist. The people were still hunters and fishermen, who made implements of bone and slate, and figures of animals, which recall the artistic tradition of the Maglemose culture, while their pottery still retains the simple forms of the Kitchen Midden period.[1] Thus the native Baltic culture tradition followed its own line of development, and ultimately gave birth to the Arctic hunting culture which extends from Northern Scandinavia far into the interior of Russia. This development, however, has nothing in common with the true Nordic culture which appears abruptly on the coasts of the Southern Baltic as a new creation of the neolithic age. It was a civilisation of agriculturalists and traders, and it is very possible that it owes its origin to the coming of adventurers in search of the amber that was so highly prized by ancient peoples. Certainly it is on the amber coast of Jutland and the Danish islands that the new culture first makes its appearance.

During the following period—the Age of the Passage Graves—the Megalithic Culture expanded from Denmark far and wide over Northern Germany, from Holland to Pomerania, and up the valleys of the Elbe and the Oder. In these regions, however, true passage graves are rare, and their place is taken by a stone chamber under a long mound, somewhat of the type

[1] This stage of culture which survived in the North down to historical times is fully described by Shetelig, *Préhistorie de la Norvège*, ch. ii. Cf. also *R.V.G.*, *s.v.* Nordischer Kreis, A, § 4.

of the English long barrow, or by a subterranean stone cist, often known as a " sunken dolmen." The expansion seems to have been a peaceful one, due to the natural increase of an agricultural population, and resembling that of the Danubian peasants into Central and Western Germany. Indeed, the two movements blended with one another in the region of the Elbe and gave birth to a series of intermediate types of culture, such as those characterised by the Walternienberg and Bernburg styles of pottery in Saxony and Thuringia, and by the Havelland culture of Brandenburg. The development of distinct regional cultures of this kind is a characteristic feature of the latter neolithic period, especially in Central Europe, and nothing is more remarkable than the contrast between this rich and varied local development of culture which was due to a settled agricultural population, and the rude undifferentiated cultures of the hunters and food-gatherers, like the Tardenoisian culture of mesolithic times, and the later Arctic culture, which preserve an almost complete uniformity throughout a wide distribution both in place and time.

The highest development of the northern Megalithic Culture, however, is to be found in its original centres in the Southern Baltic. It was during the close of the Dolmen period and the earlier part of the Passage Grave epoch that the art of pottery attained its full perfection in the north in the two phases named by S. Müller " the grand style " and " the fine style." And though the northern art has not the refinement and technical perfection of the Painted Pottery of Eastern Europe, it is impossible to deny the nobility and strength of its finest examples,[1] which are sufficient to prove the creativeness and originality of the Nordic culture. The vases are ornamented with deeply incised patterns which are quite unlike the decoration of the earlier Dolmen pottery. Professor Müller believes that the

---

[1] Reproduced by S. Müller in *Oldtidens Kunst i Danemarke*, vol. i.

new style is due to a native development of motives derived from the art of the Iberian and West Mediterranean æneolithic culture. Certainly in the later stages of the Passage Grave period there is a most remarkable resemblance between some of the vessels found in Denmark and the pottery of Los Millares, even details such as the conventionalised stags which are a typically Spanish form of ornament being also found in the north. Moreover, at the same period there is a great development of the art of flintworking, similar in technique to that of the Iberian culture, which culminated during the following period of the Stone Cists in the wonderful flaked flint daggers, which are comparable in their perfection of workmanship with the masterpieces of the predynastic Egyptian craftsman.

There can be little doubt that trading relations existed between Spain and the Baltic in the æneolithic period, for Baltic amber is found in the Iberian tombs; and indeed it is probable, as we have seen, that the very idea of the megalithic tomb itself reached the Baltic from South-western Europe by way of maritime trade. Nevertheless, it is impossible to explain the origin of the Nordic culture as a whole in this manner. The earliest pottery of the Dolmen period no more resembles the Mediterranean types than it does those of the northern Kitchen Midden Culture, while the polished stone battle-axes which are also characteristic of the Baltic region have no parallel in the Mediterranean, or in the Megalithic Culture of Western Europe.

II. The Battle-axe Culture in Jutland and its Origins

But there existed a third type of culture in the Baltic which is distinct both from the culture of the megalith builders and from that of the primitive Baltic population of hunters and fishermen. As we have seen, the dolmens are confined to the coasts. In the interior of Jutland we find a distinct type of burial, consisting of earth graves under a low mound which is surrounded by a rude wall of stone. While the megalithic graves are collective tombs, often containing scores of interments, the tombs of the non-megalithic people contain but a single burial and are therefore known as " the Separate Graves." The contents of the earliest examples are similar to those of the dolmens, but in the following period they contain a distinct type of cord-ornamental beaker pottery, as well as fine polished greenstone battle-axes and spherical maces. Evidently they belong to a distinct culture and a different people to the megalith builders, and in the course of time they seem to have dominated or absorbed the latter. Moreover a similar type of culture makes its appearance farther north, in Sweden, and across the Baltic on the coast of Finland, where the Megalithic Culture had never penetrated, while southwards it followed the earlier megalithic expansion into North-west Germany and Holland, where their separate graves take the place of the earlier megalithic tombs. Wherever it went, its presence may be traced by the battle-axes that were the characteristic weapon of the culture, and to a lesser extent by the cord-ornamented beaker pottery.

The question of the origin of this people is one of the greatest problems of European prehistory. According to the German school they are the descendants of the native Baltic population who remained unaffected by the Megalithic Culture owing to their inland position, and their expansion represents the great outward movement of the Nordic race from its original home on the Baltic, which resulted in the formation of the Indo-European peoples of Europe and Asia.

It is, however, difficult to believe that a single people, starting with the same cultural inheritance, should have created at the same time three separate cultures within the Baltic region, each with its distinct type of weapons and pottery and a different mode of burial. And in fact many of the leading Scandinavian archæologists,

PLATE III.—STONE CELTS AND BATTLE-AXES FROM CENTRAL AND
NORTHERN EUROPE

(From the British Museum)

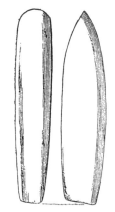

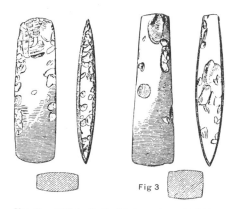

Fig 3

Fig. 1.—" Shoe-Last "
Celt or stone hoe, characteristic of the Danubian
Peasant Culture (from
near Worms, Rhineland)
($\frac{1}{3}$.)

Fig. 2.—" Thin-Butted " Axe, characteristic of
Dolmen Period in Denmark and South Sweden.

Fig. 3.—" Thick-Butted " Axe, characteristic
of Passage Grave Period in Denmark and South
Sweden (both $\frac{1}{4}$).

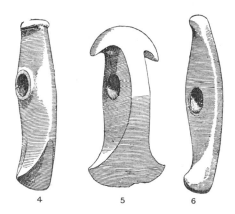

4   5   6

Figs. 4–6.—Stone Battle-axes, characteristic
of the Separate Grave culture in Scandinavia.

such as Sophus Müller, C. A. Nordmann, and Aarne Europaeus, do not accept this view, but attribute the distinctive features in the culture of the Separate Grave People in Jutland to the coming of a new people from outside the Baltic area.

They believe that the new culture is due to the first appearance in Northern Europe of the Indo-European peoples who did not originate in that area, but farther east, and reached the Baltic in consequence of a movement of expansion from Central Europe.

Now there are certainly plentiful signs of Central European influences in the Baltic cultures, even in neolithic times. Curious clay ladles of a distinctively Danubian type are found in the early passage graves, and the pedestalled dishes which are found both in the megalithic tombs and in the separate graves are probably of similar origin. Even a leading supporter of the Nordic theory, such as Åberg, admits that the later pottery of the Separate Graves, and that of the allied culture group in South Sweden, owe their style of ornament to the influence of the Danubian culture of Central Germany. Far more important, however, is the question of the origin of the battle-axe, for that is the most typical feature of the Separate Grave Culture. If the Nordic hypothesis is sound this would have to be derived from the polished stone celts, such as were used by the early megalithic people.[1] As a matter of fact, however, the farther we go back, the less do the Jutland battle-axes resemble true stone types. The thinness of the blade and the way in which its edges curve outwards are entirely unsuited to the material, and must have made it a dangerously brittle weapon. If, however, the battle-axe was an imitation in stone of a metal prototype, these peculiarities would at once find their explanation, and accordingly the majority of Scandinavian archæologists attribute the evolution of the type to this source. This, however, necessarily involves an eastern origin, for the socketed metal double-axe

[2] Cf. Plate III.

of copper, above all the type known as an " axe-adze " with its blades set transversely to one another, which is probably the model of the Nordic battle-axe, is unknown in Western Europe. It occurs plentifully in Hungary and also in South Russia,[1] and probably first originated under the influence of Sumerian types somewhere in the region of the Caucasus.

It is a far cry from the Caucasus to the Baltic. Nevertheless, the gap is bridged by a whole series of cultures, all marked by the possession of the battle-axe and by certain other common features. Thus we find, within easy reach of the Baltic, an important centre of culture in Upper Saxony and Thuringia which possesses all the main features of the Separate Grave Culture of the Baltic. The people buried their dead under large barrows. Their pottery consists of cord-ornamented beakers and amphoræ, and they used faceted battle-axes of stone which seem to be a special local development of the type used by the Separate Grave people. The importance of this region was due in part to the fact that it commands the main route from Central Europe and Bohemia to the Baltic by way of the Elbe and the Oder, and partly to the open character of its loess soil which rendered it specially suitable to agricultural settlement at a time when the greater part of Germany was covered with forest. It had been occupied earlier in the neolithic period by people of Danubian peasant culture, and they seem to have continued to exist side by side with the Battle-axe people, who may even have occupied the same settlements. The adherents of the Nordic theory naturally regard the new-comers as colonists from the Baltic on their way to the conquest of Central Europe. On the other hand, if the Battle-axe people originated in Central Europe, as many writers believe, we might look to Thuringia for the source of the Battle-axe Culture in Jutland. The

---

[1] It also occurs in Crete in the Early Minoan period, and a typical Ægean form was developed later by Period M. M. II. Cf. Evans, *The Palace of Minos*, vol. i, p. 193.

latter, however, seems the earlier of the two cultures, and it is more probable that both of them are parallel movements which have a common origin elsewhere. Certainly there is no question of the importance of the Thuringian culture. Towards the close of the neolithic period it was expanding in all directions. The barrow graves with corded beakers and faceted battle-axes extend southwards up the Elbe into Bohemia and south-westwards to the Rhine, where the Thuringian culture met and blended with that of the Bell-Beaker people from the south, as we described in Chapter X. North-eastward they extend into Brandenburg and Prussia, and even appear sporadically as far east as Kielce in Poland. The most recent student of the distribution of the culture in the region of the Oder [1] has come to the conclusion that it was introduced not by a barbarous hunting people, as was formerly believed, but that its bearers were traders who were in peaceful relations with the native peasant population, and whose culture was Central European rather than Nordic in type.

III. The Battle-axe Cultures of Central and Eastern Europe

Now the culture of Central Europe was itself undergoing important changes during the later neolithic period (Danubian II). It was no longer a simple peasant culture of the original Danubian type. The settlements are larger and in some cases, as at Lengyel in Hungary, are fortified with ditch and rampart. New ceramic types, such as the pedestalled dish, make their appearance and a crude kind of vase painting replaced the earlier incised decoration. Copper ornaments and battle-axes are also found, and there are signs of wider commercial intercourse, especially in the direction of Troy.

The majority of these new elements are apparently due to the influence of the Painted Pottery Culture

---

[1] E. Sprockhoff, *Die Kulturen der Jungeren Steinzeit in der Mark Brandenburg*, 1926.

farther east.   But there are also signs of Nordic influence.
Thus in the great cemetery at Jordansmühl in Silesia,
among the simple earth graves of the Danubian population there is one surrounded by a ring of stones, which
resembles the early Separate Graves of Jutland, and
which contains Nordic pottery of the dolmen type
together with Baltic amber.   Similar Nordic pottery is
found with amber and polygonal stone battle-axes in
the small stone cists, each containing a single interment,
which are widely distributed in Western Poland from
the region of Cracow and Lublin to the mouth of the
Vistula.   The early type of the pottery renders these
discoveries of great importance and they have been
regarded alternatively as evidence of the earliest
expansion of the Baltic peoples into Eastern Europe,
or of a migration in the reverse direction from the east
to the Baltic.   A movement of population was certainly taking place at this period, for the skulls of the
Lengyel people belong not to the old " Sudetic " type
of the Danube region, but are distinctly Nordic.   Thus
it is possible that the changes in the later Danubian
culture were due to an invasion by new warrior peoples.
The great settlement of the Painted Pottery people at
Erösd in Transylvania was destroyed about this time,
and it has been suggested that this was due to the same
movement of invasion which afterwards reached the
Middle Danube bringing with it elements of Transylvanian culture.

In the following period (Danubian III), the peasant
cultures of Central and Eastern Europe undoubtedly
underwent a series of invasions on the part of the
warrior peoples.   Not only the Battle-axe peoples
from the north, but the Bell-Beaker people from the
west were pressing down upon the Upper Elbe and the
Middle Danube.   And farther west similar changes
were at work among the lake-dwelling population of
the Rhineland and the Eastern Alps.   In the former
region the invaders were the Battle-axe people of

Thuringia and the Bell Beaker peoples from the south-west, and it was from the blending of these diverse influences that the later South-west German culture of the early Bronze Age arose.   In the Eastern Alps, on the other hand, the invaders used polygonal stone battle-axes of the Silesian type, and must have come by way of Moravia or Bohemia across the Danube. Under the leadership of these warriors, the lake-dwelling people assumed a more warlike character, and began to expand at the expense of the neighbouring peoples, eastwards into Carinthia and Hungary, and southwards across the Alps into Italy, where their settlements are found on the shores of Lakes Maggiore and Como.   The stone battle-axes, however, have a much wider distribution, extending southwards as far as the Abruzzi and the valley of the Tiber, and possibly bearing witness to the first invasion of Italy by Nordic warriors.

Owing to the multiplicity of invading movements and the rapid alternation of cultures, the whole of Central Europe seems a vast welter of confusion, and the only clear impression that we receive is that some great migration of peoples was taking place like that which swept over Europe in the days of the decline of the Roman Empire.   Indeed, there is good reason to believe that this wave of invasions marks the first great expansion of the Indo-European peoples in Europe. That expansion can hardly have taken place earlier than the close of the neolithic period, for, as we have already seen, the common elements in the Indo-European languages presuppose a certain community of culture which is not found in the earlier neolithic cultures of Europe, while, on the other hand, a later date is hardly possible in view of the historical evidence for the existence of Aryan peoples in Asia in the second millennium, and the absence of any great movement of migration from Asia into Europe during the Bronze Age.   The Battle-axe peoples are a typical example of that warlike pastoral type of society to which we have assumed that the original Indo-Europeans belonged, and the rapid and relatively simultaneous character of their expansion broke down the barriers between the old settled cultures and caused a mingling of peoples and cultures, which may well have been accompanied by the diffusion of a common type of language among the conquered peoples. For the spread of a common language does not involve a common racial origin. Indeed, it is more often the work of a comparatively small class of conquerors, like the Arabs in the early days of Islam, or the Aryans in India.

Moreover, the regions affected by the invasions of the Battle-axe peoples were just those which were to be the later centres of Indo-European culture, and the subsequent development of the Bronze Age cultures of Central and Northern Europe was directly based upon the foundations that were laid during this age of invasion. But we have still to find the source of the whole movement. On the German hypothesis, it is easily explained as due to the expansion of the Nordic peoples of the Baltic and Northern Germany, but, as we have seen, there are serious difficulties in the way of the view that the culture of the Battle-axe people originated in North-western Europe. On the other hand, it is also difficult to find a source for the movement in any part of Central Europe itself, for even in Thuringia and Silesia the Battle-axe people are not the original inhabitants of the land, but were posterior to the Danubian peasants.

The only remaining alternative is to look to the east, which we have already mentioned as the probable source of the battle-axe itself. Now the steppe region of Eastern Europe was inhabited from very early times by a nomad population of hunters who used flint implements and whose traces are found in the sand dunes and by the banks of the rivers, such as the Volga and the Dnieper, wherever the country was free of forest. Their culture is mesolithic in type, and may

even represent a continuous development from the
later palæolithic age. In the late neolithic period,
however, a considerable change of culture took place
in this region. All over the eastern steppes from
Bessarabia and Volhynia to the Caspian and Western
Siberia, the appearance of the new culture is marked
by the round barrows, known as Kurgans, in or under
which the dead were buried with their weapons and
ornaments. The bodies and sometimes the grave itself
were daubed with red ochre, a practice which is a characteristic feature of the culture. The people who made
these tombs were Nordic in race, and possessed a type
of culture similar to that of the Battle-axe peoples of
Central and Northern Europe. They were in contact,
on the one hand with the primitive nomad population,
and on the other with the neighbouring peoples of higher
civilisation, the Painted Pottery people of South-west
Russia, and the metal-working peoples of the Caucasus,
from whom they derived some elements of the higher
culture. Thus from the latter they no doubt acquired
the use of metal and of such Sumerian weapons as the
copper battle-axe.

This is not mere speculation, for at Maikop and elsewhere in the Kuban valley to the east of the Black
Sea there is material evidence of this process of
cultural interchange. The great Kurgan at Maikop
contains literally hundreds of gold and silver ornaments
as well as vases and weapons, which clearly show the
influence of Western Asiatic art and industry, and which
must belong to a Caucasian culture which was related
to that of the Sumerians. But at the same time the
tomb contains other and more primitive objects—stone
implements and pottery—which prove that its occupants,
in spite of their riches, belonged to the ruder culture of
the people of the steppes. Evidently it is the monument of warrior chieftains who dominated a more
advanced society, or, as Professor Tallgren has said,
" Nordic barbarians who had occupied the seats of

Oriental kings." The latter writer dates the Kuban culture at about 2000 B.C., and compares it to that of the Second City of Troy, which probably flourished between 2500 and 1800 B.C. At Troy also we have another instance of the amalgamation of a rich Asiatic culture with another element probably of European origin, the representatives of which used great stone battle-axes as ceremonial emblems.

Moreover, copper battle-axes of the same type as those found in the Kuban graves also appear in Transylvania and Eastern Hungary, and suggest that the Painted Pottery Culture had also been conquered by an invasion of the same people, just as the flourishing Russian civilisation of the Ukraine fell a victim to the raids of the nomads from the steppes in the twelfth and thirteenth centuries A.D.

These, however, are not the only signs that link the Kurgan people of Southern Russia with the great movement of peoples that was taking place about this time. In the very heart of Russia, on the Upper Volga and the Oka, from Tver to Nizhni Novgorod, there existed a culture which both in type and in geographical situation stands midway between that of the South Russian Kurgan people and that of the Battle-axe people of the Baltic. The people of Fatyanovo, as the culture has been named, used stone battle-axes of the Baltic type and sometimes surrounded their graves with rings of stone, like the Separate Graves of Jutland. Their pottery shows a considerable resemblance to the globular amphoræ of Eastern Germany and the corded beakers of Denmark and Thuringia, but it is even more closely allied to that found in the Kurgans of South Russia and the Kuban valley. A close connection between the Fatyanovo culture and that of South Russia is, in fact, admitted by all who have studied them. On the other hand, the links between Central Russia and the west are equally clear, for the Fatyanovo people possessed amber from the Baltic and axes of

Galician or Podolian banded flint, while their battle-axes are distributed through Western Russia as far as Finland and the shores of the Baltic.

Thus there seems to have existed a line of communication between the Black Sea and the Baltic which will serve to explain the transmission of cultural influences from one region to the other. We are so accustomed to regard Scandinavia as the outermost land of Europe that we are apt to forget that the Baltic has served throughout history as a kind of back-door to Asia. The Viking hoards are full of oriental coins struck in the mints of Central Asia, which reached Denmark from the Caspian and the Volga, and in this way examples of oriental art,[1] like the silver-gilt cup found on a Lancashire moorland, which so curiously resembles in its animal decoration the silver vase from Maikop 3,000 years earlier, penetrated even to this country.

IV. The Battle-axe Cultures and the Question of Indo-European Origins

But while the German and Scandinavian archæologists fully admit this connection between the Black Sea and the Baltic in prehistoric times, they see in it but another instance of the eastward expansion of the Nordic culture. In their eyes the South Russia culture is a step in the advance of the Indo-European peoples from Northern Europe to Asia. It is only English archæologists, like Professor Myres, Mr. Peake, and Mr. Gordon Childe, who have looked on Southern Russia as the original source of the whole movement. Yet there is no doubt that the Russian steppe fulfils all the requirements of the linguistic evidence regarding the native land of the Indo-European peoples, much better than does the Baltic. We have seen that the ancient Aryans were pre-eminently a race of horsemen, and that all the Indo-European languages (except perhaps Armenian) preserve common words not only for the

---

[1] From Halton Moor, now in the British Museum.

horse itself, but also for the chariot or waggon and its different parts.   Now the wild horse is a native of the steppe region, where it had been the quarry of the hunter as early as the palæolithic period, and from the earliest historical times the peoples of the steppe have been essentially peoples of the horse, dwelling like the Scythians in their waggons and drinking the milk of their mares.   And that this was the case also in prehistoric times is shown by the presence of horses' bones in their graves, and by the clay model of a waggon that has been found in one of the Kurgans of the Kuban region.

Moreover, the number of common words in the Indo-European languages that are apparently derived from a Sumerian or Babylonian origin, words for metals,[1] domestic animals, weapons, etc., suggest that the home-land of the Aryans must have been situated somewhere within the radius of Mesopotamian cultural influence, a condition which is far better fulfilled by South Russia which was in contact with Asiatic culture through the Caucasus than by Northern Europe.   Again, the Indo-European languages possess a common word for a town or stronghold—the Greek polis, Lithuanian pilis, and Indo-Iranian pur.   Now in the Baltic anything of this nature was unknown until late in the Iron Age, whereas in South-eastern Europe the Painted Pottery people who dwelt on the margin of the steppe region possessed important fortified settlements, like Erösd, as early as neolithic times.

Thus the philological evidence, as admitted even by German writers such as Schrader and Feist, is in favour of an eastern origin for the Indo-European peoples, and if this is once admitted, it is easy to see how the whole series of Indo-European migrations can be explained as an expansion of the warlike horsemen of the steppes.

[1] Cf. Chapter VI, p. 133.   The borrowing of the Sumerian word for copper—urud—is not, however, conclusive, since it might have reached Northern Europe from the Mediterranean by sea.   In fact, the Basque word for copper—urraida—is even closer to the Sumerian than the Latin raudus or the Old Norse raudi.

Eastward they would have penetrated through the Caucasus into Western Asia, southwards through Bulgaria to Troy, and northwards into Central Russia and the Upper Volga, while to the west they would have passed along the Danube into Hungary, and along the corridor of open lands to the north of the Carpathians, to Silesia, and then down the Elbe to Thuringia, and down the Vistula and the Oder to the Baltic. But in spite of the plausibility of this view there remain strong objections to it on archæological and chronological grounds. The German and Scandinavian archæologists are agreed on the priority of the western development. For example, they regard the Swedish Battle-axe Culture as later than the Danish, and that of Finland as later still. In the same way they treat the Thuringian corded ware as later than that of the Separate Graves, and the South Russian as the most recent of all. It is possible to date the graves of the Kuban and the Donetz region approximately by the traces that they show of Trojan and Ægean influence. For example, they contain idols and phallic beads of the Cycladic type, and a copper dagger that probably belongs to the Middle Minoan period. This suggests a date in the latter part of the third millennium or the early part of the second, whereas the origins of the Battle-axe Culture in the north are usually placed much earlier. On the other hand, prehistoric chronology is notoriously fluid, and it is possible to reverse the typological series and explain the primitive forms of Northern Europe as a degeneration from more complex originals. Thus Mr. Gordon Childe has suggested that the silver flask with a gold ring round the neck found at Maikop may supply a prototype of the clay " collared flasks " of the Danish dolmens, and in the same way the stone battle-axes may be viewed as imitations of the copper axes of the Kuban, and the Nordic tumulus grave as a descendant of the Russian Kurgan. The remarkable likeness both in form and in contents between the double dolmen,

the chambers of which are divided by a holed-stone, at
Tsarevskaya on the Kuban and the similar tomb at
Baalberg in Thuringia is equally capable of a two-fold
explanation.   On the whole the archæological evidence
seems to point to the Battle-axe Culture having developed in the northern part of Central Europe—in
Poland, Galicia, and Silesia—rather than either in the
Baltic region or in Southern Russia.   Nevertheless, the
problem is hardly capable of a definite solution, until
the chronology of the later neolithic cultures of Northern
and Central Europe can be more fully correlated with
those of the Ægean and the Near East.   Moreover,
archæological evidence, even under the most favourable
circumstances, is never capable of representing the
whole of the facts.   We have only to look at a known
historical movement like that which accompanied the
fall of the Roman Empire, in order to see the infinite
complexity of reality.

Here was a movement somewhat similar to that of
the Battle-axe peoples in prehistoric times, but one
which we could never reconstruct from purely archæological evidence.   Actually we know that the Gothic
peoples advanced from the Baltic to the Black Sea,
and afterward turned westward to the valley of the
Danube and the Northern Balkans, finally invading
Italy, Southern Gaul, and Spain.   But they were
accompanied in these later migrations by Sarmatian
tribes of Iranian culture from the Black Sea region,
such as the Alans, and it is from this source that the
Germanic peoples of the period of the migrations
acquired their characteristic style of art.   And all this
is only a part of the movement.   There is also the
advance of the West German peoples across the Rhine
and the North Sea, and the vast catastrophe of the
Hunnish invasion, which sweeps down out of Central
Asia over a great part of Europe, and ebbs as suddenly
as it had arisen, leaving practically no archæological
evidence to mark its path.

Now for aught we know, the movements that took place in later neolithic times may have been equally complex. There may have been an almost simultaneous expansion of the Baltic peoples from the north and the Steppe people from Southern Russia, and the two movements may have met and crossed one another, thus accounting for the occurrence of common features in widely separated groups of cultures.

V. The Interaction of the Warrior and the Peasant Types of Culture, and the Two Elements in the Religion and Culture of the Scandinavian North

Nevertheless, whatever the origins and the complexity of the movement, its general meaning and importance are fairly clear. In the first place there is a very strong probability that the invasion of the Battle-axe peoples marks the expansion of the Indo-European peoples in Europe.

And in the second place it is clear that the coming of the warrior peoples marks a radical change in the character of European culture. It produced a general shifting of racial and cultural boundaries, it opened up new channels of communication from east to west and from north to south, and above all it created new social types.

In place of the uniform homogeneous population of peasants or hunters, such as existed in the earlier stages of culture, there appears the warrior tribe with its chieftainship and its differences of rank. Not only was there the inequality which always exists in a pastoral clan owing to the different degrees of kinship and wealth among its members, there was also the far deeper division between warrior lord and peasant serf, which was due to the survival of elements of the older settled population of neolithic times in dependence on the conquering warrior peoples. It is this state of things which explains the extraordinary variety and intermixture of different cultural types in Central Europe at the end of the neolithic period and the beginning of the Bronze Age.   We see the hill settlements of pastoral and hunting peoples rising above the open villages of the agriculturalists in the plains, and the stately tumulus tombs of warrior chieftains standing among the simple graves of the older population.

This warlike transformation of the peasant culture continued throughout the Bronze Age, and reached its climax in the Age of Iron, when the Celtic tribes, with their great broadswords, their war chariots and their champion fighting, swept over Central and Western Europe, everywhere making themselves masters of the earlier population, and planting their great entrenched forts on every hill-top from Ireland to Bohemia.   Hence there arises a kind of duality of culture which is characteristic of societies dominated by a warrior aristocracy, and which has existed almost up to the present day in parts of Eastern Europe, where the noble landlord differed from his peasant serf, not only in his way of life and his social standards, but even in race and religion and language.

In ancient times we find this warrior society existing in ancient India, in Homeric Greece, and in the Celtic lands of Western Europe and described in the epic poetry which is so characteristic a creation of the Aryan peoples.   And in spite of the wide differences of time and place between the Homeric poems and the Mahabharata, and between the latter and the Irish prose epic, we cannot fail to be struck by the remarkable similarity in the social conditions that they depict. But below this brilliant and uniform society of the free warriors, the old life of the peasant cultures still continued to exist.   While the chariot-riding chiefs and nobles worshipped a pantheon of sky gods and war gods, the devas or " shining ones," such as Varuna and Indra and the Heavenly Twins, the peasants remained faithful to the worship of the Mother Goddess and the old chthonic deities of the vegetation religion.   This religious dualism existed even in Northern Europe and survived there to a very late period, for the traces of it are still clearly preserved in the old Norse mythology of early medieval times.   The Scandinavian gods are divided into two distinct families or races, the Vanir and the Æsir.   To the former belong the deities of the earth, of vegetation, and of sexual reproduction, such as Njördr, Freyja, and Frey ; to the latter the warrior deities, Thor, the god of thunder, Tyr, the war god, and Odin, the king of the gods who also presided over war and death, and was the patron deity of princes and nobles. These, however, were a later race than the Vanir, and they only established themselves in the north, according to tradition, after waging war with the older gods.

The earliest account that we possess of the religion of the northern peoples shows that it was a typical example of the ancient peasant religion.   According to Tacitus, the Angles and the other peoples of the far north worshipped the Great Mother under the name of Nerthus—the prototype of the later Njördr. The goddess had her dwelling in a sacred grove in an island of the ocean, and at intervals she was brought forth by her priest to travel through the land in a waggon drawn by oxen.   During her progress all strife and intertribal war must cease, and the land was full of rejoicing.   On her return, the waggon and the goddess herself were washed in a sacred lake in which the slaves who performed the office were afterwards drowned.

In later times in Scandinavia, the place of the goddess was taken by Njördr and his son Frey or Freyr, whom the Swedes worshipped as their divine king, and whose reign was marked by the Frith Frothi, the Peace of Freyr, which secured the fruitfulness of the earth and of men.   The centre of his cult was the great sanctuary at Upsala, where his ithyphallic image was placed, and whence, like Nerthus, he was carried forth in a waggon through the land accompanied by a priestess who was his human spouse. The ceremonies at Upsala were accompanied by phallic rites and ritual prostitution [1] as well as by the sacrifice of human victims who were probably the representatives of the god himself, whose death was necessary for the life of Nature.

In times of famine and distress the Swedes were wont to sacrifice the king himself, the human representative of the god, in order to restore the fertility of the land, and legend relates how the body of the great King Halfdane the Black was divided into four parts and buried in the different quarters of the land to preserve the prosperity and plenty which had accompanied his reign. Thus the later kings of Sweden were the successors and representatives of Freyr, and their office had the same sacred character that was so typical of kingship in the Archaic civilisations. As in Mesopotamia, so also in Sweden, the ruler was a priest king and the vicegerent of a god, and his royal demesne consisted of the sacred lands of the great temple of Freyr at Upsala. We cannot fail to recognise that there is an undeniably oriental and " un-Aryan " element in the religion of our Nordic ancestors. In fact, we find all the characteristic features of the ancient peasant religion reappearing in Northern Europe in comparatively recent times. Thus the cult of Nerthus finds an almost exact parallel in that of Cybele, the Mother of the Gods, in Asia Minor, who also used to make an annual progress through the land in an ox-drawn wain, and whose image was washed with the same ritual solemnity. And so, too, the oriental myths of the death of Tammuz and Adonis find their counterpart in the northern legend of the untimely death of Balder the Beautiful. Even the names are the same,

---

[1] These rites seem to have survived in a degenerate form down to modern times in the form of witchcraft, which was so prominent in Sweden in the seventeenth and eighteenth centuries. Frö or Frey actually appears by name, in a trial that took place in 1720, as the central figure in the witches' assembly at Blåkula, cf. Schütte, *Dänisches Heidentum*, p. 103.

for Balder, like Adon, signifies the Lord, and his spouse bears the name of Nanna which is one of the titles of the Babylonian Mother Goddess. It is true that partly on account of these very coincidences, German and Scandinavian scholars are inclined to regard the Balder legend as of recent origin, being possibly introduced from Thrace in the age of the migrations.[1] Nevertheless, the admittedly primitive cults of Freyr and Freyja are just as fundamentally oriental in spirit. The phallic aspect of the former suggests obvious comparisons with the Semitic fertility cult, while the tears of Freyja for the loss of her lord, Odr, were as proverbial among the northern peoples as the mourning of Ishtar for Tammuz was in the east. Moreover, the names of these deities—Freyr " the Lord," and Freyja " the Lady "— are of the same type as those of oriental divinities such as Baal and Baalath or Bel and Belit, a type which is universal in Syria and Mesopotamia, and almost unknown among Indo-European peoples.[2]

All this has an important bearing on the question of Indo-European origins, for all writers on the subject have justly laid emphasis on the existence of a common type of Indo-European religion, marked by the worship of the Sky God or Heaven Father, Dyaus-pitar, Jupiter, or Varuna, Ouranos, and on the absence of any traces in the Indo-European languages of any common cult of the Earth Mother. If the Baltic were the original home of the Aryans, we should expect this primitive religion to be exceptionally well represented there. But not only is the earliest stratum in the Nordic religion entirely devoted to the vegetation cult, there is even an absence among the later circle of deities of any clearly defined sky god. It is true that the common Indo-European name for divine beings, Tivar or Diar, " the shining ones," is applied poetically to these later

---

[1] Cf. G. Neckel, *Die Überlieferungen vom Gotte Balder* (1920).

[2] This parallelism is developed at length by Neckel, and also by Schütte in *Dänisches Heidentum*, pp. 112–16.

gods rather than to the old chthonic deities, but their usual title—the Æsir—suggests a comparison with the Etruscan Aisar, rather than with any Indo-European word. Odin, their leader, is admittedly recent, and was himself in origin probably a chthonic god of the dead. Thor is the only figure in the pantheon which is certainly celestial in character, but even he seems to have a closer affinity with the old Ægean or Anatolian thunder god, whose emblems were the double axe and the bull, rather than with Zeus or Jupiter. Montelius has even identified the famous Hammer of Thor with the Double Axe of the Ægean culture, and has traced the coming of the new cult by means of the rock engravings of the Bronze Age from the Mediterranean to South-western Scandinavia.[1]

These rock carvings, which are most numerous in Bohuslan and the adjoining regions of South-west Scandinavia, and which have some resemblance to the rock carvings of the Maritime Alps, apparently owe their origin to influences which reached the Baltic by the western maritime route. They represent ships and scenes of ploughing, fighting and religious ceremonies, as well as isolated symbols such as the axe and the wheel or sun disk. It is generally agreed that they possess a religious or magical significance, and various attempts have been made to explain them in relation to the cult of the dead or the vegetation religion.[2] The phallic figures and the representations of ploughing certainly point to the latter, and as the two cults are closely connected, the rival explanations are not mutually exclusive. On the other hand, the axe which is the symbol of the thunder god plays a very important part in the majority of the carvings, and there is evidence of a solar cult which also appears in the metal sun disks that are so common in the Baltic area, as well as to a lesser degree in the British Isles, during the Bronze Age.

Thus the religion of Scandinavia in the Bronze Age

---

[1] Cf. O. Montelius in *Folklore*, 1910, pp. 60–78.
[2] Cf. esp. O. Almgaen *art*. Felsenzeichnung in *R.V.G.*, vol. iii.

Map showing the Invading Movements of Warrior Peoples in Europe at the end of the Neolithic Period.

FATYANOVO B.A. CULTURE

KURGAN PEOPLE

FINLAND B.A. CULTURE

SWEDISH B.A.C.

JUTLAND B.A.C.

POLISH B.A. CULTURE

THURINGIAN B.A.C.

E. ALPINE CULTURE

E. HUNGARIAN COPPER B.A.C.

SPANISH BEAKER CULTURE

Don

Donetz

Kuban

Maikop

Dnieper

Danube

Danube

Troy

Oder

Vistula

Jordans-mühl

Elbe

Saale

L. Constance

Zurich

ALMERIA

Carmona

Scale of Miles
0   100 200 300 400 500

B.A.C. = Battle Axe Culture

= Spanish Beaker Culture

= Battle Axe Culture

Emery Walker Ltd. sc.

seems already to have been of a composite character, and it is difficult to correlate it with the later mythology of the historical period.   One might be tempted at first sight to identify the two elements in the Nordic mythology with the different phases of prehistoric culture, and to assign the worship of the Vanir to the neolithic agriculturalists and that of the Æsir to the coming of the warrior peoples, but neither the evidence of the rock carvings nor the late date of the literary tradition gives any warrant for such an assumption. Indeed, the very closeness of the parallels that we have traced between the later Scandinavian religion and the oriental cults seems to preclude any very distant origin. But they do show that the ancient oriental cultures exercised a much more persistent influence on pre-historic Europe than is usually supposed.   We shall see that the beginnings of the Age of Iron in Central and Southern Europe were accompanied by a fresh wave of oriental influence.   Northern Europe was brought into contact with this stream of culture through the new trade route which ran from the Gulf of Dantzig —the Sinus Veneticus of the ancients—to the territory of the Veneti at the head of the Adriatic.   This connection may explain not only the oriental character of the bronze female idols that appear in the north during the early Iron Age, but also the oriental elements in the later Scandinavian religion.[1]

It is possible that the Eastern Baltic had a much larger influence on the development of the later Scandinavian culture than is usually supposed ; for during the decline in the prosperity of Northern Europe that took place in the Iron Age, the centre of Baltic culture shifted to the south-east, so that Prussia occupied somewhat the same position during the Iron Age that Jutland had possessed in the earlier period.

---

[1] On the traces of oriental influence in Prussia cf. Bezzenberger, " Bronzezeitliche Beziehungen OstPreussens zum Kaukasus," in the *Proceedings of the Russian Archæological Congresses*, 1911, Tr. xv, Ac. i."

CHAPTER XIII

THE AGE OF EMPIRE IN THE NEAR EAST. EGYPT, ASIA MINOR, AND SYRIA.

CHAPTER XIII

THE AGE OF EMPIRE IN THE NEAR EAST. EGYPT, ASIA MINOR, AND SYRIA

I. The Near East in the Second Millennium. The Rise of the Egyptian Empire

THE decline of the Archaic Culture and the invasions of the warrior peoples at the beginning of the second millennium was followed by a period of darkness and confusion during which there is an almost entire absence of historical records. When the Near East begins once more to emerge from obscurity in the sixteenth century B.C., we find ourselves in a new world. Throughout Western Asia, from the highlands of Cappadocia to the Persian Gulf, the conquering peoples have established themselves as the overlords of the native populations and the rulers of powerful states. The most important of these, though it does not come into the full light of history until the fourteenth century, was the Hittite power, which had its centre in Cappadocia, at Boghaz Keui east of the River Halys. To the south-east, in Northern Mesopotamia and the foothills of Kurdistan, lay the powerful state of Mitanni, in which the ruling element was of East Aryan origin, though the bulk of the population belonged to the native Asianic stock. The same Aryan element was also dominant in many parts of Syria as far south as Palestine, though these regions never formed part of the kingdom of Mitanni in historical times. In Babylonia the traces of Aryan influence are much slighter, but there also the native Semitic population was ruled by a conquering race, the Kassites, who originated in the mountainous region to the north-east of the Tigris. The culture tradition of Mesopotamia was still strong enough to impose itself upon its conquerors, but it was weakened and impoverished by the loss of its independence, and Babylonia no longer occupied its old position of undisputed primacy in Western Asia. Only in Egypt, which lay farthest from the centre of invasion, had the native culture been able to reassert its independence by the expulsion of the foreign conquerors and the restoration of the national monarchy under a native dynasty with its centre at the old capital of Thebes.

But the new state in Egypt was not that of the Old Kingdom or even that of the Twelfth Dynasty. For the first time in history it appears as a great military power. The Egyptians had learnt from their conquerors the new methods of warfare, above all the use of the horse and the war chariot, and when once the resources of the organised Egyptian state were directed to warlike ends, it was possible for them to maintain a more formidable professional army than any other single power. The wealth of Egypt in chariots and horses and spearmen and bowmen remained proverbial from this age to the days when the Israelites put their trust in the chariots and horses of Pharaoh " because they were many." And the professional military class now takes its place by the side of the bureaucracy, the priesthood, and the peasantry as one of the four main orders of the kingdom. The old feudal nobility of the Middle Kingdom had been practically crushed out of existence during the Hyksos period and the wars of liberation, and the profession of arms had become the chief path to social advancement, and the origin of a new military nobility. The power of this new element in Egyptian society counterbalanced the static influence of the priestly class, and favoured a policy of war and expansion, and henceforward for 400 years the eyes of the rulers of Egypt were fixed on the wealth of Asia and the glory of foreign conquest.

The imperialist policy achieved its first successes under Thothmes I in the sixteenth century (1545–1513 B.C.), who was the first Pharaoh to lead the armies of Egypt through Syria as far as Naharin, "the Land of the Rivers," and who set up his boundary stone on the banks of the Euphrates itself. "I made the frontier of Egypt," he says, "as far as the circuit of the sun. I made Egypt to become the sovereign and every land her slave."

Nevertheless, the supremacy of the military party did not go unchallenged. Thothmes I himself owed his claim to the crown to his marriage with a princess of the old royal house, and the tradition of the theocratic monarchy of divine right was so strong that his daughter by this princess, Hatshepsut, was regarded as the true representative of the royal line in preference to the sons of the king by his other wives. There appears to have been a struggle between the two parties at court which resulted in the proclamation of Hatshepsut as queen and her marriage to her half-brother Thothmes III. But the latter was little more than a prince consort, and the real power was in the hands of his wife. For the first time in history Egypt was governed by a woman —a female Pharaoh—and the old royal titles were given a feminine termination. She was " the female Horus," " the seed of the gods," the child and representative of the Sun God, while her husband, Thothmes III, was merely described as the son of the king. Thus the reign of Hatshepsut represents the victory of the priestly party and the reassertion of the peaceful tradition of the theocratic monarchy against the secular imperialism of Thothmes and the military party. Instead of sending conquering armies into Syria, she imitated the Pharaohs of the Old Kingdom by dispatching a great expedition to the Holy Land of Punt in the far south to bring back incense and precious things for the service of the gods. Her greatest achievement was the splendid temple of Deir el Bahri, the inscriptions of which celebrate her glory, and describe how she was begotten by no earthly father, but by the god Amon Re himself when he visited her mother in human form.

On her death in 1479 B.C. all this was changed. Thothmes III, the submissive consort, who had been kept in the background throughout the lifetime of Hatshepsut, revealed himself with dramatic suddenness as the greatest conqueror and military genius that Egypt was ever to know. He revenged himself for the years in which he had been kept in tutelage by doing all that was in his power to obliterate the memory of the dead queen. Her name and portrait, and those of her favourites, were obliterated on the walls of the temples that she had built, and her great obelisks were sheathed in shells of masonry which bore the titles of her husband Thothmes alone.   All this symbolised the revolution that had taken place in Egyptian policy and the victory of the military party over the adherents of the conservative and theocratic tradition.

The spirit of the new regime is reflected in the Hymn of Victory which Thothmes caused to be inscribed on a slab in the great temple of Amon at Karnak.   The Sun God Amon Re, who is the speaker, has changed with the spirit of the times.   He is a war god and a giver of victory.

" I have come : I have caused thee to smite the princes of Syria,
I have hurled them beneath thy feet among their mountains.
I have caused them to see thy majesty as a lord of radiance ;
Thou hast shone in their face like my image.

" I have come : I have caused thee to smite the lands of the west ;
Keftiu and Cyprus are in terror.
I have made them see thy majesty as a young bull,
Firm of heart, ready of horn, irresistible.

" I have come : I have caused thee to smite those who are in their
    isles ;
Those who are in the midst of the great sea hear thy roarings.
I have made them see thy majesty as the Slayer,
Rising upon the back of his slain victim.

" I have come : I have caused thee to smite the uttermost ends of the
 lands.
The circuit of the Great Curve is enclosed in thy grasp.
I have made them see thy majesty as a soaring hawk,
Seizing that which he seeth, as much as he desires." [1]

The whole of the remainder of Thothmes' reign consisted of a series of great campaigns, some sixteen in
number, in which he subdued Syria from end to end,
destroying Kadesh, the most powerful city state north
of Lebanon, and receiving tribute and embassies from
the more distant lands of Mitanni, Cilicia, and Cyprus.

When the great king died in 1447 B.C., Syria was practically an Egyptian province, and the frontiers of the empire extended as far as the Euphrates and Mount Taurus.
In Phœnicia and Palestine, Egyptian civilisation was
strongly established. Egyptian gods were worshipped
and temples were erected in the Egyptian style to local
divinities, as for example the temple of Ashtart recently
excavated at Bethshan in Palestine. The same process
went on also to the south of Egypt in Nubia, and
during the Eighteenth Dynasty the land between the
cataracts became almost entirely Egyptian in culture,
an event which left its mark on the whole of the subsequent history of that region.

This extension of Egyptian influence into Asia brought
Egypt into immediate contact not only with the dependent states of Syria, but also with the rival Hittites and
Mitannian kingdoms, and ultimately also with Assyria
and Babylon. Thus there grew up for the first time
an organised system of diplomacy and international
intercourse, of which plentiful evidence exists in the
rich archives of the fourteenth and thirteenth centuries,
discovered at Tell el Amarna and at the Hittite capital,
Boghaz Keui. The great powers contracted alliance
with one another by embassies and gifts, and by the
intermarriage of the royal houses, so that in this age
foreign princesses, such as Nefertiti, the beautiful queen

[1] Tr. Breasted, *History of Egypt.*

of Ikhnaton, came to play a considerable part in the life of the Egyptian court. The relations between Egypt and the land of Mitanni were especially close, but even distant Assyria and the powerful rulers of Babylon were not ashamed to be pensioners on the bounty of Pharaoh, in whose land gold was held to be " as common as dust."

II. Egyptian Culture and Religion under the Eighteenth Dynasty

Under the succession of Thothmes IV, during the next three-quarters of a century, the Egyptian Empire was at the height of its prosperity. The earlier barbarian invasions had injured Babylonian trade, and had to a great extent isolated Mesopotamia from the regions to the west. Consequently the trade that used to flow to the Lower Euphrates and the Tigris was now diverted to the Nile, and Egypt was the centre of commercial intercourse in the Near East. Sea trade with the coast cities of Phœnicia was especially active, and the sphere of Egyptian influence extended farther to Cilicia and Cyprus, and to Keftiu and " the islands of the sea," by which name the Egyptians referred to Minoan Crete and the other civilised peoples of the Ægean. This movement reached its climax under Amenophis III, the great-grandson of Thothmes IV, who reigned from 1411 to 1376 B.C. His mother was a princess from Mitanni in the far north, and this is characteristic of the cosmopolitanism which now marks Egyptian culture. He was no warrior prince, like his ancestors, but a luxurious oriental monarch, devoted to the building of palaces and temples, and the pomp of a magnificent court life. It was in this period that Thebes attained the splendour that was proverbial for more than a thousand years afterwards. Diodorus in 57 B.C. describes how the kings of Egypt devoted themselves to the adornment of the city. " So that there was no city under the sun so adorned with so many and stately monuments of gold, silver, and ivory, and multitudes of colossi and obelisks, each cut out of one entire stone.

Thus the age of Amenophis III was of exceptional importance for the development of architecture and art. It saw the rise of the classical types of temple which were to remain characteristic of the Egyptian culture as long as the latter survived. The smaller type with its base and pillared portico recalls in its simplicity of form the peripteral Greek temple of classical times, while the vast temples of Karnak and Luxor, with their monumental gateways flanked by towering pylons, their colonnaded courts, and their great pillared halls, sometimes consisting of a central nave, lit by a clerestory, and two lower aisles, are comparable rather to the medieval cathedrals of the west, with which they are indeed ultimately connected through the tradition of the Hellenistic and Roman basilica.

The decoration of these buildings was as magnificent as their design. The walls and pylons were covered with painting and sculpture, the gates and pillars were overlaid with gold and the floors with silver which to the Egyptians was a metal hardly less precious than gold itself.

The same luxury characterised the court life of the age. The contents of the royal tombs, such as that of Tutenkhamon, have shown us the splendour of the jewellery and ornaments, the wonderful inlaid furniture, the carved ivory, the glazed pottery, and the beautiful opaque polychrome glass which was a special invention of the period. The bodies of the kings were no longer laid to rest in pyramids, but in the great rock-cut corridor tombs which line the cliffs of the Valley of the Kings on the edge of the desert west of Thebes. Nevertheless, the cult of the dead remained no less elaborate than in the days of the Old Kingdom. Indeed, it was in this period that the cult of Osiris and the religion of the celestial hereafter attained its full development, and became the common heritage of the whole Egyptian people.

But the most remarkable religious development of the imperial age was the attempt of Amenophis IV to create a new state religion and to replace the official cultus of the old royal god Amon Re of Thebes by the worship of the Aton or Sun Disk. Even at this time the priesthood of Amon was the wealthiest and most powerful corporation in the state, and in order to free himself from its influence the young king took the drastic step of abandoning the old capital of Thebes, and founding a new city, dedicated to the new worship, at Akhetaton, " The Splendour of the Aton," the modern Tell el Amarna. In conformity with the same idea he changed his own name from Amonhotep, " Amon rests," to Ikhnaton, " the Aton is satisfied," and encouraged his family and his courtiers to do the same.

Nor was he content with this formal recognition of the supremacy of the new divinity. He did all that was in his power to overthrow the old cults, and above all that of Amon, by the disendowment of their temples and priesthoods, and even by erasing the name of Amon from the monuments.

The iconoclastic violence of these proceedings shows that something more was at stake than the addition of a new divinity of the old type to the Egyptian pantheon. It was a religious revolution which differed from anything that had gone before in its exclusive and monotheistic spirit. The Aton was not a sun god of the type of Re and Horus and Amon. It was conceived by Ikhnaton as the one vital principle, creating and informing the whole universe.

> " Creator of the germ in woman,
>   Maker of seed in man,
>   Giving life to the son in the body of his mother,
>   Soothing him that he may not weep,
>   Nurse even in the womb,
>   Giver of breath to animate everyone that he maketh !
>   When he cometh forth from the body on the day of his birth,
>   Thou openest his mouth in speech,
>   Thou suppliest his necessities.

" When the fledgling in the egg chirps in the shell,
Thou givest him breath therein to preserve him alive.
He cometh forth from the egg to chirp with all his might,
He goeth about upon his two feet
When he hath come forth therefrom.
" How manifold are thy works !
They are hidden from before us,
O sole God whose power no other possesseth.
Thou didst create the earth according to thy heart
While thou wast alone.
" Thou alone shining in thy form as living Aton,
Dawning, glittering, going afar and returning.
Thou makest millions of forms
Through thyself alone ;
Cities, towns and tribes, highways and rivers.
All eyes see thee before them,
For thou art Aton of the day over the earth." [1]

In these utterances we can see the beginnings of a wider and more spiritual type of religion than the Archaic Culture had ever known. The pessimism and intellectual distress of the preceding age had prepared the way for a more profound conception of life, which was to find its full expression in the great world religions and philosophies of the following millennium. It is true that the cult of the Aton had its more material aspect. Professor Breasted has said that " in the Ancient East monotheism was but imperialism in religion," and the Aton cult with its three sacred cities in Egypt, in Syria, and in Nubia, was the spiritual counterpart of the Egyptian imperial expansion—one God in heaven, as there was one king on earth. Nevertheless, the religious element in Ikhnaton's policy far outweighed the political. He was profoundly convinced of his personal mission and inspiration, and the power and prosperity of the Egyptian Empire was a secondary consideration with him.

" Thou art in my heart (says the great hymn),
There is none that knoweth thee
Save thy son Ikhnaton,
Thou hast made him wise
In thy designs and in thy might."

[1] Tr. J. H. Breasted, *Development of Religion and Thought in Ancient Egypt*, pp. 324–8.

And the manifestation of " the Truth " to his chosen
followers and his subjects seems always to have been
the principal preoccupation of his life. He was in fact
a contemplative and an artist rather than a politician.
The beautiful naturalistic art of the new capital at Tell
el Amarna seems to have been due to his personal
inspiration and to his desire for the visible embodiment
of " the Truth." Nothing can give us a clearer idea of
the contrast between the spirit of the new movement
and that of the old imperial tradition than the portraits
of the king and his family, which in their morbid refinement and their exotic charm resemble the creations of
the Buddhist art of Ajanta and Sigiri far more than the
powerful and virile figures of the old warrior kings.

III. The Decline of the Egyptian Empire

As a personality Ikhnaton is certainly the most
interesting and significant character among the rulers
of Egypt, but from a material standpoint his reign was
disastrous for Egypt. He thoroughly offended the
traditional feeling both of priests and people, he neglected the military organisation of the empire, and left
the distant provinces to their own devices. The Tell
el Amarna archives are full of the pressing appeals of
the faithful vassals and governors of Egypt in Syria for
reinforcements and help. The whole country was in
confusion. The Hittite power of Eastern Asia Minor
was advancing into North Syria, and the Amorite ruler
Abdashirta threw off his allegiance to Pharaoh and
made war upon the faithful cities. In the south a
horde of Semitic tribes from the desert—Habiru—burst
into Palestine plundering and burning in all directions.
Thus the Asiatic Empire of Egypt fell to pieces even
during the lifetime of Ikhnaton, and on his death in
1362 his work of religious reform was equally undone.
His son-in-law Tutenkhaton—for he left no son—
returned to Thebes, changed his name to Tutenkhamon,
and restored the supremacy of the priests of Amon,

and the old traditional cults. In its turn the name of
the new deity was erased from all the monuments, and
the dead king Ikhnaton was condemned as a heretic
and an enemy of the gods. The great reformer went
down to posterity under the name of " the criminal of
Akhetaton."

Thus ended the Eighteenth Dynasty, the most powerful and successful that had ever reigned in Egypt. Its
place was taken by a new dynasty (Dynasty XIX, 1346–
1210 B.C.), founded by a capable noble named Harm-
hab, who had the support of the priesthood of Amon,
now the greatest power in the land. This was followed
by a renewal of imperial expansion. After a period of
rest and recuperation Egypt once more advanced to the
conquest of Syria, which had become a dependency of
the Hittite Empire. Seti I in 1314 reconquered Palestine and Phœnicia, and his son, Rameses II the Great,
attempted to reconquer the whole country, and actually
defeated the Hittites in a great battle at Kadesh in
1288. But the two empires were now evenly matched,
and after sixteen years of war a settlement was reached
by which Egypt held Southern Syria as far as Lebanon,
and the Hittites kept the north. This settlement was a
permanent one, and the Egyptian control over Palestine
and Phœnicia was not threatened again until the great
invasion of peoples from the north, which proved fatal
to the Hittite Empire itself.

Rameses II, 1300–1233 B.C., was one of the greatest
builders in Egyptian history, and has left his mark on
the country to this day. The art of the period was
already decadent—far inferior to what it had been
under the Eighteenth Dynasty—and was marked by a
taste for the colossal rather than the beautiful. But
Egypt was still wealthy, and the trade of the Near East
flowed into the Nile valley no less than it had done
during the time of Amenophis III. In fact, the cosmo-
politan tendency was stronger than ever. The court
was full of Syrian slaves and favourites, and the adminis-

tration was largely in their hands. The army was now almost purely a mercenary one, it was recruited widely from among the peoples of the Mediterranean. The Shardana—probably the same people who occupied Sardinia at this period—were especially important, and formed the royal bodyguard.

At the same time that the monarchy was becoming more and more denationalised and dependent on external support, the power of the priesthood within the country was steadily growing. In the time of Rameses III, 1204–1172, the temples owned more than half a million acres of land and 100,000 slaves, as well as towns and properties in Syria and Nubia and fleets of galleys with which to maintain communication with them. And the vast majority of this mass of wealth was the property of the priesthood of Amon which was becoming a power in the land hardly second to that of Pharaoh himself. As the monarchy declined, the priesthood grew in political power, until finally, at the end of the Twentieth Dynasty, c. 1100 B.C., the High Priest of Amon added the royal dignity to his other prerogatives and became ex-officio Pharaoh.

This is the final term of Egyptian constitutional development. Egypt was now a theocracy in the strict sense of the word, ruled by a priest king, a sort of Grand Lama, who united in himself both secular and religious authority. But from the military point of view he was almost powerless ; the imperial power of Egypt was at an end, and the Delta itself fell into the hands of Libyan invaders from the west. The beginning of the Dark Ages had come.

Thus the fundamental weakness of the New Kingdom in Egypt was revealed in its ultimate consequences. The combination of the ancient theocratic culture with the warrior state of the Bronze Age proved a failure because no organic union of the two was possible. The military class remained external to the civilisation which it defended, as a parasitic growth with no roots in the life of the nation.   The native tradition of Egyptian culture reasserted itself in the victory of the priesthood, but from a military point of view it was impotent, and consequently Egypt fell a victim to military adventurers and foreign mercenaries, as in the days of the Memluk rule.   Henceforward the leadership of the civilised world was to lie in the hands of peoples who were able to combine their cultural development with a high standard of military efficiency.

IV. The Peoples and Languages of the Hittite Empire

Already during the Bronze Age we see an example of a new type of military state in the Hittite Empire, the great rival of Egypt throughout this period, which differed from the earlier states of the Archaic Culture in the fact that it consisted of a federation of many different peoples and cities, held together by a common military organisation.

The land of Hatti itself, the core of the empire, lay in Western Cappadocia with its capital at Hattushash, the modern Boghaz Keui, east of the River Halys, and it was surrounded by a group of client states, Arzawa to the south, Hanigalbat or Milid to the east, and Kissuwadna, probably to the north, as well as many others of lesser importance.   The partial decipherment of the Hittite archives from Boghaz Keui has revealed the existence of at least five different languages which were apparently current in the territories of the Hittite Empire.   The official language, in which the majority of the documents are written, undoubtedly contains Indo-European elements and is perhaps the oldest known Indo-European language.   But although this was the speech of the ruling people of the empire, it is not strictly speaking Hittite, for the documents themselves reserve the name of Hittite or Hattic for a totally different language, which has no connection with any other linguistic group, and which was no doubt the original speech of the natives of the country. The official language of the empire has been named by its discoverers Nashili [1] or Kanesian ; but since the ruling people have always been known as the Hittites, it seems better to retain the same name for their language and to describe the native Hattic tongue as Old Hittite.

In addition to these languages and to the Babylonian, which was the common medium of diplomacy and trade throughout the Near East, the Hittite archives also refer to three other tongues, Luvian, Palaic, and Harrian or Churrite. Of the first two of these little is known, though Luvian seems to show some connection with Hittite (i.e. with the official language), but the third, Harrian, is practically identical with the language of the people of Mitanni, the most powerful state of Northwest Mesopotamia.

We have already seen that the dominant element in Mitanni was Indo-European, or rather Indo-Iranian, in origin, but there is no trace of this in the Harrian language, which is purely Asianic or Caucasian in type.

Consequently the same dualism of speech and race must have existed in Mitanni as in the Hittite realm, and in each case the native population was dominated by a ruling class of Indo-European origin. This parallelism in the development of the Hittite and the Mitannian States was not, however, due to a single Indo-European invasion. The Indo-European element among the Hittites is totally different to that which appears in the land of Mitanni. The latter no doubt had its origin to the eastward in Iran, while the former came either southward from the Caucasus or eastward from the Balkans across the Bosphorus, just as in later times we find the same region becoming the meeting-ground of the Persians from the east and the Greeks and Romans from the west. The hypothesis of a Caucasian

[1] The word Nashili only occurs in one text, and Hrozny's interpretation of it, as meaning " our language," is not certain.

origin for the Hittites is perhaps favoured by the existence of the peculiar hieroglyphic script, which makes its first appearance under the Hittite Empire. A script of so primitive a type could hardly have been evolved at that period in a region like Cappadocia in which the highly developed Babylonian cuneiform had been in u.e since the twenty-third century B.C. On the other hand, like the cuneiform script, the Hittite hieroglyphics seem ultimately to be derived from the original pictographic script of the Sumerians and consequently must have arisen in some region which was within the Sumerian zone of influence. Now we know from the style of the tomb furniture at Maikop in the Kuban that the Caucasian culture was already under Sumerian influence as early as the end of the third millennium, and it seems not improbable that the Kuban region was the original cradle of the Hittites before they invaded Cappadocia.

But this is not the only possible explanation of the appearance of the Hittite script. It might also be due to the survival of a native Anatolian script which originated under the influence of the Sumerian culture at a very early period, and which continued to be used as a sacred writing after the introduction of the Babylonian cuneiform for commercial and official purposes.

The military character of the Hittite power is shown by the important place occupied by the army which appears to have consisted of a kind of feudal militia, holding its lands on the condition of military service. The army was composed of so many different elements that it can have possessed little national feeling, but it was bound together by a sense of personal loyalty to the king and queen, which is highly characteristic of Hittite society, and which found expression in a military oath, like the Roman sacramentum, which was administered to the troops with every accompaniment of ritual solemnity.[1]

[1] Cf. the text translated by J. Friedrich in *Der Alte Orient*, xxv. ii. 16.

V. HITTITE CULTURE AND ITS RELATION WITH MESOPOTAMIA

Apart from these feudal and military elements, however, the Hittite culture was almost entirely dependent on the tradition that it had inherited from the older Sumerian-Babylonian civilisation. We have seen (in Chapter VI) that the region that was afterwards to be the centre of the Hittite realm was already in the twenty-third century B.C. an outlying province of the Mesopotamian culture ; indeed, many of the sacred cities of the Hittite Empire, such as Kanesh and Zalpa, appear by name in the cuneiform documents of the earlier period from Kara Euyuk.

Thus the Hittite military monarchy of the fourteenth century was built on the foundation of these older city states of the Mesopotamian type, and their survival in the new imperial organism secured the continuity of the higher city culture. This explains the high economic development of Hittite society, for the organisation of trade and industry followed the same lines as in the Babylonian period. As in Mesopotamia the state took a leading part in the regulation of economic life ; it was a great landowner and trader, and possessed state monopolies in certain articles such as leather.

Considerable light is thrown on the social and economic conditions of Hittite society by the code of laws discovered at Boghaz Keui, which probably dates from the fourteenth century. Like the code of Hammurabi, it contains a detailed tariff for the regulation of prices and wages, but it differs from the former, and still more from the later Assyrian legislation, in the comparative mildness of its penalties. The laws refer to a number of different trades and industries, as well as to the peasant crafts of vine-dressing, arboriculture, and bee-keeping to which the Hittites seem to have attached particular value.

The most important industries of the Hittite realm,

however, were mining and metallurgy. As far back as
the third millennium the lands west and north of Mt.
Taurus had been renowned for their wealth in copper,
silver, and lead, and had already attracted the merchants
of Babylonia and Assyria.

Under the Hittites, the mineral resources of the region
were still further developed, and it is to them or to one
of the neighbouring peoples that we owe the epoch-
making discovery of the working and smelting of iron.
In the early part of the thirteenth century Rameses II
was writing to his ally the King of the Hittites for
supplies of the new metal, and we possess the reply of
King Hattushil stating that at the moment the magazines in the land of Kissuwadna were empty.

The source of the metal was probably in the mountains
of Northern Pontus, the land of the Chalybes, to whom
the Greeks attributed the first discovery of iron, and
since it was already an article of export in the early
thirteenth century, it is probable that the discovery
goes back at least to the previous century.[1]

In the sphere of religion, the Hittite culture was no
less dependent on the tradition of the Archaic civilisation. The temple and the priestly order played a
leading part in Hittite society, and it is probable that
the holy cities of the Empire were temple states, like
Comana or Pessinus in later times, ruled by the representative of the god or the goddess.

The national deity of the Hittites was the war god
Tarkhon who was apparently identified with Teshub
the chief god of Mitanni, and with the Egyptian Sutekh.
The famous treaty between Rameses II and the Hittite
monarch mentions a whole series of gods of this name,
one for each of the principal divisions of the empire,
along with the other chief Hittite divinities, the Sun
God or Goddess of Arinna, " Ishkara the mistress of the

---

[1] In the recent excavations at Ur, however, a surprising discovery of
fragments of wrought iron was made in a grave (No. 580) belonging to
the earliest period, dated by Mr. Woolley about 3500 B.C.

mountains and rivers of the land of the Hittites," the Divine Lords of the Oaths, the Lady Goddess of the Soil, the Mistress of the Oath, and many more. Nevertheless, the ancient Peasant Cult of the Mother Goddess and her spouse, the god of vegetation, retained its power over the people of Asia Minor, and tended ultimately to absorb the more masculine and warlike element in the Hittite religion. The great rock sculpture of Yasili Kaya, the holy place which adjoined the Hittite capital, portrays in an impressive manner the fusion of the two cults. Two solemn processions advance to meet one another. On the one side the Great God of the Hittites with his sceptre in his hand,[1] on the other the Mother Goddess of Asia, crowned with towers and standing on the lion, followed by her attendant, the God of the Double Axe, and two other goddesses. It represents the Sacred Marriage of the two great powers of the Hittite religion—a union in which the Goddess proved to be the predominant partner, so that ultimately, as at Komana, she absorbed the attributes of the Hittite War God and reigned alone as a Warrior Goddess.

This preponderance of the female element in Anatolian religion and culture, which is symbolised by the reversal of the attributes of the sexes in the eunuch priests and armed priestesses of the Great Goddess, became characteristic of the later Hittite culture and made a deep impression on the minds of the neighbouring peoples. In Greek tradition the memory of the Hittite Empire survived in the legend of the Amazons who, from their home on the banks of the River Thermodon in Northeast Asia Minor, issued forth to war with the Phrygians and the Trojans, and who were the foundresses of the cities of Ionia, Smyrna, Ephesus, Cyme, and Myrina. Thus the legend of the battles of Heracles and Achilles against the Amazons, which remained one of the favourite

---

[1] Some writers have seen in this figure the Hittite king himself, but if this were the case, he would almost certainly be portrayed on a smaller scale than the Goddess. Moreover, he is accompanied by the goat, which was the sacred animal of Tarkhon.

motives of Greek art, expresses in a mythical form the
opposition between the spirit of the old civilisation of
the Asiatic Mother Goddess and that of the young
warrior peoples of Europe. Nor is this tradition
without an historical element, for the figures of the
colossal Hittite warrior carved on the cliffs of the Pass
of Karabel between Ephesus and Smyrna, as well as
other monuments of the region, prove that the Hittite
power really did extend as far west as Ionia, and the
documents of Boghaz Keui show that the Hittite
monarchs were in relation with the princes of the
Achæans, the Aḫḫiyava, who were raiding the coasts of
Caria and Cilicia in the thirteenth century. Consequently the Hittite culture acquires a special importance,
as the intermediary between the Archaic Civilisation of
Western Asia and the early Hellenic culture, and as the
possible foundation of the higher development that had
its centre in the Ionian cities. It is as yet impossible
to say how far this influence extended. We know that
Babylonian literature and learning were cultivated by
the Hittites; for example, there was a Hittite version
of the epic of Gilgamesh; and it is by no means improbable that through this channel influences originating in
Mesopotamia may ultimately have affected the culture
of the Greeks and other European people. In one
instance that has already been mentioned this communication of culture is practically certain, for the
practice of Hepatoscopy or divination from the liver
of the sacrificial victim, which reached Asia Minor from
Mesopotamia, was carried by the Etruscans to Italy,
where it became an important element in the official
Roman religion. There can be no doubt that the Hittite
culture, situated, as it was, on the north-western
frontier of the older civilised world, played an important
part as the intermediary between the Archaic Culture
of Asia and the dawning civilisation of Europe, though
our ignorance of what was passing during the Bronze
Age in Western Asia Minor, and still more in the

Caucasus, renders it a vanished chapter of history. There is indeed no more fitting symbol of the age-long march of culture from east to west than the imperial emblem of the Hittite power—the double-headed eagle which had its origin in the Sumerian city state of Lagash thousands of years earlier, and was passed on thousands of years later from Asia Minor to Europe, where it became in turn the standard of the new empires which governed the fate of Central and Eastern Europe down to our own times.

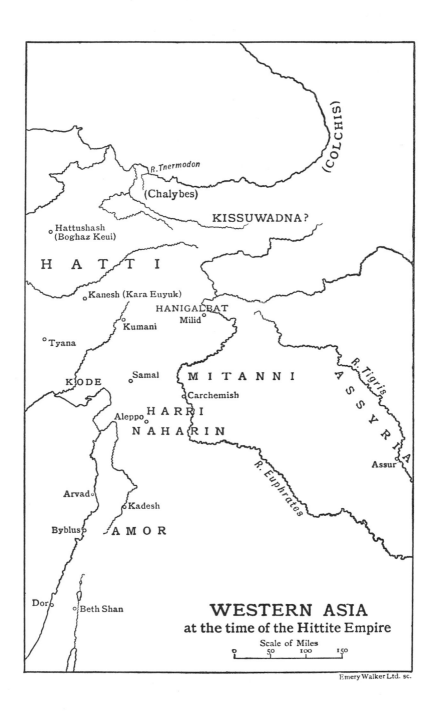

(COLCHIS)

R. Thermodon

(Chalybes)

KISSUWADNA?

Hattushash
(Boghaz Keui)

H A T T I

Kanesh (Kara Euyuk)

HANIGALBAT

Kumani   Milid

Tyana

MITANNI

Samal   R. Tigris

KODE

Carchemish

HARRI

Aleppo

NAHARIN

ASSYRIA

Arvad

Kadesh   R. Euphrates

Byblus   AMOR   Assur

Dor

Beth Shan

WESTERN ASIA
at the time of the Hittite Empire

Scale of Miles

0   50   100   150

Emery Walker Ltd. sc.

CHAPTER XIV

THE BRONZE AGE IN CENTRAL EUROPE AND THE FORMATION OF THE INDO-EUROPEAN PEOPLES

THE EUROPEAN BRONZE AGE AND ITS ORIGINS.

THE BRONZE AGE IN CENTRAL EUROPE. THE AUNJETITZ CULTURE.

THE BRONZE AGE IN GERMANY AND THE BALTIC. THE CELTIC AND GERMANIC PEOPLES.

THE BRONZE AGE IN EASTERN EUROPE. THE THRACIANS AND THE ILLYRIANS.

THE BRONZE AGE IN ITALY AND THE TERREMARE CULTURE.

THE TERREMARE CULTURE AND THE ORIGINS OF THE ITALIC PEOPLES.

THE LATER PHASES OF THE BRONZE AGE IN CENTRAL EUROPE. THE URN CEMETERIES AND THE LAUSITZ CULTURE.

CHAPTER XIV

THE BRONZE AGE IN CENTRAL EUROPE AND THE FORMATION OF THE INDO-EUROPEAN PEOPLES

I. THE EUROPEAN BRONZE AGE AND ITS ORIGINS

THE Age of Empires in the Near East finds its counterpart in Europe in the Mycenæan period of Greece and the continental Bronze Age. This is an important phase of the development of European culture, for it marks the transition between the prehistoric and the historic worlds. During its course the peoples and cultures which emerge into the light of history in the following epoch were already in the process of formation. Moreover, it was during this age that Europe first acquired a certain measure of cultural unity. The earlier neolithic peasant cultures and the hunting and food-gathering cultures of a yet more primitive type were almost entirely self-sufficing and, like the savage peoples of modern times, could follow the same unchanging course of existence for ages. But the use of metal at once brought with it a wide extension of trade and intercommunication, and led to the diffusion of common types of weapons and implements, and thus the carliest centres of metal-working became also centres of cultural influences which penetrated far and wide through Europe.

In this way the achievements of the early metal-working cultures of the Near East were gradually diffused throughout the length and breadth of Europe, and gave the initial impetus to the development of the different regional types which became characteristic of the later phases of the Bronze Age.

Thus European culture acquired a much more complex character than it had possessed in neolithic times. While the old cultures were, so to speak, simple and uniform organisms, those of the Bronze Age were made up of a number of different elements.

In the first place the cultures of the previous age still remained as a kind of permanent substratum which underlies all the later developments. This peasant foundation was an indispensable condition in the existence of a higher type of culture, and where it was absent, as in Central Russia for example, we see the new metal-using culture making a temporary appearance and passing away again without leaving any permanent mark on the culture of the region. On the other hand, it was in Central Europe, where the peasant culture of the Danubian type was most firmly established, that the subsequent development of the Bronze Age was most important and had the widest influence on the rest of Europe. And the distinction between the main types of neolithic culture—that of the Danubian peasants, that of the Alpine lake-dwellers, and that of the western megalith builders, survived to some extent into the new age and formed one of the principal elements in the evolution of the new regional cultures. Nevertheless, the new development of civilisation did not proceed directly from these peasant populations. The Bronze Age was preceded, as we have seen in Chapter XII, by a series of invasions by warrior peoples, which broke through the old cultural frontiers, and, by their conquest of the native neolithic population, formed new mixed types of peoples and cultures. To a certain extent these invasions were destructive of the Peasant Culture, and in some parts of Europe agriculture declined and the population shifted to the uplands and the fringes of the forest which were more suited to the life of a pastoral and hunting people. But the change was not wholly retrograde. The warrior chieftains were richer and more powerful than the old peasant com-

munities. They needed horses, and weapons, and ornaments, and thus they were the element in the population
that had most to do with the use and diffusion of the
new metals. It is even possible that their conquests
may have been influenced to some extent by economic
motives : that the Beaker people penetrated to Bohemia
on account of its wealth in minerals, and that the amber
of Jutland and the salt deposits of Thuringia first
attracted the Battle-axe people to those regions. Indeed,
we have seen in a previous chapter that the Battle-
axe people of Thuringia appear on the Lower Oder as
traders rather than migratory barbarians. In any case,
when the power of the warrior peoples was once established, their influence would tend to stimulate trade
and lead to the opening up of new routes and the
working of local metals.

The third element in the culture of the Bronze Age
was supplied by the higher civilisations of the Near East.
It was in that region that the knowledge of metal-
working first originated, and it is probable that the
discovery of bronze was made somewhere in the same
area during the third millennium B.C. The Sumerians
had been accustomed from very early times to make
alloys of gold and silver, copper and lead, and copper
and antimony, and in this way they may have learnt
to alloy copper with tin and produce bronze. Tin,
however, is a metal of rare occurrence in the Near East,
and it is very doubtful from what source the ancient
oriental peoples first obtained their supplies.[1] Europe,
however, possesses rich supplies of tin, in Cornwall and
Bohemia, as well as to a lesser extent in Etruria and
Portugal, and as soon as these native resources began
to be exploited, Europe became one of the main sources

---

[1] The ancient word for tin, which is found both in Greece and India—
Gr. kassiteros ; Sans. kastira-m—may throw some light on the subject.
Pokorny has shown that there is no ground for the belief that this
word is of Celtic origin, but that it is probably derived from the Elamite
word kassi-ti-ra, " from the land of the Kassites," and this suggests
that the metal first reached Mesopotamia from the north-east .

of supply for the ancient world. But there is no reason to suppose that the discovery of the new metal was of European origin. The influence of the metal-using cultures of the Near East had been gradually penetrating into Europe from the Ægean, throughout the æneolithic period, and it was in this way that the prehistoric cultures of Europe acquired not only the knowledge of the working of metals, but also the main types of tools and weapons and ornaments which served as the models of their own dawning industry.

The two main avenues by which these influences reached Europe was by way of the Mediterranean to the Iberian Peninsula, and up the valley of the Danube from Troy and the Ægean. The former region became, as has been shown in Chapter X, the source of the Bronze Age culture of the west, while the latter was the foundation of the Central European development. The Second City of Troy, which flourished in the second half of the third millennium B.C. (c. 2500–1900), was an important centre of trade and possessed a distinctive type of art and metal-working. We have already seen how the traces of Trojan commerce are to be seen from the Black Sea to the Ægean, and farther still in the Western Mediterranean and perhaps even as far as Southern Portugal (Nora). But their influence was not limited to the sea-ways, for distinctively Trojan types of pottery and copper ornaments are to be found along the course of the Danube and the Theiss, and as far into Central Europe as Bohemia, Silesia, and Thuringia. No doubt the first centre of attraction in this movement was the goldfields of Transylvania, which may have been the source from which the Trojans obtained their plentiful supplies of that metal. And it is accordingly in the settlements of the lower Maros region, near Arad, that the signs of Trojan influence, such as the two-handled " hour-glass " cups which are so common at Troy, are most numerous. Nevertheless, similar types are found as far north as Bohemia and Thuringia, and the earliest

traces of metal in that region, and in Hungary, such as
the copper ornaments in the form of a double spiral
found at Lengyel, the spiral earrings and the so-called
" knot-headed " pins, also resemble Trojan forms.   All
this points to the existence of a trade route connecting
Troy with Central Europe, and since we know that the
Trojans possessed bronze which was, for the period,
exceptionally rich in tin, it is by no means improbable
that Trojan influence was responsible for the first
opening up of the tin deposits of Bohemia, and the
beginnings of metallurgic industry in Central Europe.[1]
On the other hand, there also existed a link between
Bohemia and the earliest centre of metal-using culture
in Western Europe—the Iberian Peninsula.   We have
seen how the Beaker people, who were the dominant
element in Spain during the flourishing period of
æneolithic culture, expanded into Central Europe, and
established themselves on the Rhine and the Elbe.   They
probably reached Bohemia in the second part of the
third millennium B.C., at the same time that the
Second City of Troy was at the height of its prosperity,
and they seem to have combined with the warrior
peoples who entered Bohemia and Moravia from the
north, to form the ruling element in the population.

II. The Bronze Age in Central Europe.   The Aunjetitz Culture

These changes were the prelude to the development
of the new Bronze Age culture which arose in Central
Europe about the beginning of the second millennium.
This culture, which takes its name from the great cemetery at Aunjetitz or Unetics, close to Prague, is the
first original creation of the continental Bronze Age,
though in its origins it owed a considerable debt to
external influences alike from the south-east and the
south-west.   From the one quarter were derived the

[1] Cf. " The Danube Thoroughfare and the Beginnings of Civilization
in Europe," by V. G. Childe, in *Antiquity*, vol. i, i.

earliest types of ornaments, such as the spiral earrings and knot-headed pins mentioned above, while the weapons, such as daggers and axes, belong to the West European forms. The bronze halberd, which is common in Thuringia and Saxony, is a local development of a distinctively western type of weapon which originated in Spain, and which seems to have reached Central Europe by the round-about route by way of the British Isles and North Germany. There is also a remarkable resemblance between the Aunjetitz pottery, especially in the case of the angular cup which is one of the most popular forms of vessel, and that of the contemporary Spanish culture of El Argar, nor does it seem impossible that this is due to Spanish influence, since the Bell Beakers which appear in Bohemia in the previous period undoubtedly originated in that region.

The domain of the Aunjetitz Culture covered a large part of Central Europe, including Northern Bohemia, Moravia, Silesia, Lower Austria, and Thuringia, and extended northwards into Posen and Brandenburg, westwards to Magdeburg and Weimar and up the Danube to Straubing and Regensburg. A great part of this region seems to have enjoyed a high degree of prosperity in this period. Indeed, it has been estimated that in some districts the population must have been as large as it is in modern times. No doubt this prosperity was founded on the agriculture which was exceptionally flourishing in this region during the neolithic period, but trade and the development of the mineral resources also played an important part. Copper was imported into Bohemia from Slovakia in the shape of copper torques of a similar form to those found at Byblos and elsewhere in Syria. Large hoards of these occur in Central Europe, and seem to have formed the raw material which was alloyed with the tin of Bohemia to produce bronze. The products of this bronze were exported in all directions, and axes, pins, and bracelets of the Aunjetitz type are found as far north as Denmark

and Southern Sweden. In return the Baltic amber
was imported into Central Europe, and is frequently
found in the shape of necklaces of amber beads in the
graves of the Aunjetitz people.   A secondary centre of
the culture grew up in Thuringia which owed its importance to the salt deposits of the Saale, and above all to
the fact that it was the meeting-point of the trade
routes from South Germany and Bohemia to the Baltic.
In spite of the absence of local supplies of metal it
developed a bronze industry of its own which had great
influence on the North German lands, and the importance
of the region during the Early Bronze Age is shown by
the great tumulus graves of the Thuringian chieftains at
Helmsdorf and Leubingen which are rich in bronze and
in ornaments of Hungarian gold, and by the great hoard
of amber discovered near Dieskau, not far from Halle.

The relations of the Aunjetitz Culture with the south
were even more important than those with Northern
Europe.   The Danube route, which had been the main
link between Central Europe and the higher civilisation
of the Ægean during the previous period, had declined
in importance after the fall of Troy II, and the chief
channel of communication with the Mediterranean
world was by way of the Eastern Alps and the Brenner
Pass to North Italy and the Adriatic.   The existence of
this route probably explains the importance of the
Mycenæan settlements on the west coast of Greece,
for the tholos tombs of the Mycenæan princes at Kako-
vatos and Pylos are rich in amber which was no doubt
due to traffic with the north.   By the same way the
influence of the Italian bronze industry penetrated to
Central and Northern Europe, and even peculiarly
Ægean types like the famous Vaphio gold cups have
their counterpart in a clay vessel of similar form found
at Nienhagen in Thuringia.   Thus   the   Aunjetitz
Culture was the pivot of European commerce during
the Early Bronze Age, and the centre from which the
influence of the new culture was transmitted in all

directions. It is clear that the Aunjetitz people were one of the chief formative elements in the culture of the Bronze Age, and if only it were possible to identify them with a particular branch of the Indo-European peoples, a very important light would be thrown on the beginnings of European history. Their remains are fairly uniform in type and show strongly marked physical characteristics which are usually attributed by anthropologists to a modification of the Nordic race by admixture with the native Danubian population and with the Beaker people who had entered Central Europe from the west in the preceding period. But it is impossible to trace any connection between them and any later population of the area in historic times, although there is considerable probability that they were a people of Indo-European speech. We have seen in the last chapter that there is reason to believe that the original Indo-Europeans are to be identified with the Battle-axe people, who migrated into Central and North-western Europe in the later neolithic period, and if this is so, it will follow that the great linguistic and national groups which appear fully formed in the succeeding historical period were already in course of formation during the Bronze Age. If a people possesses a well-defined and distinctive culture, it will probably possess an equally well-marked type of language, and the differentiation of a common culture into several distinct regional types is usually accompanied by a similar process in the linguistic sphere. If a conquering people entirely exterminates the native population, it may preserve its original language and culture with little change, but, as we have seen, this did not take place to any great extent in neolithic Europe, where the Indo-European conquerors seem to have dominated the earlier population as warrior aristocracies. Hence their common culture and language would be inevitably modified by the influence of the conquered people, and a process of fusion would take place by which the culture of the conquerors and that of the conquered are amalgamated in a new unity. It is obvious that the union of an Indo-European ruling class with the subject population of Danubian peasants would produce a different result to a union of the same people with Alpine lake-dwellers or western megalith builders, and thus each of the cultural provinces of the European Bronze Age was an area of characterisation for a new social type which owed its character to the diverse elements out of which it was compounded. It was this process of differentiation which produced the different European peoples, the Celts, the Germans, the Italic peoples, the Illyrians, the Greeks, the Thracians, and the Slavs, and if only the archæological record was continuous it would be possible to connect each of these peoples with one of the prehistoric cultures of the Bronze Age. In the case of the Aunjetitz Culture, the archæological evidence is not sufficient to justify any identification of this kind, but elsewhere it is often possible to trace a definite connection between a Bronze Age culture-group and a later historical people.

III. THE BRONZE AGE IN GERMANY AND THE BALTIC. THE CELTIC AND GERMANIC PEOPLES

Thus the Early and Middle Bronze Age Culture of South-western Germany possesses clearly marked links both with the preceding and with the following periods. It owed its origins to the Beaker people who met and mingled on the Middle Rhine with the native Alpine population and with the warrior people from Thuringia who used corded pottery and battle-axes, and buried their dead in tumulus graves. It was this mixed people which invaded and colonised England from the region of the Lower Rhine at the end of the neolithic period, and there developed the new British culture of the Early Bronze Age which is represented by the Round Barrows of Salisbury Plain.

In South-west Germany the main centres of the

earlier Bronze Age Culture lay on the Middle Rhine and the Upper Danube. It was influenced by the more advanced Aunjetitz Culture as well as from Western Europe. In the Middle Bronze Age, this culture began to expand eastwards down the Danube as far as South-west Bohemia, and westwards into Burgundy and Lorraine. Thus the Vosges Mountains, which had hitherto marked the boundary between the Western and Central European groups of cultures, ceased to form a barrier, and Southern Germany and North-eastern France were united in a new territorial unity inhabited by a people of uniform culture. Like the contemporary and related population of Great Britain, the latter buried their dead under round barrows, and hence they are usually known as the Tumulus people.

This new culture-region was to prove of the greatest importance in subsequent history, for it preserved its cultural and racial unity down to the Iron Age, when it became the centre of the great movement of expansion of the Celtic peoples into Western and Southern Europe. Thus we may regard this region as the cradle of the Celtic race and the Tumulus people as the ancestors of the Celtic peoples of historical times. It does not, however, seem possible to go further than this and to distinguish in prehistoric times between the two main branches of the Celtic peoples—those who used the Q type of language like Gaelic, and those who spoke languages of the P type, like Welsh. It is true that several archæologists, such as Lord Abercromby and M. Déchelette, have attempted to identify the former with the Beaker people who invaded Britain at the close of the neolithic period ; and since these undoubtedly originated in the Rhineland and were related to the Tumulus people of South-west Germany, they may also be regarded as in a sense Proto-Celtic. But their common origin is so remote that it is impossible to draw any valid inference as to their language, and the differences in the later Celtic types of speech may be

explained equally well by the hypothesis of two waves
of invasion during the Iron Age—one in the later
Hallstatt period and the other corresponding to the
great semi-historic movement of the third and fourth
centuries B.C.   In any case the changes that took place
in the last period of the Bronze Age and the early
Hallstatt period, while they did not destroy the continuity of the culture, were sufficient to put a wide gap
between the Proto-Celts of the Bronze Age and the
later Celtic peoples.

The unity and continuity of culture which mark the
South-west German culture-province were possessed in
an even higher degree by the North-western European
region, which embraced North Germany and Southern
Scandinavia, and which has been almost universally
regarded as the area of characterisation of the Germanic
peoples.   Here there is no evidence of any change of
population between the coming of the Battle-axe people
in neolithic times and the great migrations of the
historic period, while the skeletons found in neolithic
and Bronze Age interments show that the same Nordic
racial type which characterises the region to-day was
predominant in prehistoric times.   The Age of Bronze
was of course much later here than in Central or Western
Europe, and the Baltic was still in the later phases of
the Stone Age while the Aunjetitz Culture was flourishing
in Bohemia and Silesia.   Nevertheless, when the
Northern Bronze Age began, it witnessed an exceptionally
brilliant and long-enduring development of culture.   It
received its main inspiration from Central and South-
eastern Europe, for the Western European influence
from Spain and the British Isles which had predominated
during the æneolithic period, and which had brought to
Northern Europe such characteristic western types as
the Irish gold lunulæ and the Spanish halberds, had
declined owing to the rise of the new trans-continental
trade routes.   In this way the Baltic was brought into
contact with the Bronze Age civilisation of Hungary

and acquired the highly developed metal technique and the beautiful spiral ornament that became characteristic of the Nordic art of the period.   This was the foundation of the Bronze Age industry of Scandinavia, which stands side by side with that of Hungary as the finest and most artistic style in Europe outside the Ægean world. Its later phases are contemporary with the Hallstatt culture of Central Europe, and the early Italian Iron Age, which brought new artistic influences to the north without causing any fundamental change in the development of the native culture.   Throughout the greater part of the Northern Bronze Age, which covers upwards of a millennium (c. 1600–500 B.C.), Southern Scandinavia seems to have enjoyed a very high level of prosperity, and the archæological discoveries have thrown considerable light on the culture and manner of life of the ancient population.   The graves of Jutland have yielded not only weapons and ornaments, but even articles of apparel and complete costumes, such as the woollen kirtle, sleeved jacket, and hair net found in a wooden coffin at Borum-Eshöi, and the elaborate character of the female interments suggest that women possessed a high social status.   The numerous objects of religious character, such as the gold models of boats, the gilt solar disk on a votive carriage found at Trundholm, and the sacred axes ornamented with gold and amber, not only testify to considerable artistic skill, but also show the existence of a comparatively highly developed type of religious cultus.

The prosperity of the Nordic Culture did not, however, survive the Bronze Age.   With the beginning of the Age of Iron a deterioration of climate took place in the Baltic lands which led to the impoverishment of the culture and the decline of the population.   According to Professor Sernander, who has studied the changes in the vegetation of Sweden in post-glacial times, the change seems to have been of so catastrophic a nature as to have rendered agriculture impossible, except in a few favoured regions, and to have caused the wholesale migration of a large part of the population. Now we find the peoples of the Nordic Culture advancing southward into Western Germany and Holland from the close of the Bronze Age and gradually pushing the Celtic population of the Tumulus Culture away from the Lower Rhine. Finally, in the last centuries before the Christian era a movement of peoples on a large scale took place in the north. The Cimbri left Jutland and set out on their famous raid across Europe, and the Goths and the Burgundians crossed the Baltic to find new homes in Eastern Europe, a movement which eventually brought them into collision with the Roman Empire. Thus the decline of the prehistoric Nordic Culture was the starting-point of a train of events which was ultimately to cause the downfall of the incomparably greater civilisation of the Mediterranean world.

IV. The Bronze Age in Eastern Europe. The Thracians and the Illyrians

We have now traced the history of the two great western provinces of the Central European Bronze Age. The development of the eastern provinces is far more obscure owing to the less advanced state of archæological research, and also to an almost complete ignorance of the peoples and cultures of the region in early historical times. Thus we know very little of what happened in the region of the neolithic Painted Pottery Culture during the Bronze Age. The brilliant civilisation of Erösd had already come to an end before the beginning of that period, though elsewhere, in Rumania and the Ukraine, the Painted Pottery Culture survived during the first part of the second millennium. Its downfall was no doubt due to the invasion of the Battle-axe people, indeed it is this part of Europe, particularly Rumania and Transylvania, that is the centre of diffusion for the distinctively Caucasian types of copper axes. Nevertheless, along the shores of the Black Sea in

Bulgaria and Rumania, and again in South Russia, the tradition of the Painted Pottery Culture survived in a degenerate form in later times, so that it is probable that the old peasant population survived to some extent under the domination of the warrior peoples, and contributed to the formation of the Thracian peoples and language. The little that we know of the later Thracian culture and religion bears out this view of their origin and shows that the tradition of the ancient peasant culture was still alive. It was from Thrace that orgiastic forms of the vegetation religion, like the cult of Dionysus and the worship of Bendis, penetrated into Greece, and the Thracian habit of painting the body is the survival of a custom that dates from neolithic times. On the other hand, Strabo says that the Thracians looked on the agriculturalists as the meanest of men and regarded war and plunder as the only honourable means of livelihood, sentiments which are typical of a society in which a conquering aristocracy of warriors dominates a native population of peasant serfs.

The lands to the west of the Thracian region, on the Middle Danube, form another important province of Bronze Age culture. Here the archæological evidence is much more complete, and it is clear that during this period Hungary was the centre of a brilliant development of culture which, from the artistic point of view, surpassed anything that existed elsewhere in Central Europe, though it was later in date than the Aunjetitz Culture of Bohemia that has been already described. The splendid Hungarian swords and axes, often ornamented with elaborate spiral decoration, are perhaps the finest specimens of European bronze work, and supplied the models for the similar types of the Nordic Bronze Age. The spiral patterns resemble those found in Ægean art as far back as the end of the Early Minoan period, and were probably due to southern influence. On the other hand, there is reason to believe that the

broadsword which began to come into use in the
Middle Bronze Age, and took the place of the rapier
or thrusting sword, was first developed in Hungary, and
thence spread throughout Europe and even reached
Egypt and Mesopotamia. Some writers believe that
the diffusion of this " leaf-shaped sword " during the
later Bronze Age points to a great invasion of Western
and Southern Europe by the people of the Middle
Danube. It seems more probable, however, that the
spread of the new weapon was due to its own merits,
and that the type was quickly adopted and developed
by the other metal-working cultures outside its original
region, for nothing is more rapidly borrowed than a
superior type of weapon,

No less remarkable than the metal-work is the
pottery of the region, the so-called Pannonian ware,
which is found along the banks of the Middle Danube
from the frontier of Austria to Western Bulgaria. It is
evidently based on the old traditions of the Danubian
culture, for it reproduces forms which were typical of
the neolithic culture of the region, such as the double
vases and high pedestalled dishes. Moreover, clay
images of women were still manufactured, some of them
elaborately decorated with patterns that are intended
to represent the dress and ornaments of the period.
Thus it is clear that a fusion had taken place in Hungary
during the Bronze Age between the culture of the
Battle-axe people, which had invaded the region at the
close of the neolithic period, and that of the native
Danubian population, a fusion which must have resulted
in the formation of some specific group of Indo-European
peoples and languages. This group has generally been
regarded as Illyrian, but since it is impossible to trace
the further development of the culture after the close
of the Bronze Age, and since our knowledge of the
historic people and language is extremely limited, this
derivation, even if certain, would mean very little to
us. There are some, however, who have looked on

Hungary as the original home of the Greek-speaking peoples, and who believe that the fall of the Mycenæan culture was due to the conquest of the native Mediterranean population of Greece by the Indo-European of the Danube valley. If this were indeed the case, the brilliant Bronze Age culture of Hungary would find its continuation in the historic Greek culture, and the problem of its apparent disappearance would be solved. Unfortunately it is a purely speculative hypothesis, for which there is no satisfactory archæological or historical evidence. It is far more probable, as we shall see in a later chapter, that an Indo-European element was already present in the Southern Balkans during the Bronze Age, and that the area of characterisation of the Greek people and language is to be found in Greece itself, and in the neighbouring regions of Macedonia and Epirus.

On the other hand, the Bronze Age culture of Hungary, or rather of Pannonia, certainly possesses some links that connect it with Italy, and it is probable that the very important changes that took place in the culture of Northern Italy during this period are due in part to influences that come, if not from the Danube valley itself, from the territories immediately to the west, between the Drave and the Save.

V. THE BRONZE AGE IN ITALY AND THE TERREMARE CULTURE

Northern Italy occupied an especially important position during this and the subsequent period, for it was the chief link between the Mediterranean world and the Bronze Age cultures of Central and Northern Europe. From the time of the fall of the Second City of Troy, early in the second millennium, down to the foundation of Marseilles by the Greeks, and the opening of the new trade-route up the Rhone valley, in the sixth century B.C., it was the chief link between the Mediterranean world and the cultures of Central and

Northern Europe. We have seen that the great trade route from the Baltic which passed up the Elbe and divided into several branches, passing through Bohemia and Central and Southern Germany, ultimately debouched through the Brenner Pass into North-eastern Italy ; and consequently the region between the Eastern Alps and the Northern Adriatic was the centre of the commercial intercourse between the Mediterranean and Transalpine Europe, and a focus from which cultural influences radiated in all directions.

Nevertheless, in prehistoric times Italy did not form a unitary province of culture. It was a transitional region which received currents of civilisation from different directions without creating a native culture of its own. The extreme south, with Sicily and Sardinia, belonged entirely to the Mediterranean world, and was in contact both with the Ægean and with Spain from a very early period. Northern Italy, on the other hand, developed during the Bronze Age a perfectly independent type of culture, and was in closer relations with Central Europe. But in many regions the native population still continued to live in caves and to lead the barbarous existence of hunters and food-gatherers with a culture that is sometimes hardly distinguished from that of palæolithic times.

A fully developed type of neolithic culture only existed in Sicily and in the extreme south of the peninsula, where it was due to a movement of culture from across the Adriatic, for the painted pottery of Molfetta and Matera is clearly connected with the Eastern European type of culture which also makes its appearance at Dimini in Thessaly during the second neolithic period. In the rest of Italy, however, there was no true neolithic period, for while some part of the country had advanced to the æneolithic or the full Bronze Age, the more backward regions were still in an epipalæolithic stage of culture.

The earliest metal-using culture of Northern Italy is

of a very composite character. The influence of the Eastern Mediterranean is seen in the copper daggers of the Ægean type with a mid-rib, but the Spanish type with a flat tang is equally common and became the basis of the new form of bronze-hilted dagger which was evolved in Italy and thence passed on to Central and Northern Europe. One or two examples of the Spanish halberd are also found, and the same weapon appears in the rock carvings of the Maritime Alps. But the most important evidence of West Mediterranean influence is to be found in the Bell-Beakers of the Spanish type which occur at Remedello and the neighbouring cemeteries south-west of Lake Garda on the River Chiese. As in other parts of Europe, they are accompanied by a few brachycephalic skulls, though the majority of the remains in the cemeteries belong to a long-headed population of the Mediterranean type. The exceptional richness of this region in remains of the æneolithic period suggests that the route across the Brenner was already coming into use, and this may also explain the appearance of the Beaker people so far from their other centres of settlement. At the same time other new influences were coming in from the north. Lake villages of the Alpine type were being established on the Italian Lakes, presumably by a population of northern origin. Moreover, polygonal stone axes of similar type to those found at Mondsee and elsewhere in the Austrian Alps, not only appear in the lake villages, but have a wide distribution in the rest of Italy, occurring as far south as the Abruzzi and the valley of the Tiber. Thus Italy seems to have been affected by the invasions of the Battle-axe people, and it is possible that an Indo-European element was already present in the population at this very early period.

Finally, with the Bronze Age there appears in North Italy the new and highly distinctive type of culture known as that of the Terremare. It receives its name from the peculiar pile settlements which form its characteristic feature. Unlike the lake villages the Terremare were built on dry land and surrounded by an artificial moat and rampart. In plan these structures are remarkably uniform, being trapezoidal in form with the longer sides parallel, and running roughly north and south. The whole settlement was divided into sections by two main streets which crossed one another at right angles. In the eastern half there was a small separate area divided from the rest of the settlement by an inner moat which was crossed by a bridge from the west. This quarter of the settlement was not inhabited, but seems to have been set apart for a religious purpose. It was covered by a raised platform of earth, in the centre of which a long trench was dug containing three to five covered pits. They contain fragments of pottery and bones of animals, and were apparently of a ritual character. Outside the settlement itself were situated the cemeteries of the community, usually two in number, which consisted of closely packed rows of urns containing the cremated remains of the dead.

The inhabitants of the Terremare were pre-eminently an agricultural people. But they were also skilled workers in metal, who manufactured bronze sickles as well as daggers and short swords and spears, and they also made use of bronze razors and fibulæ or safety-pins for fastening their garments. Their pottery was usually grey or black, and highly polished, and is often characterised by a peculiar crescent-shaped type of handle —the *ansa lunata*; and like the Danubian peasants they also made pottery figures of animals.

The Terremare settlements have a very limited distribution north of the Po; they appear only in the region of Mantua to the south of Lake Garda, and westwards towards Brescia and Cremona. They are most numerous, however, to the south of the river in Emilia, where they occupy the whole territory to the north of the Apennines from west of Bologna to Piacenza.

Outside these regions only a single Terramara settlement has been discovered, and that is in the extreme south of Italy at Taranto.

VI. The Terremare Culture and the Origins of the Italic Peoples

It is clear from the character of their culture that the Terremare represent a new people entirely distinct from the Italian natives who continued to live in caves and in hut villages. On the other hand, the form of the settlements shows considerable resemblance to that of the lake village type, and consequently it has often been supposed that they were due to an expansion of the earlier lake-dwelling population of Upper Italy who had continued to build their settlements on piles after they had moved southwards from the lakes. Nevertheless, except in the case of the lake villages of Lake Garda which had come within the sphere of the Terremare influence, the two groups are quite distinct in culture, though they were to some extent at least contemporary in date. Hence it is usually believed that the Terremare Culture was due to a new migration of people distinct from that of the lake-dwellers. It is, however, very difficult to find any cultural group in Central Europe from which they can be derived. They are quite distinct in culture from the people of the Eastern Alps, in the direction of which we should naturally look. The Terremare pottery with its curious types of handle finds its closest parallel in Hungary and the Balkans; and since pile dwellings occur in Hungary and at a late date in Bosnia, this seems the most probable source for the culture. Moreover, a movement from the Balkans might also explain the appearance of a solitary Terramara in the far south of the peninsula, in a region which has always attracted settlers from across the Adriatic.

On the other hand, though cremation and urn burial are also found in Western Hungary in the Middle Bronze

Age, the high development of art that we see in the Pannonian pottery has no parallel in the Terremare Culture, and the characteristic types of Hungarian bronze weapons such as the battle-axes with spiral decoration are entirely absent in Italy. Thus the Danubian origin of the Terremare people cannot be regarded as certain, and it is equally possible that the Terremare Culture arose in Italy itself owing to the fusion of the lake-dwelling population with a new element of higher culture which reached the Upper Adriatic and dominated the Italian end of the great Central European trade route. Certainly the whole structure of the Terremare bears witness to a very high sense of order and social organisation which explains the subsequent fortunes of the people. For towards the end of the Bronze Age the Terremare Culture entered on a new phase of expansion. Some of the population seems to have crossed the Apennines and moved southwards into Umbria and the valley of the Tiber. They no longer built pile settlements, but occupied ordinary hut villages like those of the aboriginal inhabitants with whom they no doubt mingled. Their progress is shown by the diffusion of the Northern Italian type of Bronze Age culture and also by the introduction of the custom of cremation in place of inhumation which was practised by all the other peoples of Italy.

An important settlement of this type is found at Pianello in the Marches, near the great pass in the Apennines that leads down into Umbria. And from thence we can follow their expansion by way of Spoleto and Todi to Tolfa in Southern Etruria and finally to Latium, where their traces reappear in the cemeteries of the Alban Hills and even on the site of Rome itself.

The majority of scholars have seen in this movement the southward advance of the ancestors of the Latin people into the territory of the earlier non-Indo-European population, and consequently they regard the region of the Terremare Culture as the cradle of the

Italic race and language, or at least of the Latin section of it, for the Italic, like the Celtic group of languages, falls into two divisions characterised respectively by their use of Q and P to represent the original *ku* sound.

And certainly this view of their origin might well explain the peculiar character of the historic Latin civilisation. The sense of order and the strict social discipline which is shown in the very form of the Terremare settlements, with their rigid adherence to the same traditional plan, seems to foreshadow the similar characteristics of the later Latin people. The intensely communal spirit of Latin society, its conservatism and instinct for order, its use of the spade and the measuring line, all suggest the inheritance of a long past of settlement and disciplined activity rather than that of the wandering life of pastoral clans, like the Ligurians or the Sabellian peoples. And the instinct of colonisation —the sending out of swarms of daughter settlements— which was the secret of the Latin predominance in Italy finds its prototype in the multiplication of the Terremare settlements—each of them an organised whole from its birth—throughout North-eastern Italy.

But the most remarkable parallel of all is that between the plan of the Terramara itself and that of the Roman camp and city, which is so close that some archæologists, such as Sergi, believed that the Terremare were actually Roman camps of the third century.

The laying out of the Roman settlement based on the fixed rectangular lines of the Cardo and the Decumanus, corresponding to the two intersecting streets of the Terremare, the tracing of the pomerium and the casting up of the agger and the vallum, all have their analogies in the Terremare. The sacred area in the eastern portion of the latter corresponds to the arx or templum, and the ritual pits with their offerings have a close resemblance to the similar pits found in Roman camps, and to the mundus or covered pit at Rome which was opened on certain solemn occasions and played an important part in the civic religion. Moreover, this system of town-planning was a sacred tradition which was carefully preserved by the members of the guild of augurs, so that it may well go back to a remote antiquity. Similarly, the Roman priestly title of pontifex or bridge-maker, which has always been a puzzle to archæologists, might also find its explanation in the bridges which were an important feature of the Terremare settlements and the construction of which may have been a sacred function.

On the other hand, this view of the origin of the Italic peoples involves several grave difficulties. If the people of the Terremare represent the earliest Indo-European element in Italy, as is assumed by the school of writers to which we have referred, it is clear that the greater part of Italy must have remained in the possession of non-Indo-European peoples down to the end of the Bronze Age, and that the spread of the Italic languages in Southern Italy must have occurred in relatively recent times. Nevertheless, apart from the Etruscans, there is practically no evidence for the existence of any non-Indo-European languages in Italy in historic times. It is true that the Ligurians of the north-west are usually believed to represent the indigenous population of æneolithic and yet earlier times, but even this view is now contested by Professor Conway,[1] who regards them as speaking an Italian language of the same type as Latin. In any case it is certain that the Siculi, who occupied Sicily before the arrival of the Greeks, spoke an Italic language ; and since there is no evidence to connect them with the Terremare people or with any later move-ment of population from North Italy, it seems evident that an Indo-European element must have been present even in Southern Italy from early times. Thus it seems probable that the first expansion of the Indo-European peoples throughout Italy dates, as in Greece, not from

[1] In *The Cambridge Ancient History*, vol. iv, ch. 13.

the beginnings of the Iron Age, but from a much earlier period.   We have already seen that there is some reason to suppose an invasion of Italy by the Battle-axe people in the æneolithic period, and if this should be admitted, we might assume the existence of an Indo-European element among the Italian population, as in the culture-provinces of Central Europe, from before the beginning of the Bronze Age.   In fact, some of the most recent writers on the subject, such as Pareti in Italy and Herbig in Germany,[1] regard the Indo-European migration into Italy as entirely independent of the Terremare Culture, and view the latter as the creation of a non-Indo-European or at any rate of a non-Italic people. Nevertheless, the older view is still maintained by the majority of scholars, and has recently been worked out in greater detail from the archæological point of view by Randall-MacIver and von Duhn.   Although the latter differ considerably in point of detail, they agree in regarding the Terremare people as the first wave of the Indo-European migration from Central Europe, which was followed at the beginning of the Iron Age by a further invasion of peoples from beyond the Alps. According to von Duhn the former are to be identified with the speakers of the Q group of Italic languages, such as the Latins, and the latter with the P group, the Oscans and the Samnites.

VII.   The Later Phases of the Bronze Age in Central Europe.   The Urn Cemeteries and the Lausitz Culture

But in order to judge the probabilities of this theory it is necessary to turn once more to Central Europe and to see whether the evidence that is to be derived from the culture of that region during the later Bronze Age is capable of throwing any light on the Italian development.   Now it is certain that a great movement of

[1] N. L. Pareti, *Le Origini Etrusche*.   Firenze, 1927.   Herbig, s.v. " Italiker " in *R.V.G.*, vol. vi.

peoples, accompanied by a corresponding change in culture, was taking place during the later Bronze Age, round about the thirteenth century B.C., in Central Europe. Southern Germany and Eastern France, the region of the Tumulus Culture, was invaded by a new people who practised cremation and buried the ashes of their dead in great urns laid out in regular cemeteries, after the manner of the Terremare people or their successors in Italy at the beginning of the Iron Age. The funeral urns are also accompanied, as in the graves of the Villanova period in Italy, by a number of smaller vessels, intended as votive offerings. Moreover, both their pottery and their bronze implements resemble those of North Italy rather than the types of the Central European Bronze Age. They were the first to introduce bronze sickles, razors, and safety-pins of Italian type into Central Europe, and there are even examples of metal-work, like the bronze buckets found at Unterglauheim in Bavaria, and the helmets that occur occasionally in finds of the later Bronze Age in South Germany, and even in North France, which may have been actually imported from Italy.

Thus the new culture of the Urn Cemeteries cannot be ascribed to a southward expansion of Central European culture, but rather represents an invading movement from the south-east. The German archæologists regard it as due to an Alpine people, " Ligurians " or " Raeti," probably of non-Indo-European origin, who advanced northwards, occupying the fertile valleys and the open lands suitable for agriculture, and leaving the hill country in the possession of the earlier Bronze Age population who continued to bury their dead under round barrows as in the previous period.

And about the same time similar changes of culture were taking place farther to the east. Throughout the old domain of the Aunjetitz Culture, from the Middle Danube to the Oder and the Saale, there appears a new type of Bronze Age civilisation, known as the Lausitz

Culture.   Here also the rite of cremation was universal, and the ashes of the dead were placed in great urns, accompanied by small votive vessels, sometimes as many as thirty-five in number, and buried in large cemeteries. The characteristic feature of this culture is the pottery, which is ornamented with grooved patterns and raised bosses or knobs, a feature which also appears in the Terremare pottery of North Italy, and in that of the Urn Cemeteries of Southern Germany, which seems closely related to the Lausitz ware.   The origin of the people who created the Lausitz Culture is no less a mystery than that of the Urn Cemetery people farther west.   Some writers consider them to belong to the Illyrian stock, while the Bohemian and Polish archæologists believe that they were the ancestors of the Slavonic peoples.   It is possible that they were the descendants of the earlier Aunjetitz population, and that the new features in their civilisation were due to cultural influences only.   This, however, is far from certain, and as the practice of cremation was almost universal, little help is to be gained from anthropological evidence.[1]

The Lausitz Culture had a very long existence in East-Central Europe, and its later stages are contemporary with the Hallstatt Culture of the Alpine lands. In its earlier phase, however, it is more or less contemporary with the Urn Cemetery Culture of South Germany and with the later stages of the Terremare Culture and the beginnings of the Iron Age in Italy.   And in fact all these three cultures though not necessarily due to a single racial stock, show considerable points of similarity. All of them may be described as " Urn Cemetery Cultures," though the title is usually applied to that of Southern Germany and Eastern France only.   It is true that the practice of cremation is so widespread and

---

[1] Of the few skulls that exist, six are said to be Nordic in type and fifteen Mediterranean.   Cf. art. " Lausitzische Kultur " in *R.V.G.*, vol. vii.

occurs at so many different epochs that it is not alone
sufficient to establish a cultural connection.   But in
the cultures that we are considering the resemblance
goes much farther.   In all of them we find the ashes of
the dead placed in an urn, often of biconical shape,
which was covered by an inverted dish or basin, and
often contained or was surrounded by a number of
smaller votive vessels.   In all of them the urns were
placed close together in regular cemeteries, sometimes
directly in the earth and later in small stone cists or
chambers.   Moreover, the resemblance in the types of
bronze implements and ornaments, such as the razor
and the fibula, are also striking, at least in the case of
Southern Germany and Northern Italy.   Nevertheless,
the existence of these parallels does little to explain
the origins of this type of culture.   It certainly does not
point to an invasion of Italy from the north of the Alps,
for the characteristic features of the culture are found
in Italy earlier than in Southern Germany or Bohemia,
while the appearance of the new type of bronze industry
north of the Alps is due in part to the influence of trade
with Italy at the beginning of the Iron Age.

The only part of Europe in which it is possible to find
antecedents for this type of culture is in Western Hungary and the adjacent regions to the south-west.   At
Vattina and other sites on the Middle Danube there
exist Urn Cemeteries dating from the Middle Bronze
Age, which contain biconical urns and pottery which has
a considerable resemblance to that of the Italian Terremare, as well as a primitive type of razor which might
be regarded as a prototype of the Italian form.[1]   Hence
it is by no means improbable that this region may be
the source of the new influences which appear in Italy
with the Terremare Culture, and in Central Europe at
a later date with the Urn Cemeteries of South Germany
and the Lausitz Culture farther east.   But though we
may admit the importance of Danubian influences in

[1] Cf. V. G. Childe in *Man,* vol. xxvi, No. 100.

the later Bronze Age cultures of Italy and Central Europe, it does not necessarily follow, as many writers believe, that the origin of the new cultures of the early Iron Age are to be explained in the same way, for the latter are accompanied by a number of new features that have no prototypes in the Danube valley or in any other part of Central Europe. But before considering this problem, we have still to deal with the most interesting and important of all the Bronze Age cultures of Europe—the Mycenæan civilisation of Greece and the Ægean.

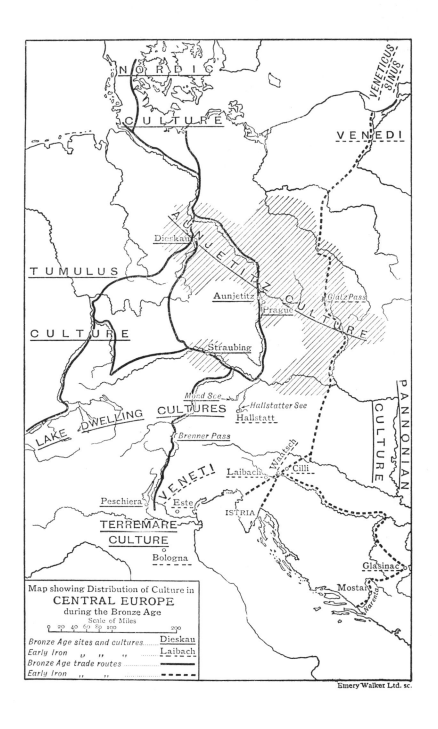

Map showing Distribution of Culture in
CENTRAL EUROPE
during the Bronze Age

Scale of Miles

0 20 40 60 80 100   200

Bronze Age sites and cultures....... Dieskau
Early Iron   „   „   „ .... Laibach
Bronze Age trade routes ....
Early Iron   „   „ ....

Emery Walker Ltd. sc.

CHAPTER XV

THE MYCENÆAN CULTURE OF GREECE AND THE AGE OF THE INVASIONS

CHAPTER XV

THE MYCENÆAN CULTURE OF GREECE AND THE AGE OF THE INVASIONS

I. The Succession of Cultures in Mainland Greece

During the later Bronze Age a new culture, contemporary with the New Kingdom in Egypt and the Hittite Empire, was arising in mainland Greece which was destined to take the place of the old Minoan civilisation that had its centre at Cnossus. It occupies an intermediate position between the barbaric cultures of the European Bronze Age and the civilised empires of Egypt and Western Asia, and affords a remarkable example of the new type of warlike society which arose from the contact between the invading Indo-European peoples and the Archaic Culture of the Near East.

Owing to its geographical position and the main lines of communication in the peninsula, Greece has been throughout its history the natural meeting-place of Mediterranean and Central European influences. As we have already seen, the earliest culture of the Southern Balkans was allied in type to the neolithic peasant cultures of the Danube region. At the beginning of the Bronze Age, however, this neolithic culture was transformed by the coming of new influences from two different directions. In the south we see the appearance of a metal-using culture of the Ægean type, similar to that of the Cyclades, which is usually termed Helladic, and which established itself on the coast in the region of Tiryns and Corinth, and thence gradually extended west and north throughout Southern and Central Greece. At about the same time a new culture of northern origin made its appearance in Thessaly. It brought with it a new type of pottery with encrusted ornament and elaborate forms of handles, far inferior from the artistic point of view to the fine painted ware of the old Peasant Culture, as well as new weapons, such as the northern battle-axe. The coming of this new culture was probably an episode in the great movement of the warrior peoples of Indo-European stock that has already been described, and consequently its bearers may have been the original ancestors of the Greek-speaking peoples ; for we have no reason to believe that either the Ægean peoples, or the original neolithic population (with the possible exception of the intrusive Painted Pottery Culture of the second Thessalian period) were speakers of Greek or indeed of any Indo-European language.

Early in the second millennium, at about the same time as the fall of the Second City of Troy and the new wave of invasions which changed the face of Western Asia, the domain of the Helladic Culture in Central Greece was also overrun by the invasion of a northern people who established themselves as far south as the Argolis.   These new-comers were probably a branch of the same Indo-European people who had settled in Thessaly during the earlier period.   Like the latter, they were a warlike people who buried their dead in cist graves, but their pottery—the so-called Minyan ware— is of a far more advanced type than that of the third Thessalian period. A similar type of pottery occurs also at Troy, though only at a later period, the age of the Fifth and Sixth Cities.

II. THE MYCENÆAN CULTURE AND THE RISE OF THE ACHÆAN POWER

This victory of the northern influence in Greece was, however, only a temporary one. In the latter part of the seventeenth century, the Ægean tradition which had already been represented by the Early Helladic Culture reasserted itself by the sudden appearance of the Cretan Culture in its fully developed form on the mainland. On the rocky hill of Mycenæ, overlooking the plain of

Argos and dominating the trade route that leads from Tiryns to the Gulf of Corinth, a small fortress was built on the site of an earlier Helladic settlement. This stronghold became the centre of a powerful state which dominated first the North-eastern Peloponnese, and later the whole mainland and the islands. The graves of the earliest princes who reigned from perhaps 1620 to 1500 B.C. have been found intact in the Grave circle at Mycenæ, and are extremely important and interesting. They are characterised by an extraordinary wealth of gold and elaborate ornaments of fully developed Minoan style, such as chased silver cups, beads of amber and amethyst, ostrich eggs and vessels of alabaster, and finest of all, the famous bronze daggers inlaid with hunting scenes in gold—perhaps the most beautiful product of Ægean goldsmiths' work in existence. In one grave was the body of a queen with her jewellery and golden toilet vessels, and by her side was the body of her baby wrapped in thin plates of gold.

All this wealth proves that the rulers of Mycenæ were powerful princes, who must have controlled a considerable territory, and the purely Cretan style of art and ornament shows that they were in close touch with the older civilisation of Cnossus. It has been suggested that they were pirate chiefs, and that their treasure was the result of their raids upon the cities of Crete. But if that was so, their culture would certainly show stronger signs of an indigenous non-Cretan element. We must in fact suppose that they were either actual settlers from Crete, provincial governors of the Minoan Empire, or else that they were chieftains in tributary dependence on the island power through whose hands passed the trade of Crete with the mainland and the Gulf of Corinth. In either case there can be no question of the thoroughly Ægean character of the new culture which is in fact nothing less than a mainland offshoot of the Minoan civilisation of Crete. Later on in the fourteenth and thirteenth centuries the Achæans appear as an historical people, and since there is no sign of a fresh invasion from the north during Mycenæan times, we must conclude that the dominant element on the mainland was already Greek.

During the fifteenth century Mycenæ was ruled by a dynasty which buried its dead in large stone-built vaulted tombs, unlike the single shaft graves of the earlier period. Unfortunately these tombs have all been robbed, so we know little about the culture of their occupants. This period, however, was one of great expansion for the Mycenæan Culture ; we find similar domed tombs spreading round the coast of Greece as far as Pylos on the west and Thessaly on the north.

Nor was this expansion of the Mycenæan power limited to the mainland. Before the close of the fifteenth century it had acquired the hegemony of the whole Ægean world, and the supremacy of the old centres of the Minoan Culture in Crete had been brought to a sudden and violent end by the destruction of Cnossus and Phæstus. It can hardly be doubted that this catastrophe was due to the conquest of Crete by the mainland princes. For at the same period that Cnossus was destroyed, the palace and citadel of Mycenæ was refounded on a grand scale. Like the palace of Cnossus it was not simply a royal residence, but a centre of government, containing storehouses, workshops, and offices which housed a whole population of soldiers, officials, and dependents ; but the existence of a northern element in the mainland culture is shown by the megara, or large halls with central hearth and outer porch, which were a characteristic type of the neolithic culture of Transylvania and its offshoot in Thessaly, and which also make their appearance in the Second City of Troy. To the time of this rebuilding belong the famous Lion Gateway and the so-called Treasury of Atreus, the great domed tomb, fifty feet high, which was the mausoleum of the royal family.

An equally imposing fortified citadel was constructed at Tiryns, the port of Mycenæ, and farther north in

Bœotia was an even larger palace, built on the island of Goulas in Lake Copais, while at Orchomenos there is another magnificent royal tomb. These two regions, the Argolis and Bœotia, seem to have been the centres of different dynasties, but the former was apparently the greater power, and enjoyed a kind of imperial supremacy throughout the Ægean world.

The period that follows, from 1400 to 1150 B.C., is known as the Third Late Minoan Period, or better, the Mycenæan Age. Mycenæan trade and influence spread far and wide, from Cyprus and Western Asia Minor to Southern Italy and Sicily. The old Minoan Culture still lived on, for in religion and art, in material culture, and industry, and even in their amusements, the Mycenæan princes simply carried on the tradition of the earlier Ægean civilisation.

Nevertheless, in spite of this continuity of material culture, the fall of Cnossus marks a real break in the development of the Ægean world, and the appearance on the stage of history of a new people, who were no other than the Achæans of Greek tradition. As early as the fourteenth century the Hittite documents of Boghaz Keui show that the Achæans were already a powerful people, who were taking their part in the war and diplomacy of the Anatolian mainland.[1] About 1330 the Hittite king greets Antaravas, king of Aḫḫiyava and La-az-pu (? Lesbos) on a footing of equality as " his brother " the Great King. A few years later another king of Aḫḫiyava, Tavagalavas, is mentioned as holding Pamphylia as vassal of the Hittite Empire, and as defending the Lycians (the Lugga) against invasion. These kings have been identified by Forrer with the two first kings of Orchomenos, Andreus and his son Eteocles ('Ετεϝοκλέϝης). Finally in the thirteenth century (c. 1250–1225) another Aḫḫiyava king, Attaras-

---

[1] The interpretations are due to Dr. Forrer and are disputed by some English scholars. Professor Sayce accepts the general interpretation, but identifies Attarassiyas with Perseus, and in place of *Kurievanies* reads Marêwanes, *i.e.* the Mariyanni or nobles of the Tell el Amarna documents.

siyas (? Atreus), again appears in Asia Minor engaged in raids or wars of conquest in Caria and Cyprus. He and his ally are entitled Kurievanies (Κοιράνοι) in the Hittite documents.

These discoveries give a remarkable support to the Greek traditions and seem to prove that the Achæans were the ruling people of the Ægean world in the Mycenæan age.[1] It does not necessarily follow, however, that they were the original founders of the Mycenæan culture, for Greek tradition itself ascribes the foundation of the Mycenæan states to strangers from Asia Minor, Egypt, or Phœnicia, such as Pelops, Cecrops, Cadmus, and Danaus, whose names often suggest a non-Indo-European origin. This tradition is in complete agreement with the archæological evidence of an abrupt break in the development of the mainland culture which accompanies the appearance of the Mycenæan Culture at the end of the seventeenth century, while the subsequent rise of the Achæan power finds a natural explanation in a gradual assimilation of the foreign minority by the native population, such as occurred in later times in the case of the Scandinavian founders of the Russian State, or the Norman conquerors of England and Sicily. It is possible that the Greek legend of the expedition of Theseus to Crete and his slaying of the Minotaur in the labyrinth at Cnossus preserves the tradition of a Mycenæan revolt against the Cretan suzerainty, for there can be no doubt that the fall of Cnossus and the rise of Mycenæ to the hegemony of the Ægean world represent the reaction of the mixed culture of the mainland, probably under Achæan leadership, against the parent civilisation of Crete.

In the Homeric poems Crete itself forms part of the Achæan world, and it is probable that Achæan dynasties from the mainland bore rule in the island from the time of the fall of Cnossus to that of the Dorian invasion.

[1] The view has been maintained by Professor Sayce and others that the Achæans were originally a people of Western Asia Minor and that the Ionians colonised mainland Greece from Asia instead of vice versa. Cf. Sayce, " The Aryan Problem," in *Antiquity*, June, 1927.

III. The Society of the Heroic Age and the Homeric Epic

Thus the fourteenth and thirteenth centuries represent a gradual transition from the rich and brilliant civilisation of the Late Minoan Period to the chivalrous but semi-barbarised world of the Homeric epic. The accumulated resources of the peaceful Ægean Culture were gradually dissipated by rulers who lived for plunder and war. For the Mycenæan Culture was, to an even greater extent than the Hittite Empire, or the New Kingdom in Egypt, that of a thoroughly warlike society. Its centres were not peaceful cities, like those of Minoan Crete, but royal burgs whose great walls of Cyclopean masonry remain to this day as a witness to the power of the princes who once bore rule there.

When Schliemann opened the shaft graves at Mycenæ they were still lying there, crowned and covered with gold, with their long swords by their sides and their gold death-masks on their faces—grim bearded faces of warrior kings, very different from the effeminate beauty of the Priest King of Crete who stands unarmed and almost naked among the flowers in the great painted relief of the Palace of Cnossus.

Thus, though their culture, their art, and their way of living were modelled upon those of Crete, it was in the same way as that in which the Ostrogothic kingdom of Italy entered into the tradition of the later Roman civilisation. The society was not the society of a sacred city state, but that of a military aristocracy. It is the heroic society of the Homeric epic, and in Homer's world there is no room for citizen or priest or merchant, but only for the knight and his retainers, for the nobles and the Zeus-born kings, " the sackers of cities." It is a society of princes and pirates.

It is true that the Homeric poems, at least in their present form, date from a much later period, long after the passing of the Mycenæan Age. Nevertheless, they

faithfully preserve the tradition of the older civilisation.
The map of the Homeric world is that of Mycenæan
Greece and the Ægean before the age of the Dorian
invasion.   The heroes of the epic are the Mycenæan
princes of Pylos and " rich Mycenæ " and " Tiryns of
the great walls."   They use bronze weapons and armour,
they fight from chariots, and their dwellings are true
Mycenæan palaces.   The tradition of the old civilisation
and its political organisation still survived, and pre-
vented the development of a true tribal society like that
of the early Dorian States.   In the Homeric Age the
leading element in society is the war leaders and their
bands of retainers who carve out new kingdoms at the
point of their swords, and who succeed to the position
of the rulers of the older civilisation, like Theodorich or
Stilicho at the fall of the Roman Empire, who were at
once leaders of barbarian war bands and Roman consuls
and patricians.   The tendency for a renowned war-leader
to attract adventurers from every quarter to his standard
naturally interferes with the strict tribal organisation,
and so we find an intertribal or supertribal society of
warrior princes and pirates, living on the plunder of the
older civilised societies, and welcoming at their courts
roving adventurers like Odysseus and wandering min-
strels like the rhapsodists who first composed the lays
of the Trojan War.   Professor Chadwick [1] has pointed
out the remarkable parallels that exist between this
Heroic Age of Ancient Greece and that of the Germanic
peoples in the fifth and sixth centuries A.D. as we see
it in the fragments of the great Teutonic epic cycle of
the Age of the Invasions.

The great hall of the Dane King at Heorot and the
Burgundian court of Worms are like the palaces of the
Homeric princes, the centres of a semi-cosmopolitan
society of champions and poets.

" I will recite before the company in the mead hall,"
says Widsith, " how the noble ones were liberal to me

[1] *The Heroic Age.*

in their generosity. I was with the Huns and with the glorious Goths, with the Swedes and with the Geats and with the south Danes. With the Burgundians I was, and there received an armlet ; Guthere gave me there a splendid jewel in reward for my song : that was no sluggish king ! Likewise I was in Italy with Ælfwine ; he had, I have heard, the promptest hand among mankind to gain praise, a heart most generous in giving of rings and gleaming armlets."

In each case the contact of a primitive warlike society with an ancient settled civilisation had set up a process of change which affected alike the culture of the conquered and that of the conquerors and produced a transitional type of society which prepared the way for a new age. It is true that the culture of the Homeric period was relatively higher and in closer contact with the older civilisation than was that of the Teutonic peoples, but nevertheless the changes that were taking place in the Mediterranean world during the twelfth and thirteenth centuries were no less destructive in their effects on the ancient civilisations of the Levant than were the barbarian invasions of the fifth century A.D. in the Roman world. The Homeric poems only lift the curtain on a corner of the stage ; a far greater drama was taking place, of the details of which we know practically nothing.

IV. THE INVASION OF THE SEA PEOPLES AND THE FALL OF THE HITTITE EMPIRE

About the close of the thirteenth century the whole of the Eastern Mediterranean was in turmoil. A great movement of peoples was taking place which entirely destroyed the Hittite Empire and almost proved fatal to Egypt. With this wave of unrest the Trojan War, which Greek tradition usually assigned to the years 1192–1182, was also probably connected. Archæological evidence shows that the Sixth City of Troy, an important stronghold belonging to the Mycenæan period,

but to an independent province of culture, was sacked
and burnt about this time or somewhat earlier, and there
is no reason to doubt the Homeric story that this catastrophe was the work of a great expedition of Achæan
peoples, led by the sons of Atreus, the king of Mycenæ.

This movement has usually been attributed to the
migration of the Indo-European peoples from Central
Europe and the valley of the Danube, which brought
the Hellenic peoples into Greece, the Thracians into
Thrace, and the Phrygians across the Bosphorus into
Asia Minor, where they were the destroyers of the
Hittite Empire.   This view, however, is not borne out
by either archæological or historical evidence.   As we
have seen, the great expansion of the Indo-European
peoples from Central Europe took place about a thousand
years before the end of the Mycenæan Culture, and it is
probable that the Balkans were already largely Indo-
Europeanised long before the beginning of the Age of
Iron.

So, too, with regard to Asia Minor; there is nothing
in the Homeric tradition to suggest that the Trojan War
was an episode in a great invasion of Indo-European
peoples.   The Phrygians appear as allies of the Trojans,
already established on Asiatic soil, and the Trojans
themselves were not a people of native Anatolian stock,
for their leaders bear good Indo-European names, and
their culture and religion are similar in type to those of
the Greeks.   Nor were the Trojans new-comers from
Europe, for the Sixth City, which is the archæological
representative of the Homeric Ilion, goes back to the
beginning of the fifteenth century, and the peoples of
the Homeric Troad, the Dardani, the men of Ilion,
and the Mysians, figure in the Egyptian records of the
Age of Rameses II, under the names of the Iliunna, the
Derden, and the Masa in the catalogue of the Hittite
levies who took part in the Syrian campaign of the
year 1288.

Hence there is no reason to suppose that the fall of

the Hittite Empire was due to a new migration of peoples from Thrace at the beginning of the Iron Age. The great movement of invasion seems to have come not from the land but from the sea, and to have been due to the Mediterranean peoples who were known to the Egyptians as " the Peoples of the Sea." These consisted of a large number of different peoples, whose names appear on the Egyptian monuments. There were the Luka or Ruka, the Ekwesh or Akaiwasha, the Shardana, the Shakalsha or Shekelesh, the Tuirsha or Teresh, the Danuna, Danaua or Denyen, the Pulesati or Peleset, the Washasha, and the Zakal, Thekel or Zakaray. Of these it is almost universally agreed that the Luka are Lycians, the Akaiwasha are Achæans, the Tuirsha are Etruscans, and the Pulesati Philistines. The other names have received different interpretations according to whether their place of origin was looked for in Asia Minor or farther west.

Thus the Shardana are alternatively Sardinians or men of Sardes ; the Shakalsha, Siculi from Sicily or Sagalassians from Pisidia ; the Washasha, Oassians from Caria, Axians from Crete or Oscans from Italy ; and the Danuna, Danaans from Greece or Daunians from Apulia. With the exception of the Achæans, however, all these peoples first appear in relation with Egypt and not with the Hittites, as one might expect had they been natives of Asia Minor. As early as the fourteenth century the Luka, the Danuna, the Shardana, and the Shakalsha make their appearance on the coasts of Syria, either as piratical raiders or as mercenaries in the Egyptian service. Later in the year 1221, the Shardana, the Shakalsha, the Tuirsha, the Luka, and the Akaiwasha, " Northerners coming from all lands," as the Egyptian record describes them, joined with the Libyans in a great invasion of Egypt which was met and defeated by King Merneptah in the Western Delta. Finally, about the year 1194 at the beginning of the reign of Rameses III there took place the last and greatest of

these movements, a veritable migration of peoples.   In
the words of the Egyptian inscription : [1]

" The Isles were troubled, disturbed among themselves at one and the same time.   No land stood before
them, beginning from the land of the Hittites, Cilicia,
Carchemish, Arvad, and Cyprus.
" They destroyed them all and fixed their camp in
one place in the land of Amor (Syria).   They desolated
its people and its land like that which is not.   They
came with fire prepared before them, forward to Egypt.
Their main strength was of the Pulesati, the Zakaray,
the Shakalsha, Danuna, and Washasha.   These lands
were united and they laid their hands upon the land as
far as the Circle of the Earth.   Their hearts were confi-
dent, full of their plans."

The main host marched by land with their women and
children in ox carts, while their fleet sailed along the
coast, but they were met and defeated by the forces of
Egypt both by land and sea.   In the reliefs of the temple
of Rameses III at Medinet Habu we see the incidents of
the struggle—the attack of the Sardinian mercenaries on
the ox wagons of the Philistine army, the fight for the
ships, and the procession of captive warriors, whose
strikingly European faces, as well as their armour and
plumed head-dress, present a remarkable contrast to
the other types represented on the Egyptian monuments.
Later tradition is almost unanimous in deriving the
Philistines from Crete, " the remnant of the island
of Caphtor " as Jeremiah says.   But though they
may have been accompanied by Cretan elements, their
dress and armament are so different from those shown
in Cretan art that it is difficult to accept them as genuine
Minoans, and the recent tendency has been to regard
them as a people of South-western Asia Minor who had
been driven to migrate by the invasion of the Phrygians,
or more probably the Greeks.   However this may be,
there are grounds for thinking that at least some of the

[1] Breasted, *Ancient Records of Egypt*, vol. iv.

invading peoples came from much more distant lands than Asia Minor. If the Shardana were really natives of Sardes, they must have been in contact with the Hittite culture, for that region shows more signs of Hittite influence than any other part of Western Asia Minor. But the Shardana of the Egyptian monuments are by no means Anatolian in appearance, and are entirely different to the Hittite warriors whose figures are carved on the rocks of Karabel. On the other hand, the bronze statuettes of warriors that have been found in Sardinia bear a close resemblance to the figures on the Egyptian reliefs with their great swords, their body armour, and their strange horned helmets ; and though the former may be later in date, they certainly belong to the tradition of the Bronze Age culture of Sardinia, which goes back without a break to æneolithic times. But if the Shardana came from the Western Mediterranean, we have no reason to reject the hypothesis of a western origin for the other peoples, so that the Shakalsha may be Siculi, the Washasha Oscans, and the Danuna Daunians. The fact that the Peoples of the Sea were associated with the Libyans rather than with the Hittites in their invasion of Egypt is on the whole more favourable to the western theory. Moreover, Greek tradition preserved a vague memory of a great invasion from the west. According to Myrsillus of Lesbos,[1] the " Pelasgian Tyrrheni " owing to disturbances in Italy returned eastwards to Greece and other lands in the second generation before the Trojan War, and Plato's story of the great expedition of the empire of Atlantis, at the head of all the peoples of the west as far as Libya and Tyrrhenia, against Egypt and Greece, seems to represent a similar tradition.

Certainly great changes were taking place at this time in the Western Mediterranean, no less than in Asia Minor and the Balkans. Only in Sardinia does the older culture of the Bronze Age continue to exist undisturbed.

[1] In *Dionysius Halic*, i, 68.

Elsewhere there is an abrupt hiatus, due perhaps to the interruption of the old Mediterranean and western megalithic trade routes of the Bronze Age by the coming of new continental influences. We know little of what was happening in Spain at this period, owing to the dearth of archæological evidence, but in Italy the Terremare type of Bronze Age culture was expanding southward, owing perhaps to the expansion of the Italic peoples, and in Sicily the Bronze Age closes with the destruction of the settlements that had been in contact with the Mycenæan Culture in the south-east of the island [1] and the desertion of their sites. Thus the great invasions of Syria and Egypt at the close of the Bronze Age might be due to the fall of the old thalassocracy of the Anatolian Peoples of the Sea who had dominated the Mediterranean and the western trade routes since the third millennium. Heracles, the Gilgamesh of the West, who had set forth a thousand years earlier, in the strength of his youth, to set up his pillars on the threshold of the Atlantic world, to rob the oxen of the Sun from Tartessus and the golden fruit from the garden of the Hesperides, was returning to the lands of his birth, old and hard pressed by the wild peoples of the North, but still strong enough in his death to shake the two pillars of the eastern world, Hatti and Egypt.

For whatever the source of the movement of the Sea Peoples, there can be no doubt that it marks an epoch in the history of the Near East. From this moment the Hittite Empire vanishes for ever, and though it is extremely improbable that the Sea Peoples actually penetrated into the Hittite homelands, their defeat of the Hittite armies at Carchemish or elsewhere in Northern Syria may well have led to the collapse of the kingdom, and its replacement by the Phrygians as the leading power in Asia Minor. The victories of Merneptah and

[1] Sir Arthur Evans believes that Sicily had been actually settled by Cretan colonists in Late Minoan times, as Greek tradition maintained.

Rameses III saved Egypt herself for a time, but her control over Southern Syria gradually lapsed. The Israelite tribes established themselves in the interior of Palestine, while the coasts fell into the hands of the remnants of the Philistine and Zakaray invaders, whose " fenced cities " became the chief centres of civilisation in Southern Palestine.

At the same time a similar process was taking place in Western Asia Minor and the neighbouring islands. As we have seen, the Trojan War probably formed part of the same great movement of the Peoples of the Sea which caused the Philistine invasion of Syria and Egypt, and the subsequent Hellenic colonisation of Æolis and Ionia is a parallel phenomenon to the settlement of the Philistines in Palestine.

V. The Passing of the Mycenæan Age and the Dorian Invasion

These events seem to have prepared the way for the final decline of the Mycenæan Culture and the Dorian invasion of Greece and Crete. We do not know to what extent the Achæan attacks upon Asia Minor and Egypt were due to pressure from the rear, or whether it was that their energies were so absorbed in foreign wars that their powers of resistance were weakened. Certainly it is possible to trace, during the Heroic Age, the gradual infiltration of new cultural elements, and the substitution for the naturalistic art of the Ægean tradition of a new geometrical style, similar to that which also prevailed in Northern Italy and Central Europe during the early Iron Age. This new style did not, however, originate in Central Europe, and in Greece it finds its highest development in Attica, where the population was of the same stock as the Greeks of Ionia. Moreover, the introduction of iron and the practice of cremation may have been due to Anatolian rather than European influence. But there are other elements, such as the use of the brooch or fibula and the substitution of the

broadsword for the rapier, which are probably of northern or Adriatic origin and point to a new movement of
population which culminated in the eleventh century with
the coming of the Dorians. The new-comers were
closely related to the other Hellenic peoples in race and
language, and it is improbable that they originated
farther north than Macedonia or Epirus. Nevertheless
they came from outside the limits of the Mycenæan
culture-province,˙ and consequently their occupation of
the centres of Ægean civilisation in the Argolis, Sparta,
and Crete, involved the destruction of the older culture.
Their relation to the Achæans was like that of the
Lombards to the Ostrogoths, or that of the Allemanni
to the Burgundians, and, as with the second wave of
Germanic invasion in the Roman Empire, their coming
marked the complete victory of the warlike tribal
society and the temporary disappearance of the higher
city culture. The Ægean world was only saved from
complete barbarisation by the survival of the tradition
of the older culture on the coast of Asia Minor, in Æolia,
and above all in Ionia, where the Asiatic element in
Greek culture was strongest.

It was on the coasts and islands of Asia Minor that the
Hellenic civilisation of classical times had its origins,
gradually returning westward to European Greece with
the revival of trade and economic prosperity in the
seventh and eighth centuries. Thus the rise of classical
civilisation was to a great extent the renaissance of the
old Ægean culture. It did not proceed in equal measure
from all Greek-speaking peoples. On the contrary, it was
practically confined to those regions which had already
taken part in the Mycenæan development. Outside
this area—in North-west Greece, for example, the Greeks
remained a semi-barbarous population of warlike tribesmen and peasants, without literature, without science,
and without the city state. For the Greek city was
the heir of the immemorial tradition of the Archaic
culture of Western Asia. Like the old oriental sacred

city, it had its centre in the shrine of the city goddess—
the temple of Artemis at Ephesus, the temple of Aphrodite at Corinth, or the temple of Athene at Athens—and,
at least in the case of Ephesus, there is a direct continuity
between the Greek temple and the pre-Greek sanctuary
of the great goddess of Anatolia.

Nevertheless it would be a mistake to look upon the
Greeks as mere barbarians who owed all their culture
to the higher civilisation that they had conquered, like
the Kassites in Babylonia, or the Mongols in China.
They brought with them not only new blood, but new
institutions, new ideals, and a new spirit. If the Greek
city was ancient and oriental, Greek citizenship was
new and European. The city state, the greatest and
most original creation of the Greek genius, owes its
existence to the marriage of the oriental sacred city with
the Indo-European warrior tribe. From the one parent
came the religious feeling that inspired such intense
devotion to the Hellenic city with its splendid buildings,
its great temples, and its wealth of statuary ; from the
other the strict discipline, the sense of civic solidarity
and common kinship which made every city a kind of
large family, and gave birth to a tribal loyalty very
different from the passive obedience of an oriental
people to its god, and his human representative, the
priest king. The latter attitude eventually triumphed
even in the Greek world, but the greatest achievements
of both Greece and Rome were made when the tribal
spirit was yet strong. The culture-tradition of the
Mediterranean world remained largely oriental, and
retained its contact with Western Asia, but there came
into it as a new leaven the tribal society from the
north, and the consequent process of fermentation
resulted in the production of the classical culture of the
ancient world, and the rise of a true European civilisation.

CHAPTER XVI

ITALY AND THE BEGINNINGS OF THE IRON AGE IN EUROPE

363

CHAPTER XVI

ITALY AND THE BEGINNINGS OF THE IRON AGE IN EUROPE

I. The Early Iron Age Cultures in Italy and the Origin of the New Style

THE changes that passed over the ancient world in the twelfth and thirteenth centuries B.C. were not confined to the Eastern Mediterranean. At the same time that the Mycenæan Culture was passing away in Greece and the Ægean, a great change was also taking place in Italy. The Terremare Culture of the Po valley came to an end and its place was taken by a group of new cultures, all of which were characterised by the use of iron and by a new geometrical style of art. The most important of these, the Villanova Culture, occupied the northern slopes of the Apennines from Bologna to Ravenna and Rimini, whence it gradually expanded over the mountains into Etruria and southwards as far as the Lower Tiber. The allied culture of Este lay farther north in Venetia, while a third group—that of Novilara —appeared on the west coast of the Adriatic in Picenum. Finally the Golasecca Culture occupied the territory of the old Lake Settlements in Lombardy, round Lake Como and Lake Maggiore. All these new culture-provinces are regarded by Professor Peet and many other scholars, such as Pigorini, Colini, Pareti, and Helbig, as a direct continuation and development of the Terremare Culture, while MacIver and von Duhn ascribe them to a new migration of Italic peoples from across the Alps.

Now it is certainly possible to trace some connection between the culture of the Early Iron Age and that of the previous period, for the cemeteries of Bismantova and

Fontanella Mantovana in the north represent a survival
of the Terremare Culture, and belong to the same stage
of culture as that of the southward expansion of the
Terremare Culture into Umbria and Latium, which we
described in a previous chapter.   Moreover, the Terremare types of safety-pins and razors find a direct continuation in those of the Early Iron Age cultures, and

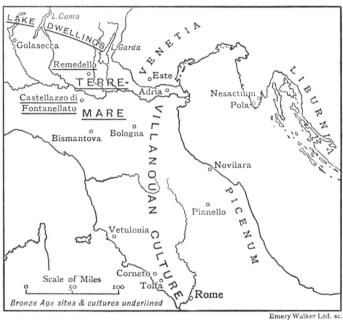

Emery Walker Ltd. sc.

THE CULTURES OF NORTHERN AND CENTRAL ITALY DURING THE
BRONZE AND EARLY IRON AGES.

even the peculiar crescent-shaped handle or *ansa lunata*
of the Terremare pottery reappears at Este.

Above all, the rite of cremation and the use of urn
cemeteries characterise all the new cultures, except that
of Novilara, though the urns were now placed in small
separate graves or cists, instead of side by side in the
earth.

Nevertheless, a number of new elements now make
their appearance in the culture of North Italy, which

have no antecedents in the Terremare Culture of the Bronze Age. With the introduction of iron came a new artistic style, characterised by the use of geometrical decoration, such as the meander pattern, and of animal ornament, consisting of figures of horses, oxen, and birds. All these elements are equally characteristic of the new culture that was making its appearance in Greece about this time, and of the Hallstatt culture in Central Europe.

The discovery of the great cemeteries at Hallstatt in the Austrian Alps, and the importance of that region as an iron-producing centre in ancient times, have led many writers [1] to regard it as the centre of the new influences and the source from which they reached both Italy and the Ægean. There has been a tendency among archæologists and historians to treat Central Europe as a kind of conjuror's hat out of which any missing factor in the development of culture in other regions could be produced, and in this way it has been resorted to in order to explain not only the beginning of the Iron Age, but the fall of the Mycenæan civilisation in the Ægean and the rise of the Geometrical style. It must, however, be clearly realised that iron was coming into use in Greece considerably earlier than in the west, and in Italy earlier than at Hallstatt, and it is probable that the knowledge of the new metal first reached Central Europe from North-eastern Italy or the head of the Adriatic rather than vice versa.

So, too, with the new style of art. It is true that this represents a complete break with the great art which dominated the Ægean world during the Bronze Age, and for that reason it has been assumed to be a new importation from Central Europe. Nevertheless, the appearance of the new style in Central Europe equally marks a break with the past, for as F. van Scheltema, the greatest living authority on prehistoric European art, has pointed out, the new art of the Iron Age is entirely different in spirit to that of the European Bronze Age,

[1] E.g. Ridgeway, *The Early Age of Greece.*

and has no roots in the earlier development.   In place
of the flowing patterns, the abstract designs and the
organic unity of the decoration that marked the native
styles, the art of the Iron Age is characterised by its
employment of figured animal and human ornament,
often in plastic form, which is applied externally with
little regard for the organic unity of the design.   There
is also a complete absence of the naturalism that characterised Ægean art; the figures are stiff and often geometrical in form, and they are arranged symmetrically
in formal rows or in pairs.

This type of design has no antecedents, either in Central
Europe, or in the Middle Danube region which was the
home of the abstract spiral type of ornament.   On the
other hand, it has a long history in the east, where it
goes back to the earliest period of Sumerian and Elamite
art.[1]   It flourished above all in the lands between the
Black Sea and the Caspian, where it continued to develop
from the time of the Early Copper Age culture of the
Kuban valley to that of the Scythians and the Sarma-
tians.   In the Late Bronze Age and the Early Iron Ages
this art is represented by the great cemeteries of Caucasia, such as Koban and Helenendorf, which are dated
by Professor Tallgren from 1300 to 900 B.C.   Here the
resemblances to the art of the Early Iron Age in Central
Europe and North Italy are so evident that they cannot
be ignored.   Not only is there the same predominance
of animal ornament and stylised human figures, but even
the details of execution are often the same, as in the
case of the figures on the pottery of Helenendorf in
Caucasia and of Oedenburg in West Hungary,[2] the safety-
pins and pendants in the form of animals, the engraved
bronze girdles, and the highly decorated bronze bits

---

[1] It also appears in the Bronze Age art of the Ægean, but only in
the Cyclades which stood in close relations to the culture of Asia
Minor, not in Crete.

[2] Cf. also the figures on the geometrical vase from Narce in the
Faliscan territory illustrated in *Monumenti antiche*, vol. iv, fig. 147
(pp. 291 ff.).

and horse trappings. A few examples of this style of art also appear sporadically in Eastern Europe, e.g. at Pasa Kjöj in Bulgaria, at Podgortsa in the Ukraine, and above all in the great treasure of Michalkova in Galicia. These isolated finds stand entirely apart from the contemporary culture of the steppe region, and Tallgren[1] regards them as foreign imports due to commercial intercourse with the Caucasus and Armenia. For the animal style of ornament and the new style of working in metal represent the development of a native tradition in the Caucasus, whereas in Europe they appear abruptly, together with the use of iron, as a new phenomenon which has no organic connection with the earlier culture. Moreover, the metal industry of the Caucasus possesses a far higher technical development, and the technique of inlaying sword hilts and girdles with coloured enamels was already in wide use. On the other hand, there are other signs which point to influence from the west, such as the bronze-hilted daggers of Italian form, the swords, with antennæ handles, and the so-called Bismantova type of safety-pin, which appears to have been developed in North Italy from the earlier " violinbow " type which already occurs in the Terremare.

Moreover, the appearance of amber in some of the Caucasian tombs also suggests the existence of relations with the west.

This double series of parallels between North Italy and the Caucasus can only be satisfactorily explained by a movement of trade or migration which brought the two regions into contact, for if it was due to the parallel evolution of two kindred peoples, the resemblance in points of detail could hardly be so exact.

II. The Adriatic and the Venetian Culture

Now both philological evidence and legendary tradition do tend to establish a certain connection between the coasts of the Adriatic and the eastern shore of the

[1] Tallgren, *La Pontide Préscythique*, pp. 219, 221–7.

370 ITALY AND EARLY IRON AGE [CH. XVI

Black Sea. The former are associated with the legend of the Argonauts who sailed as far as the River Timavus, and Pola and the islands of the Absyrtides are said to have received their names from the Colchians who came from the Caucasus in pursuit of Medea and established a colony there. It is of course possible that the resemblance between the place-names of the two regions which has impressed modern philologists was also the source of these Greek legends. For example, we have the River Apsorus in Colchis, and the island of Apsorus off the coast of Istria, the River Rhizon in Colchis and the Rhizonic Gulf in the Adriatic, the Caucasian tribe of the Dizeres and the River Dizeres in Illyria, the Chaoi in the Caucasus, and the Chaones on the coast of Epirus, the Albanian Mountains and the later Albania east of the Adriatic, and the Albania of the Caucasus. Moreover, it is remarkable that the region in which these names occur is also the habitat of a very remarkable type—the so-called Dinaric race—which has a marked resemblance to the Armenoid peoples of Asia Minor and which probably arose in this region owing to the mingling of a brachycephalic Anatolian stock with a European people of Nordic origin. This type prevails to-day throughout Bosnia, Herzegovina, Montenegro, and Albania, and is characterised by its exceptionally tall stature, and its broad and lofty form of skull.

Of course both the linguistic and anthropological parallels might be explained by a movement of peoples in early prehistoric times. There is, however, I believe, no evidence for the occurrence of the Dinaric type in the neolithic period, and it seems probable that the earliest population of the region was a dolichocephalic people of the same type that we find in the Danubian lands.

On the other hand, if a migration of peoples from Northern Asia Minor to the Adriatic had taken place at the beginning of the Iron Age, it would explain the appearance of the new cultural influences that we have described in the latter area. At first sight the idea of any direct connection between two such outlying regions seems incredible. Nevertheless it must be remembered that in those times the Caucasus was not so remote from the highways of the world trade as it is to-day. As early as the third millennium merchants from Mesopotamia were visiting Armenia and Cappadocia in search of metal, and in the second half of the following millennium, under the Hittite Empire, North-eastern Asia Minor had become one of the great centres of world-power and possessed a flourishing trade and industry. It was here, in the land of the Chalybes on the south-eastern coast of the Black Sea, that tradition places the origin of iron-working, and this is borne out by the recent discovery of a document which shows that iron was already being exported by the Hittites as early as the thirteenth century. It is probable that the knowledge of the new metal reached Europe, as well as Western Asia and Egypt, from this quarter, for even in classical times Æschylus still speaks of it as " the Chalybian stranger," and " the stranger from across the sea."

Now in Central Europe the new type of metal-working and the new style of art had their earliest centres at the head of the Adriatic, and it was from here that their influence was diffused along the trade routes into Carniola, Austria, and Bosnia, as well as over the Apennines into Central Italy. This focal region was occupied in historic times by the Veneti, who are generally believed to be a people of Illyrian origin who conquered the country in the eleventh or twelfth century B.C. The ancients, however, regarded them as the same people as the Eneti of Asia Minor, who dwelt to the west of the Chalybes on the coast of the Black Sea and who were believed to have migrated to the west after the Trojan War.[1] The historic Veneti were a people of traders and metal-workers, who were the chief intermediaries

---

[1] With the exception of Strabo, who traces their origin to the Veneti of Southern Brittany. The latter were also a trading people, renowned for their skill in seamanship.

between the Mediterranean peoples and the amber-producing regions of the north.

At this period the Great Bronze Age trade-routes across Central Europe had begun to decline. The chief source of amber-producing was no longer in Jutland, but had shifted to West Prussia, and the amber was now exported by way of the Vistula and the Oder to the head of the Adriatic. The neighbouring district of Carniola is extraordinarily rich in amber antiquities, as well as in examples of Venetic metal-work, and from this region the trade passed across the Adriatic to North-eastern Italy and Etruria, where it also appears in very large quantities by the seventh century B.C.

The rise of this Adriatic trade undoubtedly accounts for the sudden appearance of new cultural influences in Central Europe from the Eastern Alps to the North-west Balkans at this period. For the great development of Iron Age culture and art which is represented by the famous cemeteries at Hallstatt and Dürrnberg and Wezelach belongs to the later phases of the so-called Hallstatt period, i.e. from the eighth to the fifth century, and it is separated from the earlier culture of the region by a distinct cultural hiatus which suggests an actual change of population. The new culture is attributed by Austrian archæologists[1] to the direct influence of the Veneto-Illyrian people from the south, who inaugurated the salt workings at Hallstatt and Hallein, as well as the new amber route to the north. Where this route strikes the Danube, we have evidence of the same cultural influences in the Kalenderberg culture of Lower Austria, with its remarkable pottery decorated with ornament in relief and with plastic figures of men and animals. Still further north, in Moravia, the rich iron deposits in the region of Brünn were exploited, like the Hallstatt salt-mines, by colonists from the south, who introduced a fully developed

[1] E.g. O. Menghin and G. Kyrle. For the Moravian development cf. Červinka in *R.V.G.*, vol. ii, p. 96.

Hallstatt industry among the native bronze-using population, and whose remains are to be seen in the famous chariot burial of the Byčiskala cave.

Finally the opening up of trading relations between the Adriatic and the Eastern Baltic was accompanied by new developments of culture in the latter region and by the appearance of exotic types such as the curious anthropomorphic " Face Urns " that are found in West Prussia on the Lower Vistula. So, too, the bronze figures of women which were mentioned in Chapter XII, and which bear a striking resemblance to the figures from Novilara and Villanova, probably reached Scandinavia by the same route. These undoubtedly have an oriental prototype, and are connected with the agricultural religion of the Mother Goddess which, according to Scandinavian archæologists, had a great expansion in the Northern Lands during the Iron Age.[1] This cult was especially characteristic of the Eastern Baltic, where, as late as the age of Tacitus, the inhabitants of the amber coast were still renowned for their devotion to the Mother Goddess by their skill in agriculture and the cultivation of fruit trees.

It can hardly be mere coincidence that these foreign influences had their centre in the region that was the northern terminus of the trade route that led from the Venetic territory at the head of the Adriatic, and it may even be possible that the Venedic Gulf, the Gulf of Dantzig and the Venedi of the north, owed their names to this connection.[2]

[1] Cf. H. Rydh in *R.V.G.*, vol. ix, p. 92.

[2] It is true that in the age of Tacitus the Venedi were an inland people, and the amber coast was inhabited by the Aestii. But this may be only another example of the way in which the names of peoples outlast the peoples themselves. In this very area the Prussian name still survives, though the Old Prussian language and people have disappeared, while the Aestii, whose language, according to a surprising remark of Tacitus, resembled that of the British, have passed on their name to the Finno-Ugrian people of Esthonia. Whatever the Venedi may have been it is generally agreed that they were not the ancestors of the Slavonic Wends who, however, seem to have inherited their name.

But leaving aside such doubtful questions, there is ample evidence to prove that the Veneti were one of the great trading peoples of antiquity and that it was through them that the new artistic influences of the Italian Iron Age were introduced into Central Europe, and thence diffused in a modified form to the west and north. The products of their workshops had a wide distribution in the lands to the north of the Adriatic during the later Hallstatt period, above all the situlæ or pails of beaten bronze, which are the most characteristic product of Venetic industry.

These situlæ are elaborately decorated with friezes consisting of rows of figures, and the scenes of feasting and boxing and chariot racing which they depict throw some light on the social life of the people.

Moreover, the Veneti seem to have attained some skill in architecture and stone carving, for the remains of a temple have been discovered at Nesactium in the south of Istria which appears to date from the Early Iron Age, since it was already in ruins when the Iron Age cemetery on the site was in use. The ruins contain remarkable statues of twin figures (? the Dioscuri), ithyphallic horsemen, and a goddess of birth, as well as numerous stone slabs decorated with finely executed spiral and geometrical patterns.[1]

Thus the art of the Veneti, while distinctly barbarous in comparison with that of Ancient Greece, belongs to a far more advanced stage than that of the other native European peoples. In this respect it may be compared with the art of the Etruscans, though the latter in its developed stage was much more strongly influenced by the culture of the Ægean and the Near East. On the other hand, there can be no doubt that the art and culture of the Veneti has its roots in the same tradition as that of the Early Iron Age culture of Villanova, as well as of the

---

[1] The worship of a triad consisting of the Mother Goddess and the two divine horsemen was still prevalent in Pannonia during the Roman period.

third culture-group which appears on the Adriatic coasts
in the region of Novilara. If we could regard all these
three cultures as due to the transformation or modification of the North Italian cultures of the Bronze Age
under the influence of a movement of trade and migration from Asia Minor, it would afford a much more
satisfactory explanation of their development than either
the hypothesis of a direct evolution from the Terremare
Culture or that of a new movement of peoples from
Central Europe or the Danube. It is true that the latter
view has in its favour the supposed Illyrian character
of the Venetic language. But our knowledge of the
Illyrian languages is so slight that it is dangerous to
base far-reaching conclusions on the linguistic evidence.[1]
In fact, Professor Conway, whose knowledge of the
Italic dialects is unrivalled, is inclined to regard the
Venetic language as the most primitive member of
the Italic group, and as the possible representative of
the speech of the Terremare people. Now the earliest
evidence for the Venetic language dates from the sixth
century, and there is ample time between that date and
the beginning of the Iron Age for a conquering minority
to have adopted the language of the native population,
just as they had adopted the native burial rites and
some features of the native pottery. Moreover, there
do exist traces of a non-Indo-European type of speech,
resembling Etruscan, throughout the Venetic area, and
in the neighbouring regions to the north and north-east of
the Adriatic. Indeed, many of the elements common to
Venetia and Illyria seem to be derived from this source
rather than from a common Indo-Germanic stock.[2]

---

[1] The question is fully discussed by Jokl in *R.V.G.*, s.v. " Illyrier."
[2] As we have already remarked, our knowledge of the Illyrians is
infinitesimal. It is possible that they were originally a mere conquering aristocracy who enslaved a native population of Thracian
stock. Theopompus speaks of the Illyrian Ardiæans as ruling over a
vast population of Thracian serfs whom he compares to the Spartan
helots. Cf. Rostovtzeff, *Social and Economic History of the Roman
Empire*, chap. vi, note 58.

III. The Etruscans and their Relation to the Villanovan Culture

It is of course universally admitted that the historical Etruscans occupied North-eastern Italy as far as Mantua and Verona, and inscriptions in the Etruscan script, and some of them perhaps in the Etruscan language, occur as far north as Lake Como, and through the Trentino to the Brenner, so that there is some reason to believe that the Raeti who inhabited the Eastern Alps were partially Etruscanised, even if they were not themselves, as Livy and Pliny believed, a people of Etruscan speech. There has, however, always been a great difference of opinion among scholars as to the interpretation of these facts. The majority of modern writers accept Herodotus's tradition of the Lydian origin of the Etruscans. They believe that the latter first landed on the coast of Tuscany in the eighth or ninth century B.C., and gradually extended their power northwards to the valley of the Po which they dominated from the close of the sixth century down to the Gallic invasion. Thus the Etruscan period in North Italy can have lasted little more than a century. On the other hand, the opposite theory of Dionysius of Halicarnassus, according to which the Etruscans were a native European people, has also found a number of supporters in modern times. The majority of historians, such as Niebuhr and Mommsen, Beloch and de Sanctis, have favoured the view that the Etruscans first entered Italy from the region of the Alps, and that their occupation of Northern Italy preceded that of Tuscany. This theory has recently been put forward in a new form by Pareti who identifies the Etruscans with the people of the North Italian lake-dwellings, and of the Terremare, and regards the Villanova Culture of the Iron Age as a step in the continuous evolution which leads from the Terremare to the Etruscan civilisation of historic times.[1]

[1] N. L. Pareti, *Le Origini Etrusche*, 1926.

But the linguistic and cultural evidence in favour of the Asiatic origin of the Etruscans is too strong to be easily refuted. It is true that the Etruscan language is different from that of the Lydians or from any Asiatic language that is known to us at present, but it is distinctly Asiatic in character and entirely unlike any European tongue. The very name of the people— Tursenna or Turranna—is Anatolian in type and is the same as the Greek word for tyrant—Turannos, which has a non-Indo European and possibly Lydian origin.[1]

Even the name of Tarchon, the chief god of the Hittite Empire, plays an important part in Etruscan legend. The Greek traditions with regard to the presence of Etruscans in the Ægean, in Attica, and at Lemnos, are borne out by the discovery of an inscription which has considerable resemblance to Etruscan in the latter island, while the old name for the Attic Tetrapolis— Ὑττηνία—seems clearly derived from hut—the Etruscan word for four.

Moreover, the whole character of the historic Etruscan society and culture is entirely consistent with the hypothesis of their Asiatic origin. It was the civilisation of a city-dwelling aristocracy who had reduced the native peasant population to a state of serfdom, and it early blossomed into a premature urban luxury, like that of the Ionian and Lydian cities. In comparison with the Latins and even with the Greeks, the Etruscans seem an old people whose roots lay in the past and whose culture had already become stationary and unprogressive while the Hellenic world was still in the vigour of youth. And their religion leaves a similar impression of oriental archaism, with its strict ritual formalism and its elaborate development of divination and the science of augury, a tradition which had its origin in Sumerian

[1] Thus the name of the Etruscans would be not a racial appellation, but a title—" the Lords," like Arya " the Nobles." The same word appears in Etruscan religious usage. The goddess is Turan, " the Lady," and the war-god is Maristuran, " Mars the Lord."

Mesopotamia and had thence passed west into Asia Minor and had been assimilated by the Hittite culture.

Thus there are strong grounds for the prevalent modern view in favour of the Asiatic origin of the Etruscans. Yet on the other hand there are grave difficulties with regard to the date of the movement. If the Etruscan colonisation did not begin until the end of the ninth century, as the archæologists usually maintain, it is difficult to see how their culture can have struck such deep roots in Italy. The Greek movement of colonisation in Southern Italy and Sicily is little later, and the influence of the Greek colonies was always limited to the coasts and failed to absorb the native population entirely, even in Sicily. Yet the Greeks were in permanent contact with their mother country, and a continuous stream of immigrants was passing into Italy for centuries, while the Etruscans had no home population on which to draw and their numbers must have been recruited only from the descendants of the small band of the original conquerors of the later ninth and early eighth centuries.

Now the evidence for this late date rests almost entirely on the changes of culture that appear in this period at the Villanovan sites in Southern Etruria, such as Corneto and Vetulonia. First there is an advance in civilisation marked by an increase in wealth and new types of art which show oriental and Ægean influences. Secondly there is the change in the burial rite from incineration to inhumation.

The latter change, however, might equally well be explained as due to the revival of the burial rite of the native population of Central Italy which had been replaced for a time by the burial rite of the conquering Villanovans from the north. And so, too, the growth in wealth and the new artistic influences do not necessarily imply the coming of a new population, but mark the influence of a new expansion of trade and culture from the Near East, which is equally seen in Greece with the appearance of orientalising motives, and the change of artistic style that accompanied them. Moreover, as Pareti has pointed out, there is no lack of evidence for the survival of Villanovan elements in the early Etruscan culture. There is no break in the occupation of the sites which is continuous from the Villanovan period down to the time of the Etruscans. Moreover, the Villanovans were already skilled workers in metal, and the ornamental vessels of beaten bronze, the swords and helmets, and the engraved bronze girdles, and the use of animal and human figures in ornament, were equally characteristic of the Villanovan and the Etruscan periods. There is, in fact, no more cultural hiatus between the Villanovan and the Etruscan cultures than there is between the geometrical culture in Greece and that of the orientalising period. Finally, those very points in the culture of the Romans which have been held to prove their connection with the Terremare people are just the elements which were admitted by Roman tradition itself to have been a cultural borrowing from the Etruscans.

Thus, while we must admit the eastern origin of the Etruscans, there seems to be no conclusive reasons against placing their arrival as early as the beginning of the Iron Age—a period which was marked by a distinct break in the development of Italian culture and by the appearance of new influences of Asiatic origin. Such a movement of migration is, after all, more appropriate to the age that followed the fall of the Hittite Empire, and which witnessed the break-up of the Mycenæan power and the Dorian invasions, than to the ninth century when the Ægean world had settled down to a condition of relative stability. Moreover, it is in agreement with ancient tradition which placed both the Etruscan invasion and the coming of the Veneti in the age of confusion that followed the Trojan War, while it will also explain the resemblance in culture between the Etruscans and the Veneti, and will give room for the assimilation of the native culture of Northern and Central Italy by the new-comers, and the wide expansion of their influence in the region of the Po and the Northern Adriatic. On this hypothesis the rise of the Villanova Culture would be due to the Etruscans, and that of the culture of Este and Venetia to the Veneti, while the older Italic population of the Terremare Culture, who might perhaps be identified with the Umbrians, would in both cases form the underlying element in the population.

In the Third Iron Age culture of the Adriatic coast—that of Novilara and Picenum—the foreign origin of the new culture is even more clearly evident, for here it has no relations with an earlier Bronze Age culture of the Terremare type, but appears abruptly in the midst of the primitive population of æneolithic culture which had occupied the region from time immemorial. Yet it is marked by the same characteristics—the same advanced type of metal-work, and the same use of animal ornament and human figures as in the Etruscan and Venetic area. It is, moreover, in this region that we find the earliest inscriptions, written in a remarkable alphabet of a very primitive type which is not derived from Etruscan or Chalcidic Greek prototypes. It seems probable that this culture is to be attributed to the Liburnians from across the Adriatic, who are known by historical evidence to have possessed settlements on the eastern coast of Italy in this region. The Liburnians, like the Etruscans, were a sea-people who were noted in later times both for their seamanship and their piracy, and it is possible that they also, like the Etruscans and the Veneti, belong to the group of Anatolian peoples who migrated to the Adriatic from Asia Minor at the beginning of the Iron Age.[1]

It is impossible to say whether the new influences

[1] Jokl in the article mentioned above considers the termination -URN to be typical of a non-Indo-European language of the same type as Etruscan. The language of the Novilara inscriptions is as yet undetermined.

that appear at Hallstatt in Austria and Glasinatz in Bosnia are to be attributed to a similar movement of population, or merely to cultural influence from the Adriatic, but the remains from these sites bear witness to a mixture of racial types and it is by no means improbable that the appearance of the new type of culture was due to the coming of a foreign minority.[1]

IV. The Influence of the Etruscans on the Development of the Higher Culture in Italy

But whatever may be the ultimate conclusion with regard to the date and extent of the Asiatic or Anatolian migration to Europe, it is impossible to exaggerate its importance. Whether the Villanovans were, as we have supposed, Etruscans from the beginning, or whether the latter invaded Central Italy during the second period of the Villanova Culture, there is no doubt that the whole of the Villanovan territory was ultimately Etruscanised, and that this was the foundation on which the higher culture of the Italian Peninsula was based. As in the Ægean, the union of the oriental city with the tribal society of Bronze Age Europe gave birth to a new type of civilisation. The mingling of the two streams of culture is to be seen most clearly in the case of the Latium, where the native element was not so completely absorbed by the Etruscan conqueror as in the Villanovan territory proper. Here the southward expansion of the Etruscans about the seventh century B.C. led to the foundation of the early city state of Latium, such as Præneste and Rome herself. Even the name of Rome— Ruma—and those of the three original tribes, the Ramnes, Tities, and Luceres, are clearly of Etruscan origin, and the same influence is to be traced not only in the names of the early Etruscan kings, but in

[1] The most important Iron Age cemeteries in Jugo-Slavia are found along the ancient trade-route from the Adriatic to the region of Sarajevo by way of the Narenta valley and Mostar.

such common Roman names as Aulius, Tullius, and Cassius.

Thus the Roman State and its culture was due to the fusion of two distinct elements—the Etruscan city state and the Italic peasant community. From the one side came the city itself and all the institutions of city life—the magistracy with its insignia, such as the curule chair, the purple toga, the ivory sceptre, and the rods and axes of the lictors.[1] Etruscan also were the triumphal procession and the public games which played so large a part in the life of the Etruscans, and also of the Veneti.   No less important was the influence of Etruria in the sphere of religion and art, for it was from the Etruscans that the Romans learned their science of augury and probably much of their religious ritual, as well as the plan of their temples and the knowledge of statuary.   Finally, not only the Romans, but all the Italic peoples, were indebted to the Etruscans for their knowledge of the alphabet and the art of writing—the most decisive mark of the attainment of true civilisation.

On the other hand, the Latin stock contributed its peasant solidity and virility, its courage and laboriousness, qualities which were possessed in equal measure by other Italic peoples, such as the Samnites, but which were lacking in the more highly civilised cities of Etruria. If the Roman and Prænestine nobles of the earlier period had shared in the personal luxury of the Etruscan Culture, the prevailing ideal during the age of the early Republic was one of peasant simplicity and military severity and discipline.   Indeed, the Latin reaction against Etruscan culture may be compared to the somewhat earlier Dorian reaction against the luxurious Ionian

---

[1] The last were said by tradition to have come to Rome from Vetulonia, and a double axe surrounded by a fascis of eight iron rods has actually been found in an eighth-century tomb on this site—a remarkable justification of tradition.   Cf. Randall-MacIver, *Villanovans and Early Etruscans*, fig. 56.

culture in Greece.   Alike in Greece and Italy, we can
trace the conflict between a relatively advanced city
culture and a simple tribal culture, out of which there
arose a new type of society unlike anything that had
existed before.   Nevertheless, in both cases the rise of
the classical city state was due, not to a spontaneous
development of the European tribal society, but to a
direct inheritance from the old West Asiatic and Ægean
culture of the Bronze Age, the tradition of which had
survived in Asia Minor whence it was transmitted to
Europe, on the one hand by the Ionian Greeks, and on
the other by the Etruscans.

Thus the Early Iron Age witnessed a complete fusion
between the culture of the warrior peoples and that of
the ancient city.   In Asia, the Assyrian Empire represents the complete militarisation of the Archaic sacred
monarchy, while in Europe the union of the sacred city
and the warrior tribe gave birth to the new city state
of classical times.   But this new Iron Age type of
culture did not possess the stability which is so impressive
a feature of the Archaic Culture as we see it in Egypt
or Babylonia, perhaps because it was a hybrid form
which failed to achieve internal equilibrium, or because
the predominance of the military element produced a
premature exhaustion of the class of citizen soldiers
which was the foundation of this type of society.   Thus
the Etruscan Culture, and the Assyrian and Persian
Empires were all notably short-lived, and even the Greek
city and the Latin peasant republic, in spite of their
immense achievements, experienced an almost equally
rapid decline.   The new cultures, in fact, represent an
intermediate transitional stage between two more
permanent forms of religion-culture—between the
Archaic Civilisation of the ancient East, and the new
World-Religions which were already coming into
existence during this period.   Throughout the pre-
Christian Iron Age from the Assyrian to the Roman

Empires, the military element was predominant, but the following period witnessed a return to the purely religious conception of life and to a theocratic ideal of the state, such as we find in Sassanian Persia and in the Byzantine Empire, and above all in Islam and in medieval Christendom.

BIBLIOGRAPHY

A. GENERAL

1. ENCYCLOPÆDIAS AND PERIODICALS

Ebert, *Reallexikon der Vorgeschichte* (Berlin, 1924–). 8 vols. published (to N). Cited as *R.V.G.* Indispensable.

Hastings, *Encyclopædia of Religion and Ethics*, cited as *E.R.E.*

Hoops, *Reallexikon der Germanischen Altertumskunde.* 4 vols., 1911–13.

O. Schrader, *Reallexikon der Indo-Germanischon Altertumskunde.* 2nd ed. in course of publication. 1st ed., 1901.

The following are some of the most important and easily accessible periodicals :

Der Alte Orient (Leipzig), cited as *A.O.*

L'Anthropologie.

The Antiquaries' Journal, cited as *A.J.*

Archæologia.

Bulletino di Paletnologia Italiana, cited as *B.P.*

The Journal of the Royal Anthropological Institute, cited as *J.R.A.I.*

The Journal of Egyptian Archæology, cited as *J.E.A.*

The Journal of Hellenic Studies, cited as *J.H.S.*

The Liverpool Annals of Archæology and Anthropology, cited as *Liverpool Annals.*

Man. A Monthly Record of Anthropological Science.

Monumenti Antichi dell' . . . *Accademia dei Lincei,* cited as *Mon. Ant.*

Prähistorische Zeitschrift (Berlin), cited as *P.Z.*

Proceedings of the Royal Irish Academy, cited as *P.R.I.A.*

Syria (in French).

Wiener Prähistorische Zeitschrift, cited as *W.P.Z.*

Zeitschrift für Anthropologie, Ethnologie und Urgeschichte, cited as *Z.E.*

2. ANTHROPOLOGY AND THE DEVELOPMENT OF CULTURE

F. Birkner, *Die Rassen und Volker der Menschheit.* 1912.
J. Brunhes, *La Géographie Humaine.* 3rd ed., 3 vols., 1925.
L. D. Buxton, *The Peoples of Asia.* 1925.
L. D. Buxton, *Primitive Labour.* 1924.
L. Febvre, *La Terre et l'Évolution Humaine.* 1922 (vol. 4 of series "L'Évolution de l'Humanité," cited henceforward as *E.H.*).[1]
H. J. Fleure, *The Peoples of Europe.* 1922.
F. Graebner, *Die Methode der Ethnologie.* 1911.
A. C. Haddon, *The Races of Men and their Distribution.* 2nd ed., 1925.
E. Huntingdon, *Civilization and Climate.* 3rd ed., 1924.
B. Kidd, *Social Evolution.* 1894.
A. L. Kroeber, *Anthropology.* 1923.
P. G. Leplay, *Les Ouvriers Européens.* 6 vols., 1877–1879.
E. de Martonne, *Géographie Physique.* 3rd ed., Vol. III, *Biogéographie,* 1927.
E. Meyer, *Geschichte des Altertums,* Vol. I, pt. I, *Einleitung, Elemente der Anthropologie.* 3rd ed., 1911.
W. J. Perry, *The Growth of Civilization.* 1924.
E. Pittard, *Les Races et l'Histoire.* (Vol. 5 of series *E.H.*). 1924.
H. Pinard de la Boullaye, *L'Étude Comparée des Religions.* 2 vols., 1922–5.
F. Ratzel, *Anthropogeographie.* 2 vols., 1st ed., 1882–1891. English translation :
F. Ratzel, *The History of Mankind.* 3 vols., 1896–1898.
W. H. R. Rivers, *The History of Melanesian Society.* 2 vols., 1914.
W. H. R. Rivers, *Psychology and Politics.* 1923.
W. H. R. Rivers, *The Contact of Peoples* (in Essays and Studies presented to William Ridgeway). 1913.
G. Elliot Smith, *The Migrations of Early Culture.* 1915.
W. Schmidt and W. Koppers, *Völker und Kulturen.* I. *Gesellschaft und Wirtschaft der Völker.* 1926.

[1] This series is in the course of translation into English under the title of " The History of Civilisation."

G. Schwalbe and E. Fischer, "Anthropologie" in *Die Kultur der Gegenwart*. 1923. (Sections on Prehistory by Hoernes, and Ethnology by Graebner.)

E. B. Tylor, *Primitive Culture*. 2 vols., 1889.

J. Vendryes, *Le Langage: Introduction linguistique à l'Histoire*. (Vol. 3 of series *E.H.*) 1921.

O. Wissler, *Man and Culture*. N.D. (1923.)

3. THE PREHISTORIC CULTURE OF EUROPE IN GENERAL

British Museum Guide to the Antiquities of the Stone Age. 3rd ed., 1926.

British Museum Guide to the Antiquities of the Bronze Age. 2nd ed., 1920.

British Museum Guide to the Antiquities of the Iron Age. 2nd ed., 1925.

V. G. Childe, *The Dawn of European Civilization*. 1925. (From mesolithic times to the middle of the Bronze Age. The best and most complete work on the subject. Full bibliographies.)

J. Déchelette, *Manuel d'Archéologie préhistorique, celtique et gallo-romaine*. 4 vols., 1908–1914. (Vol. 1 Stone Age, Vol. 2 Bronze Age, Vols. 3 and 4 Iron Age.)

M. Hoernes, *Kultur der Urzeit*. 3 vols., 1912 (pub. in Sammlung Goschen). 1. *Steinzeit*; 2. *Bronzezeit*; 3. *Eisenzeit*.

M. Hoernes, *Natur und Urgeschichte des Menschen*. 1909.

M. Hoernes, *Urgeschichte der bildenden Kunst in Europa*. 2nd ed., 1915. 3rd ed. with notes, etc., by O. Menghin, 1925. (Indispensable.)

G. G. MacCurdy, *Human Origins*. 2 vols., 1924. (Covers all the prehistoric periods.)

J. de Morgan, *L'Humanité Préhistorique*. 1924. (Vol. II of series *E.H.*)

J. L. Myres, Chapters I and II of *Cambridge Ancient History*, Vol. I.

H. Schmidt, *Vorgeschichte Europas*, I. 1924. (A short sketch of the Stone and Bronze Age cultures by a leading authority on the subject.)

C. Schuchardt, *Alt Europa in seiner Kultur- und Stil-entwicklung*. 1919. (2nd ed., 1926.) (A learned and interesting book, written from a strongly "Occidentalist" point of view.)

4. The History of the Ancient East in General

J. H. Breasted, *Ancient Times*. 1914.

The Cambridge Ancient History. Vol. I to 1580 B.C. 1st ed. 1923. Vol. II to 1000. (1924.) Vol. III The *Assyrian Empire*. (1925.) Indispensable. Cited as *C.A.H.*

G. Fougère, G. Contenau, R. Grousset, P. Jouguet and J. Lesquier, *Les Premières Civilisations*. 1926. (In series *Peuples et Civilisations*.)

H. H. Hall, *The Ancient History of the Near East from the Earliest Times to the Battle of Salamis*. 6th ed., 1926. (The standard textbook.)

Hartmann's *Weltgeschichte*. Vol. I, pt. I. *Geschichte des Alten Orients*, von E. G. Klauber und C. F. Lehmann-Haupt. 3rd ed., 1925. (To the fourth century B.C. Brief but valuable.)

G. Maspero, *Histoire ancienne des peuples de l'orient*. 6th ed., 1904.

G. Maspero, *The Dawn of Civilization : Egypt and Chaldœa*. 5th ed., 1910.

G. Maspero, *The Struggle of the Nations*. 2nd ed., 1910.

E. Meyer, *Geschichte des Altertums*. Vol. I, pt. II. 3rd ed., 1913. (A fundamental work, embracing the history of the Ancient East to the sixteenth century B.C., and a brief survey of neolithic European culture.)

A. Moret, *Des Clans aux Empires*. 1923. (Vol. 6 of series *E.H.*)

J. L. Myres, *The Dawn of History*. N.D. (A brilliant introductory sketch.)

J. de Morgan, *Les Premières Civilisations*. 1909.

W. Otto, *Kulturgeschichte des Altertums*. 1925. (A valuable survey of the recent literature on the subject.)

G. Perrot and C. Chipiez, *Histoire de l'Art en l'antiquité*. 9 vols., 1882–1911. (There is an English translation of the earlier vols.)

M. Rostovtzeff, *A History of the Ancient World*. Vol. I, *The Orient and Greece*. 1926. (Very fully illustrated.)

B. SPECIAL BIBLIOGRAPHY
1. Chapter I

M. Boule, *Les Hommes Fossiles*. 2nd ed., 1923. (English translation, 1923.)

C. E. P. Brooks, *The Evolution of Climate.* 2nd ed., 1925.

Burkitt, *Prehistory.* 1921.

Burkitt, *Our Forerunners.* N.D. (In Home University Library.)

A. P. Coleman, *Ice Ages : Recent and Ancient.* 1926.

H. J. Fleure, " Some Early Neanthropic Types in Europe and their Modern Representatives," in *J.R.A.I.*, 1920, Vol. 50.

J. Joly, *The Surface History of the Earth.* 1925.

A. Keith, *The Antiquity of Man.* 2nd ed., 2 vols., 1925.

R. A. S. Macalister, *Text Book of European Archæology*, I. 1921.

H. Obermaier, *Der Mensch der Vorzeit.* 1912.

H. Obermaier, *El Hombre Fosil.* 1st ed., 1912. Translated with some alterations by H. F. Osborn as *Fossil Man in Spain.* 1924. (A somewhat misleading title, as the book has a much wider scope.)

H. Obermaier, Articles on Diluvial-Chronologie, -Fauna, -Flora, -Geologic, in *R.V.G.*, Vol. II.

H. F. Osborn, *Men of the Old Stone Age.* 2nd ed., 1918.

H. Peake and H. J. Fleure, *Hunters and Artists.* 1927.

G. Elliot Smith, *Primitive Man.* 1916.

W. J. Sollas, *Ancient Hunters and their Modern Representatives.* 3rd ed., 1924.

W. B. Wright, *The Quaternary Ice Age.* 1914.

2. CHAPTER II

R. F. Benedict, *The Concept of the Guardian Spirit in North America* (Memoirs of the American Anthropological Association, 29). 1923.

M. A. Czaplica, *Aboriginal Siberia.* 1914.

E. Durkheim, *Les Formes Élementaires de la Vie Religieuse.* 1912. (English translation.)

J. G. Frazer, *The Golden Bough.* 3rd ed., 1907, etc. 12 vols.

J. G. Frazer, *Totemism and Exogamy.* 4 vols., 1910.

W. Jochelson, *The Koryak* (Memoirs of A.M.N.H.,[1] X). 1905–8.

A. Leroy, *La Religion des Primitives.* 1909.

R. H. Lowie, *Primitive Religion.* 1925.

---

[1] A.M.N.H. = American Museum of Natural History.

T. Mainage, *Les Religions de la préhistoire: L'Age Paléolithique*. 1921.

R. R. Marett, *The Threshold of Religion*. 2nd ed., 1914.

A. G. Morice, " The Canadian Dene " (*Annual Archæological Report*, Toronto). 1906.

A. G. Morice, " The Great Dene Race," in *Anthropos*, V. 1910.

W. Schmidt, " L'Origine de l'Idée de Dieu," in *Anthropos*, III–IV. 1908–9.

N. Söderblom, *Das Werden des Gottesglaubens*. German translation, 1916.

J. R. Swanton, *The Social Condition, Beliefs and Linguistic Relations of the Tlingit Indians* (Bureau of American Ethnology 26th Report, 1908.

3. CHAPTER III (see also CHAPTER XII)

There is, unfortunately, no single work devoted to the Peasant Cultures of Neolithic Europe. The best treatment of the subject is to be found in the general works by V. G. Childe and M. Hoernes mentioned in the General Bibliography, A. 3.

M. C. Burkitt, *Our Early Ancestors*. 1926. (An introductory sketch of the mesolithic, neolithic, and æneolithic periods.)

V. G. Childe, " Schipenitz : a Late Neolithic Station with Painted Pottery in Bukowina," *J.R.A.I.*, Vol. LIII, 1923.

M. Hoernes, W. Radimsky, and F. Fiala, *Die Neolithische Station von Butmir bei Sarajevo*. 2 pts., 1895–1898.

M. Hoernes, " Die Neolithische Keramik in Österreich," in *Z.E.*, Vol. 35, 1903.

T. D. Kendrick, *The Axe Age*. 1925.

G. Kossinna, *Die deutsche Vorgeschichte*. 3rd ed., 1918.

L. Kozlowski, " L'Époque Mesolithique en Pologne," in *L'Anthropologie*, Vol. 36, 1926.

J. L. Myres, " The Alpine Races in Europe," in *Geographical Journal*. 1906 (Dec.). (Maintains the thesis of the origin of the neolithic culture of lake dwellings among the Alpine peoples of Anatolia.)

R.V.G. articles on Böhmen-Mähren, Mitteldeutschland, Nordischer Kreis, etc.

H. Reinerth, *Chronologie der Jungeren Steinzeit Suddeutschlands.* 1924.

A. Schliz, *Das steinzeitliche Dorf Grossgartach.* 1901.

H. Schmidt, "Ausgrabungen in Cucuteni, Rumanien," in *Z.E.*, Vol. 43, 1911.

C. Schumacher, *Siedelungs- und Kultur-geschichte der Rheinlande,* I. 1921. (Includes the whole prehistoric period, but is specially valuable for neolithic culture.)

H. Shetelig, *Préhistoire de la Norvège.* 1926. (Also includes the whole prehistoric period down to Christian times.)

J. M. Tyler, *The New Stone Age in Northern Europe.* 1921.

Verworn, "Kulturkreis der Bandkeramik," in *P.Z.*, II.

A. J. B. Wace and M. S. Thompson, *Prehistoric Thessaly.* 1912.

M. Wosinsky, *Das prähistorische Schanzwerk von Lengyel.* 1888–1891.

G. Wilke, *Spiralmäanderkeramik und Gefässmalerei.* 1910.

4. CHAPTER IV

1. On the Asiatic Painted Pottery Cultures in General.

V. G. Childe, *The Aryans*, Ch. V, § 2. 1926.

H. Frankfort, *Studies in the Early Pottery of the Near East.* I. *Mesopotamia, Syria and Egypt and their Earliest Interrelations.* 1924.

E. Pottier, in *Mémoires de la Délégation en Perse*, Vol. XIII. 1912.

2. *Anau*

R. Pumpelly (with H. Schmidt and others), *Explorations in Turkestan.* 3 vols., 1905–8. (Published by the Carnegie Institution.)

3. *China*

J. G. Andersson, *An Early Chinese Culture.* (Reprint from *Bulletin of Geological Survey of China*, No. 5. 1923.)

T. J. Arne, *Painted Stone-Age Pottery from the Province of Honan.* 1925. Cf. also *L'Anthropologie*, Vol. XXXV, pp. 63 and 351.

D. Black, *The Human Remains from the Sha Kuo T'un Cave Deposit.* 1925.

4. *Elam*

Mémoires de la Délégation en Perse (ed. J. de Morgan), 17 vols., 1900–1923. (Cf. esp. Vols. I and VII to XIII.) Moussian is dealt with in Vol. VII, 1906 (by Gautier and Lampre), and Bender Bushire on the Persian Gulf in Vol. XV, 1914 (by Pézard.)

5. *India*

There are, as yet, no full reports of the discoveries in the Indus valley. See, however, the articles by Sir John Marshall in the *Illustrated London News*, September 20, 1924, and February 27 and March 6, 1926 (with numerous illustrations).

6. *Mesopotamia*

W. Andrae, *Die archaischen Ištar-Tempel in Assur.* 1922.

W. F. Albright on Tell Zeidan Pottery in *Man*, Vol. XXVI, 3. 1926.

H. R. Hall, on Ur, Eridu, and Tell el 'Obeid, in *Proceedings of the Society of Antiquaries.* 1919.

S. H. Langdon, on The Excavations at Kish. 1925, etc.

S. H. Langdon, in *C.A.H.*, Vol. I, Ch. X.

E. Mackay, " Report on the Excavation of the ' A ' Cemetery at Kish " in *Field Museum of Natural History, Anthropology Memoirs*, I. 1925.

M. von Oppenheim on Tell Hallaf, in *A.O.*, X, 1. 1909.

F. Sarre on Painted Pottery from Samarra (the Hertzfeld expedition), in *Der Islam.* 1914, V, p. 190.

R. C. Thompson on Abu Shahrein (excavations of 1918), in *Archæologia*, Vol. 70.

7. *Syria, Anatolia, and the Caucasus*

E. Chantre, *Mission en Cappadoce.* 1898.

G. Contenau, *La Glyptique Syro-Hittite.* 1923.

J. Garstang on Sakje Geuzi in *Liverpool Annals*, I.

R. S. Macalister, *The Excavations at Gezer.* 3 vols., 1912.

J. L. Myres, " The Early Pot Fabrics of Asia Minor," in *J.R.A.I.*, Vol. 33, 1903.

H. Vincent, *Canaan.* 1907.

C. L. Woolley, " Asia Minor, Syria and the Ægean," in *Liverpool Annals*, IX. 1922.

8. *Seals, Pictographs, and Art*

G. Contenau, op. cit. supra, § 7.

A. J. Evans, *Scripta Minoa*, I. 1909.

L. Heuzey, *Les Origines Orientales de l'Art*. 1891–1915.

D. G. Hogarth, *Hittite Seals*. 1920.

W. M. F. Petrie, *Scarabs and Cylinders with Names*. 1917.

S. H. Langdon, " The Religious Interpretation of Babylonian Seals," in *Revue d'Assyriologie*, Vol. XVI.

W. H. Ward, *The Seal Cylinders of Western Asia*. 1910.

O. Weber, *Altorientalische Siegelbilder*. 2 vols., 1920 (in *A.O.*).

9. *Sumerian Origins, etc.*

C. J. Ball, *Chinese and Sumerian*. 1913.

S. H. Langdon, " Sumerian Origins and Racial Characteristics," in *Archæologia*, Vol. 70.

E. Meyer, *Sumerier und Semiten in Babylonien*. 1906.

M. Rostovtzeff, " The Sumerian Treasure at Astrabad," in *J.E.A.*, Vol. 6.

M. Tseretheli, " Sumerian and Georgian," in *Journal of the Royal Asiatic Society*. 1913–1916.

5. CHAPTER V

W. W. F. Baudissin, *Adonis und Eshmun*. 1911.

G. Contenau, *La Déesse Nue Babylonienne*. 1914.

L. R. Farnell, *The Cults of the Greek States* (esp. Vol. III, 1907).

J. G. Frazer, *The Golden Bough*, Pt. IV, *Adonis, Attis and Osiris*. 3rd ed., 2 vols. Pt. V, *Spirits of the Corn and of the Wild*. 3rd ed., 2 vols.

E. Hahn, *Die Entstehung der Pflugkultur*. 1909.

E. Hahn, *Haustiere*. 1896.

E. Hahn, *Hacke und Pflug*. 1919.

V. Hehn, *Kulturpflanzen und Haustiere in ihrem Übergang aus Asien nach, Europa*. 8th ed., 1911.

M. J. Lagrange, *Études sur les Religions Sémitiques*. 1905.

S. H. Langdon, *Tammuz and Ishtar : A Monograph upon Babylonian Religion and Theology*. 1914.

S. H. Langdon, *Sumerian and Babylonian Psalms*. 1909.

S. H. Langdon, *Babylonian Liturgies.* 1913.
W. Mannhardt, *Wald- und Feld-Kulte.* 2 vols., 1875–7, 2nd ed., 1904–5.
M. P. Nilsson, *Greek Religion.* 1925.
W. M. Ramsay, "The Peasant God," "Asia Minor : The Country and its Religion," in *Luke the Physician and other Studies.* 1908.
W. M. Ramsay, article on Religion of Asia Minor in Hastings' *Dictionary of the Bible,* Vol. VI.
W. M. Ramsay, "Phrygians," in *E.R.E.*
W. R. Smith, *Lectures on the Religion of the Semites.* 2nd ed., 1894.
E. J. Thompson and A. M. Spencer, *Bengali Religious Lyrics, Sakta.* 1923.
H. Whitehead, *The Village Gods of South India.* 1921.

6. CHAPTER VI

W. F. Albright, "Magan, Meluhha and the Synchronism between Menes and Nasam-Sin " in *J.E.A.,* VII, 1921.
A. T. Clay, *The Empire of the Amorites.* 1919.
G. Contenau, *La Civilisation Assyro-Babylonienne.* 1922. (A brief sketch.)
G. Contenau, *La Civilisation Phénicienne.* 1926.
F. Cumont, *Astrology and Religion among the Greeks and Romans.* 1912.
L. Delaporte, *La Mésopotamie.* 1923. (Vol. 8 of series *E.H.*)
P. Dhorme, *La Religion Assyro-Babylonienne.* 1910.
P. Dhorme, *Textes Religieux Assyro-Babyloniens.* 1907.
H. de Genouillac, *Tablettes Sumeriennes archaïques* (with introduction). 1909.
H. Grimme, *Mohammed* (contains a good sketch of the early civilisation of South Arabia). 1904.
A. Grohmann, *Göttersymbole und Symboltiere auf Südarabischen Denkmälern.* (*Denkschrift der Kaiserliche Akademie, Wien.*) 1919.
P. S. Handcock, *Mesopotamian Archæology.* 1912.
M. Jastrow, *Religious Beliefs in Babylonia and Assyria.* 1911.
M. Jastrow, *Die Religion Babyloniens und Assyriens.* 3 vols., 1905–12.

A. Jeremias, *Handbuch der altorientalischen Geisteskultur.* 1913. (Written from the standpoint of the " Pan Babylonist " school.)

C. Jeremias, " Die Vergöttlichung der babylonisch-assyrischen Könige," in *A.O.* 1919.

F. X. Kugler, *Sternkunde und Sterndienst in Babel.* 1907-1924.

L. W. King, *History of Sumer and Akkad.* 1910.

L. W. King, *History of Babylonia.* 1915.

B. Landsberger, " Assyrische Handelskolonien in Kleinasien," in *A.O.* 1925.

S. H. Langdon, *The Babylonian Epic of Creation.* 1923.

S. H. Langdon and R. C. Thompson in *C.A.H.*, Vol. I.

J. Lewy, art. " Kappadokische Tontafeln," in *R.V.G.*, VI. 1925.

B. Meissner, *Babylonien und Assyrien.* 2 vols., 1920–25. (Very important.)

A. T. Olmstead, *History of Assyria.* 1923.

R. C. Thompson, " The Influence of Babylonia," in *C.A.H.*, III (ch. XI).

O. Weber, " Arabien vor dem Islam," in *A.O.* 1904.

E. Weidner, *Handbuch der babylonischen Astronomie.* 1915.

E. Weidner, *Der Zug Sargons von Akkad nach Kleinasien.* 1922.

H. Winckler, *Mussri, Melucha, Ma'in in Mitteilungen der Vorderasiatischen Gesellschaft.* 1897, I.

C. R. L. Woolley, Annual Reports on Excavations at Ur, 1922–1927, in *Antiquaries' Journal.*

7. CHAPTER VII (AND CHAPTERS XI AND XIII)

(See also Chronological Tables I and II, Authorities)

J. H. Breasted, *History of Egypt.* 2nd ed., 1909.

J. H. Breasted, *Development of Religion and Thought in Ancient Egypt.* 1912.

J. H. Breasted, *Ancient Records of Egypt.* 5 vols., 1906–7.

J. Capart, *Les Débuts de l'Art en Égypte.* 1909. (English translation.)

A. Erman, *Aegypten und Aegyptisches Leben.* 2nd ed. (ed. Ranke), 1922–4. English translation of 1st ed. as *Life in Ancient Egypt.* 1894.

A. Erman, *Die Aegyptische Religion.* 2nd ed., 1909. (English translation.)

A. Erman, *Die Literatur der Aegypter*. 1923. (English translation, 1927.)

A. H. Gardiner, on " Osiris Cult," in *J.E.A.*, II, 1915.

S. Langdon, " The Early Chronology of Sumer and Egypt and the Similarities in their Culture," in *J.E.A.* VII, 1921.

G. Maspero, *The Art of Egypt (Ars Una)*. 1921.

A. Moret, *Le Nil et la Civilisation Égyptienne*. 1926. (Vol. 7 of series *E.H.*)

A. Moret, *Du caractère religieux de la Royauté pharaonique*. 1903.

J. de Morgan, *Recherches sur les origines de l'Égypte*. Vol. I, 1896 ; Vol. II, 1909.

P. E. Newberry, " The Petty Kingdom of the Harpoon," in *Liverpool Annals*, I.

W. M. F. Petrie, *History of Egypt,* Vols. 1 to 3 (many editions).

W. M. F. Petrie, *Prehistoric Egypt*. 1920.

W. M. F. Petrie, *Social Life in Ancient Egypt*. 1923.

W. M. F. Petrie, *Arts and Crafts of Ancient Egypt*. 1923.

H. Schäfer, *Von Aegyptischer Kunst*. 1922.

A. Scharff, *Grundzüge der Aegyptischen Vorgeschichte*. 1927.

G. Elliot Smith, *The Ancient Egyptians and their Influence on the Civilization of Europe*. 2nd ed., 1923.

G. Caton-Thompson " The Neolithic Industry of the Northern Fayum Desert," in *J.R.A.I.*, Vol. 56, 1926.

A. Wiedemann, " Der Tierkult der alten Aegypter," in *A.O.*, XIV, 1.

W. Wreszinski, *Atlas zur altaegyptischen Kultur*. 1914, etc.

8. Chapter VIII

C. Autran, *Tarquoundemos*. 1923.

C. Autran, *Les Phéniciens*. 1920.

A. Debrunner, art. " Griechen " (Sprache), in *R.V.G.*, IV, ii, 1926.

W. Dörpfeld, *Troja und Ilion*. 2 vols., 1902.

C. Dugas, *La Céramique des Cyclades*. 1925.

R. Dussaud, *Les Civilisations préhelléniques dans le bassin de la mer Égée : études de protohistoire orientale*. 2nd ed., 1914.

R. Eisler, " The Introduction of the Cadmeian Alphabet," in *Journal of R. Asiatic Soc.*, 1923.

A. J. Evans, *Scripta Minoa*, Vol. I, 1909.

A. J. Evans, *The Palace of Minos*, Vol. I, 1921.

A. J. Evans, " Mycenæan Tree and Pillar Cult," in *J.H.S.*, Vol. 21, 1901.

A. J. Evans, " The Early Nilotic, Libyan and Egyptian Relations with Minoan Crete," in *J.R.A.I.*, Vol. 55, 1925.

D. Fimmen, *Die Kretische-Mykenische Kultur*. 1921.

G. Glotz, *La Civilisation Égéenne*. 1923. (Vol. 9 of series *E.H.*)

H. R. Hall, *Ægean Archæology*. 1915.

G. Karo, art. " Kreta," in *R.V.G.*, VII, 1926.

August Köster, *Das antike Seewesen*. 1923.

August Köster, *Schiffahrt und Handelsverkehr des östlichen Mittelmeeres im 3 und 2 Jahrtausend vor C.* (Beiheft I to *A.O.*)

M. J. Lagrange, *La Crète Ancienne*. 1908.

R. von Lichtenberg, *Ägaische Kultur*. 1918. (A brief sketch.)

A. Philippson, *Das Mittelmeergebiet*. 1904.

H. Schliemann, *Ilios*. 1880.

R. B. Seager, *Excavations in the Island of Pseira*. 1910.

R. B. Seager, *Explorations in the Island of Mochlos*. 1912.

C. Smith, etc., *Excavations at Phylakopi*. 1904.

J. Sundwall, art. " Kretische Schrift," in *R.V.G.*, VII, 1926.

A. J. B. Wace and others, " Excavations at Mycenæ," in *Annual of British School at Athens*, Vol. 25.

S. Xanthudides and J. P. Droop, *The Vaulted Tombs of the Messara*. 1924.

9. Chapter IX

1. *The Megalithic Culture in General*

E. Baumgärtel, *Dolmen und Mastaba*. 1926.

J. Ferguson, *Rude Stone Monuments in All Countries*. 1872.

J. H. Hutton, " The Use of Stone in the Naga Hills," in *J.R.A.I.*, Vol. 56, 1926.

O. Montelius, *Orient und Europa*. 1899.

T. E. Peet, *Rough Stone Monuments and their Builders*. 1912.

W. J. Perry, *The Children of the Sun*. 1923.

W. J. Perry, " The Relationship between the Geographical Distribution of Megalithic Monuments and Ancient Mines," in *Proceedings of Manchester Literary and Philosophic Society.* Vol. 60, 1915.

G. Elliot Smith, " The Evolution of the Rock-cut Tomb and the Dolmen," in Essays presented to ·W. Ridgeway. 1913.

G. Wilke, *Südwesteuropäische Megalithkultur und ihre Beziehungen zum Orient.* 1912.

2. *Palestine*

P. Karge, *Rephaim.* 1917.

D. Mackenzie, " Megalithic Monuments of Rabbath-Ammon," in *Palestine Exploration Fund.* 1911.

P. Thomsen, art. " Megalith-Grab " (*Palästina-Syrien*), in *R.V.G.*, VIII, 1927.

H. Vincent, *Canaan.* 1907.

3. *Malta*

T. Ashby and others in *Papers of the British School at Rome,* VI, 1913.

L. H. D. Buxton, " The Ethnology of Malta and Gozo," in *J.R.A.I.*, LII, 1922.

A. Mayr, *Die Insel Malta.* 1910.

M. A. Murray, *Excavations in Malta.* 1925.

T. Zammit, articles in *Archæologia,* Vols. 67, 68, and 76, 1916–20.

T. Zammit, articles in *Liverpool Annals,* Vols. 3, 4, etc.

T. Zammit, articles in *J.R.A.I.*, Vol. 54, 1924.

T. Zammit, *Guide to the Valletta Museum.* 1919.

10. CHAPTER X

1. *Spain and Portugal*

N. Åberg, *La Civilisation Énéolithique dans la Péninsule Ibérique.* 1921.

P. Bosch Gimpera, " La Arqueologia preromana Hispanica. (Appendix to the Spanish edition of A. Schulten's *Hispania.* 1920.)

P. Bosch Gimpera, art. " Glockenbecherkultur," in *R.V.G.*, IV, ii, 1926.

P. Bosch Gimpera, art. " Megalithgrab (West Europa),"
in *R.V.G.*, VIII, 1927.

P. Bosch Gimpera and L. Pericot, " Les Civilisations de la
Péninsule Ibérique," in *L'Anthropologie*. 1925 (Dec.).

E. T. Leeds, " The Dolmens and Megalithic Tombs of Spain
and Portugal," in *Archæologia*, 70, 1920.

S. Reinach, on the evora gorget and Irish gold lunulæ,"
in *A.J.*, 1925.

A. Schulten, *Tartessos. Ein Beitrag zur ältesten Geschichte
des Westens*. 1922.

A. Schulten, *Numantia*, I, 1914.

L. Siret, *Questions de chronologie et d'ethnographie Ibériques*.
1913. (The chief account of Almerian culture.)

H. and L. Siret, *Les Premiers Ages du Métal dans le Sud-est
de l'Espagne*. 1887.

2. *Sardinia*

G. Patroni, " L'Origine del Nuraghe Sardo e le Relazioni di
Sardegna con l'oriente," in Vol. 19 of *Atene e Roma*.
1916.

R. Pettazzoni, *La Religione Primitiva in Sardegna*. 1912.

G. Pinza, in *Mon. Ant.*, XI, 1902.

A. Taramelli, numerous articles in *Mon. Ant.* 1908, etc.,
esp. on the nuraghic temple of S. Vittoria di Serra in
Vol. 23, 1915 ; and on the nuraghic temple of S.
Anastasia in vol. 25, 1919.

A. Taramelli, on Anghelu Ruju, in *Notizie dei Scavi*,
1904 ; and in *Mon. Ant.*, Vol. 19, 1908.

3. *France*

P. Bosch Gimpera and J. de Serra Rafols, art. " Frankreich,"
in *R.V.G.*, IV.

J. Déchelette, *Manuel*, Vol. I, op. cit. A. 3.

H. J. Fleure on " The Breton Megaliths," in *Archæologia
Cambrensis*. December 1924.

C. Daryll Ford, on " The Breton Megaliths," in *Man*, August
1926, and *A.J.*, 1927.

4. *England and Wales*

J. Abercromby, *A Study of the Bronze Age Pottery of Great
Britain and Ireland*. 2 vols., 1912. (Deals especially
with the Beaker Culture.)

O. G. S. Crawford, *The Long Barrows of the Cotswolds.* 1925.

O. G. S. Crawford, " The Distribution of Early Bronze Age Settlements in Britain," in *Geographical Journal*, Vol. 40, 1912.

C. Fox, *The Archæology of the Cambridge Region.* 1923.

W. Greenwell, *British Barrows.* 1877.

T. Rice Holmes, *Ancient Britain.* 1907.

T. D. Kendrick, *The Axe Age.* 1925.

A. Keith, on " The Racial Origins of the Beaker People " in *J.R.A.I.*, Vol. XLV.

E. H. Stone, *The Stones of Stonehenge.* 1924. Cf. also Reports on recent excavations (by Col. Hawley), in *A.J.*, VI, 1926.

J. Thurnam, "Ancient British Barrows," in *Archæologia*, Vols. 42–3.

R. E. M. Wheeler, *Prehistoric and Roman Wales.* 1925.

5. *Scotland and Ireland*

J. Anderson, *Scotland in Pagan Times*, Vol. I, *Stone and Bronze Ages.* 1886. Vol. II, *Iron Age.* 1883. (Still a most valuable book.)

W. C. Borlase, *The Dolmens of Ireland.* 3 vols., 1897.

G. Coffey, *New Grange and other Incised Tumuli.* 1912.

G. Coffey, *The Bronze Age in Ireland.* 1903.

Leabhar Gabhala, *The Book of the Conquests of Ireland.* Ed. R. A. S. Macalister and J. MacNeill, Pt. I. N.D.

R. A. S. Macalister, *Ireland in Pre-Celtic Times.* 1921.

R. A. S. Macalister, article on Carrowkeel, in *P.R.I.A.*, sect. c., Vol. 29, 1912.

J. MacNeill, *Some Phases of Irish History.* 1919. (On the ethnological question and the early traditions, cf. also in *P.R.I.A.*, sect. C, Vol. 28, pp. 123 seq., and Vol. 36, pp. 265 seq.)

Proceedings of Society of Antiquaries of Scotland, especially articles on the Brochs, in Vols. 46, 48, and 49.

T. J. Westropp, on " The Stone Forts of the Aran Is.," in *P.R.I.A.*, Vol. 28.

T. J. Westropp, on " The Fair of Tailltin," in *Folklore*, Vol. 31, 1920.

11. Chapter XI

V. G. Childe, *The Aryans : a Study of Indo-European Origins.* 1926.

S. Feist, *Kultur, Ausbreitung und Herkunft der Indo-germanen.* 1913.

S. Feist, art. "Indogermanen," in *R.V.G.*, VI, 1925.

J. G. Frazer, *The Worship of Nature*, Vol. I, 1925.

J. Friedrich, art. "Altkleinasiatische Sprache," in *R.V.G.*, I, 1924.

A. H. Gardiner, *The Admonitions of an Egyptian Sage.* 1909. (Leipzig.)

P. Giles, in *C.A.H.*, Vol. II, chs. I and II, and in *Cambridge History of India*, Vol. I.

H. Hirst, *Die Indogermanen : ihre Verbreitung, ihre Urheimat und ihre Kultur.* 2 vols., 1905–7.

F. Hrozny, *Die Sprache der Hethiter. Boghazköi Studien*, I. 1917.

Ipsen, "Sumero-akkadische Lehnwörter, in Indogermanischen," in *Indogermanische Forschungen*, XLI.

S. Konov, *The Aryan Gods of the Mitanni People.* 1921.

A. Meillet, *Introduction à l'étude comparative des langues indo-européennes.* 5th ed., 1923.

T. Peisker, "The Asiatic Background " (on nomadism), in *Cambridge Medieval History*, I, 1911.

W. J. Perry, "An Ethnological Study of Warfare," in *Proceedings of Manchester Literary and Philosophical Society.* 1917.

W. J. Perry, *War and Civilization.* 1918.

R. Pettazzoni, *Dio. I. L'Essere celeste nel Credenze dei Popoli Primitivi.* 1922.

A. H. Sayce, in *Anatolian Essays and Studies* presented to Sir William Ramsay. 1924.

O. Schrader, *Reallexikon, ut supra*, A. 1.

O. Schrader, *Die Indo-Germanen.* 1911.

O. Schrader, art. "Aryan Religion," in *E.R.E.*

I. Taylor, *The Origin of the Aryans.* 1889.

12. Chapter XII

N. Åberg, "*Das Nordische Kulturgebiet, in Mitteleuropa.*" 2 vols., 1918. (Important.)

O. Almgren, art. " Felsenzeichnung," in *R.V.G.*, III, 1925.

V. G. Childe, " When did the Beaker Folk Arrive ? " in *Archæologia*, Vol. 74, 1925. (A chronological study of the cultures of Central and Northern Europe.)

V. G. Childe, works cited above, A. 3 and B. 11.

M. Ebert, *Sud Russland im Altertüm.* 1922.

A. Götze, Höffer, and Zschiesche, *Die vor- und früh-geschichtlichen Altertümer Thüringens.* 1909.

G. Kossinna, *Die Indogermanen.* 1921.

G. Kossinna, *Das Weichselland ein uralter Heimatboden der Germanen.* 1919.

E. H. Minns, *Scythians and Greeks.* 1913. (On South Russia, including prehistoric remains.)

O. Montelius, *Kulturgeschichte Schwedens.* 1906.

O. Montelius, *Minnen från vår Forntid*, I, 1917.

S. Müller, *Oldtidens Kunst i Danmark.* I. *L'Art de l'âge de pierre.* 1918. (In Danish, with summary in French. Fine illustrations.)

S. Müller, " L'âge de la pierre en Schlesvig," in *Mémoires de la Société Royale des antiquaires du Nord.* 1913–14.

S. Müller, *Nordische Altertümskunde.* 2 vols. (German edition), 1905.

G. Neckel, *Die Überlieferungen vom Gotte Balder.* 1920.

Art. " Nordischer Kreis," in *R.V.G.*, IX, 1927.

C. A. Nordman, " Some Baltic Problems," in *J.R.A.I.*, 1921.

M. Rostovtzeff, *Iranians and Greeks in Southern Russia.* 1922. (With a full account of the Kuban Culture.)

F. A. van Scheltema, *Die Altnordische Kunst.* 1923.

C. Schumacher, op. cit., B. 3.

G. Schütte, *Dänisches Heidentum.* 1923.

H. Shetelig, op. cit., B. 3 (prehistory of Norway).

E. Sprockhoff, *Die Kulturen der Jüngeren Steinzeit in der Mark Brandenburg.* 1926.

K. Stjerna, *Före Hallkisttiden.* 1911.

A. M. Tallgren, *La Pontide Préscythique après l'Introduction des Métaux.* 1926. (Important.)

A. M. Tallgren, " Zur frühen Metalkultur Sudrusslands " in *Götze-Festschift.* 1925.

A. M. Tallgren, *The Copper Idols from Galich and their Relatives.* 1925.

A. M. Tallgren, articles on Ananyino, Fatyanovo, Finnland, Kaukasus, Kuban, etc., in *R.V.G.*, passim, and in the *Journal of the Finnish Society of Archæology of Helsingfors* (in French or German).

13. CHAPTER XIII

J. Capart, *Thèbes, la gloire d'un grand passé*. 1925.
G. Contenau, *Éleménts de Bibliographie Hittite*. 1923.
G. Contenau, op. cit., B. 4, § 7. (*La Glyptique Syro-Hittite*.)
A. E. Cowley, *The Hittites*. 1918.
J. Friedrich, "Aus Hethitischen Schrifttum," in *A.O.*, 1924, Heft 3, and 1925, H. 2.
J. Garstang, *The Land of the Hittites*. 1910.
A. Gustavs, art. "Mitanni" (Sprache), in *R.V.G.*, VIII, 1927.
H. R. Hall, "Egypt and the External World," in *J.E.A.*, VII, 1921.
D. G. Hogarth, in *C.A.H.*, Vol. II, Ch. XI and Vol. III, Chs. VI and VII.
D. G. Hogarth, *Kings of the Hittites*. 1926. (On the Southern Hittites.)
D. G. Hogarth, op. cit., B. 4, § 8. (Hittite Seals.)
D. G. Hogarth and C. L. Woolley, *Carchemish*, Pt. I, 1914 ; Pt. II, 1921.
F. Hrozny, *Code Hittite*. 1922.
F. Hrozny, op. cit., B. 11 (on Hittite languages).
S. H. Langdon and A. Gardiner, "The Treaty between Hattusshil and Rameses II," in *J.E.A.*, VI, 1920.
E. Meyer, *Reich und Kultur der Chetiter*. 1914.
E. Pottier, "L'Art Hittite." Articles in *Syria*, Vols. I, II, and V.
A. H. Sayce, *The Hittites : the Story of a Forgotten Empire*. 1888. 4th ed., 1925.
O. Weber, "Die Kunst der Hethiter," in series *Orbis Pictus*, IX, 1921.
A. E. P. Weigall, *The Life and Times of Akhenaton*. 2nd ed., 1923.
C. L. Woolley, "Hittite Burial Rites," in *Liverpool Annals*, VI.

14. CHAPTER XIV

G. Behrens, *Bronzezeit Süddeutschlands*. 1916.
G. Behrens, art. "Mittel- und Süddeutschland," in *R.V.G.*, V II, 1927.

V. G. Childe, " The Danube Throughfare and the Beginnings of Civilization in Europe " in *Antiquity*, I, 1. 1927.

G. A. Colini, " Il sepolcreto di Remedello Sotto, nel Bresciano, e il periodo eneolitico in Italia," in *B.P.*, Vols. 26–28. 1900–1902.

G. A. Colini, " La civiltà del Bronzo in Italia," in *B.P.*, Vol. 29, 1903.

F. von Duhn, *Italische Gräberkunde*, I, 1924.

F. von Duhn, art. " Italien," in *R.V.G.*, Vol. VI.

J. Evans, *The Ancient Bronze Implements, Weapons, and Ornaments of Great Britain*. 1881.

M. Mayer, *Molfetta und Matera*. 1924. (On the neolithic and æneolithic culture of Apulia).

O. Montelius, *La Civilisation primitive en Italie*. 5 vols., 1895–1904.

O. Montelius, *Die Vorklassische Chronologie Italiens*. 2 vols., 1912.

O. Montelius, Cf. also Chronological Tables. III.

S. Müller, *L'Age du Bronze en Schlesvig*. 1914–15. Cf. *supra*, B. 12.

S. Müller, *Oldtidens Kunst in Danmark*. II. *L'Art de l'Age du Bronze*. Cf. *supra*, B. 12.

J. M. de Navarro, " Prehistoric Routes between Northern Europe and Italy defined by the Amber Trade," in *Geographical Journal*, Vol. 66, 1925 (December). (With good maps.)

H. Peake, *The Bronze Age and the Celtic World*. 1922.

T. E. Peet, *The Stone and Bronze Age in Italy*. 1909.

L. Pigorini, on the Terramara of Castellazzo di Fontanellato, in *Mon. Ant.* 1892.

G. Pinza, *Storia delle Civilta Antiche* (Paletnologia d'Italia). 1923.

B. von Richthofen, *Die ältere Bronzezeit in Schlesien*. 1926.

K. Schumacher, op. cit., B. 3 (on Rhineland).

H. Seger, art. " Aunjetitzer Kultur," in *R.V.G.*, I, 1924.

H. Seger, art. " Lausitzische Kultur," in *R.V.G.*, VII, 1926.

R. Sernander, " Die Schwedischen Torfmooren als Zeugen postglazialer Klimaschwankungen " in *Die Veränderung des Klimas seit . . . der letzen Eiszeit*. 1910.

15. Chapter XV

T. W. Allen, *The Homeric Catalogue of Ships*. 1921.

J. Beloch, *Griechische Geschichte*, Vol. I, 1912–13.

V. Bérard, *Les Phéniciens et l'Odyssée*. 2 vols., 1902–3.

J. B. Bury, in *C.A.H.*, Vol. II (Ch. XVII, " The Achæans and the Trojan War " ; Ch. XVIII, " Homer.")

S. Casson, *Macedonia, Thrace, and Illyria*. 1926.

S. Casson, on Excavations in Macedonia, in *A.J.*, VI, 1926 ; and in the *Annual of the British School at Athens*, Vol. 24 (1919–21).

S. Casson, " The Dorian Invasion Reviewed," in *A.J.*, I.

H. M. Chadwick, *The Heroic Age*. 1912.

V. G. Childe, " Date and Origin of Minyan Ware," in *J.H.S.*, Vol. 35, 1915.

P. Dhorme, " Les Achéens dans les textes de Boghaz-Keui," in *Revue Biblique*, Vol. 33, 1924.

A. J. Evans, " The Ring of Nestor," in *J.H.S.*, 1925. (On Mycenæan art and religion.)

H. R. Hall, " The Peoples of the Sea " in *Mélanges Champollion*. 1922.

H. R. Hall, in *C.A.H.*, Vol. II, Ch. XII (" Keftians, Philistines and Peoples of the Levant ").

C. Heurtley, on Excavations in Macedonia, in *Liverpool Annals*, Vol. 12 and elsewhere.

D. G. Hogarth, *Ionia and the East*. 1909.

D. G. Hogarth, on " Hellenic Settlement in Asia Minor," in *C.A.H.*, Vol. II, Ch. XX.

R. A. S. Macalister, *The Philistines*. 1913.

G. Murray, *The Rise of the Greek Epic*. 2nd ed., 1911.

W. M. Ramsay, *Asianic Elements in Greek Culture*. 1927.

G. Rodenwaldt, *Tiryns*, II. 1912.

A. H. Sayce, " The Aryan Problem—50 Years Later " in *Antiquity*, Vol. I, ii.

H. Schliemann, *Mycenæ*. 1878.

H. Schliemann, *Tiryns*. 1886.

C. Tsountas and J. I. Manatt, *The Mycenæan Age*. 1897.

A. J. B. Wace, in *C.A.H.*, Vol. II, Ch. XVI (" Crete and Mycenæ ").

H. T. Wade-Gery, in *C.A.H.*, Vol. II, Ch. XIX (" The Dorians ").

W. Weber, *Die Staatenwelt des Mittelmeers in der Frühzeit des Griechentums*. 1925.

R. Weill, "Phéniciens, Égéennes et Hellènes dans la Mediterranée Primitive," in *Syria*, Vol. II.

16. Chapter XVI

C. Blinkenberg, "Le Pays Natal du Fer," in *Mémoires de la Société des Antiquaires du Nord*. 1920–4.

E. Chantre, *Recherches anthropologiques dans le Caucase*, 4 vols., 1885–7.

R. S. Conway, in *C.A.H.*, Vol. IV, Ch. XII, "The Etruscans ; Ch. XIII, "The Indo-European Communities."

R. S. Conway, *Italic Dialects*. 1897.

von Duhn, op. cit., B. 14.

A. Gnirs, *Istria Præromana*. 1925.

A. Grenier, *Bologne Villanovienne et Étrusque*. 1912.

G. Herbig, art. "Etrusker" (Sprache), in *R.V.G.*, III, 1925.

G. Herbig, "Etruskisches Latein," in *Indogermanische Forschungen*, Vol. 37, 1917.

M. Hoernes, op. cit., A. 3 (on the art of the Iron Age).

M. Hoernes, "Zur Chronologie der Gräberfunde von Wätsch," in *W.P.Z.*, I. 1914.

M. Hoernes, "Krainische Hügelnekropolen der jüngeren Hallstattzeit," in *W.P.Z.*, II, 1915.

N. Jokl, art. "Illyrier" (Sprache), in *R.V.G.*, VI, 1925.

D. Randall-MacIver, *Villanovans and Early Etruscans*. 1924.

B. Modestov, *Introduction à l'Histoire Romaine*. 1907.

O. Montelius, op. cit., B. 15.

J. de Morgan, *Mission Scientifique au Caucase*. 2 vols., 1889.

L. Pareti, *Le Origini Etrusche*, I, 1926.

C. Pauli, *Altitalische Forschungen*, Vol. III, *Die Veneter*. 1891.

F. Poulsen, *Der Orient und die frühgriechische Kunst*. 1912.

P. Reinecke, "Die Goldfunde von Michalkow und Fokoru," in *Z.E.*, Vol. 31, 1899.

P. Reinecke, "Zur Geschichte der ältesten Fibeln," in *Götze-Festschrift*. 1925.

W. Ridgeway, *The Early Age of Greece*. 1901.

A. Rosenberg, *Der Staat den alten Italiker*. 1913.

BIBLIOGRAPHY 407

M. Rostovtzeff, op. cit., B. 12 (on origins of the " Animal
    Style ").
E. von Sacken, *Das Gräberfeld von Hallstatt.* 1868.
F. A. von Scheltema, articles " Figurliche Darstellung " and
    " Hallstattstil," in *R.V.G.*, III and V.
W. Schulze, *Geschichte der lateinischen Eigennamen.* 1904.
A. M. Tallgren, articles " Kaukasus " and " Koban " in
    R.V.G., VI and VII.
A. M. Tallgren, *La Pontide Préscythique.* 1926.
R. Virchow, *Das Gräberfeld von Koban im Lande der Osseten.*
    1883.
G. Wilke, " Archäologische Parallelen aus dem Kaukasus,"
    in *Z.E.* 1904.
O. Menghin, Ürgeschichte Niederösterreiches. 1921.

ADDENDA

G. Contenau, *Les Tablettes de Kerkouk et les origines de la
    Civilisation Assyrienne.* 1927.
F. Hommel, *Ethnologie und Geologie des alten Orients.* Pt. I.
    2nd ed. 1904.
D. Nielsen, F. Hommel and N. Rhodokanakis, *Handbuch
    der altarabischen Altertümskunde.* 1927.
K. Sethe, Die altägyptischen Pyramidentexte. 1908 and
    1922.

CHRONOLOGICAL TABLES

In the present state of our knowledge, it is not possible to give a fixed and absolute chronology of the prehistoric cultures of Europe or even of the earliest historical civilisations of the Near East. But although a prehistoric chronology may seem to be a contradiction in terms, it has considerable practical value as a standard of comparison to show the approximate contemporaneity and succession of the different cultures. This, however, is only the case with the relatively advanced cultures of the later neolithic and bronze periods, for it is impossible to estimate the duration of a really primitive culture like that of the South African Bushmen or of the food-gatherers and hunters of prehistoric Europe by the scanty evidence of their tools and weapons. And this is even more impossible in the case of the cultures of palæolithic times, where our only guide is the succession of glacial phases and the raised beaches of ancient seas. The attempt to interpret this geological evidence in terms of years and thus to fix the duration of the palæolithic cultures has indeed often been made, but the scale is so vast and the element of uncertainty so great that the results remain almost as hypothetical as the Sumerian calculation of the length of the dynasties that reigned before the Flood. In comparison with these remote periods, the later neolithic and bronze age cultures are semi-historical, and though the element of uncertainty is still present, it is reduced to manageable dimensions. Wherever possible I have given a double series of dates so as to show the approximate limits of this uncertainty. The maximum figures represent the chronology generally accepted by Continental archæologists and are largely based on the work of the pioneer of prehistoric chronology, the late Professor Montelius, while the minimum dates are for the most part those given by Mr. Gordon Childe in his *Dawn of European Civilization*. I have followed the same dual system in dealing with the early oriental civilisations, for, as it will be seen, the different systems of Egyptian chronology differ in some cases even more widely than those of the writers on European prehistory.   Nevertheless the objections to the higher chronology of Borchardt, and still more to that of Sir Flinders Petrie, are very great, while the " short chronology " of Edward Meyer, which is accepted by so many Egyptologists, also has the great advantage of being reconcilable with the Mesopotamian evidence.   In the case of Mesopotamia, there is now a considerable measure of agreement between the different systems, and at least from the age of Sargon onwards the dates of the Mesopotamian dynasties may be regarded as fixed within the limits of little more than a century.

NOTE ON SOUTH ARABIAN CHRONOLOGY

[see pp. 115–6]

THE early chronology of the South Arabian States rests on the data of the Assyrian inscriptions.   In 715 B.C. an inscription of Sargon mentions the tribute of the Sabæan It'i-amara, and in the last years of Sennacharib, c. 685 B.C., Ka-ri-bi-ilu, king of the land Saba'i, sends precious stones and incense as an offering for the Bit-Akîtu.   Professor Hommel identifies these rulers with Jit'î-Amara Bajin and Kariba-ilu Watar, the two mukarribs of Saba who conquered Ma'in and founded the Sabæan power.   On this assumption, the period of the kings of Ma'in must fall before the seventh century B.C., and we have the following chronology:

> Kings of Ma'in, c. 1300–700 B.C.
> Mukarribs of Saba, c. 985–650 B.C.
> Kings of Saba, c. 650–115 B.C.
> Kings of Saba and Dû Raidân, 115 B.C.–340 A.D.
> First conquest of South Arabia by the Abyssinian kings of Axum, 340–375 A.D.

The alternative synchronisms which Hommel rejects would place the fall of Ma'in, either in 620, 800, or 890 B.C. ; cf. *Handbuch der Altarabischen Altertümskunde*, ed. D. Nielsen, vol. i, Copenhagen (1927).   The same work contains a full description of the organisation of the South Arabian state and temple-corporation by N. Rhodokanakis.

TABLE I

THE DYNASTIES OF MESOPOTAMIA AND EGYPT

AUTHORITIES

1. *Mesopotamia*

S. Langdon, in *Cambridge Ancient History*, Vol. I, ed. 2, based on his edition of the chronological prism in : *Oxford Editions of Cuneiform Texts*, II ; *The Weld Blundell Collections*, Vol. II ; *Historical Inscriptions* (Oxford, 1923).

E. F. Weidner, " Die Könige von Babylonien und Assyrien," in Meissner, *Babylonien und Assyrien*, Vol. II, pp. 438 ff., 1925.

D. Opitz, art. " Herrscherliste," in *R.L.V.*, Vol. V, 1926.

E. Meyer, *infra*.

For the astronomical evidence see F. X. Kugler, S.J., " *Sternkunde und Sterndienst, in Babel*," Vol. II.

2. *Egypt*

E. Meyer, *Geschichte des Altertüms*, Vol. I, 2, 2nd ed., 1913, as revised in *Die Ältere Chronologie Babyloniens, Assyriens und Aegyptens*, 1925.

L. Borchardt, *Die Annalen und die zeitliche Festlegung des Alten Reiches des Aegyptischen Geschichte*, 1917.

H. R. Hall, in *Cambridge Ancient History*, Vol. I.

S. Breasted, *Records of Ancient Egypt*, Vols. I and II.

A. Scharff, *Grundzüge der Aegyptischen Vorgeschichte*, 1927 (a strong advocate of the minimum chronology).

From the beginning of the New Kingdom the differences of date are inconsiderable, and I have followed the *Cambridge Ancient History*, Vol. II.

1. MESOPOTAMIA

The earliest remains of the developed Sumerian culture recently
discovered by the expeditions to Ur and Kish are estimated by Mr.
C. L. Woolley to date from about 3500 B.C.

1. First Dynasty of Kish, legendary.
2. First Dynasty of Erech, legendary.
3. First Dynasty of Ur, historical, circ. 3100–3000 B.C.
4. Dynasty of Awan, traditional.
5. Second Dynasty of Kish, traditional.
6. Dynasty of Khamazi, traditional.
7. Second Dynasty of Erech, traditional.
8. Second Dynasty of Ur, traditional, 108 years.
9. Dynasty of Adab, traditional, 90 years.

	Langdon.	Weidner.	
10. Dynasty of Maer or Mari	3103	136 years	Period of the early Patesis of Lagash, Ur Nina and his successors.
11. [Third Dynasty of Kish]	} to {	100 years	
12. Dynasty of Akshak		93 years	
13. Fourth Dynasty of Kish	2777	97 years	
14. Third Dynasty of Erech	2777–2752	2662–2638	Fall of Lagash.
15. Dynasty of Akkad (Semitic)	2752–2571	2637–2582	
Sargon	2752–2697	2637–2582	
Naram sin	2675–2619	2557–2520	
16. Fourth Dynasty of Erech	2571–2542	2456–2427	Period of Gudea of Lagash ?
17. Dynasty of Gutium	2541–2416	2426–2302	Period of Barbarian Rule.
18. Fifth Dynasty of Erech	2416–2409	2301–2295	
19. Third Dynasty of Ur	2409–2328	2294–2187	Period of the Cappadocian Tablets (cf. ch. vi).
20. First Dynasty of Isin	2357–(2069)	2186–1961	
21. Dynasty of Larsa	2357–(2040)	2187–1901 (or 1925)	
22. Dynasty of Amurru (or First of Babylon)	2169–1870	2057–1758	
Hammurabi	2067–2024	1955–1913	Unification of Babylonia.
23. First Dynasty of the Sea Land		1884–1517	
(Hittite raid on Babylon	c. 1870	c. 1758)	
24. Kassite Dynasty	1746–1169	1746–1171	
25. Second Dynasty of Isin (or Pashe)	1169–1039	1170–1039	

TABLE I   413

2. EGYPT

	E. Meyer.	Borchardt.	Cambridge Ancient History.
I. The Old Kingdom :			
Dynasty I, Thinite .	3197	4186	3500
Dynasty II, Thinite .	(2982)	(3936)	3350
Dynasty III, Memphite	2778	3643	3190
Dynasty IV, Memphite	2723	3427	3100

(The Age of the Pyramids and the full development of the Art of the Old Kingdom.)

Dynasty V, Memphite .	2563	3148	2965

(The Age of Heliopolitan influence and of the great Solar temples.)

Dynasty VI, Memphite	2423	2920–2720	2825–2631

(The Decline of the Old Kingdom and the Rise of Feudalism.)

I*a*. Transition Period between Old and Middle Kingdoms :

	–2243	2720–2220	2621–2500

II. The Middle Kingdom

	E. Meyer	Borchardt	C.A.H.
Dynasties IX and X, Heracleopolitan .	2242	2200	2500
Dynasty XI, Theban .	—	2040	2375
Dynasty XII, Theban .	2000	1996	2212
Dynasty XIII, Theban	1788–1660	—	2000
Dynasty XIV, Decay and Division of the Middle Kingdom .	—	—	–1800
The Hyksos Invasion .	c. 1660	—	c. 1880

II*a*. The Hyksos Period :

Dynasties XIV or XV–XVII . . .	1660–1580	—	1800–1580

(Dynasties XV and XVI, Hyksos Kings of Xois.
Dynasty XVII, Vassal Dynasty of Thebes.)

III. The New Kingdom (Theban), 1580–1100 :

Dynasty XVIII, The Imperial Age of Egypt, 1580–1346.
Dynasty XIX, Decline of Egyptian Empire, 1346–1210.
Dynasty XX, End of Egyptian Empire, 1210–1100.

III*a*. Dynasty XXI, Priest Kings at Thebes, and independent Kingdom of the Delta, 1100–942.

TABLE II

THE ÆGEAN CULTURES (TO CHAPTERS VII AND XV)

AUTHORITIES

A. P. Evans, *Scripta Minoa*, Vol. I, 1909 ; *The Palace of Minos*, Vol. I, 1921.

D. Fimmen, *Die Kretisch-Mykenische Kultur*, ed. 2, 1924.

C. Dugas, *La Céramique des Cyclades*, 1925.

A. J. B. Wace and M. S. Thompson, *Prehistoric Thessaly*, 1912.

V. G. Childe, *The Dawn of European Civilization*.

CRETE	CYCLADES	MAINLAND GREECE	THESSALY	TROY
First Period (Neolithic), c. 3000 B.C. Incised pottery.	*First Period* 3000–2400. Early Cycladic I and II. Predominance of incised pottery.	*First Period,* –2600 Neolithic Peasant Culture of continental type. Black pottery.	*First Period,* –2600 Neolithic Peasant Culture. Red painted pottery. Clay figurines.	*Troy I,* –2500 Neolithic or æneolithic Peasant Culture of Anatolian type.
Second Period (Age of Copper), c. 3000–2100 B.C. Painted pottery and stone vases. Period of Mochlos and Messara Tombs. Early Minoan I, 3000–2700 (3400–2800). Early Minoan II, 2700–2400. Early Minoan III, 2400–2100. Rise of polychrome pottery with spiral decoration and of the pictographic script.	*Second Period* 2400–1900. Early Cycladic III. The Age of the expansion of the Cycladic Culture. Predominance of geometrical painted pottery. Marble idols. Phylakopi I.	*Second Period,* 2600–1900 Early Helladic II and III. Appearance of Ægean type of culture with affinities to Cyclades. Incised pottery and geometrical painted ware. Orchomenos II.	*Second Period,* 2600–2400 Appearance of Dimini culture, an offshoot of the painted pottery culture of Eastern Europe. Polychrome pottery with spiral ornament. Fortified settlements. Megaron type of house.	*Troy II* (Early Bronze Age), 2500–1900 Troy an important walled settlement with wide commercial relations. "The Treasure of Priam," rich in gold, silver, and bronze. Stone battle-axes and Megaron type of house, pointing to European influences. Pottery—Face Urns, etc.
Third Period (Early Bronze Age), 2100–1750 The first Palace of Cnossus (2000–1750). Middle Minoan I, 2100–1900. Development of polychrome pottery with spiral ornament and of pictographic script. Middle Minoan II, 1900–1750. Period of Kamares pottery. The climax of the polychrome curvilinear style.	*Third Period,* 1900–1400 Age of Cretan Influence. Middle Cycladic, 1900–1600. Curvilinear style of pottery (influence of Kamares ware). Phylakopi II. Later Cycladic I and II, 1600–1400. Creto-Cycladic style of pottery. Cretan fresco painting.	*Third Period,* 1900–1600. Middle Helladic. Appearance of Minyan culture of continental origin. Grey polished "Minyan ware" and matt painted pottery. Orchomenos III. *Fourth Period,* 1600–1200 Late Helladic or Mycenæan Age. Period of Cretan influence.	*Third Period,* 2400–1800 Æneolithic period. Appearance of new culture of northern origin. Stone battle-axes. Plain pottery with high handles. (? Related to Minyan culture of Central Greece.) Artistic decline.	*Troy III-V,* 1900–1500 Ruin of the city. Unimportant village settlements.

TABLE II 417

Fourth Period (Later Bronze Age), 1750–1400	Phylakopi III. Incised pottery of Syros.	Mycenaean I, 1600–1500. Shaft Grave Dynasty.	Fourth Period (Bronze Age), 1800–1100	Troy VI, 1500–1200
The Age of Cretan Expansion. The second Palace of Cnossus (1700–1400). Middle Minoan III, 1750–1580. Beginnings of naturalistic style and of the linear script. Late Minoan I, 1580–1450. Climax of naturalistic style and of Cretan art and architecture. Late Minoan II, 1450–1400. Decline of naturalistic art. The "Baroque" "Palace Style," of pottery. Fall of Cnossus, c. 1400.	*Fourth Period* 1400–1200. Late Cycladic III. Age of Mycenaean Predominance. Importation of Mycenaean pottery, Mycenaean "Palace" at Phylakopi.	Appearance of Minoan culture and art in Greece. Rise of Mycenae. Mycenaean II, 1500–1400. Tholos Tomb Dynasty at Mycenae. Spread of Mycenaean culture in Greece. Tholos tombs at Vaphio, Pylos, Kakovatos, etc. "Palace style" of pottery.	Stagnation of Thessalian culture during this period. Pottery rude and inartistic. During Mycenaean III, 1400–1200. The influence of the Mycenaean culture spreads to coastal region of Thessaly.	Rebuilding of Troy on a larger scale. Strong fortifications. Close relations with Ægean world and the Mycenaean culture. The Trojan War and the fall of the city, c. 1200 (traditional date of Eratosthenes, 1192–1183).
Fifth Period (close of Bronze Age), 1400–1200. Late Minoan III. Period of Mycenaean predominance. Decline of Cretan Culture. Conventionalism in art. Introduction of iron.		*Fifth Period* 1400–1200. Mycenaean III. The Imperial Age of Mycenae. Rebuilding of Mycenae. The Lion Gate and the "Treasury of Atreus." Foundation of fortresses of Tiryns and Goulas. Fresco painting at Tiryns and Mycenae. Conventional style of pottery. Beginnings of the Heroic Age.		

TABLE III

THE PREHISTORIC CULTURES OF WESTERN EUROPE

AUTHORITIES FOR PREHISTORIC EUROPE
(TABLES III AND IV)

The first attempt to provide a scientific chronology of the prehistoric cultures of Europe was due to the late Professor Montelius, whose work still forms the basis of all the modern chronological systems. His most important contributions to the subject are :

" Die Chronologie der ältesten Bronzezeit in Norddeutschland und Scandinavien (*Archiv für Anthropologie*, 25–26, 1898 and 1900).

Die Vorklassische Chronologie Italiens, 1912.

" La Chronologie Préhistorique en France et en d'autres pays Celtiques " (*L'Anthropologie*, 1901).

" The Chronology of the British Bronze Age " (*Archæologia*, 61, 1908).

Minnen från vår Forntid, Vol. I, 1917.

For the minimum chronology I have followed V. G. Childe, *The Dawn of European Civilization*, and his article " When did the Beaker Folk Arrive ? " in *Archæologia*, Vol. 74.

Cf. also *Reallexikon der Vorgeschichte, passim.*

H. Reinerth, *Chronologie der jüngeren Steinzeit*, 1924.

H. Schmidt, *Vorgeschichte Europas*, Vol. I.

C. Schumacher, *Siedelungs-und Kultur-geschichte der Rheinlande*, Vol. I, 1921.

—	IBERIAN PENINSULA	WEST MEDITERRANEAN, ITALY, AND THE ISLANDS
Neolithic, –2700 (Maximum date, 5th–4th millennia.)	A. Neolithic culture of Almeria in south-east. B. Cave culture in Central and Southern Spain and in Catalonia. C. Rise of megalithic culture in Portugal (Dolmen period).	Rise of megalithic culture in Malta. Neolithic culture in Sicily (Stentinello) and in Apulia (Molfetta to Matera). Painted pottery, with curvilinear (spiral) decoration.
Early Æneolithic, 2700–2500.	A. Beginnings of metal (copper) in Almeria, C. Passage graves in Portugal.	
Full Æneolithic or Copper Age, 2500–2000. (Max. 3000–2500, Min. 2200–1700).	The Age of Cupola Tombs and Bell Beakers. A. Los Millares culture in Almeria. Fortified settlements. Cupola tombs. Bell beakers. Signs of relations with Eastern Mediterranean and the west. Gold, ivory, amber, callais, and jet. B. Bell beaker culture in Southern and Central Spain (Carmona and Ciempozuelos). Cupola tombs and passage graves in the south. Importance of Andalucia and Grenada. C. Palmella culture in Portugal. Cupola tombs and later passage graves. Stone cists. Bell beakers. Schist idols. Gold and callais. Expansion of megalithic culture eastwards into Spain and northwards to the Pyrenees. D. Rise of megalithic culture in Catalonia and the Pyrenees. Bell beakers, but no cupola tombs. Stone cists.	Later megalithic culture in Malta. Later neolithic culture of Sicily (Villafrati). Incised pottery. Bell beakers. Æneolithic culture of Sardinia (Anghelu Ruju). Rock-cut tombs. Bell beakers. Marble idols. Copper daggers. Early megalithic tombs. "Giants' graves" and dolmens. Æneolithic culture of North Italy (Remedello). Bell beakers. Appearance of lake-dwelling culture in north.
Early Bronze Age, 2000–1500. (Max. 2500–2000, Min. 1700–1200).	El Argar culture in Almeria. Fortified settlements. Bronze and silver plentiful. Daggers, short swords, and halberds. Silver diadems. Burial in small cists and jars. Dark polished pottery. Expansion of El Argar culture throughout coastal regions. Copper mining in south and in Algarve and Asturias. Disappearance of Megalithic culture, with the exception of some megalithic cist graves in Portugal, Andalucia, and Catalonia.	Æneolithic and Early Bronze Age in Sicily and South Italy (overlapping previous period). Siculan I (Castelluccio). Rock-cut chamber tombs. Painted pottery. Signs of contact with the Ægean and Troy II. In South Italy. Rock chamber tombs and unpainted pottery (Pulo di Molfetta). Megalithic tombs in the extreme south-east (Otranto). North Italy. Beginnings of Terremare culture. Sardinia. Beginnings of Nuraghic culture.
Later Bronze Age, 1500–1000. (Max. 2000–1000, Min. 1200–1000).	End of El Argar culture. Scanty evidence for this period. South Spanish culture prosperous (Tartessus) with wide commercial relations (the Huelva hoard).	Siculan II in Sicily. Rock tombs. Relations with Ægean. Mycenæan imports. "Mycenæan Palace" at Pantalica. South Italy. Terramara of Tarentum. North Italy. Later Terremare culture and its expansion into Central Italy. Beginnings of Iron Age (early Villanova culture) Nuraghic culture in Sardinia and Talayot culture in Balearic Islands.

TABLE III 421

—	FRANCE	BRITISH ISLES
Early Neolithic.	Flint culture in north and centre (Campignian). Cave culture in south. (Related to Spanish cave culture.)	
Later Neolithic and Æneolithic, 2600–2100. (Max. 3000–2500, Min. 2300–1900).	Megalithic culture in France. A. Breton culture of mixed character. Passage graves and covered galleries. Bell beakers. Callais, amber, and some copper gold. Stone battle-axes. Cremation. B. Pyrenean culture extending east to the Rhine. Covered galleries and stone cists. Cupola tombs (Collorgues). Subterranean galleries. Bell beakers. Some copper and gold. Callais.	Megalithic culture in British Isles. Dolmens and passage graves in Ireland. Long barrows in England. At close of period invasion of Beaker people from the Rhineland.
Bronze I, or later Æneolithic, 2100–1800. (Max. 2500–1900, Min. 1950–1750.)	Later megalithic culture in Brittany and South France. The great tumulus graves of Mont St. Michel, Tumiac, etc., with jadeite axes. Seine–Oise–Marne culture in north, based on neolithic Flint culture. Covered galleries and artificial grottos with sculptured figures.	Round barrows and corded beakers in Britain. Stone battle-axes. Bronze celts and daggers. In Ireland bronze daggers and halberds. Gold lunulæ. Stone circles and dolmens and cist graves in Ireland, Scotland, and Wales.
Bronze II, 1800–1500.	Tumulus graves of North Brittany and West Normandy (related to round barrow culture of England ?). Latest megalithic culture of South Brittany (? period of stone avenues of Carnac) and of South France (dolmens and grottos of Cevennes). Appearance in East France of Tumulu culture from West Germany.	Round barrows and Food Vessels in Britain. Erection of Stonehenge. Introduction of cremation. Development of bronze weapons. Stone battle-axes. Gold and amber and jet. Beads of Middle Minoan III type. In Ireland the cupola tombs of New Grange, Lough Crew, etc., and in Scotland Maeshowe, etc. Bronze daggers and flanged celts. Spears. Gold disks (sun disks).
Period III, 1500–1200.	Further development of bronze industry, characterised by more advanced types of bronze celts (with stop ridge), thrusting swords (rapiers), and socketed spears (British). Gold armlets and torques.	
Period IV, 1200–900.	Eastern France (region of Tumulus culture) affected by coming of Urn Cemeteries people. New types of pottery and bronze work. Broadswords, razors, sickles, safety-pins. Socketed celts.	Beginning of later Bronze Age. Changes of culture. Broadswords. Palstaves.
Period V, 900–600 (in Ireland, –350).	Early Iron Age, Hallstatt I, in France. Razors. Revival of Tumulus burial in east, and expansion of Tumulus culture south-west to the Pyrenees.	Broadswords and socketed celts. Razors. Bronze buckets and cauldrons. In Ireland this period sees the highest development of Bronze Age culture. Bronze swords and trumpets. Safety-pins, sickles, and razors. Gold gorgets and bracelets.

TABLE IV

THE PREHISTORIC CULTURES OF CENTRAL AND NORTHERN EUROPE

AUTHORITIES

As above, p. 419.

For the minimum chronology of the Bronze Age in Northern Europe, I have followed that given by S. Müller in his Bronzealdems Kunst in Danmark (1914–15). He divides the Bronze Age into 9 periods of a century each, so that Period II in the following table includes his Periods 2, 3 and 4, and Period III corresponds to his Periods 5 and 6.

TABLE IV

CENTRAL EUROPE

Neolithic

	Maximum.	Minimum.
Danubian I. Early Peasant Culture. Spiral meander ware and stroke ornamented ware. Shoe-last celts. Rise of Painted Pottery Culture in Eastern Europe. Erösd, Cucuteni A, Tripolye A	–3000	–2500
Danubian II. Later Peasant Culture. Crusted ware with painted ornament. Lengyel and Jordansmühl. End of Erösd. Period B at Cucuteni and Tripolye . . .	3000–2500	2500–2200
Danubian III. Invasion of Central Europe by warrior peoples. Corded ware and bell beakers. Marschwitz culture. Mondsee culture in Eastern Alps. End of Painted Pottery Culture in Eastern Europe . .	2500–2100	2200–1750

Bronze Age

	Maximum.	Minimum.
Early Bronze Age I. Aunjetitz culture in East. Adlerburg culture in West . .	2100–1700	1750–1400
Middle Bronze Age II. Tumulus culture in West. End of Aunjetitz culture in East. Bronze Age culture of Hungary. (Axes with spiral ornament. Broadswords. Pannonian pottery.)	1700–1300	1400–1200
Later Bronze Age III. Urn cemeteries culture in West. Early Lausitz culture in East. Sickles, razors, and safety-pins (fibulæ). Embossed pottery (Buckelkeramik). Beginnings of Iron Age in North Italy and of Hallstatt period in Central Europe	1300–900	1200–900

TABLE IV

425

NORTHERN EUROPE

Neolithic

	Maximum.	Minimum.
Nordic I. Pre-dolmen period . . .	−3500	—
Nordic II. Dolmen period. Dolmen pottery. Thin butted celts	3500–2500	2500–2200
Nordic III. Passage graves. Thick butted celts. Climax of artistic development in pottery. Relations with Western Europe. Separate grave in Jutland. Battle-axes. Corded beakers	2500–2100	2200–1650
Nordic IV. Long stone cists. Flint daggers. Decline of pottery. Beginnings of knowledge of metal	2100–1800	1700–1500

Bronze Age

	Maximum.	Minimum.
I. Bronze celts and daggers. Simple ornament of neolithic style	1800–1550	1400–1300
II. Rise of spiral ornament. Hungarian influence. Battle-axes and broadswords with spiral decoration. Invention of Nordic fibula. Introduction of cremation	1550–1300	1300–1000
III. Decline of first style of Nordic Bronze Age (spiral ornament). Socketed celts. Disappearance of battle-axes. Bronze vessels. Cremation general . . .	1300–1100	1000–800
IV. Transition to second style of Nordic Bronze Age. Italian influence . .	1100–950	800–700
V. Full development of second style. (Stylised spiral and meander patterns and concentric circles. Ornamental representations of ships, etc.)	950–750	700–600
VI. Transition to Iron Age. Decline of Nordic culture	750–600	600–500

TABLE V

THE AGE OF EMPIRES IN THE NEAR EAST

Authorities as for Table I, and especially the "Cambridge Ancient History," Vol. II.

427

TABLE V

EGYPT	WESTERN ASIA
The decline of the Middle Kingdom.	*c.* 1900–1700 B.C. The invasions of the northern peoples, Hittites, Mitannians, Kassites, etc.
The Hittite invasion of Egypt (? eighteenth century).	1870 or 1759. Great Hittite raid on Aleppo and Babylon. Fall of Dynasty of Babylon.
c. 1580. The expulsion of the Hyksos.	1746–1169. The Kassites in Babylonia. The power of Mitanni on the Upper Euphrates. Aryans in Syria and Palestine. Power of Aleppo in North Syria.
1580–1346. *Dynasty XVIII.*	
1545–1514. Thothmes I. Conquests in Syria.	
1501–1479. Hatshepsut.	Mitannians and Hittites in relation with Egypt. *c.* 1450. Shaushatar of Mitanni and Dudkhalia II of Hatti.
1501–1447. Thothmes III.	
1479. Battle of Megiddo and foundation of Egyptian Empire in Syria (1479–1447).	Friendship of Egypt with Mitanni and marriage alliances. Artatama, Shuttama, and Tushratta.
1447–1380. Prosperity of the Egyptian Empire.	Expansion of Hittite power (*c.* 1400–1350). Subbiluliuma (1380–1350). Conquest of North Syria. Decline of Mitanni between Hatti and Assyria.
1447–1420. Amenophis II, 1420–1412 ; Thothmes IV, 1412–1376 ; Amenophis III.	
The Tell el Amarna period. Close diplomatic relations between Egypt and the Asiatic Powers—Mitanni, Hatti, Alashiya, Assyria, Babylon, etc.	*c.* 1359. Mitanni becomes dependent on Hittites.
	c. 1355. Murshil II of Hatti.
1375–1362. Amenophis IV (Ikhnaton). Religious revolution. Great artistic development. Decline of the Egyptian Empire. Habiru and other invading peoples in Palestine.	*c.* 1329. Mutallu of Hatti.
	1289. Hittite league against Egypt.
	1288–1255. Hattushil III.
	1272. Treaty between Hatti and Egypt. Division of Syria.
1346–1210. *Dynasty XIX.*	1259. Hattushil visits Egypt. Dudkhalia III.
1321–1300. Seti I. War with Hittites in Syria.	Rise of Assyria.
1300–1233. Rameses II the Great.	1242. Assyrian conquest of Babylonia.
1288. Battles of Kadesh. Temporary revival of Egyptian Empire.	*c.* 1200. *Fall of the Hittite power.* Philistine settlement in Palestine.
1233–1223. Merneptah. First attack of the sea peoples on Egypt (1221).	1170. Fall of Kassite Kingdom of Babylon before an Elamite invasion.
1205–1100. *Dynasty XX.*	1170–1039. Dynasty of Pashe (Isin II).
1204–1172. Rameses III.	1115–1102. Tiglath-Pileser. Imperial power of Assyria.
1194–1187. The great invasions of the Libyans and the Sea Peoples. Final decline of Egypt. Predominance of the priests of Amon. Independent kingdom in the Delta.	*c.* 1100. Decline of Assyria. The Aramæans in North Mesopotamia and Syria. The Chaldæans in Babylonia.

1100–900, *The Dark Ages.*

INDEX

A

ACHÆANS, 307, 346–55
ACHEULEAN CULTURE, 7–8
ADONIS, 98, 282–3
ADRIATIC, 286, 319, 329–30, 367, 369–75, 381
ÆGEAN CULTURE, general, 170–90, 345–61; origins, 76–7, 174–6; race and language, 187–90; religion, 76–7, 101, 113–14, 175, 177; its decline, 353, 359; revived in classical Greek culture, 360. Its contacts with Egypt, 175, 178, 182; with Asia Minor, 76, 175, 187; Ægean influences in Black Sea, 183, 185, 277; in Western Mediterranean, 186, 216–20; in Scandinavia, 284; in Central Europe, 316, 319, 326. See also Cycladic Culture, Helladic Culture, Minoan Culture, Mycenæan Culture, Peoples of the Sea, Trojan Culture
ÆNEOLITHIC CULTURES. See Neolithic
ÆSIR, 281, 284, 286
AFRICA, NORTH, see also Libya(ns). Megaliths in, 195, 205
AGRICULTURE, 52, 54–5, 57, 68–9, 72, 89–93, 155, 172, 304, 331; origin of, 89–90, 92–3. See also Peasant Culture and Vegetation Cult
AHA, 153
AHURA MAZDA, 244
AKAIWASHA, 35
ALMERIAN CULTURE, 212–13; contact with Megalithic Culture, 213; dolichocephalic race, 216; pottery, 221; continued in El Argar Culture, 226
ALPINE LAKE-DWELLING CULTURE, 52–3, 220–1, 270–1, 330, 332
ALPINE RACE, 46, 52, 67, 77–8, 81, 84, 86, 145, 188, 215–16, 218, 330, 337, 370
AMAZONS, 306
AMBER, 171, 215, 220–1, 263, 265, 270, 274, 315, 318–19, 347, 372–3
AMENEMHAT I, 251–2
AMENEMHAT III, 252
AMENOPHIS III, 294–5
AMENOPHIS IV (Ikhnaton), 296–9
AMERICAN (NORTH) INDIANS, 26–8, 30–1, 32 n., 33–40, 91
ANATOLIA, 76, 98–9, 101, 114, 183. See also Cappadocia, Hittites, Caria(ns), Lycia(ns), Lydia(ns), Phrygians, Pisidia, Troy, Etruscans, Ægean Culture, Ionia, and Mother Goddess
ANAU, 69, 71
ANGHELU RUJU, tombs, 218–19
ANIMALS :

(A) Sacred, 29–32, 39–40, 146, 156; (agricultural) 106–7
(B) Domestication of, 49, 52–4, 57, 70, 72, 92–3, 107, 240–1, 253–4, 275–6

ANIMAL GUARDIAN SPIRITS, 32–9
ANU, 125
APACHE, 31

429

I. GENERAL

Its nature and evolution, Int., xiii ff. ; tendency to fixation of type, 323–8 ; not to be confused with race, 22 ; religious basis of, 22–3

II. TYPES OF CULTURE

(A) *Hunting*, 25–41 ; in Palæolithic and modern times, 25–6 ; art of, 31–2 ; religion of, 25 ff. See also Animal Guardian Spirits, Totemism

(B) *Peasant Agricultural*, 52–62, 89–107 ; peaceful character of, 59–238 ; social organisation based on agriculture, 8–9 ; garden agriculture, 90–1 ; higher position of women in, 90–1 ; plough agriculture, 92–3. Religion, see Mother Goddess, Vegetation Cult

(C) *Higher Culture* (*Archaic Civilisation*), rise of, in Asia, 72–80, 86 ; its theocratic character, 124–9, 153–9 ; the temple state and the sacred city, 111–18, 122–4 ; the Great State and the Divine Monarchy, 148–64 ; its economic and intellectual development, 112–13, 129–33, 237 ; the foundation of later civilisation, xx, 133–6, 237 ; its decline, 244–51, 300–1, 383 ; influence on prehistoric Europe, 169, 286, 300–1, 315, 381–3

P

PAINTED PEBBLES, Azilian, 47
PAINTED POTTERY. *See* Pottery
PAINTED POTTERY CULTURES (*Asia*), 68–72, 75–6, 80, 82, 84, 253. (1) Mesopotamia, 72–3 ; Persia, 68–9, 72 ; Turkestan (Anau), 69. (2) India, 70, 74–5, 80, 82. (3) North and West China, 69–70. (4) Syria, 75. (5) Anatolia, 75–6
PAINTED POTTERY CULTURE (*Europe*), 55–6, 62, 101–3. Origin and diffusion, 84–6. Relations to Danubian culture, 55–6, 269–70 ; and to Kurgan culture, 273. Sicilian, South Italian Culture, 329. Conquered by Battle-axe People, 270, 274, 325. Substrate of Transylvanian and Thracian cultures, 274, 326. Survival in Southern Russia, 326
PAINTING, *see also* Art. 16–18, 31–2, 36–7, 65, 179, 298
PALACE, Minoan, 176–9 ; Trojan, 184 ; Mycenæan, 348
PALÆOLITHIC CULTURES, 7–41. In Asia, 65. *See* Culture
PALESTINE, 114, 172, 195, 233–9, 289, 293, 298–9
PANNONIAN CULTURE, 326–8
PAROS, 182
PASSAGE-GRAVES, 194, 262–3
PASTORAL CULTURE, 240–4, 279–80. *See* Culture, II
PATRIARCHY, 242
PEACE, 237–40
PEASANT CULTURES, 52–62, 89–107. *See* Culture, II, *and* Religion
PELASGIANS, 188
PEOPLES OF THE SEA, 355–9
PEPI II, 160
PERSIA, 68–9, 72–3, 75, 81, 113, 117, 119–20, 368
PERU, 163

PHÆSTUS, 176–7, 180–1, 348
PHILISTINES, 355–6, 359
PHILOLOGY, 132
PHŒNICIA(NS), 115, 172, 293–4, 299
PHRYGIA(NS), 354, 356, 358
PILTDOWN SKULL, 8
PISIDIA, 177
PLOUGH AGRICULTURE, 92–3
POLAND, 50, 269–70, 278
POLISH MICROLITHIC CULTURE, 50
PONTIFEX, 335
PORTUGAL, *see also* Spain. 46, 216, 315. *Megalithic*, 199–200, 205, 211, 213 ; *Bell-Beaker*, 213–14 ; El Argar, 226 ; trade with Troy, 316
POTTERY, *Ægean*, 76, 78 ; *Almerian*, 221 ; *Alpine Lakedwellers*, 52 ; *Aunjetitz*, 319 ; *Badarian*, 143, 174 ; *Baltic Battle-axe*, 266–7 ; *Bell-Beaker*, 214, 217–18 ; *Campignian*, 49 ; *Caucasian Iron Age*, 368 ; *Cretan Neolithic*, 174 ; *Danubian* I, 54–5 ; *Danubian* II, 269–70 ; *Egyptian*, Predynastic, 144 ; New Kingdom, 295 ; *Este-Venetic*, 366, 375 ; " *Face Urns*," 373 ; *Fatyanovo*, 274 ; *Lausitz*, 338 ; *Megalithic* (Malta), 221 ; (Northern Megalithic, Baltic), 262, 264–5 ; *Minoan*, 178 ; *Minyan*, 346 ; *North Italian Æneolithic*, 330. *Painted Pottery Cultures*, Eastern Europe, 56, 58 ; *Asia*, North China, 69 ; India, 70 ; Mesopotamia, 72–3 ; Persia, 68–9, 71 – 3 ; Turkestan (Anau), 69, 71. *Pannonian*, 327 ; *Proto - Baltic*, 263 ; *Round Barrow*, 222, 225 ; *Sardinian*, 218 ; *South Italian Neolithic*, 329 ; *Terremare*, 331 ; *Thessalian*, 57, 346 ; *Thuringian Battle-axe*, 268–9; *Trojan*, 185, 316, 346 ; *Urn Cemetery*, 337